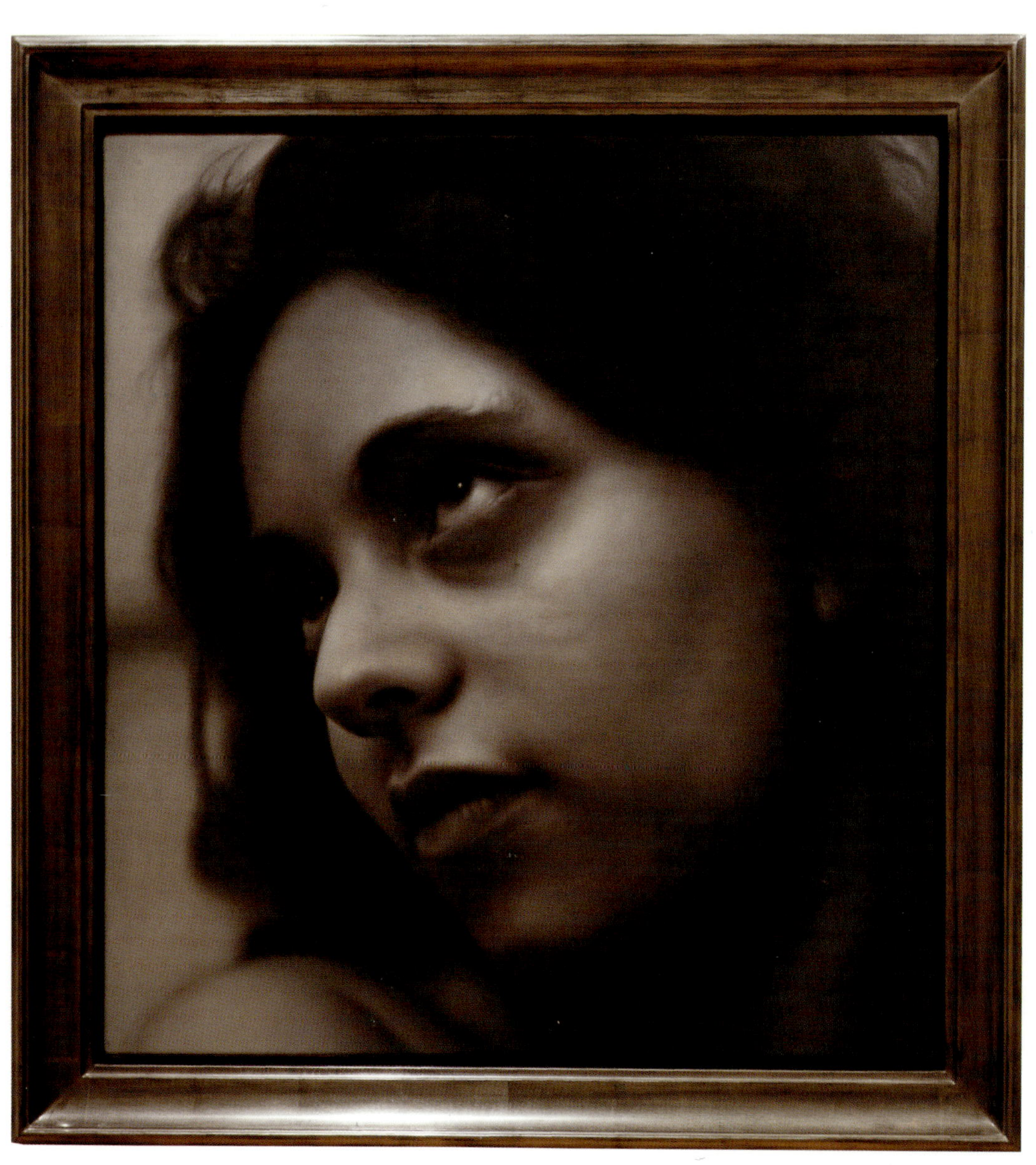

The New Neurotic Realism

Essay by Dick Price

The Saatchi Gallery

previous page: Mark Alexander *Untitled* 1997-98
oil on canvas 77 x 69.5 cm/30¹/₂ x 27¹/₂ in
opposite: Daniel Coombs *South of Birmingham* 1995
oil on canvas 228.6 x 304.8 cm/90 x 120 in
overleaf (1): Ron Mueck *Pinnocchio* 1996
polyester resin, fibreglass and human hair 84 x 20 x 18 cm/33 x 8 x 7 in
overleaf (2): Sarah Jones *Consulting Room (Couch B)* 1996
c-type photographic print mounted on aluminium 152.4 x 152.4 cm/60 x 60 in

designed and published in 1998 by The Saatchi Gallery
98A Boundary Road NW8 0RH

text © Dick Price 1998
front cover: Martin Maloney *Rave (After Poussin's Triumph of Pan)* 1997
oil on canvas 244 x 457 cm/96 x 180 in
photograph courtesy Stephen White © 1998

printed by The Pale Green Press
printed and bound in Great Britain

ISBN 0 9527 453 8 0

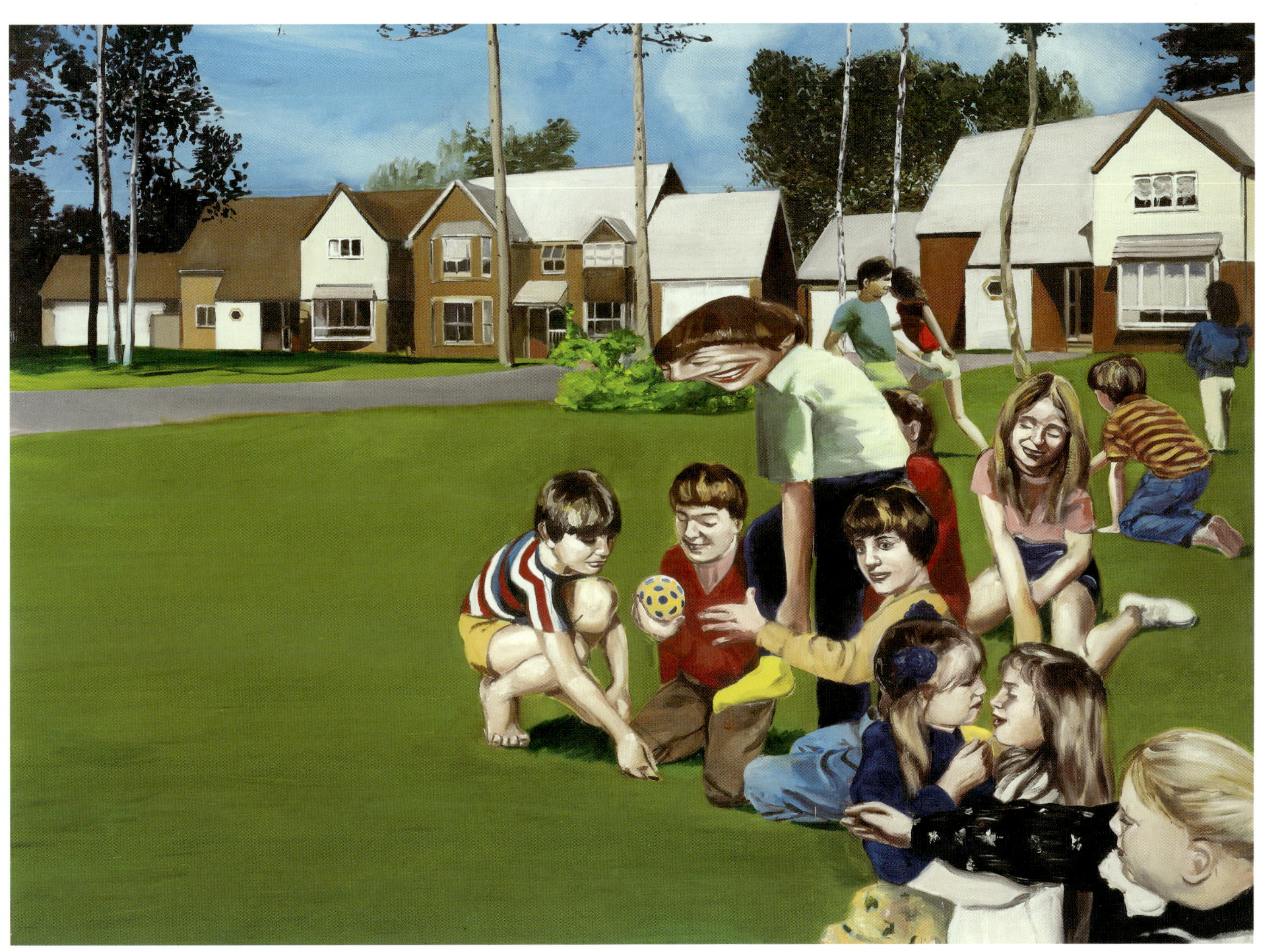

The New Neurotic Realism

David Falconer
Steven Gontarski
Brian C. Griffiths
Roger Hiorns
Mark Hosking
Ron Mueck
Tim Noble &
Sue Webster
Andreas Schlaegel
Tomoko Takahashi
Keith Wilson

Luke Gottelier
Tom Hunter
Sarah Jones
Katia Liebmann
Paul Smith
Hannah Starkey

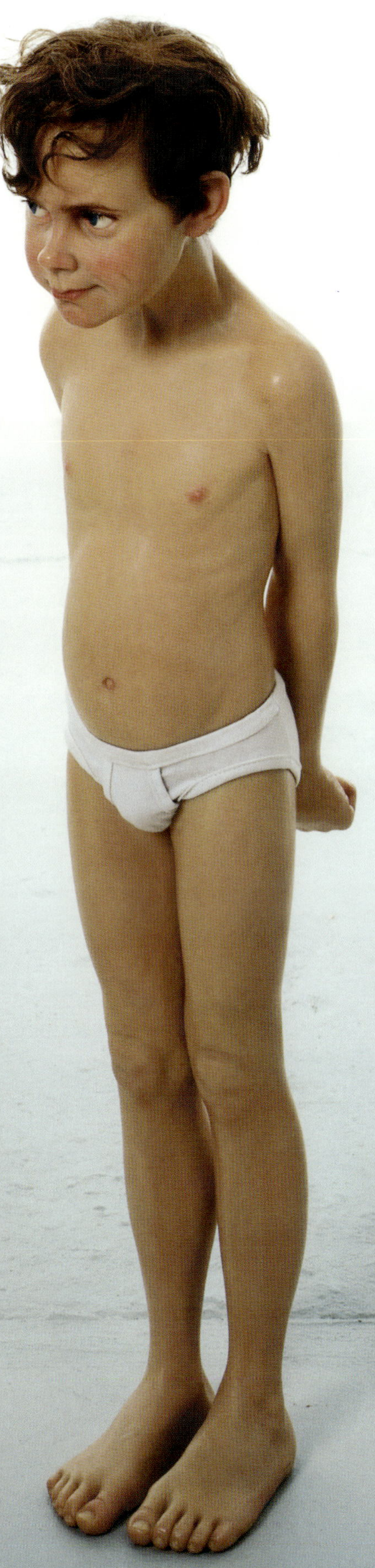

Jason Brooks
Cecily Brown
Daniel Coombs
Victoria Chalmers
Dexter Dalwood
Peter Davies
Dan Hays
Nicky Hoberman
Chantal Joffe
Felicia Larsson
Martin Maloney
Karl Maughan
Michael Raedecker
Richard Reynolds
Rosie Snell
Johnny Spencer
David Thorpe

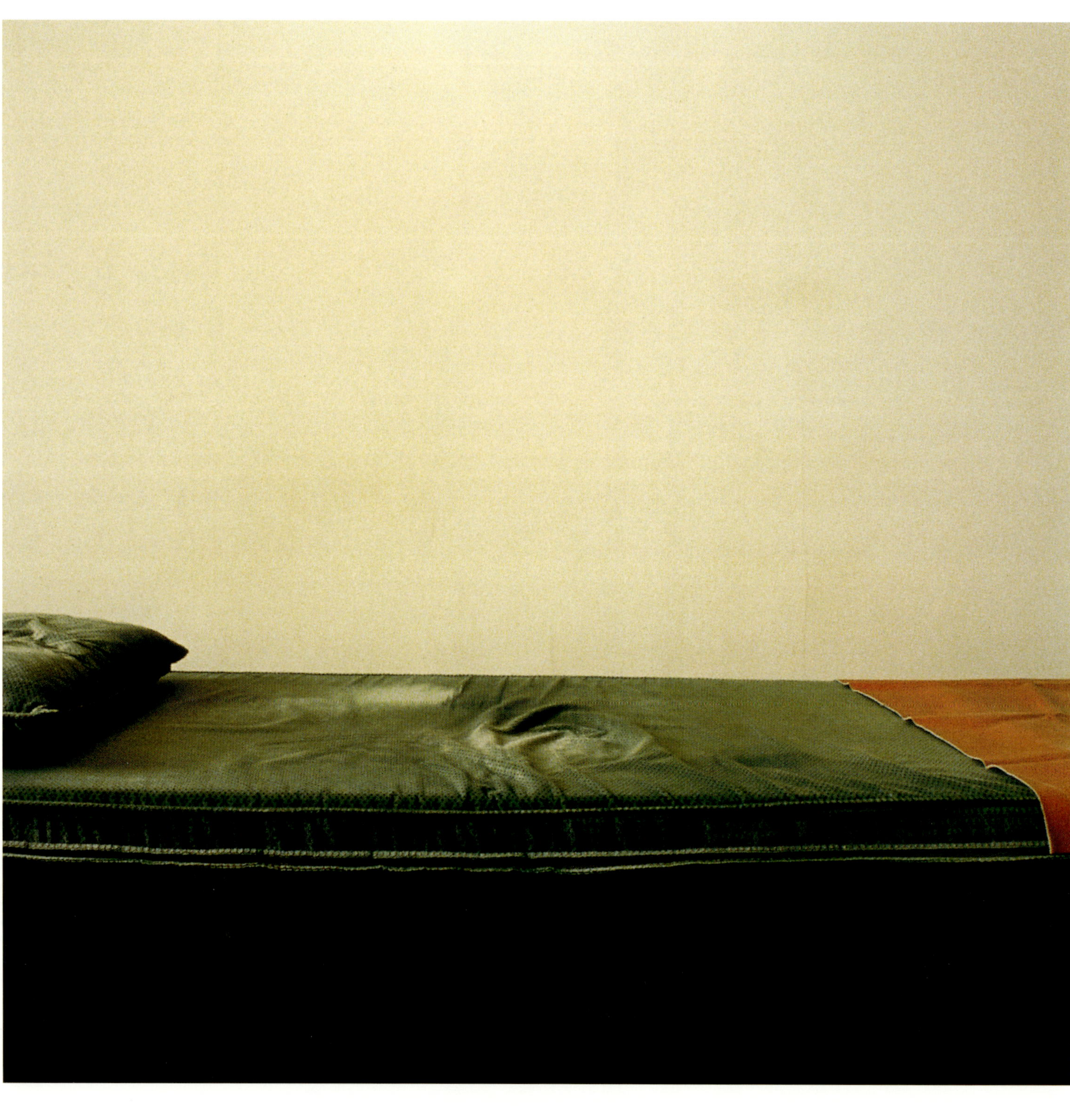

Don't stop 'til you get enough
by Dick Price

> Did it seem real to you sir?
> Its the realest thing I've ever done.... I mean that.
> *Westworld* 1973 (fig. 1)

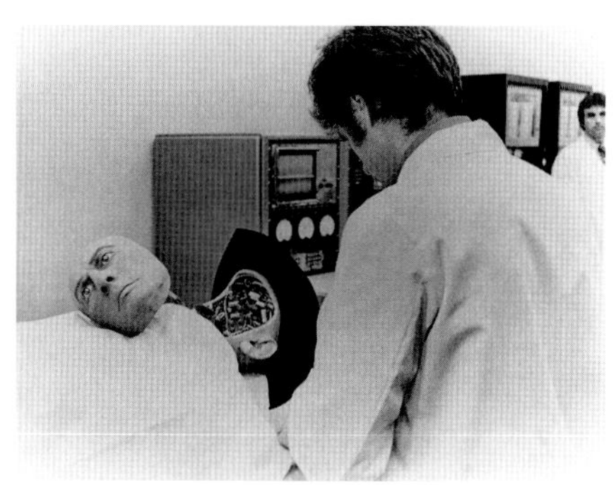

Westworld 1973 (film still)   fig. 1

The art of the last two or three years poses a different look and preoccupation to the concerns of artists at the beginning of the decade. London in the early 90s championed youthful success; what started as 'alternative' quickly became establishment. But a group of artists working in the slipstream became excited by the media attention and wanted a 'piece of the action'. Inevitably, the YBA cult of personality became tired. New artists and curators began looking elsewhere. Artists *wanted* to make art without anyone peering over their shoulders. They became enthusiastic about making things again. Art started to look like it was having more fun while artists remained serious in how they reflected their concerns. These new artists started putting themselves into the picture through low-key, improvised shows at artist-run spaces. Cynicism was finally *passé* and the art star a bore.

A recent shift in art has been away from the self as subject, with fiction becoming a common starting point rather than theory; fiction and memory, no longer separate entities, have become integrated. For example, our subjective relationship to film narrative is now second nature; we all remember both our real lives and those self-defining filmic moments within the same playback. Using the idea of collective memory, Brian Cyril Griffiths, Katia Liebmann, David Thorpe and Michael Raedecker each locate their work firmly in fiction through a diverse take on manipulation and funky working processes.

Katia Liebmann's Batgirl images, with their re-vamped Cindy Sherman *à la* fanzine mentality, dispense with subtle nuance and use self-consciousness as an anxious strength. David Thorpe takes a leaf out of the homecraft manual and cuts coloured paper to project an idealised landscape that alludes more to an opening film shot of a city at night than to the landscape in painting. Contained and claustrophobic, Michael Raedecker's paintings have a road movie wanderlust, with its image literally stitched into the present. Luke Gottelier places and then photographs objects, creating the surface of some unknown planet.

Art became less about "me myself and I" and more about collective ideas. The casually cobbled High Art object (i.e. Sarah Lucas) 'was replaced by a new

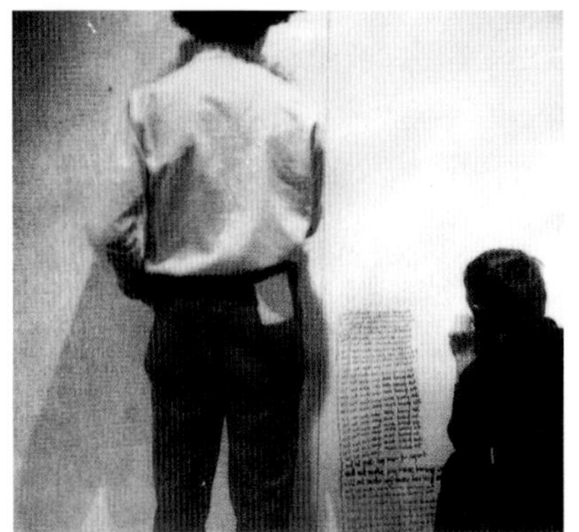

John Baldessari   fig. 2
I will not make any more boring art 1971

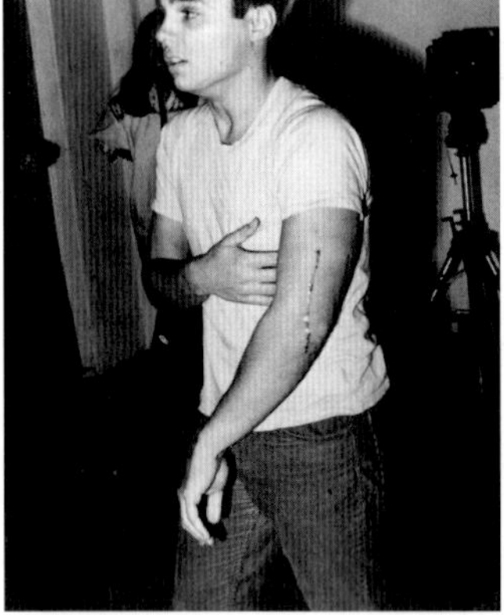

Chris Burden   fig. 3
Shoot 1971

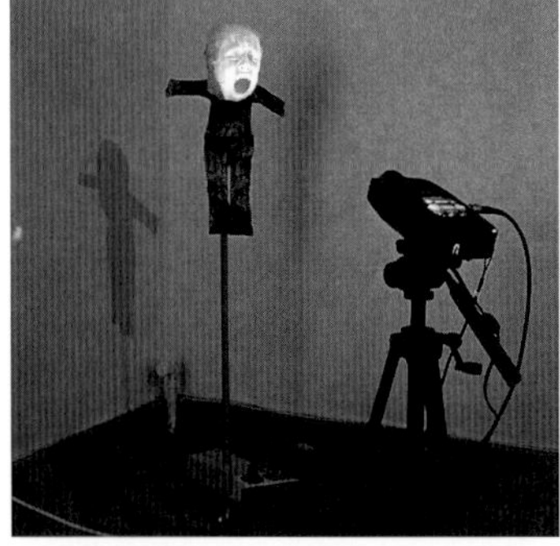

Tony Oursler   fig. 4
Horror (from Judy) 1994

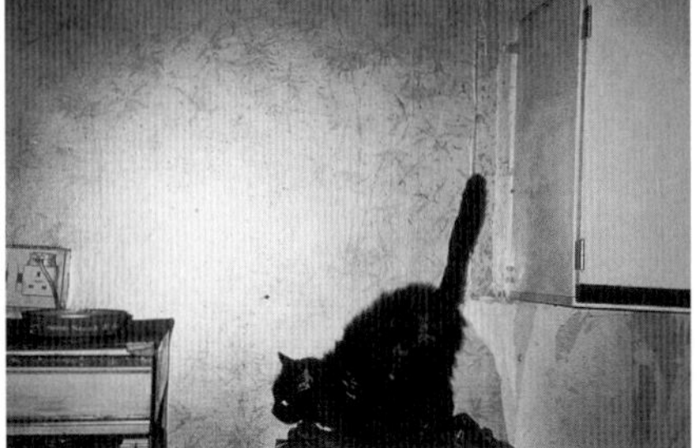

Richard Billingham   fig. 5
Untitled (Ral 38) 1995

kind of shabby-ragged realism. The legacy of pathetic, throw-away art had played itself out. In its place, elegance and sophistication reared their heads. Much of the work 'formerly known as sculpture' was well made and lovingly produced; Ron Mueck does the unthinkable and turns figurative sculpture (more akin to *Spitting Image* than Duane Hanson) into something with feeling. Brian Cyril Griffiths releases a domestic science fiction, a re-fabricated world of make-believe, plumbing the depths of Do-It-Yourself, with a Blue Peter manual and sticky-back plastic in hand. Scatter (lots of bits on the floor) had to re-invent itself. Even the organic, romantic, loss-and-decay work of Anya Gallaccio and Felix Gonzalez-Torres gave way to a new realism. Tomoko Takahashi, starting where Fischli and Weiss left off, gets in amongst rubbish and like a terrifyingly articulate toddler, lays it all out and demands we enjoy looking at it.

Both David Falconer and Mark Hosking expand a reduced aesthetic and, in their own way, pick up on familiar sculptural tropes. Hosking harks back to modernism, the object and the work of Anthony Caro with the functional objects he makes by carrying out (to the letter) U.N. directives for agricultural machinery. Falconer, like the tornado from the Wizard of Oz, whips up a column of rats, managing to reference 80s Brit sculpture (Tony Cragg) at the same time.

Two generations of American artists influenced British Sculpture: the *louche* conceptualism of John Baldessari (fig. 2), Chris Burden (fig. 3) and William Wegman and the generation who followed from their teaching milieu at Cal Arts, including Meg Cranston, Mike Kelley, Raymond Pettibon and Tony Oursler (fig. 4). Their art reflected a movie psychology, putting content forward into histrionics. Broader, youth-led and lifestyle orientated, it inspired a particular British brand of *neurotic realism* becoming more radical as the decade accelerated.

A new confidence in photography started to declare itself. Freed from the constraints of 'artyness', the photograph as art object became more relaxed. New British photography is bursting with content. Paul Smith uses realism as shock tactic: his personal experience of a stint in the army turns fact into fiction in a pseudo-documentary style. Smith fiddles with Frank Capa and Jeff Wall en-route to a street fighting Nan Goldin and his re-creation of hanging out is a scary, undesirable activity. Sarah Jones depicts an English, posh, internal world of spotless dining rooms inhabited by girls in their teens, savvy to Girl power and the implication of their patriarchal past. Her ordered world is the complete opposite of Richard Billingham's naturalism (fig. 5), and she makes the self-conscious reconstruction its *forte*.

At the beginning of the 90s painting was in disgrace due to bad behaviour in the 80s. It had to fiercely compete in the race to theorise; end game strategies were the model. Obsessed with removing the hand of the maker, the Richter-esque blurred image became the sexy fast-track; Mark Francis, Brad Lochore and Paul Winstanley chased the beautiful surface. The ersatz process painting of Gary Hume and Ian Davenport mined the Modernist seam in the search for gold. Painting, as a form, seemed a limited and reductive option. Artists became bored with process-based art and had a sneaking desire to do something else. Richter's light dimmed, claimed by all sides as the ideal model for painting, and Luc Tuymans' low-wattage bulb was switched on, shining some of his European pathos on the debate enlivened by Sigmar Polke's ragged sophistication. Suddenly, painting was forced back into the limelight, left to cope with an explosion of emerging concerns, different from the highbrow arguments about photography's relationship to painting.

Drawing as a form became an end in itself. Artists began to use drawing to reclaim imagery and this opened up a new possibility. Sue Williams' early 90s attacks on sexism are unexpectedly re-interpreted for the 'boy's bedroom' drawing habits of Paul Noble. Exhibitions at alternative spaces, like Cabinet, Cubitt, City Racing, Bank and Lost in Space, started to be dotted with drawings pinned or drawn directly onto the walls. This kind of drawing followed the creed of Raymond Pettibon, Jim Shaw (fig. 6) and Mike Kelley, learned by heart from catalogues and cult comics.

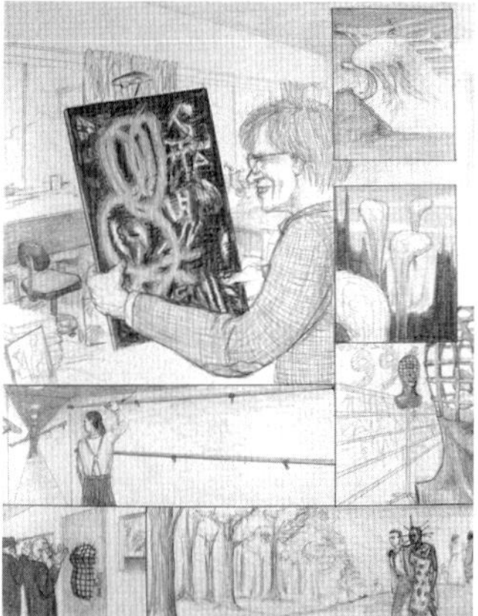

Jim Shaw   fig. 6
I'm showing Peter Saul 1993

Drawing had returned. The problem was how to make it into painting. Americans had previously managed to move the comic book style onto canvas but in Britain, cartoonish figurative painting still smelled bad. Painters in the early 90s remained a little fearful of a brush-licked surface. They were uneasy because figurative painting reminded them too much of an earlier over-wrought neo-expressionism and its derivatives.

Glenn Brown (fig. 7) had raised the stakes, and then sucked the air out of the representation debate, so others began to look further afield. Richard Patterson (fig. 8) went foraging for a synthesis of Tom Wesselmann and James Rosenquist, doffing his cap to Roy Lichtenstein and Fiona Rae. Jason Brooks put on a respirator and continued digging, pulling from the past a style so good there was no need to re-mix it. So, he copied it wholesale and in the large recent paintings of his friends he picks up from where Chuck Close left off and stays put; a bit like returning to the debris of a party, with all the expectation of making it great again. Dan Hays struggled with his Richter schooling and then emerged, first with guinea pigs and later with their cages, playful and serious at the same time. He attempts to re-vamp mid-seventies pop, breathing new life

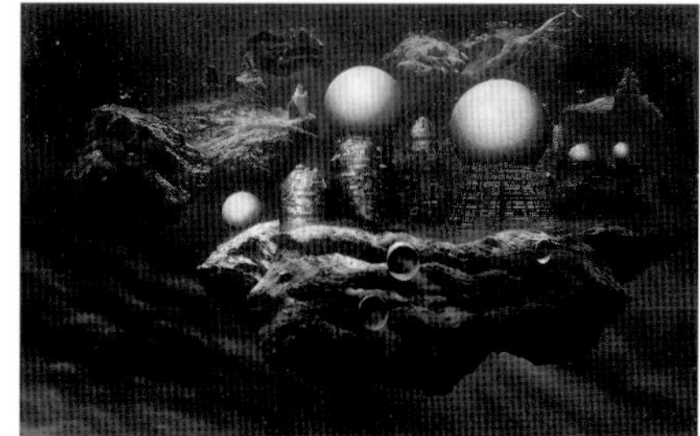

Glenn Brown   fig. 7
The Pornography of Death 1995

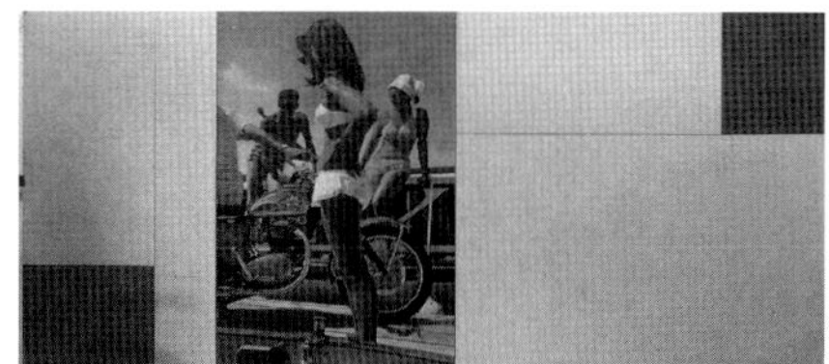

Richard Patterson   fig. 8
Culture Station – Zipper 1995

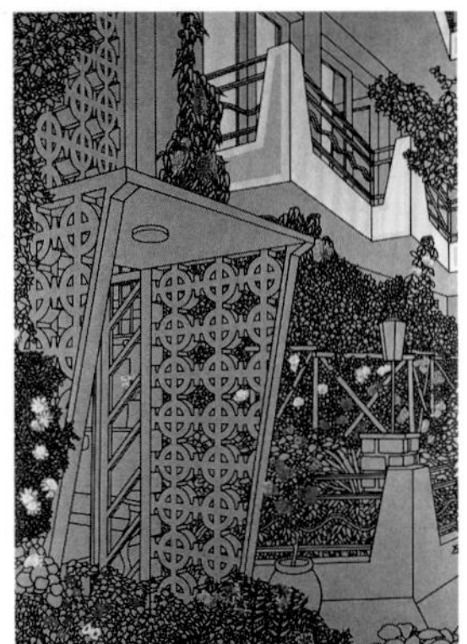
Patrick Caulfield   fig. 9
Entrance 1975

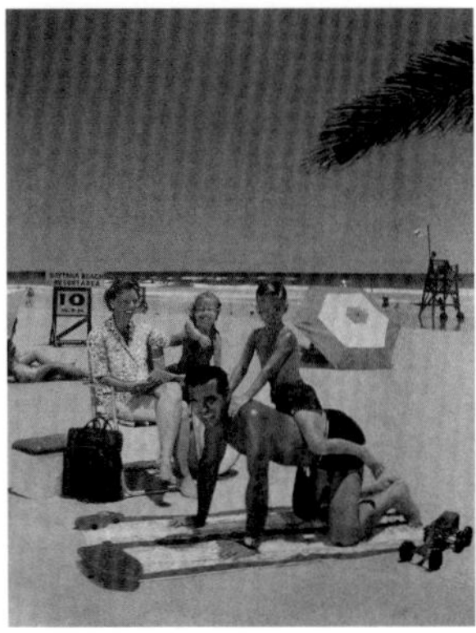
Malcolm Morley   fig. 10
Beach Scene 1968

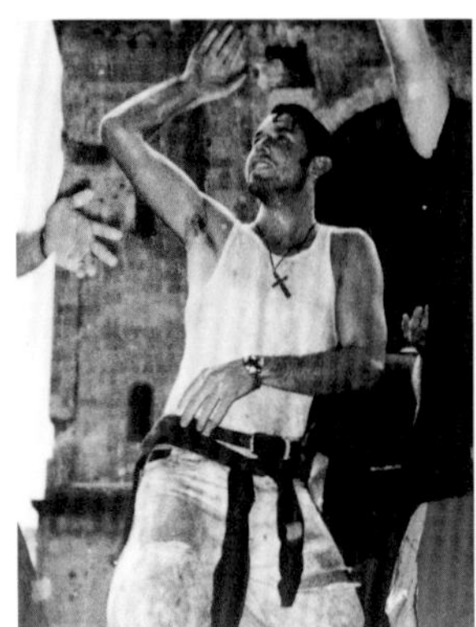
Wolfgang Tillmans   fig. 11
Love Parade 1993

into Patrick Caulfield (fig 9) and rekindling something from the apparent cul-de-sac of Op art.

Daniel Coombs takes his form from a photo realist model, seizing upon Malcolm Morley (fig 10) and giving it a David Lynch swerve. He mucks about with scale and restrained blur, then visits Richard Hamilton, keeping both Caulfield and Hockney in tow. Coombs' anxious heightened world evokes the cartoon madness of Ren and Stimpy. Such busily populated paintings are characteristic of *neurotic realism* and in the hands of Chantal Joffe and Nicky Hoberman the unspoken sexuality of children is subtly exposed. Chantal Joffe flicks and scratches her paint playfully from kids to porn and back again while Nicky Hoberman creates a world located somewhere between Malcom Morley's family group and Sue Williams' fear of abuse. Martin Maloney adopts a more carefree and enjoyable take on figuration. Maloney attacks painting with a running embrace, a genuine love for the practice. Late Picasso blends with Hockney, making a smelt down of art history's highlights. He transcribes Poussin through rave culture.

One group of these new British painters didn't look to America, but took from their own backyard. Celebrating painterly skill, they used domesticity and a familiar English type of documentary drama. Karl Maughan, Victoria Chalmers and Rosie Snell tread a realist path which does not reflect transatlantic modishness. They claim a peculiar heritage, re-visiting the skill of the deeply unfashionable Stanley Spencer. Maughan's perfect flower borders threaten in their photographic clarity. Snell's landscape paintings trace a path of American Gothic straight to Andrew Wyeth. Chalmers paints a cool portrait of nervous disturbance. By picking up on the underlying, kitchen-sink nostalgia of the Britcool phenomena, this group of painters suddenly found their documentary style a strength.

The theme of hanging out and being cool gave us an art that reflected 'real life'. Nan Goldin and Wolfgang Tillmans (fig 11) made a lot of sense, for many new artists. They appeared unself-consciously self-conscious and for this they were admired. Jack Pierson's ruggedly gay thing had a tinsel-camp slant (fig 12). Karen Kilimnik assimilated fame fetishism and neuroses into a diverse body of work: photos; paintings; drawing and installation. Elizabeth Peyton, borrowing from Alex Katz, found a 'just painting' equivalent. Peter Davies, in his list paintings, looks at the fetishism of art star fame. Like Bruce Nauman, he uses the obsessive's list to highlight the madly transient nature of life in the Hall of Fame.

The British don't find it easy to make work about hanging out. Andreas Schlaegel and Steven Gontarski, British artists by default (Schlaegel originally from Germany and Gontarski from America), provide a relaxed attitude and refreshing angle. Schlaegel offers a complete Euro-Pop package with his tongue firmly in his cheek. The monumental look of Rachel Whiteread's sculptures meet Hitler's bunker but end up at a Las Vegas themepark. Gontarski's model figures fetishise nightclub posing and distorted copulation. It's clean cut gone scary (Keanu Reeves does Cyberpunk) as these figures combine the technology of a morphed image with hands-on sewing skills. Sue Webster and Tim Noble have the Southend seaside pathos of beach detritus, mixed with the neon flavour of ultra violence. They show the beloved underbelly of English life, giving a Punch and Judy show for the modern age.

Historically, the strength of realist art has been psychological. It has been a way for the individual artist to point to something deep beyond surface appearances. The trouble, is no one is quite sure where the 'surface' lies any more. Here you have a group of artists who use strange psychology as an accepted subject. Traditional forms of making imagery have returned. The apparent Brave New World of art as a weird science, theoretical and controlled, an art for people who enjoy wearing lab coats, has been hijacked. Ordered hunting and gathering of the everyday, and the subsequent presentation in a biographical or confessional form, has given way to a healthier interest in art history. Looking to the past and celebrating it, rather than borrowing blindly, this group of new artists searches to find something which could be shared out. This transition was most dramatically played out through the function of the artist-run space that by the midpoint of the decade, realised it had fed the YBA mainstream but had left little for itself. Through documentary methods with facts sliding into fictions these artists strive to make something 'real' for us all to sink our teeth into.

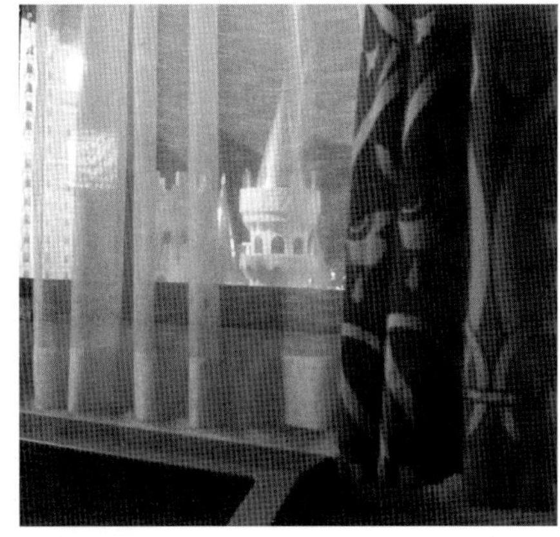

Jack Pierson   fig. 12
Excalibur 1992

Figure 1   *Westworld* 1973 directed by Michael Crichton courtesy Warner Bros. Photograph supplied by BFI
Figure 2   John Baldessari *I will not make any more boring art* 1971 lithograph on Arches paper (ed. 50)
  57 x 76.4cm/22½ x 30in Photograph courtesy of Sonnabend Gallery, New York
Figure 3   Chris Burden *Shoot* 1971 black & white photograph 20.3 x 25.4cm/8 x 10in
  Photograph by Alfred Lucjean, courtesy of Gagosian Gallery, New York
Figure 4   Tony Oursler *Horror (from Judy)* 1994 mixed media video installation
  Photograph courtesy of Metro Pictures, New York
Figure 5   Richard Billingham *Untitled (Ral 38)* 1995 SFA4 colour photograph on aluminium 80 x 120cm/31½ x 47¼in
  The Saatchi Gallery, London
Figure 6   Jim Shaw *I'm showing Peter Saul...* 1993 pencil on paper 30.5 x 23cm/12 x 9in
  Photograph Rosamund Felsen Gallery, Santa Monica
Figure 7   Glenn Brown *The Pornography of Death* 1995 oil on canvas 209.5 x 328cm/82½ x 129in
  The Saatchi Gallery, London
Figure 8   Richard Patterson *Culture Station – Zipper* 1995 oil and acrylic on canvas 213.4 x 459.7cm/84 x 181in
  The Saatchi Gallery, London
Figure 9   Patrick Caulfield *Entrance* 1975 acrylic on canvas 304.8 x 213.4cm/120 x 84in
  Patrick Caulfield all rights reserved, DACS, 1998
Figure 10   Malcolm Morley *Beach Scene* 1968 acrylic on canvas 267 x 221cm/105 x 87in
  Photograph courtesy Lida Morley
Figure 11   Wolfgang Tillmans *Love Parade* 1993 Photograph courtesy the Daniel Buchholz Gallery, Cologne
Figure 12   Jack Pierson *Excalibur* 1992 Ektacolour print (ed. 1/1) 74 x 77cm/29¼ x 30¼in
  Photograph courtesy Jack Pierson

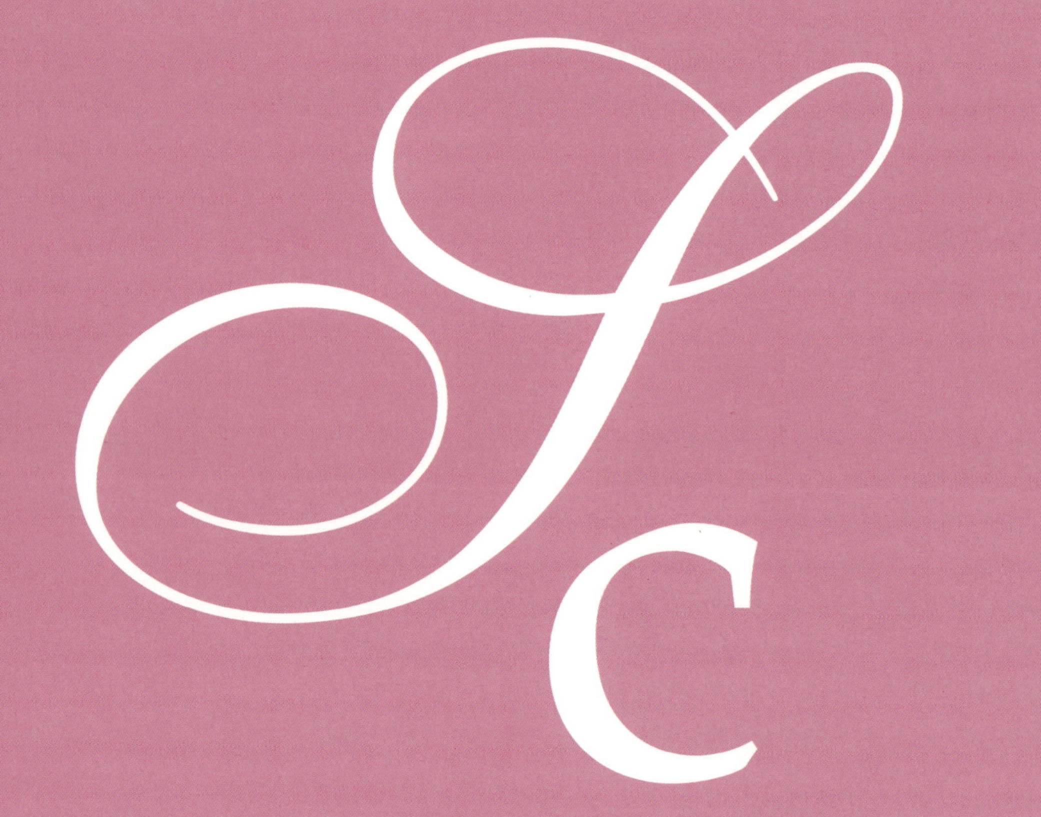

tuRE

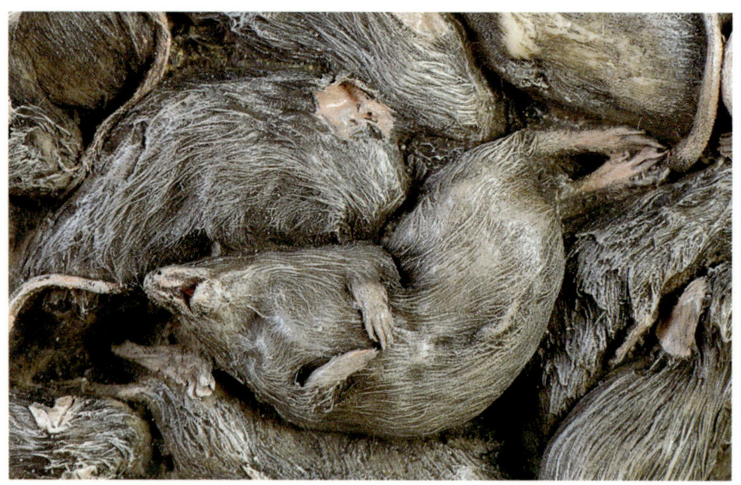

DAVID FALCONER

Vermin Death Stack 1998
cast resin, enamel paint
305 x 91.5 x 91.5cm/120 x 36 x 36in

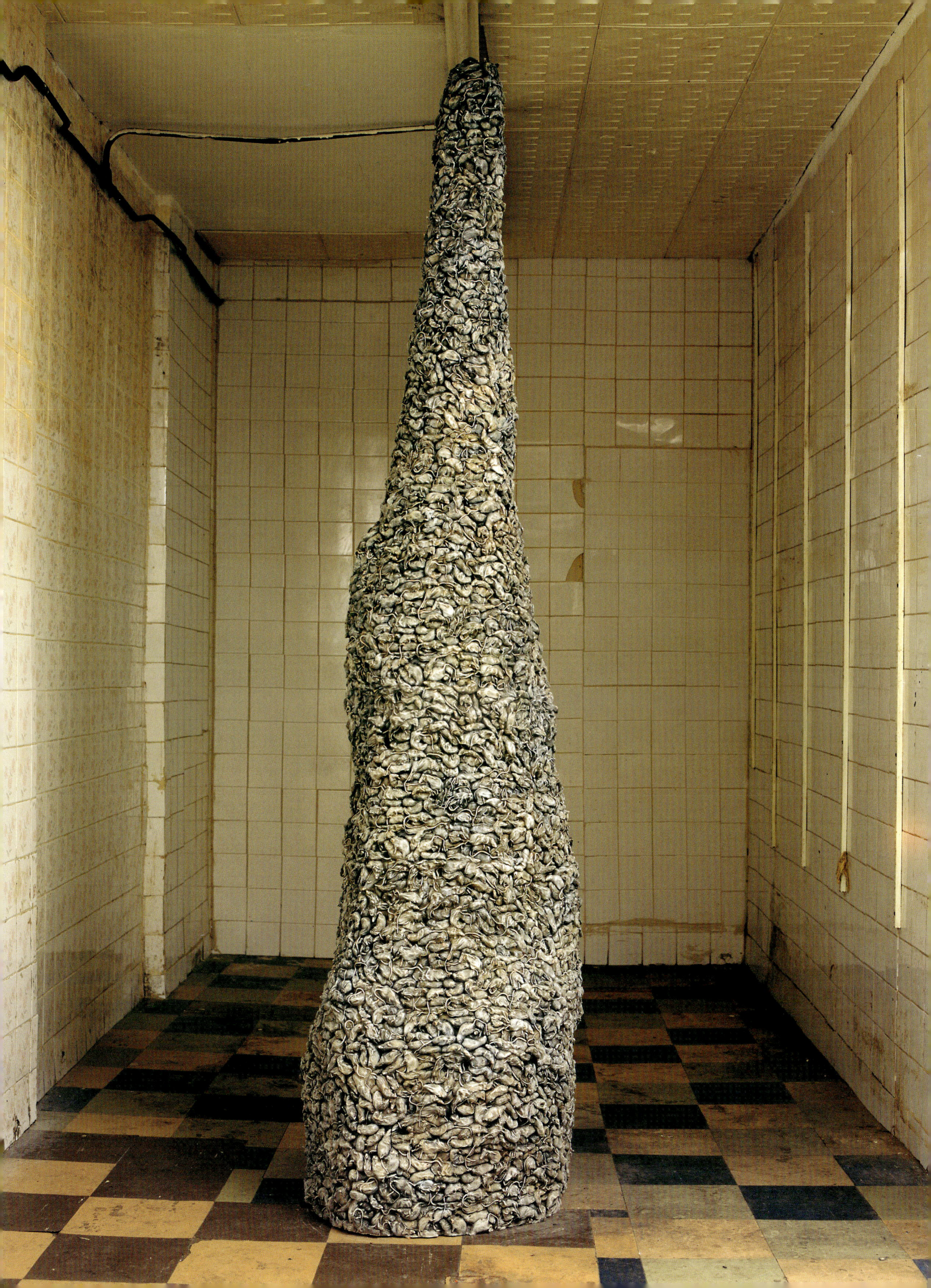

STEVEN GONTARSKI

Arbeiter Samariter 1997
pvc, synthetic hair, fabric, wadding
101.6 x 122 x 71cm/40 x 48 x 28in

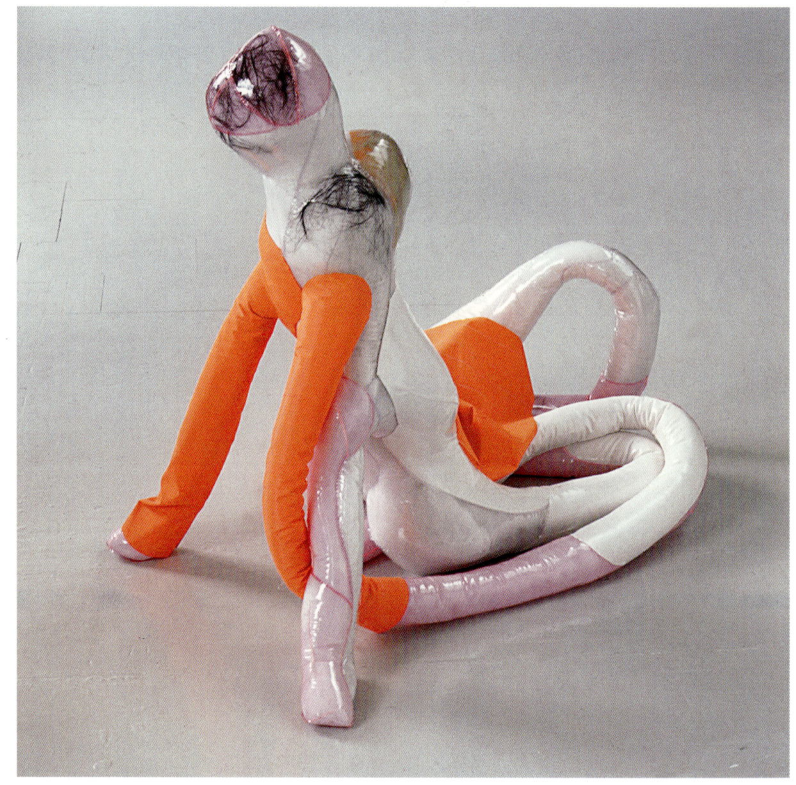

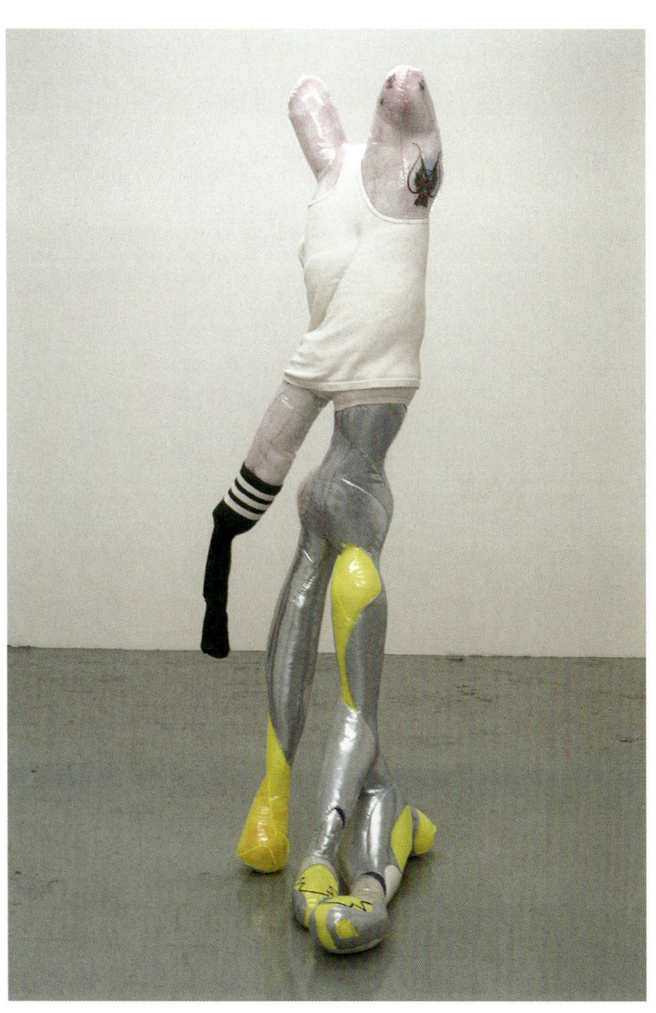

Arbeiter Samariter 1997
pvc, synthetic hair, fabric, wadding
101.6 x 122 x 71cm/40 x 48 x 28in

STEVEN GONTARSKI

Useless 1997
pvc, polyester wadding, wood, synthetic clothing, transfer tattoo
173 x 63 x 84cm/68 x 24¾ x 33in

right:
Wife 1998
pvc, polyester wadding, synthetic hair and wood
195 x 160 x 178cm/76¾ x 63 x 70in

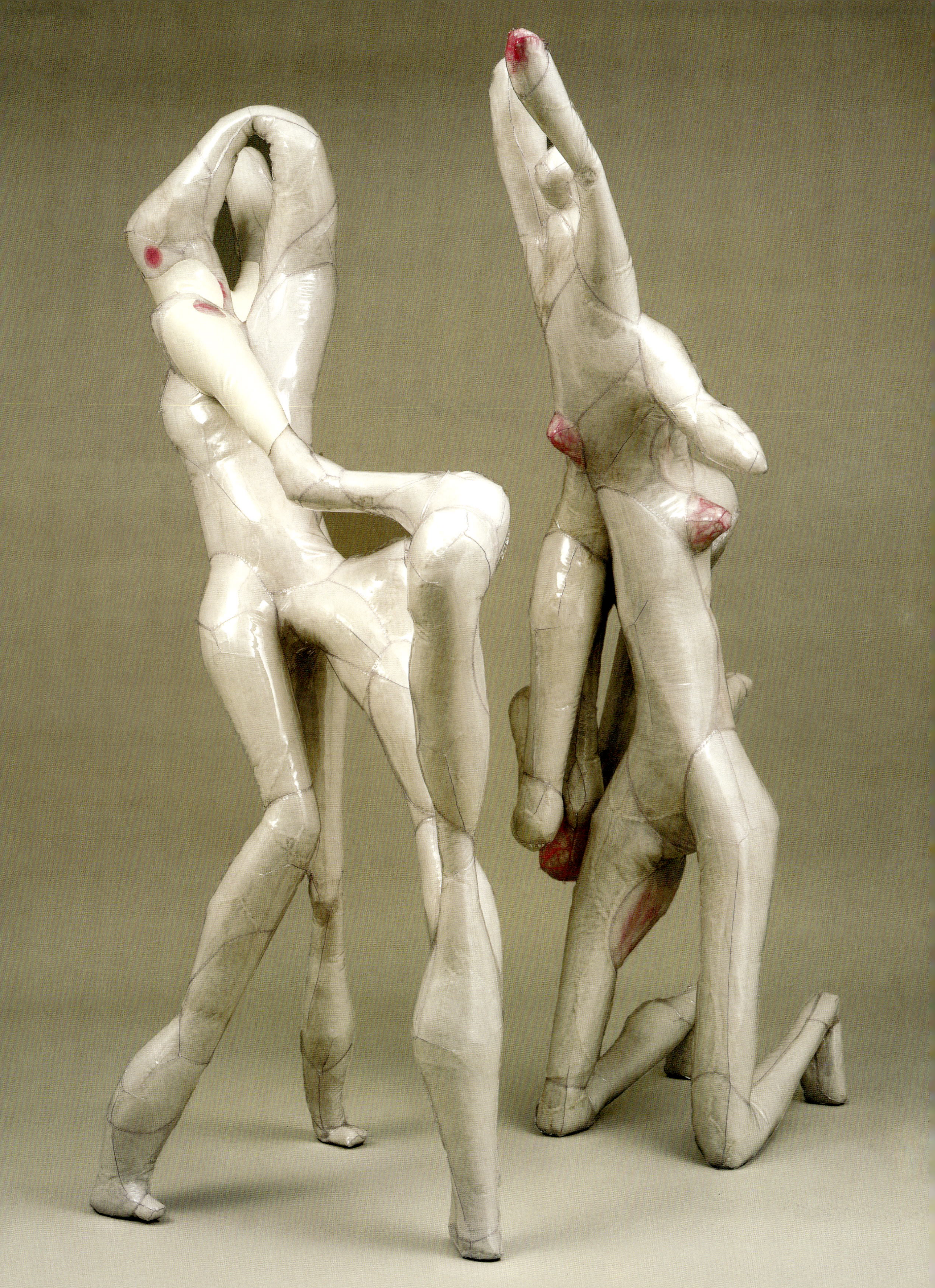

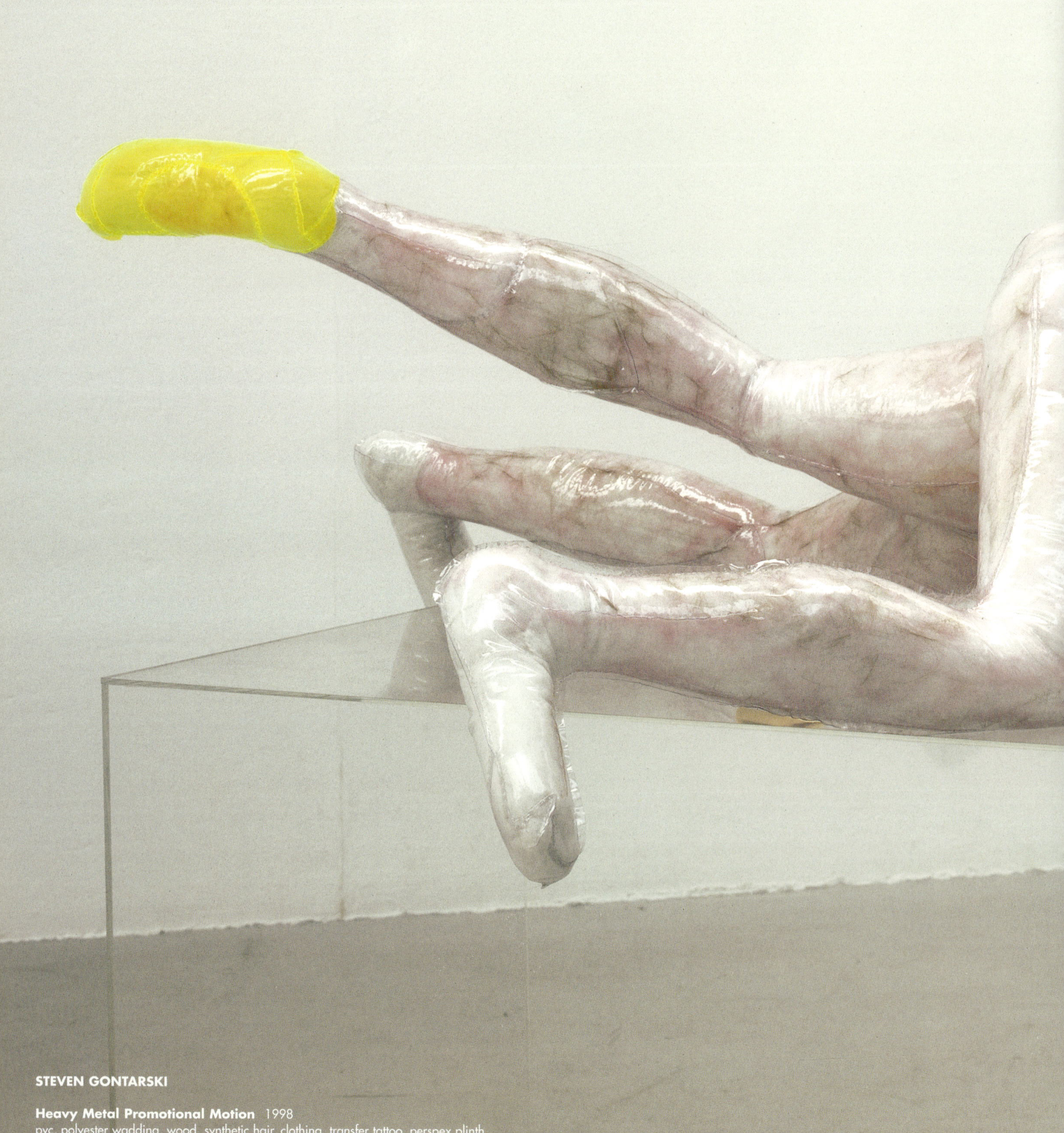

STEVEN GONTARSKI

Heavy Metal Promotional Motion 1998
pvc, polyester wadding, wood, synthetic hair, clothing, transfer tattoo, perspex plinth
dimensions including plinth: 125 x 175 x 102cm/49¹/₂ x 69 x 40¹/₄ in

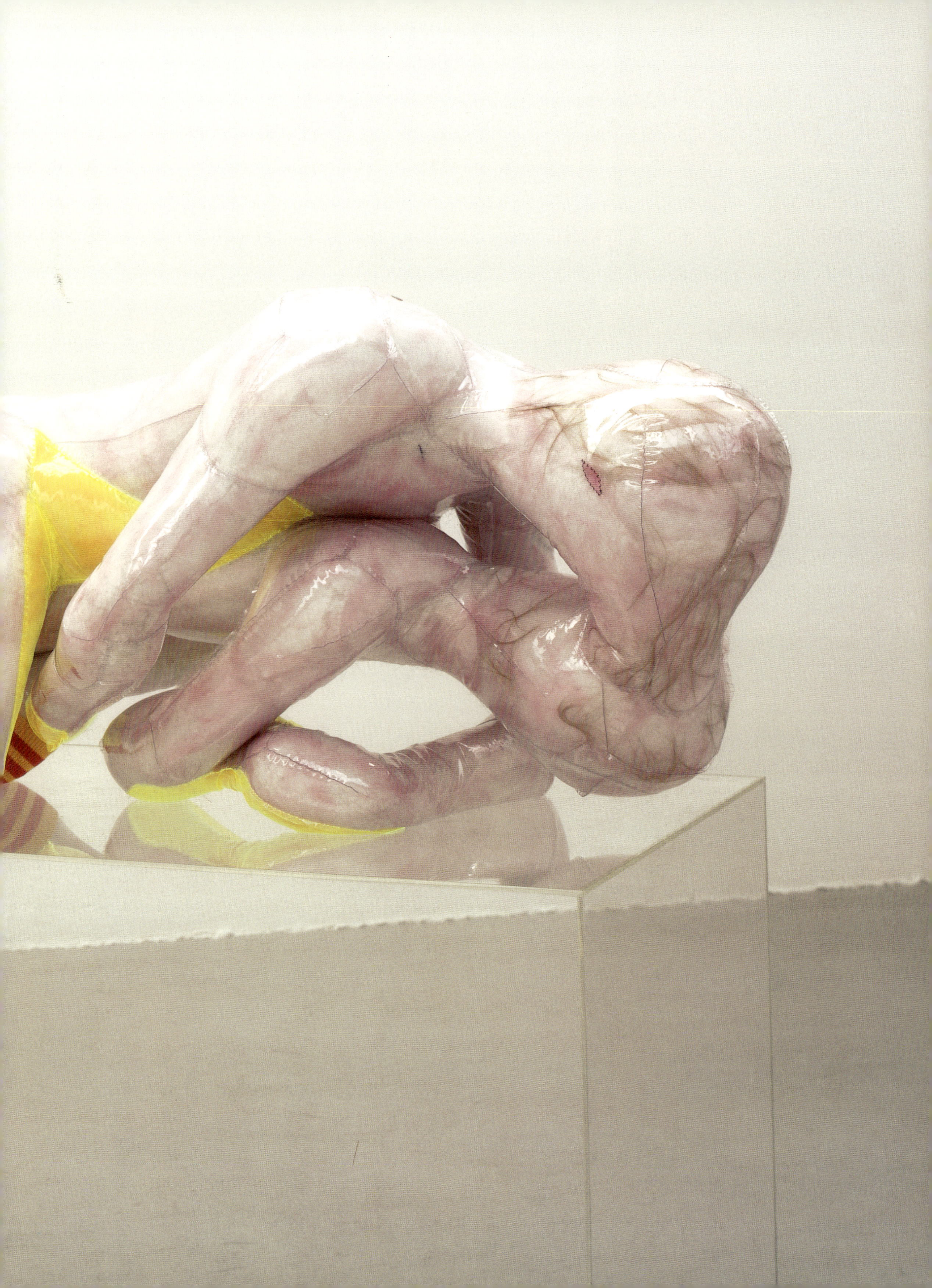

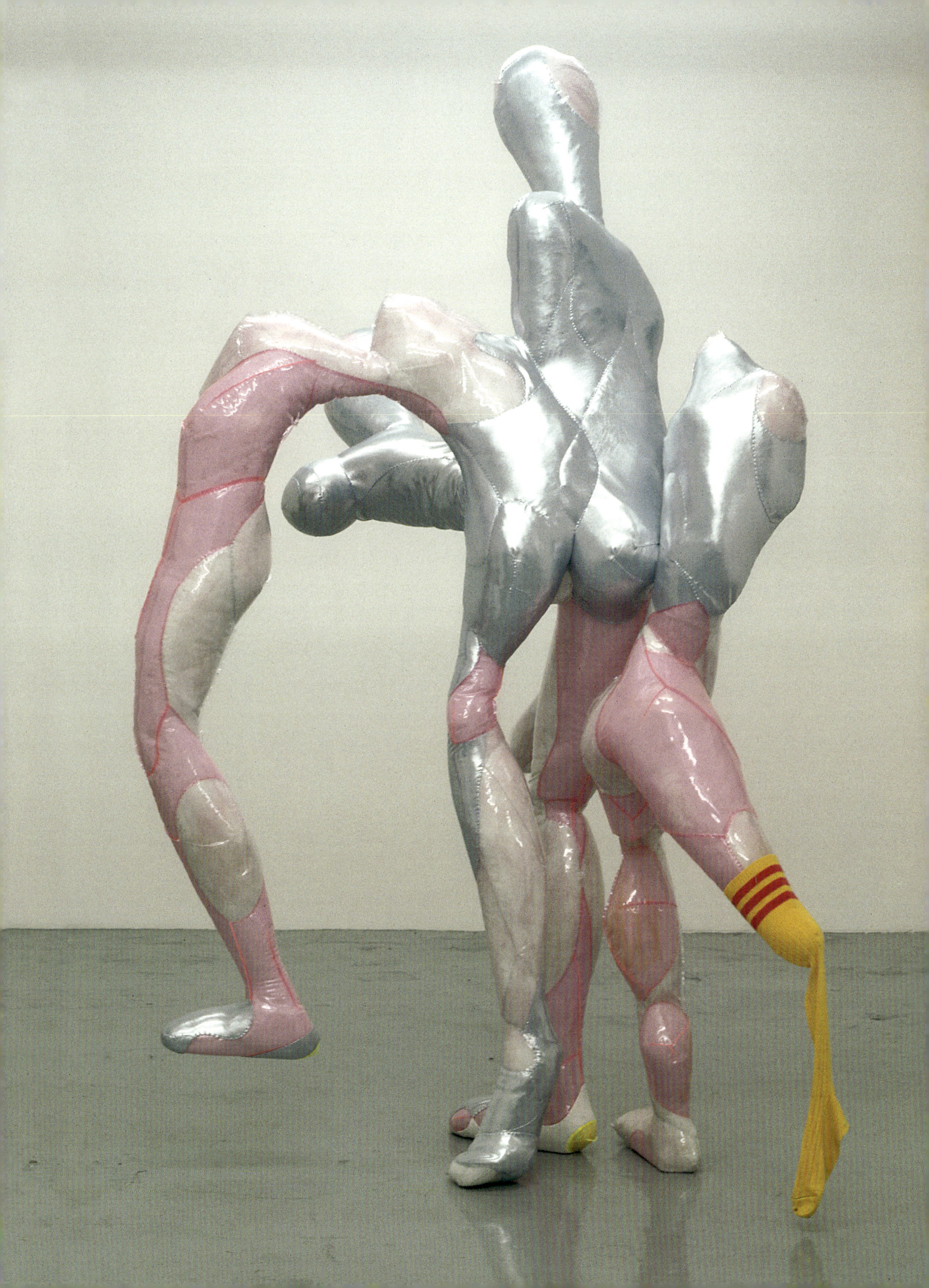

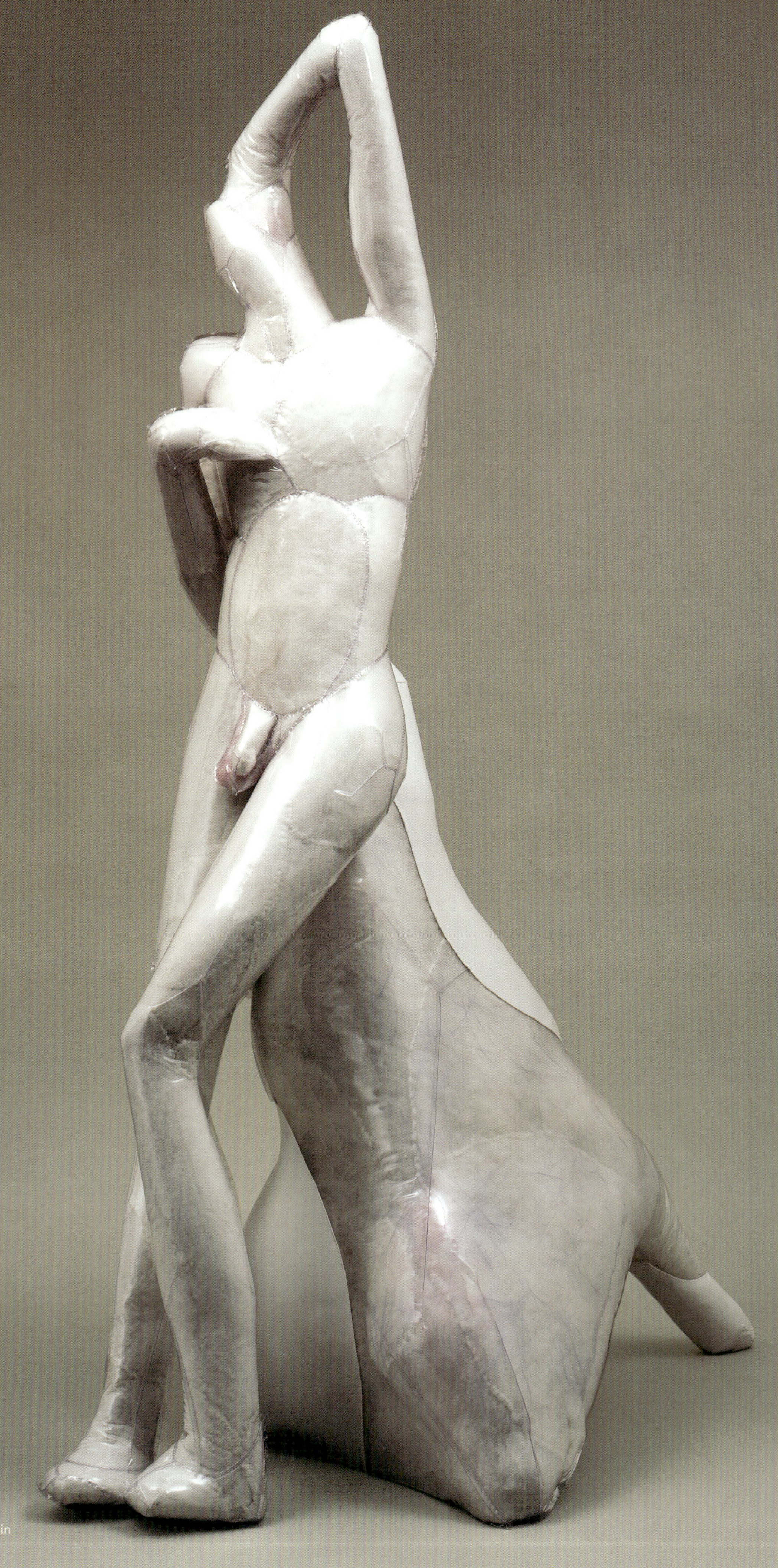

STEVEN GONTARSKI

**Lying Active
(Dying Captive)** 1998
pvc, polyester wadding,
synthetic hair and wood
193 x 193 x 53cm/76 x 76 x 21in

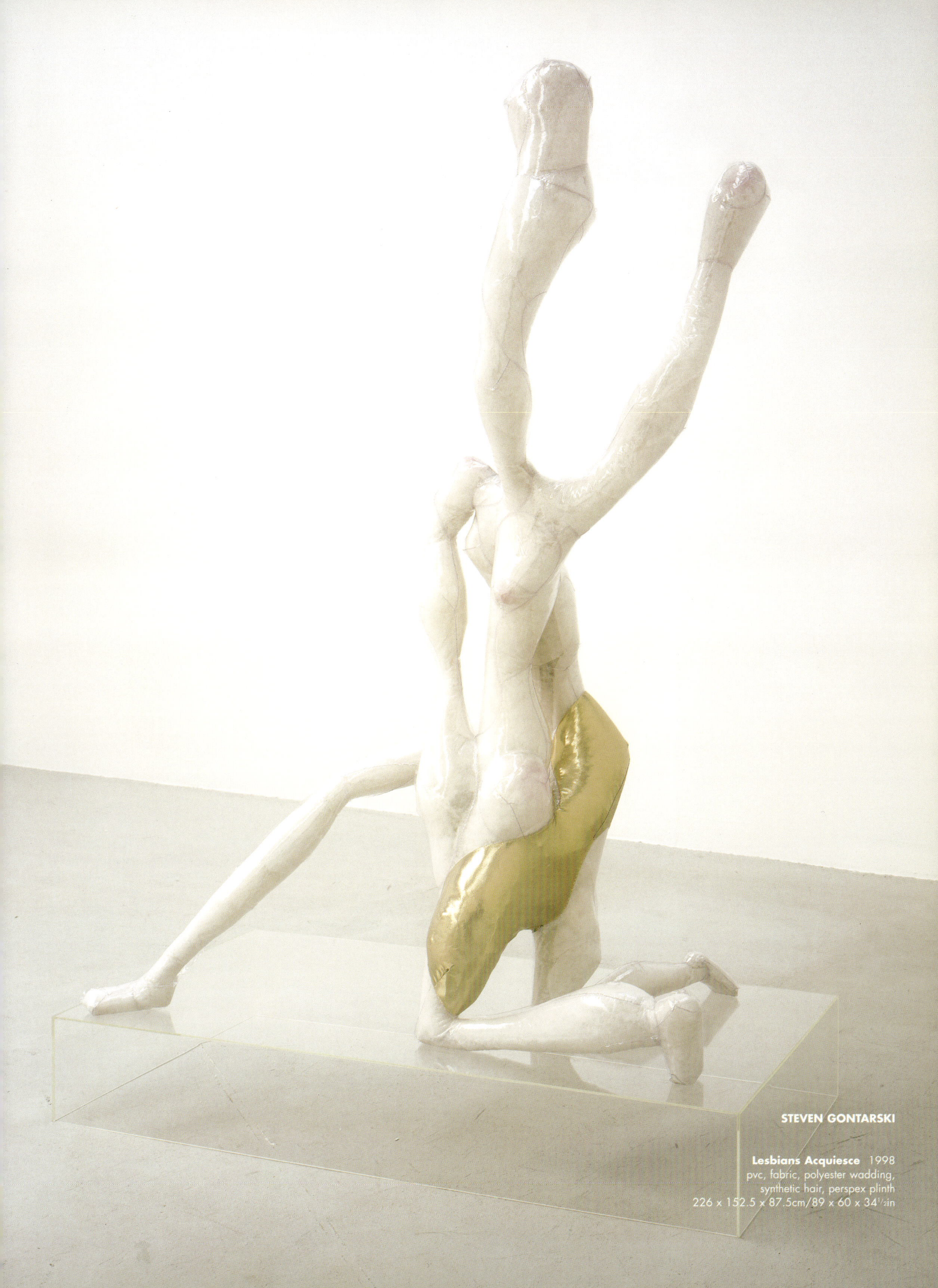

Lesbians Acquiesce 1998
pvc, fabric, polyester wadding,
synthetic hair, perspex plinth
226 x 152.5 x 87.5cm/89 x 60 x 34½in

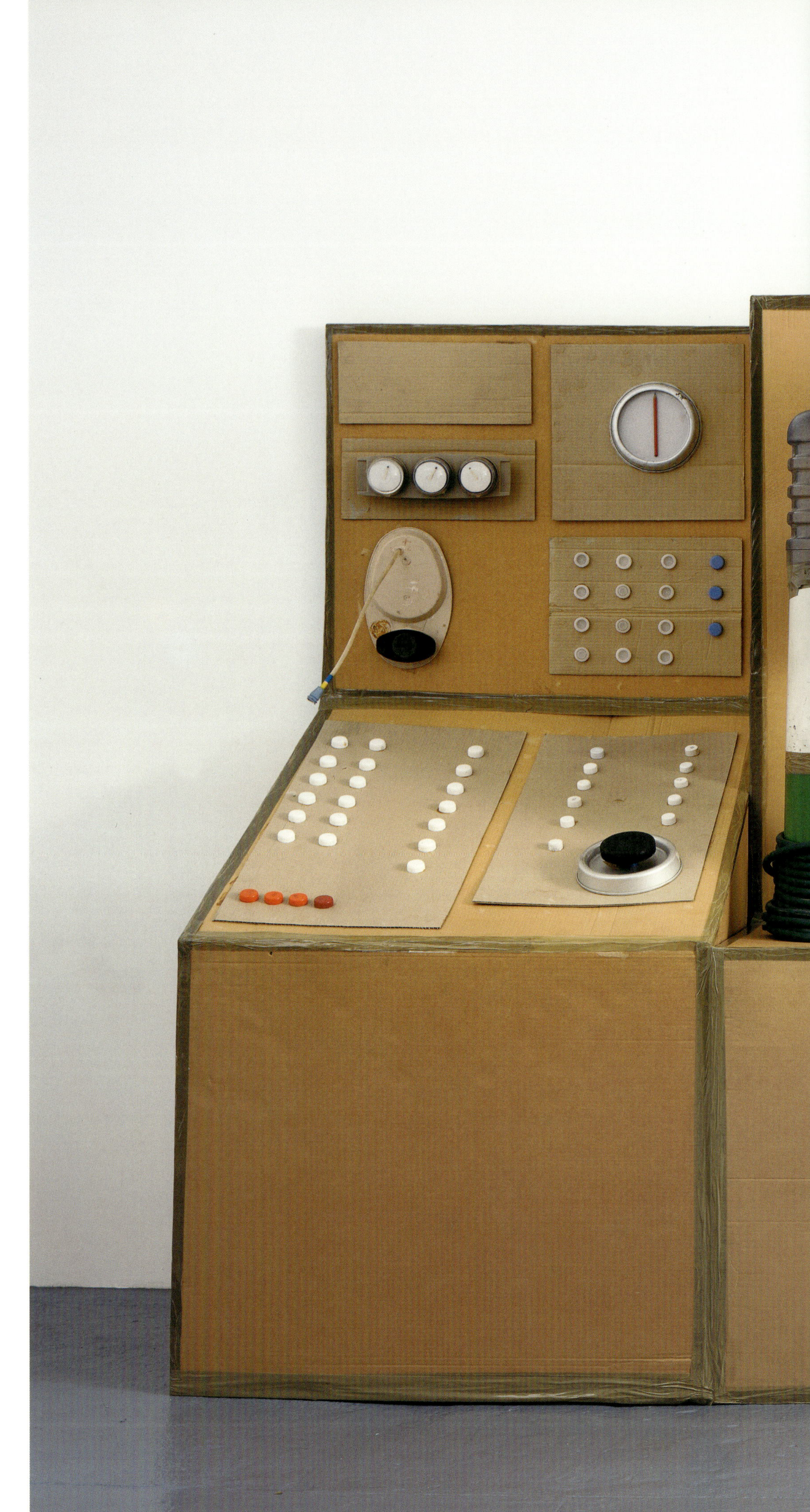

BRIAN CYRIL GRIFFITHS

Osaka 1997
cardboard boxes, office bins, water
container, umbrella, drawer, plastic
sheeting, pencils, matches, plastic cups,
whisk, tubing, egg cup, tea strainer,
hose pipe, bottle tops, tape (various)
approx: 250 x 330 x 150cm/
98$^{1/2}$ x 130 x 59in

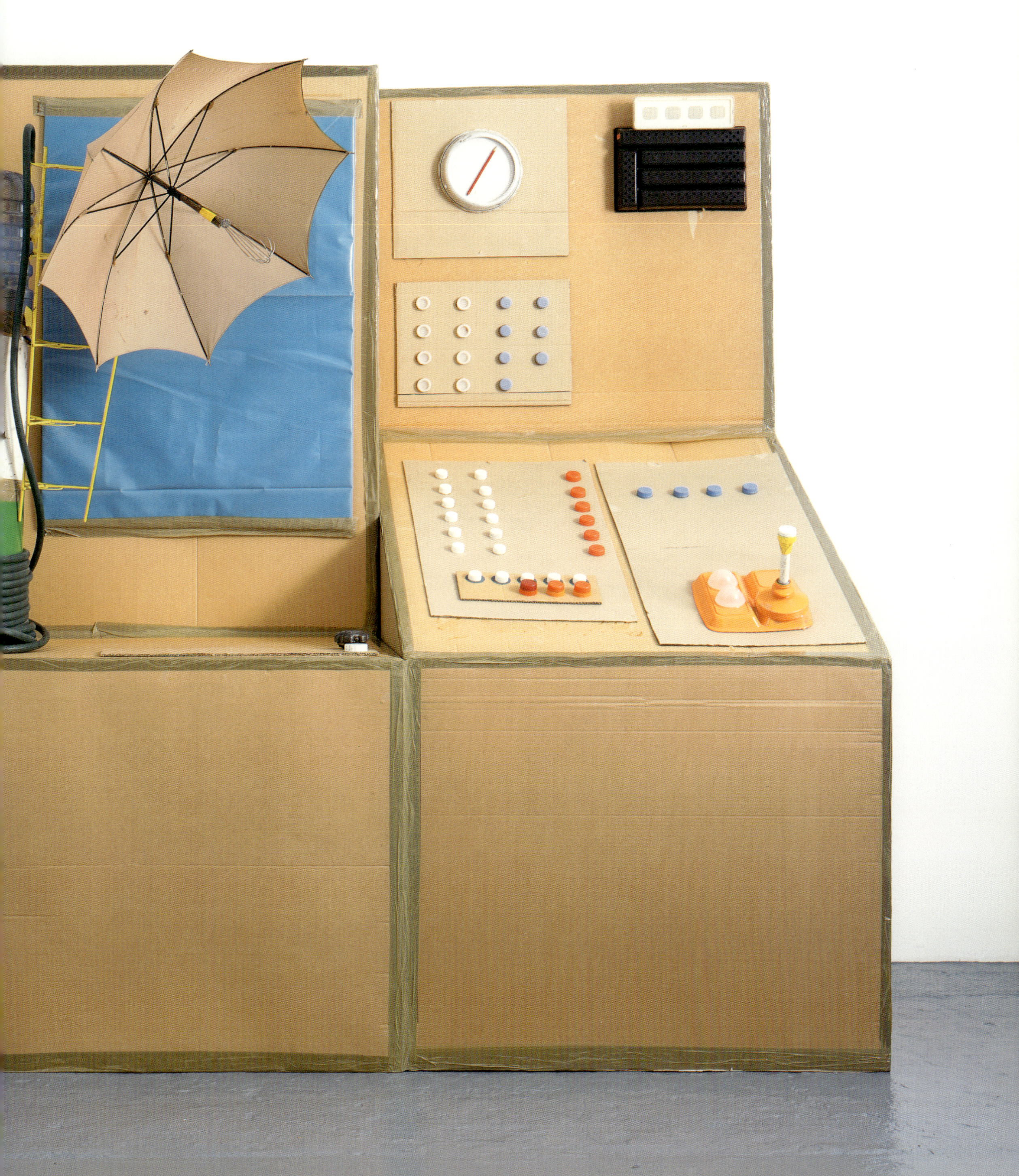

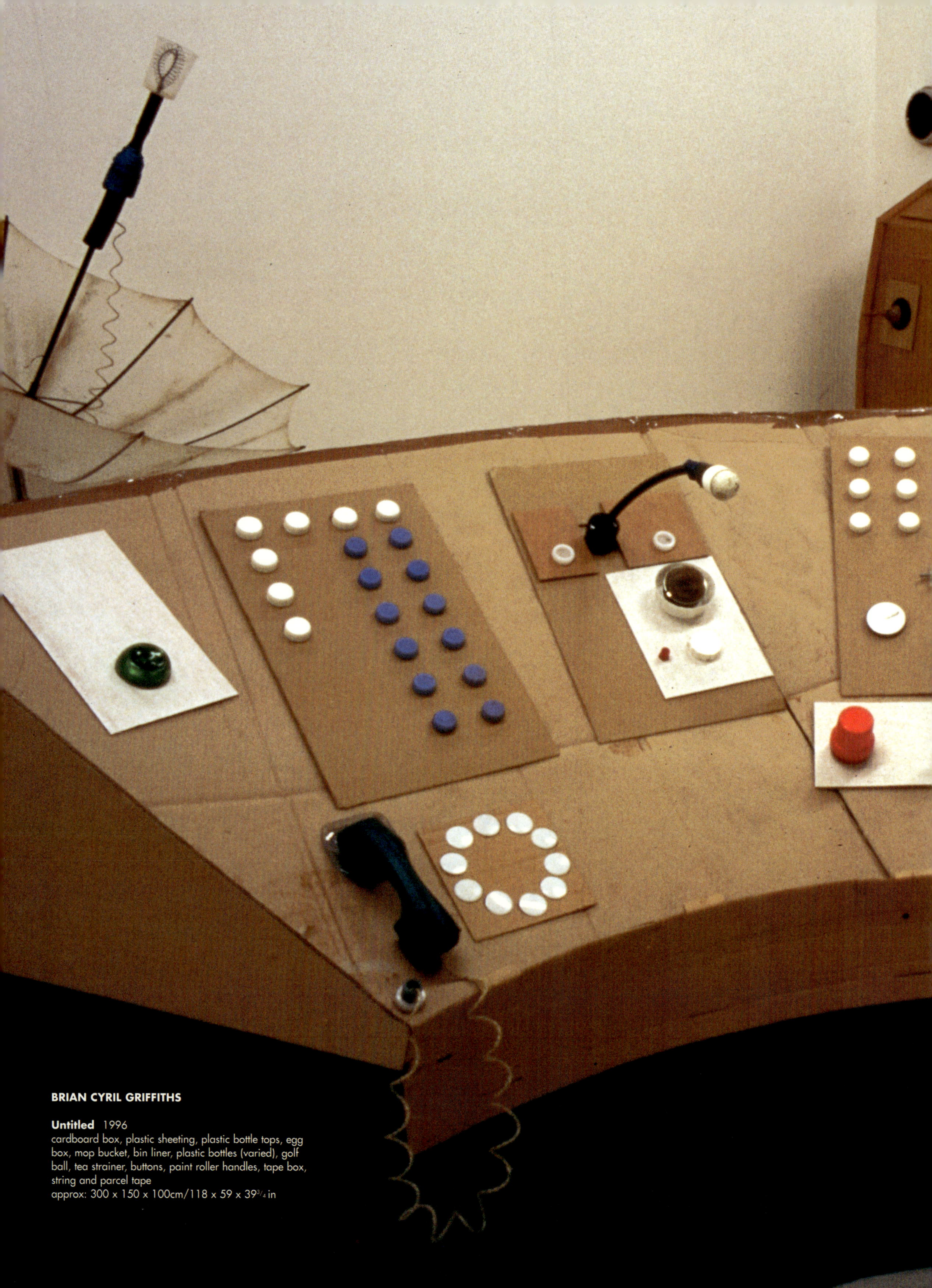

Untitled 1996
cardboard box, plastic sheeting, plastic bottle tops, egg
box, mop bucket, bin liner, plastic bottles (varied), golf
ball, tea strainer, buttons, paint roller handles, tape box,
string and parcel tape
approx: 300 x 150 x 100cm/118 x 59 x 39¾ in

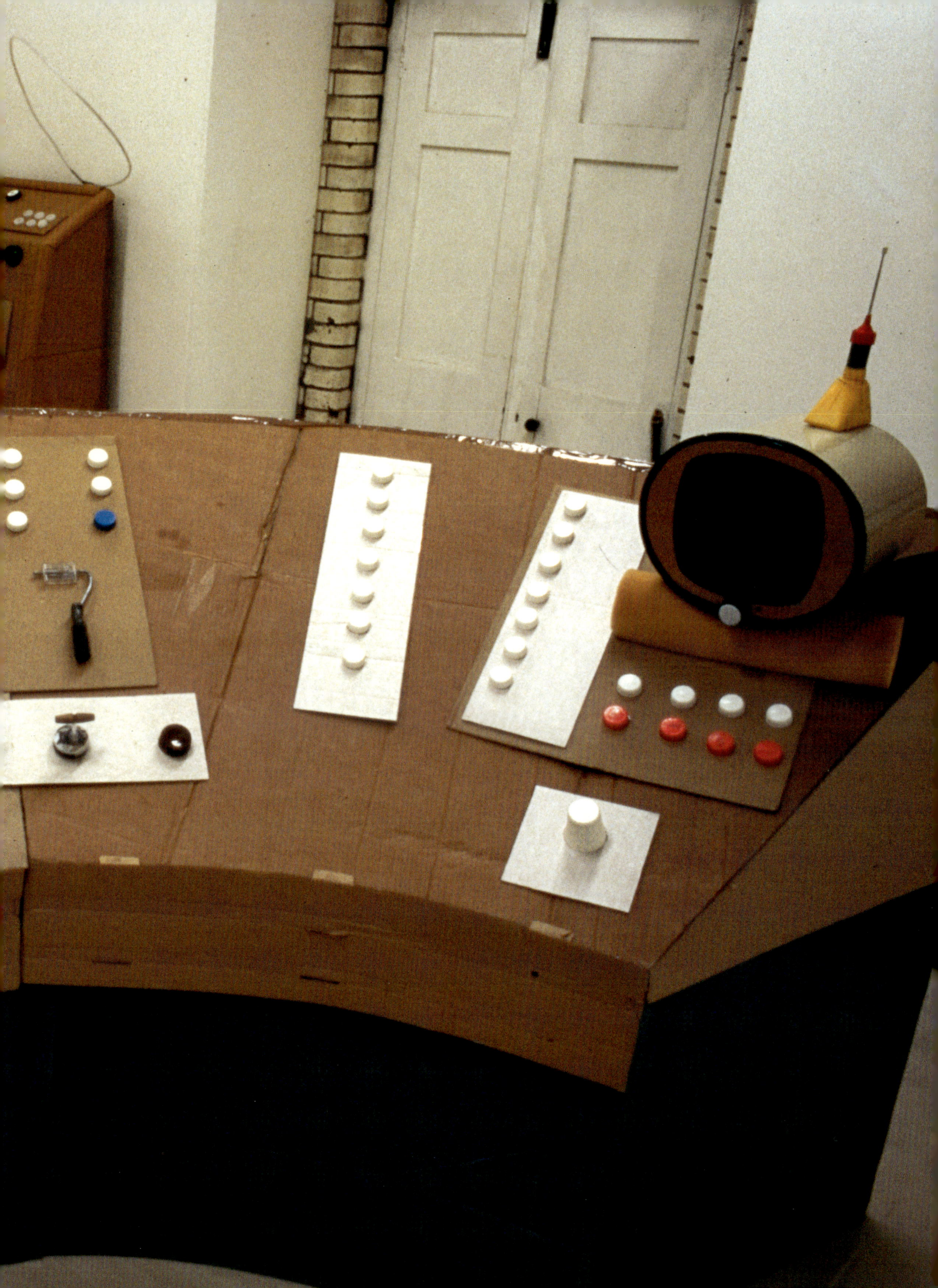

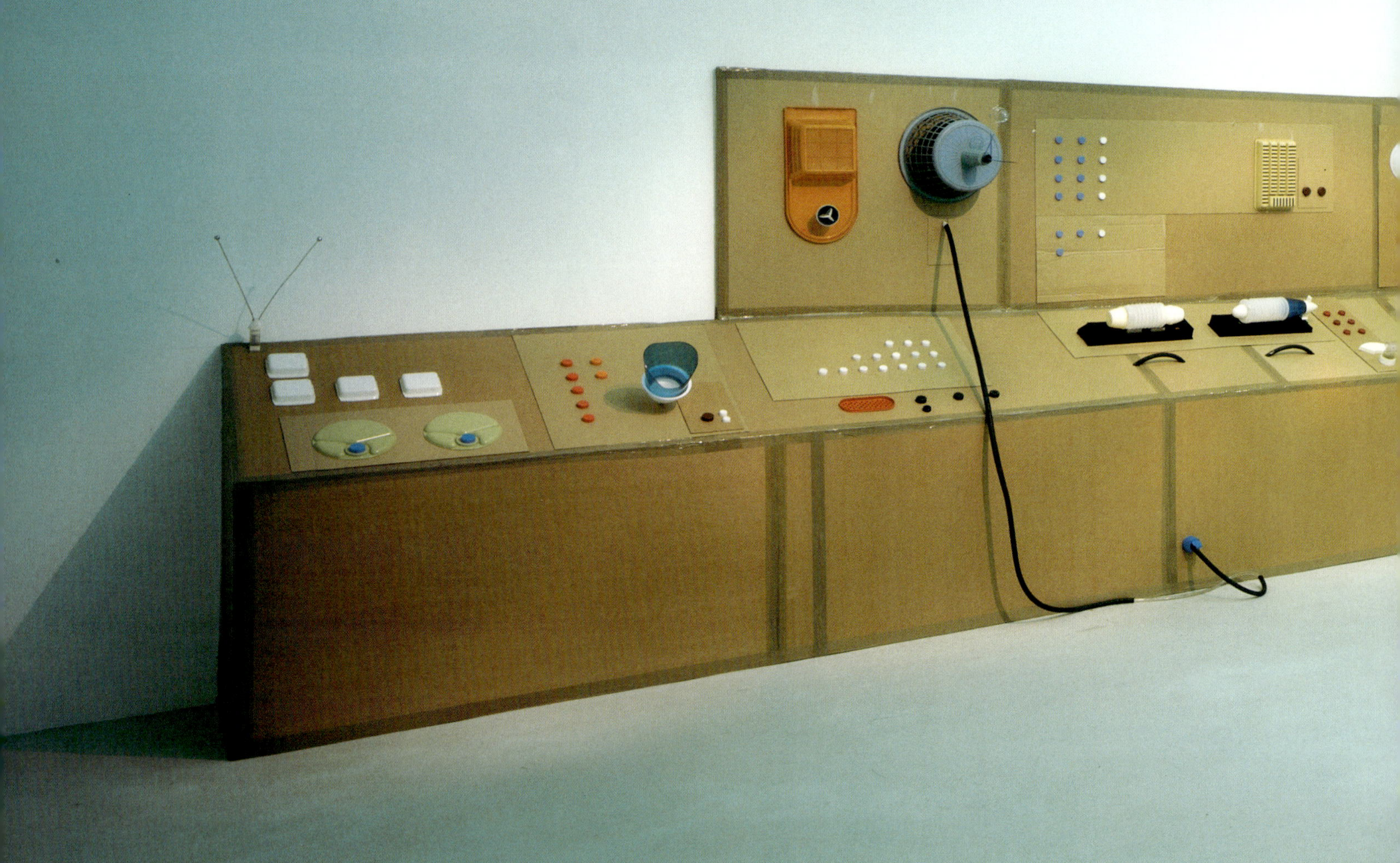

BRIAN CYRIL GRIFFITHS

Osaka, Taylan and Ron 1998
mixed media
dimensions variable

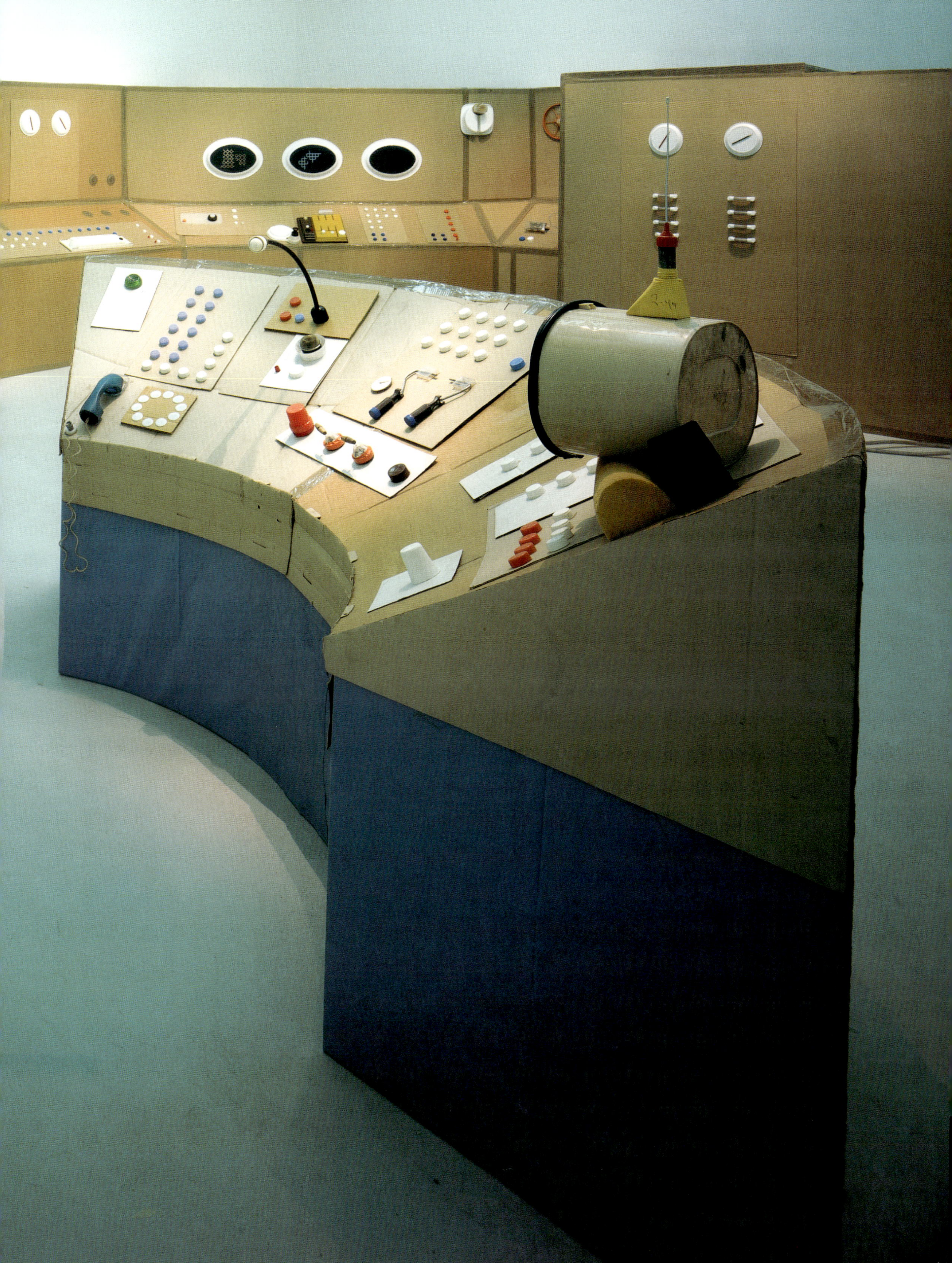

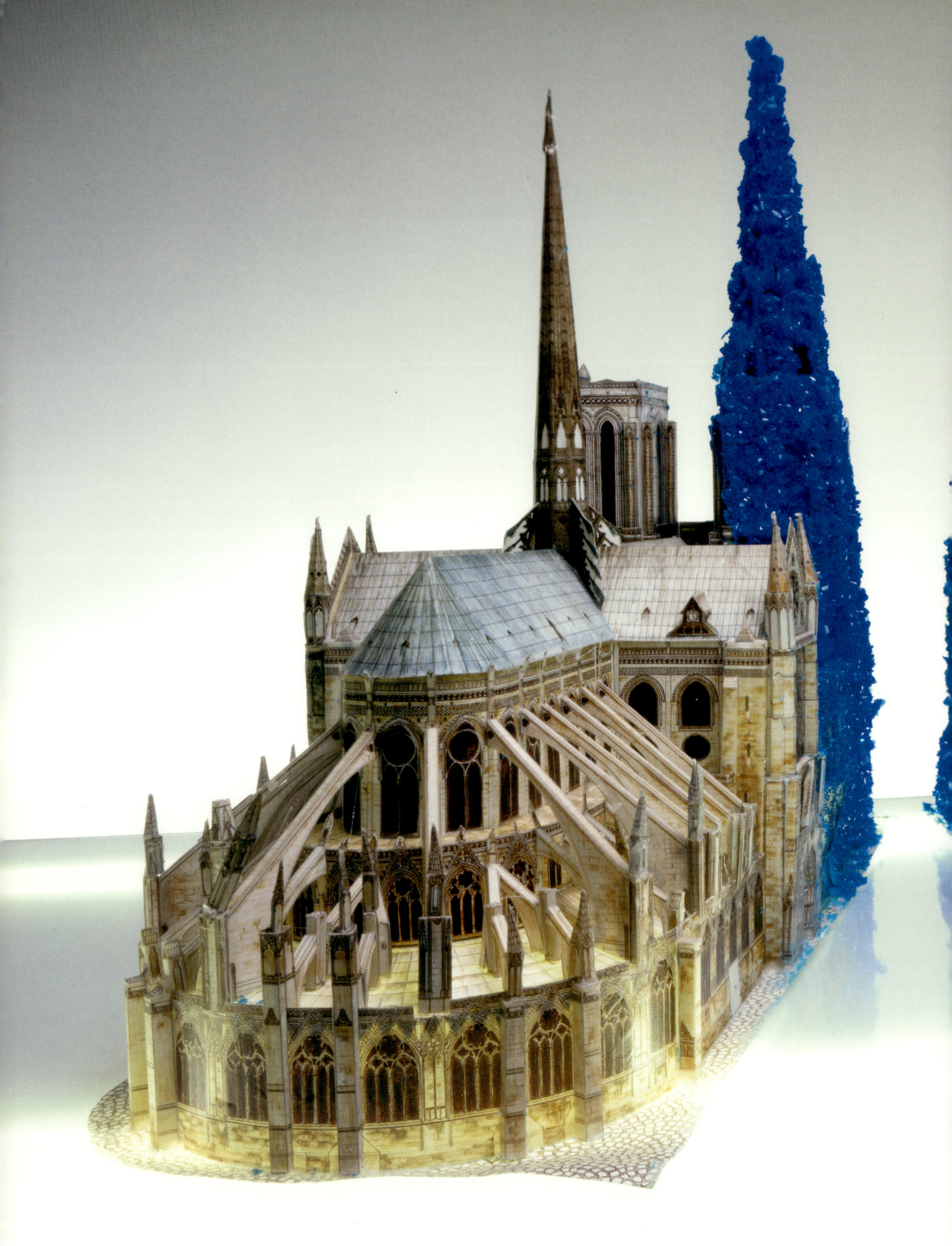

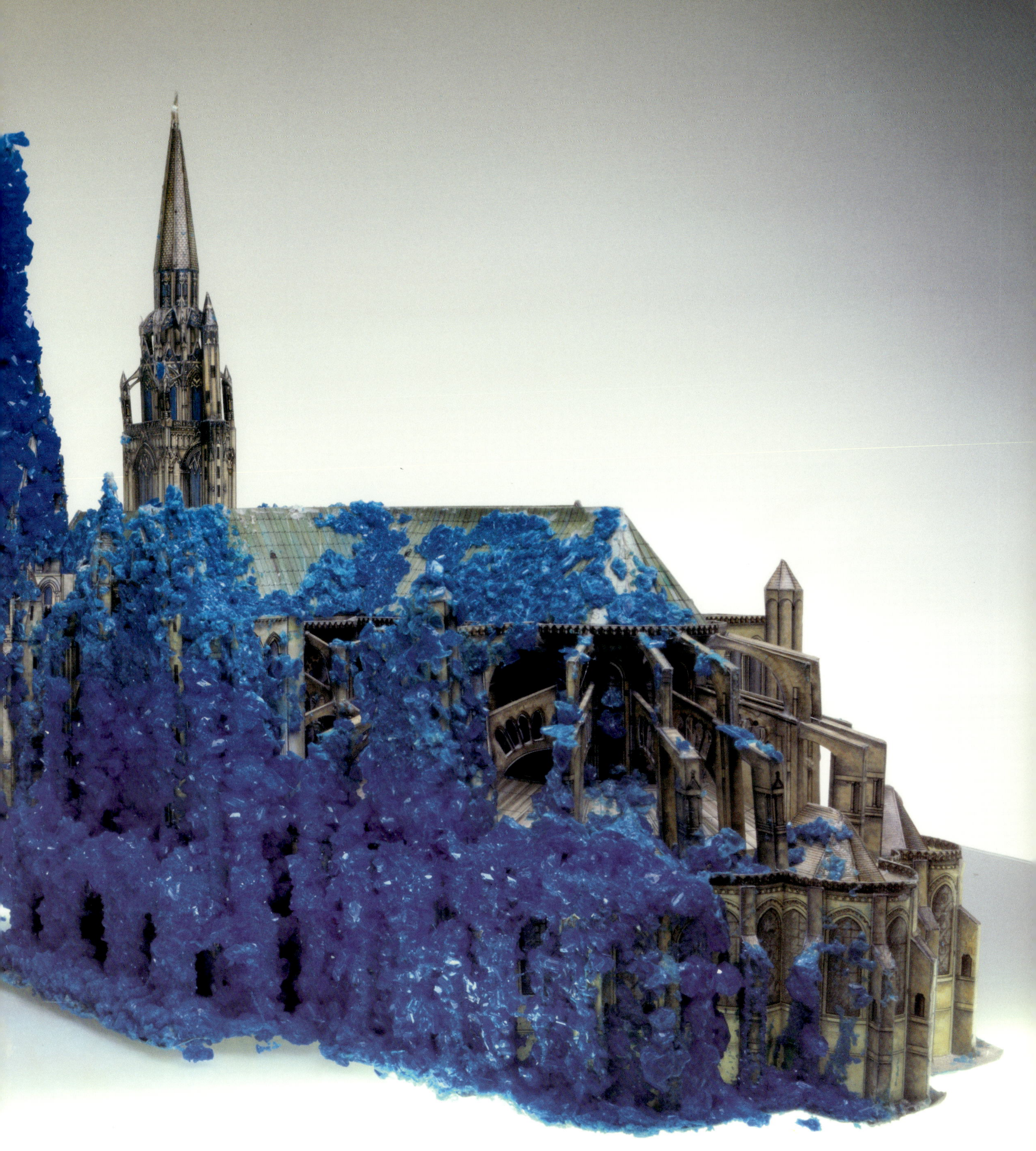

ROGER HIORNS

Copper Sulphate Chartres & Copper Sulphate Notre Dame 1996
card construction with cobalt and copper chemical growth
mounted on glass and wood trestle table with perspex cover underlit by two strip lights
137.2 x 124.5 x 64.8cm/54 x 49 x 25³/₄ in

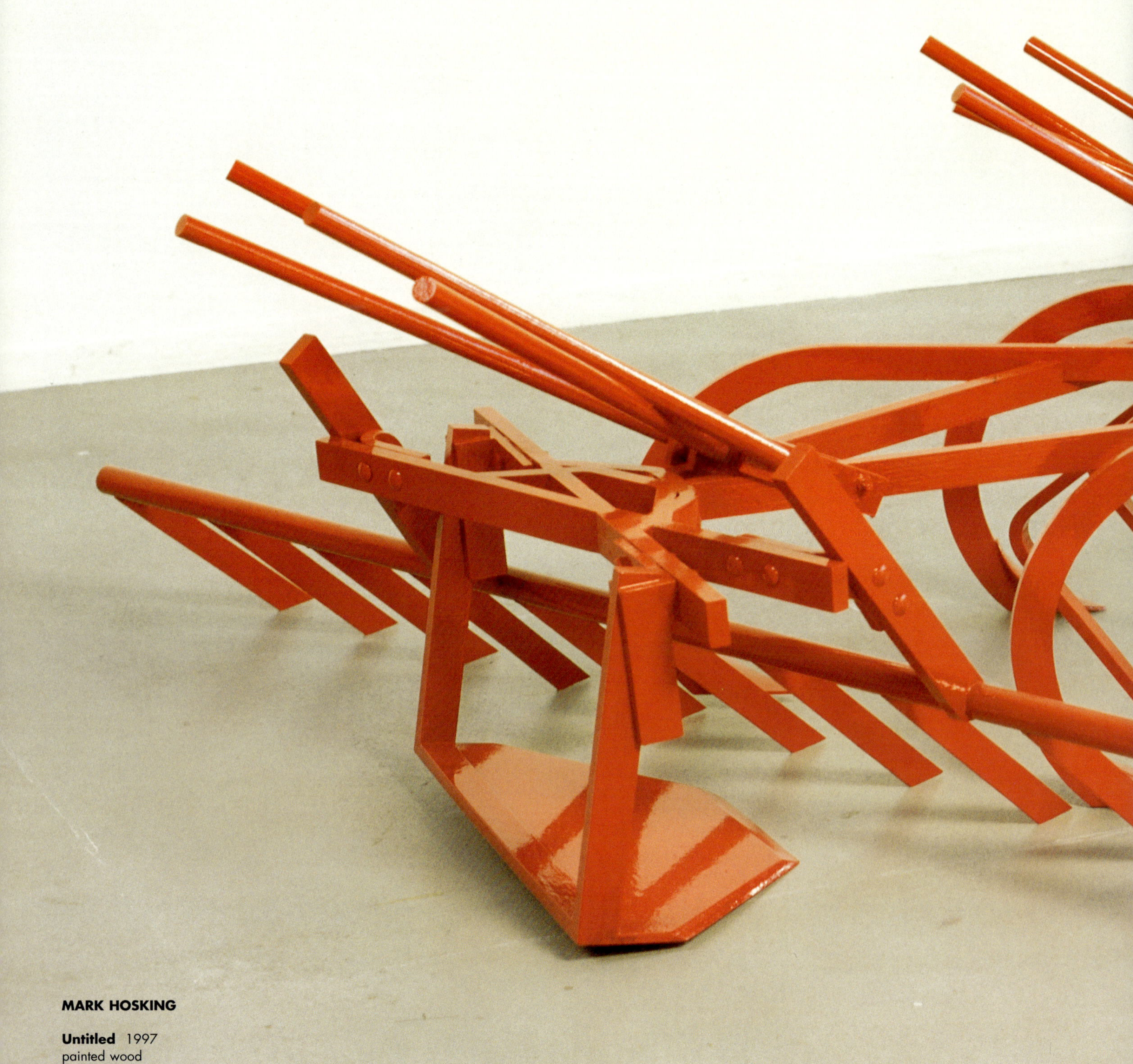

MARK HOSKING

Untitled 1997
painted wood
76 x 202 x 202cm/30 x 79$^{1}/_{2}$ x 79$^{1}/_{2}$in

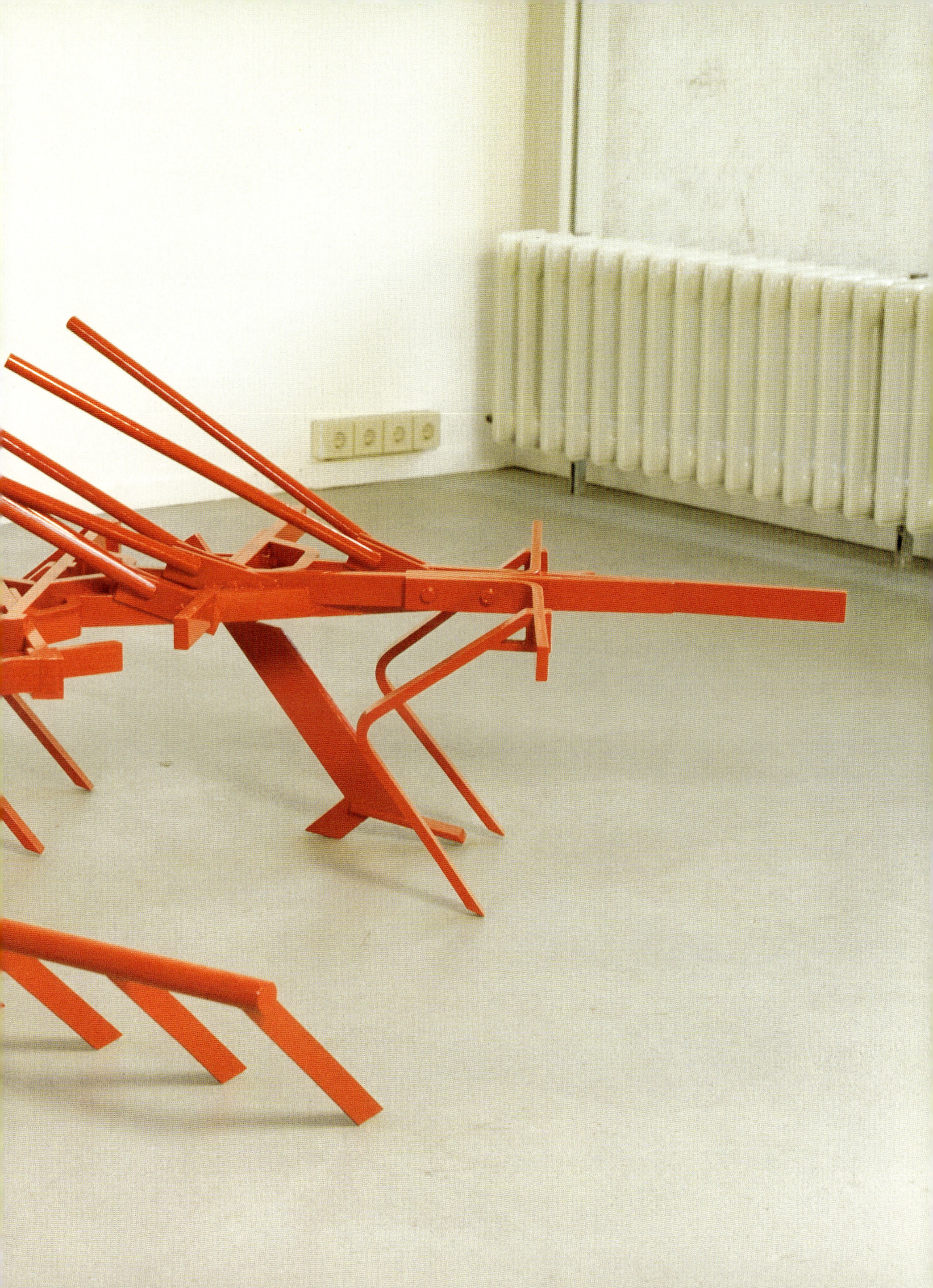

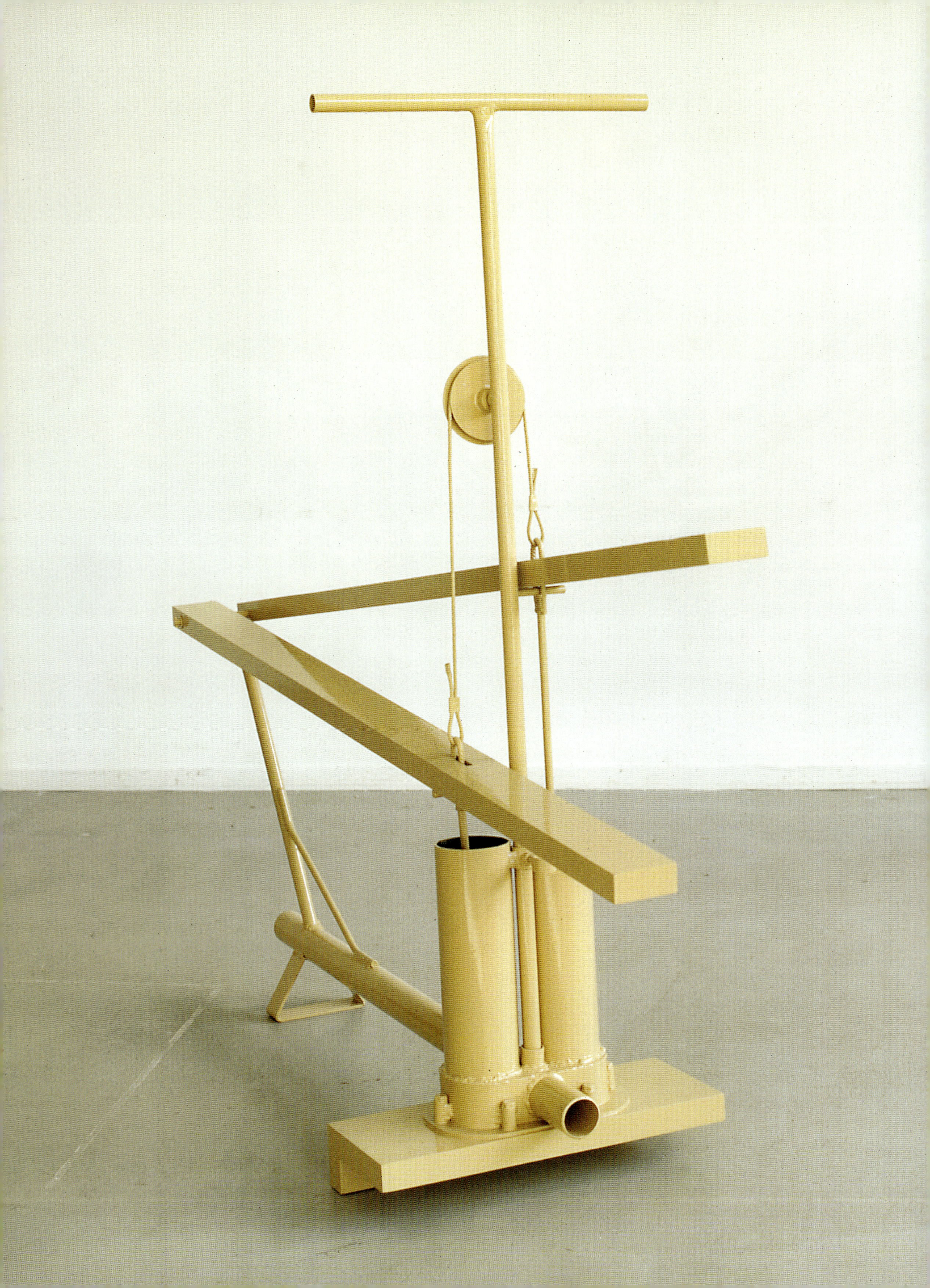

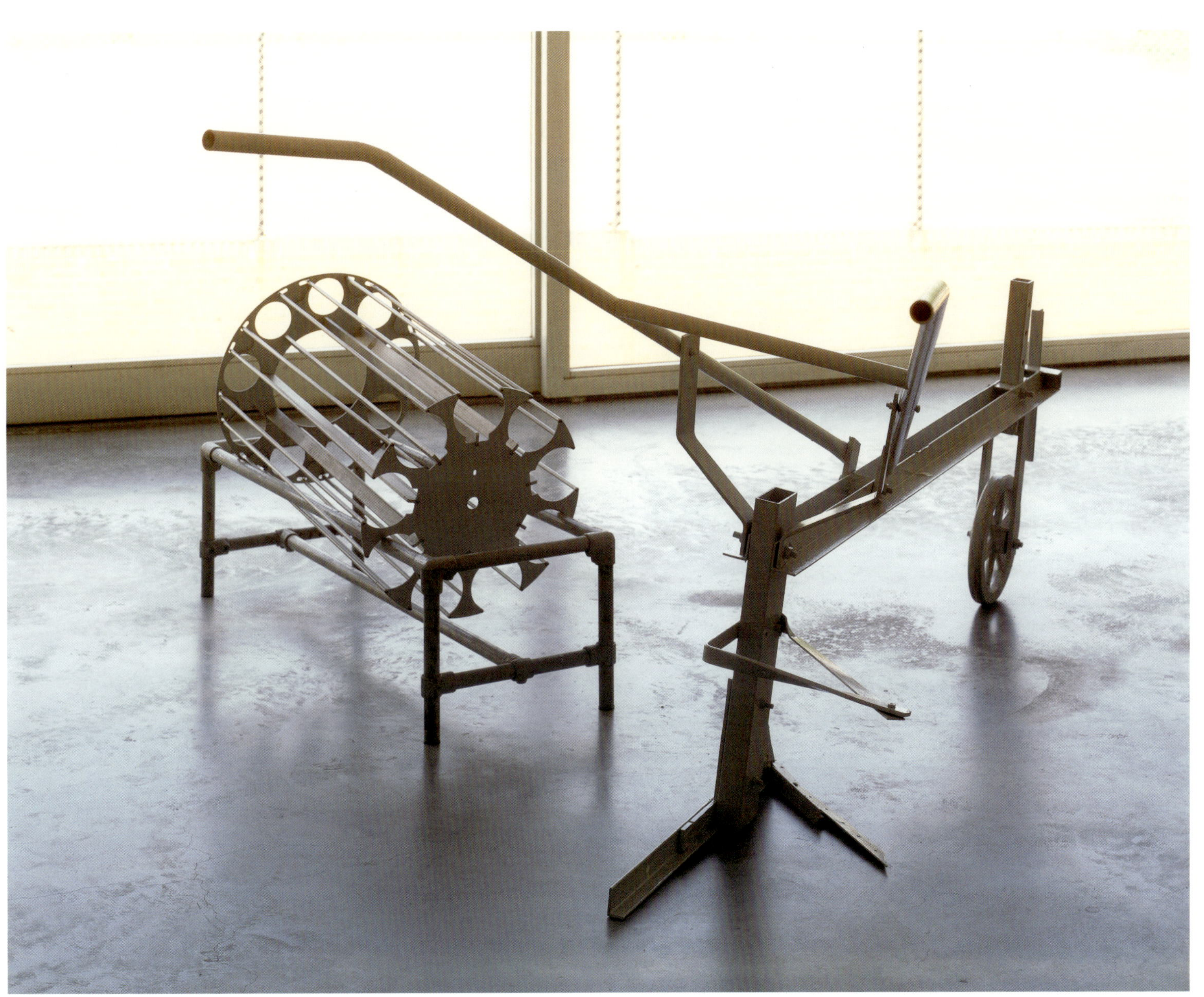

MARK HOSKING

Untitled 1995
steel and aluminium
2 parts: 112 x 262 x 92cm/72 x 101 x 44cm
44 x 103¹/₄ x 36¹/₄/28¹/₄ x 39³/₄ x 17¹/₄in

left:
Untitled 1997
painted steel and wood
155 x 54 x 71cm/61 x 21¹/₄ x 28in

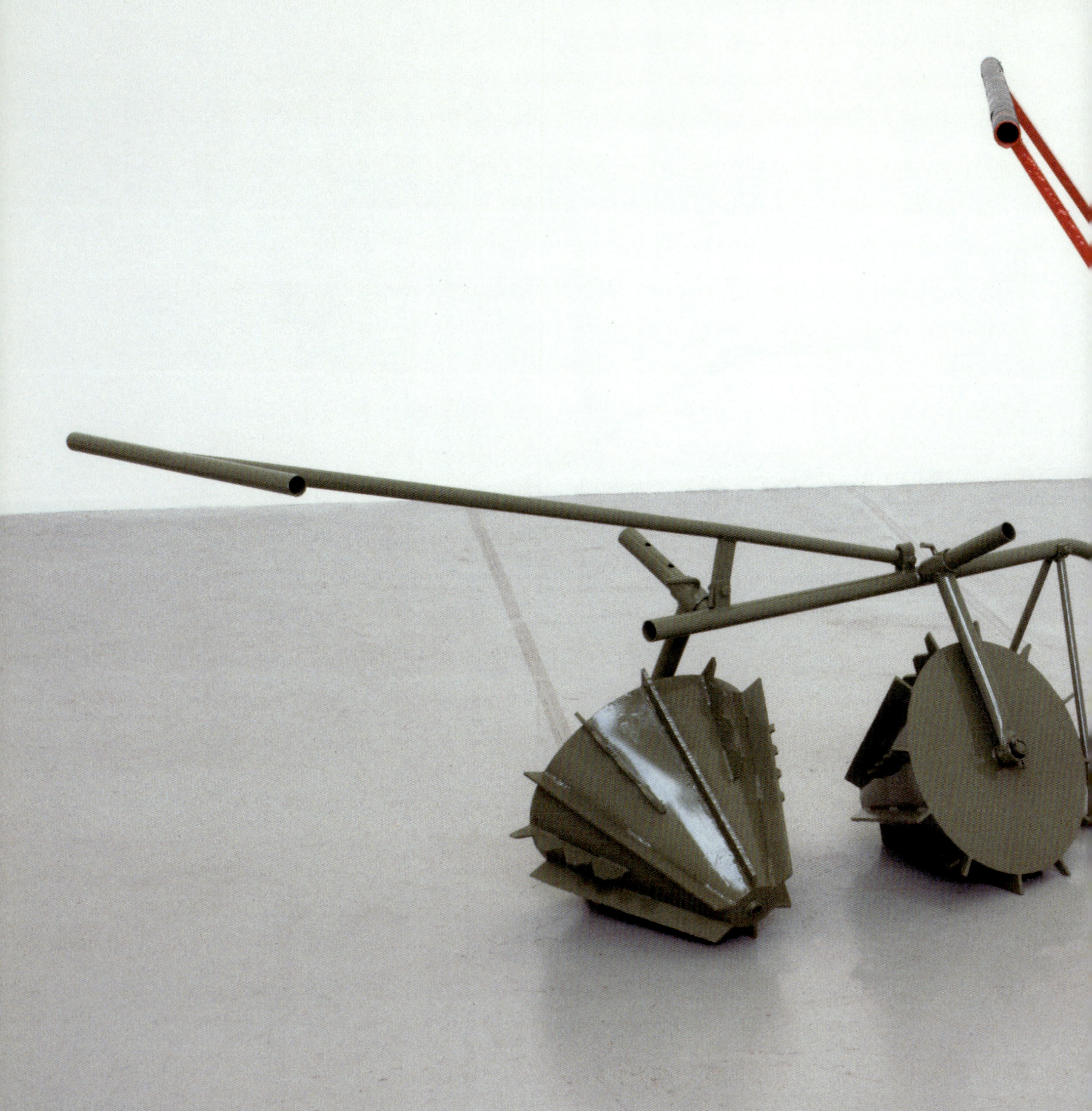

MARK HOSKING

Untitled (Lowland Rice) 1998
painted steel
300 x 350cm/118 x 137³/₄in

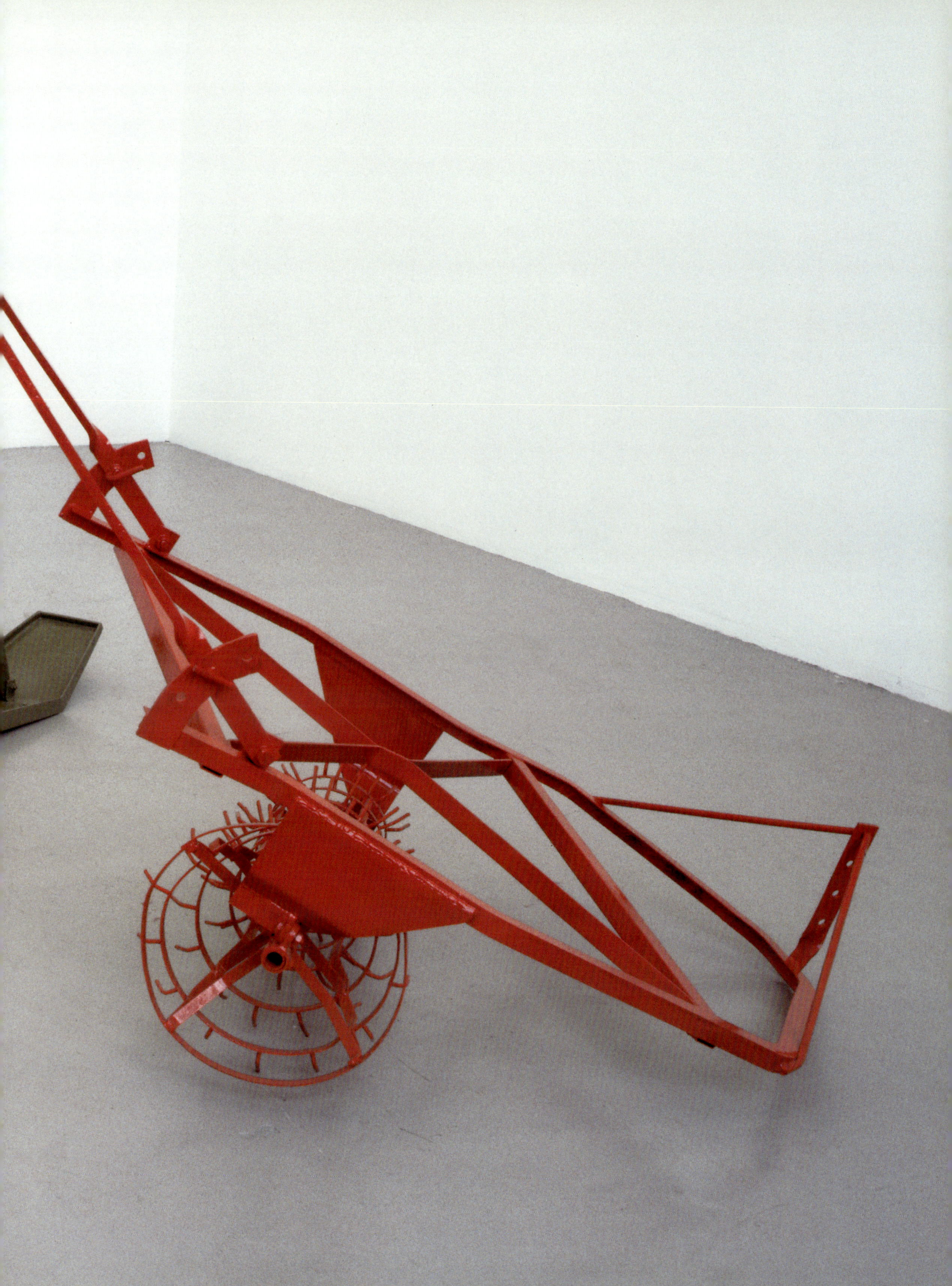

RON MUECK

Mask 1997
polyester resin and mixed media
158 x 153 x 124cm/62 x 60 x 49in

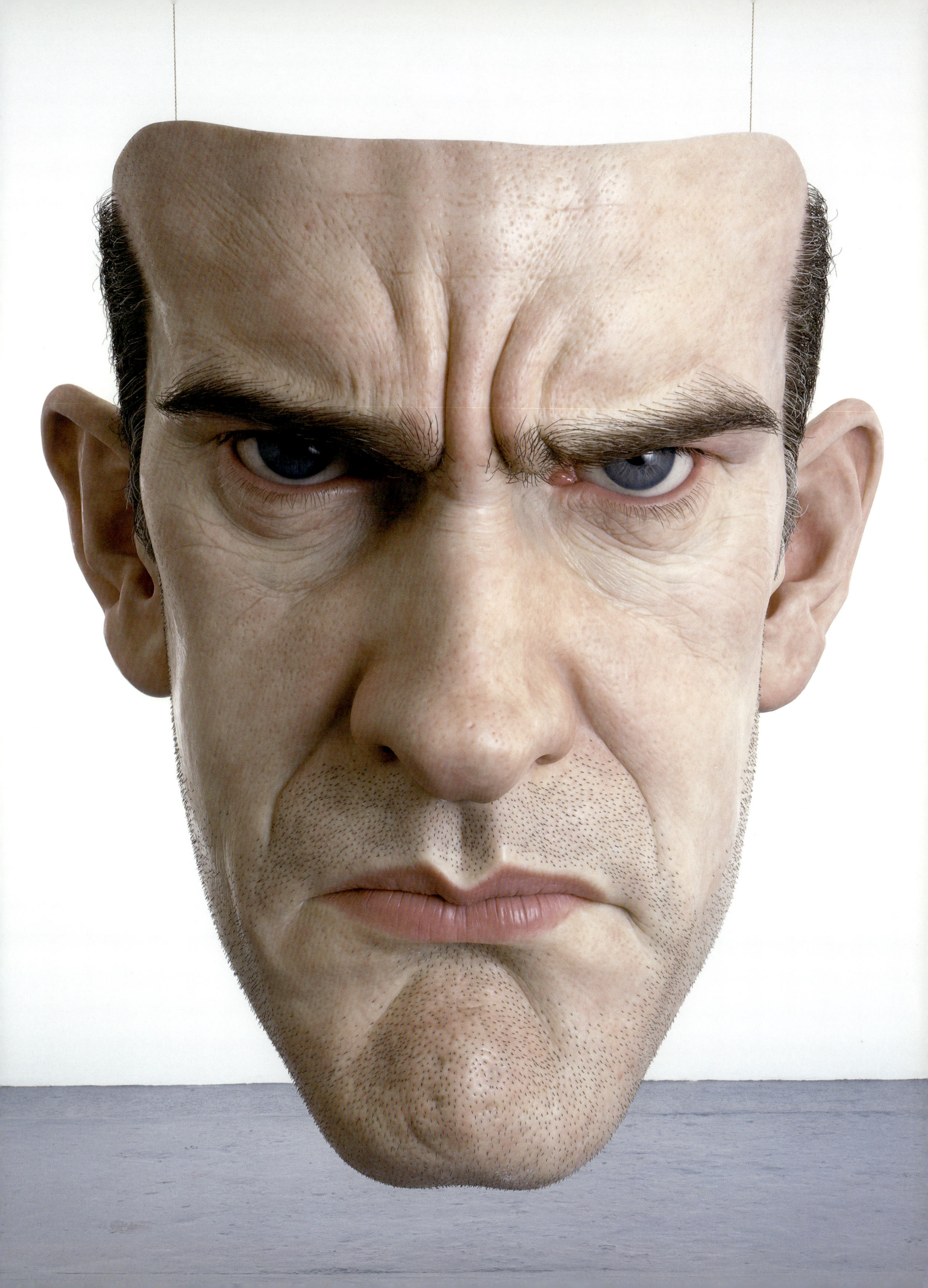

RON MUECK

Angel 1997
silicone rubber and mixed media
110 x 87 x 81cm/43¼ x 34¼ x 31¾in

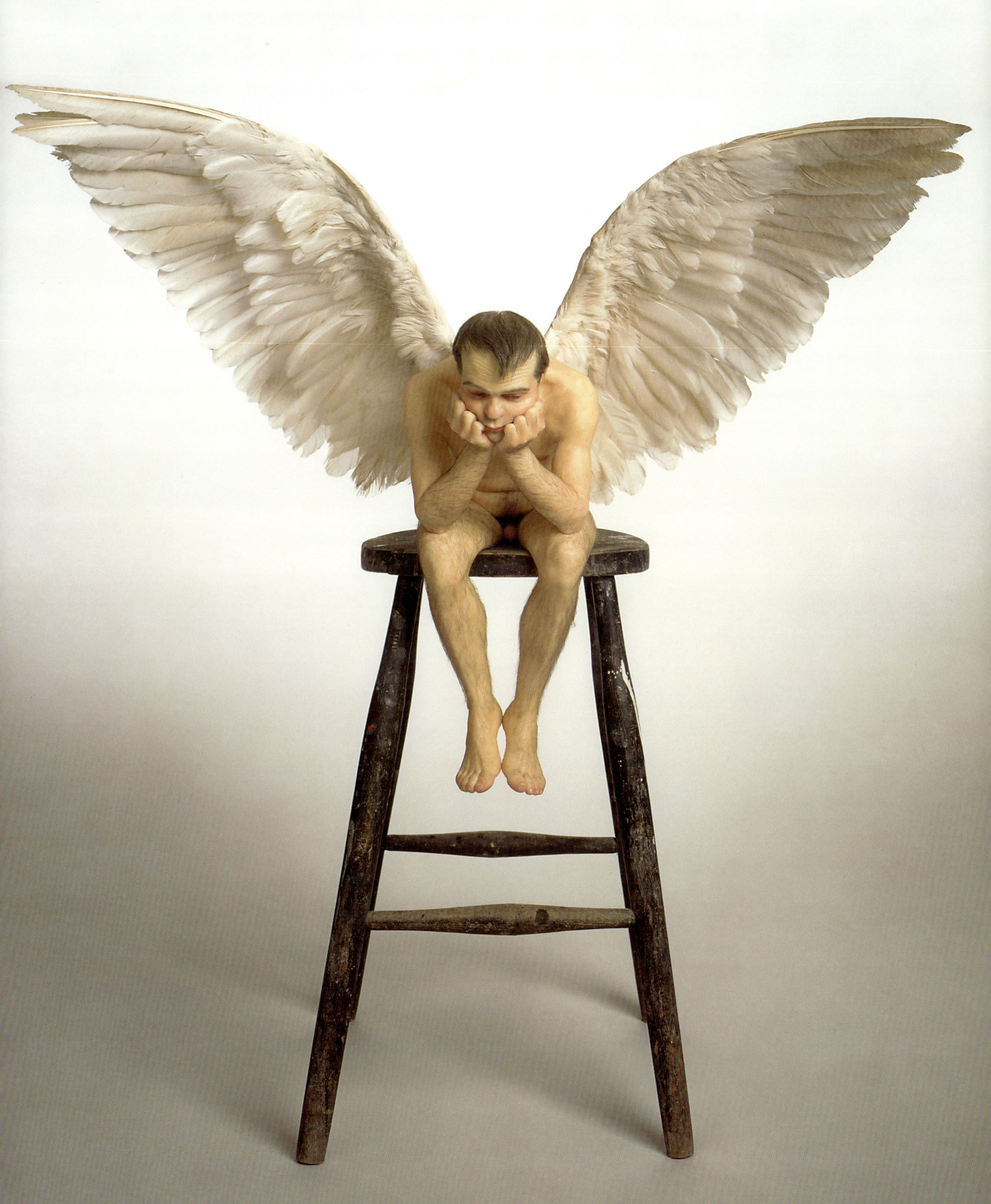

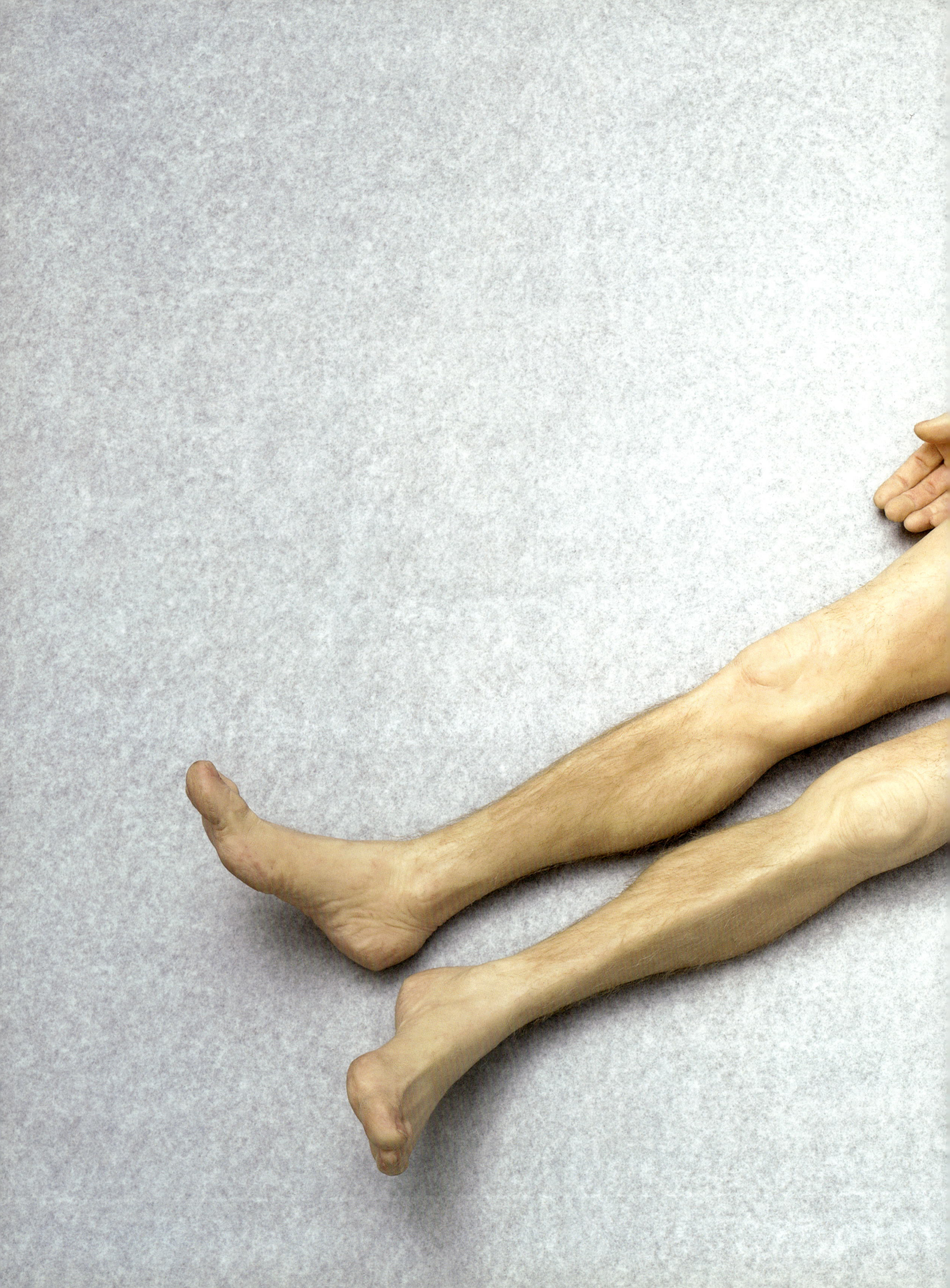

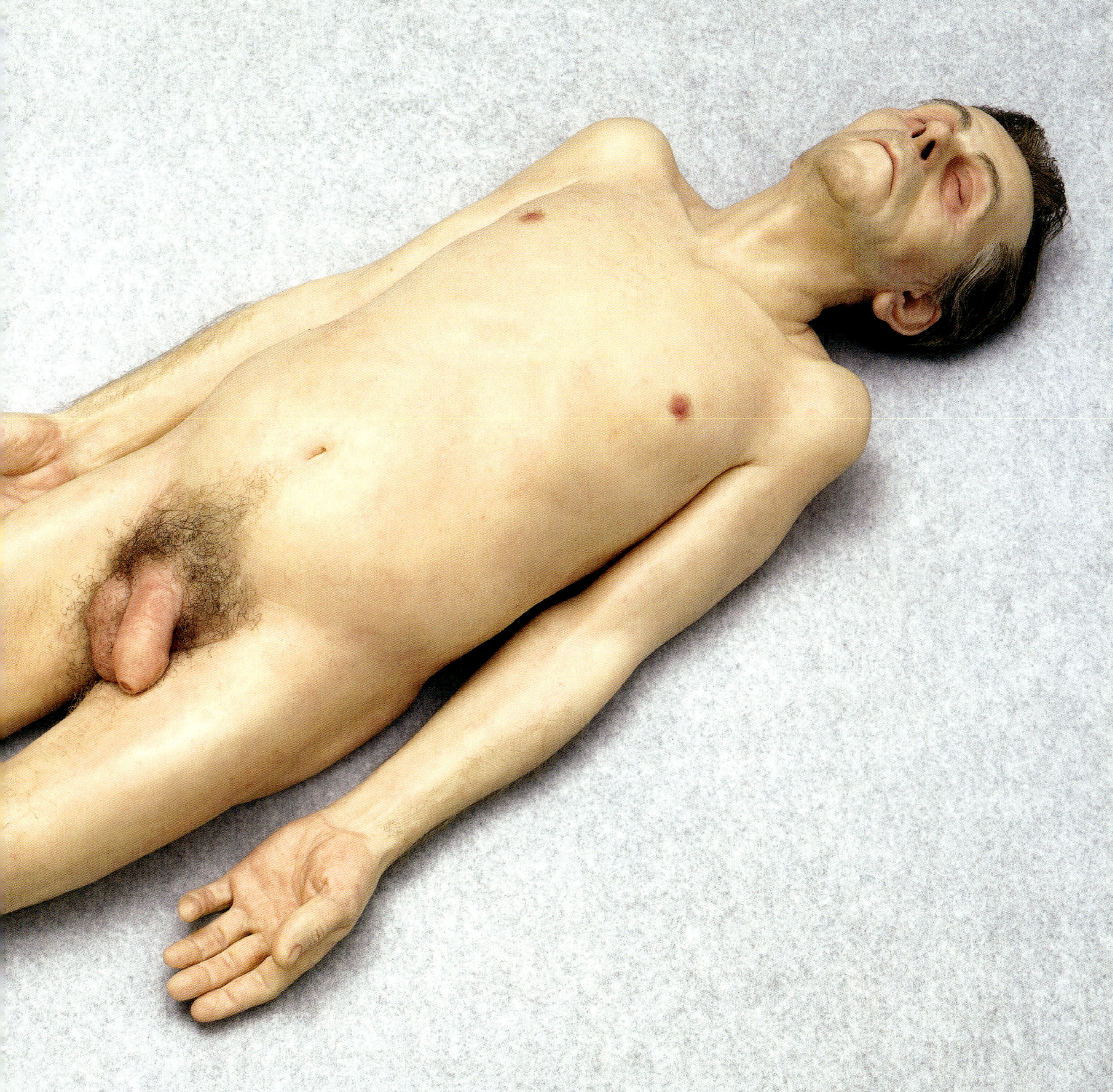

RON MUECK

Dead Dad 1996-97
silicone and acrylic
20 x 102 x 38cm/8 x 40 x 15in

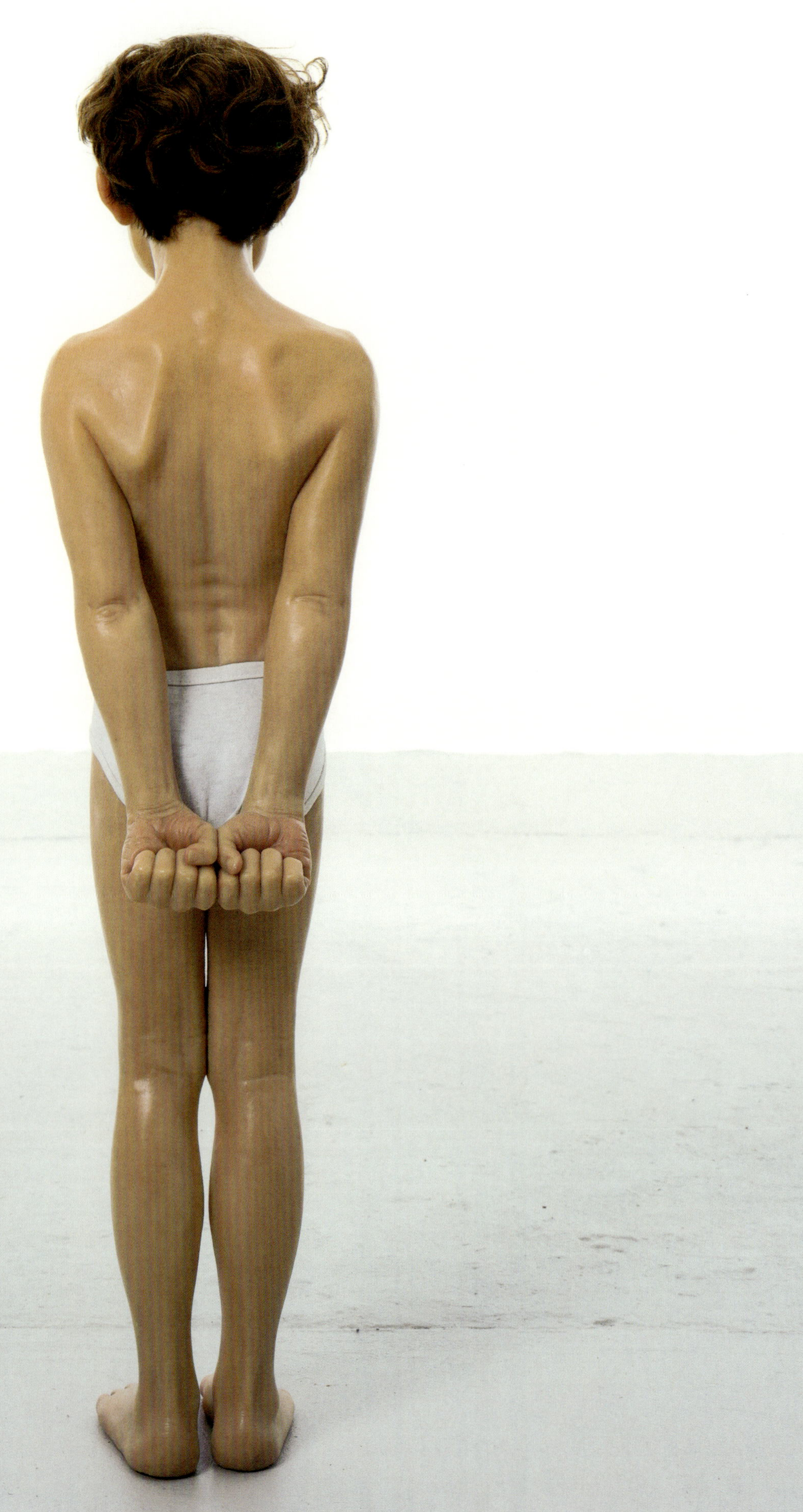

RON MUECK

Pinnochio 1996
polyester resin, fibreglass and human hair
84 x 20 x 18cm/33 x 8 x 7in

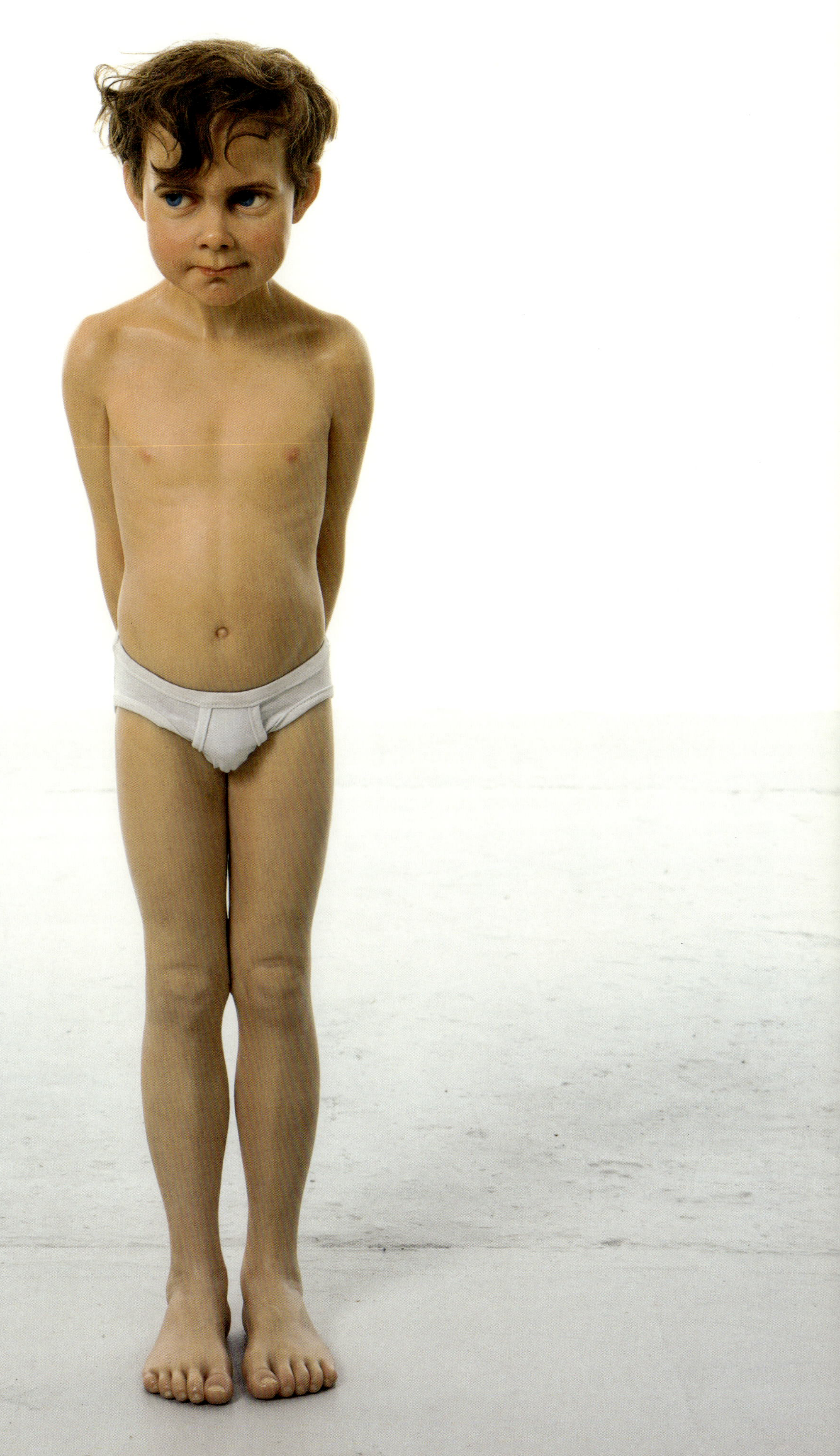

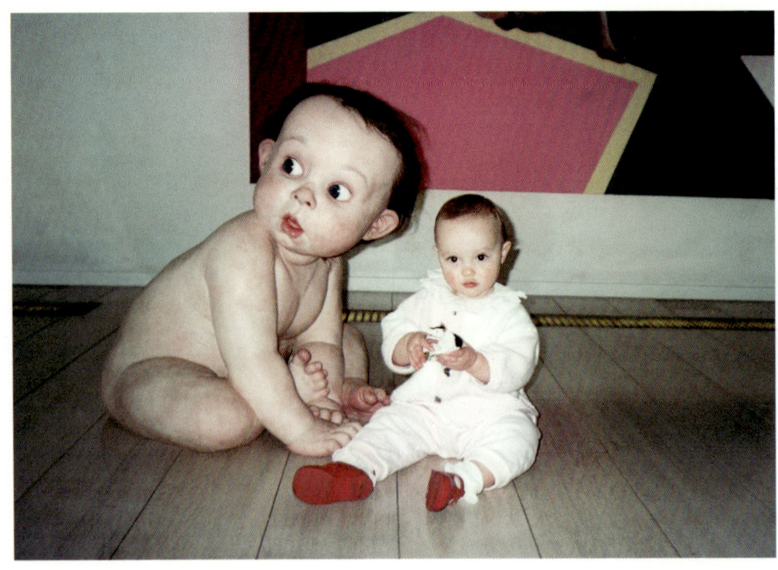

RON MUECK

Big Baby 1996
polyester resin, fibreglass and human hair
85 x 71 x 7cm/33½ x 28 x 27½in

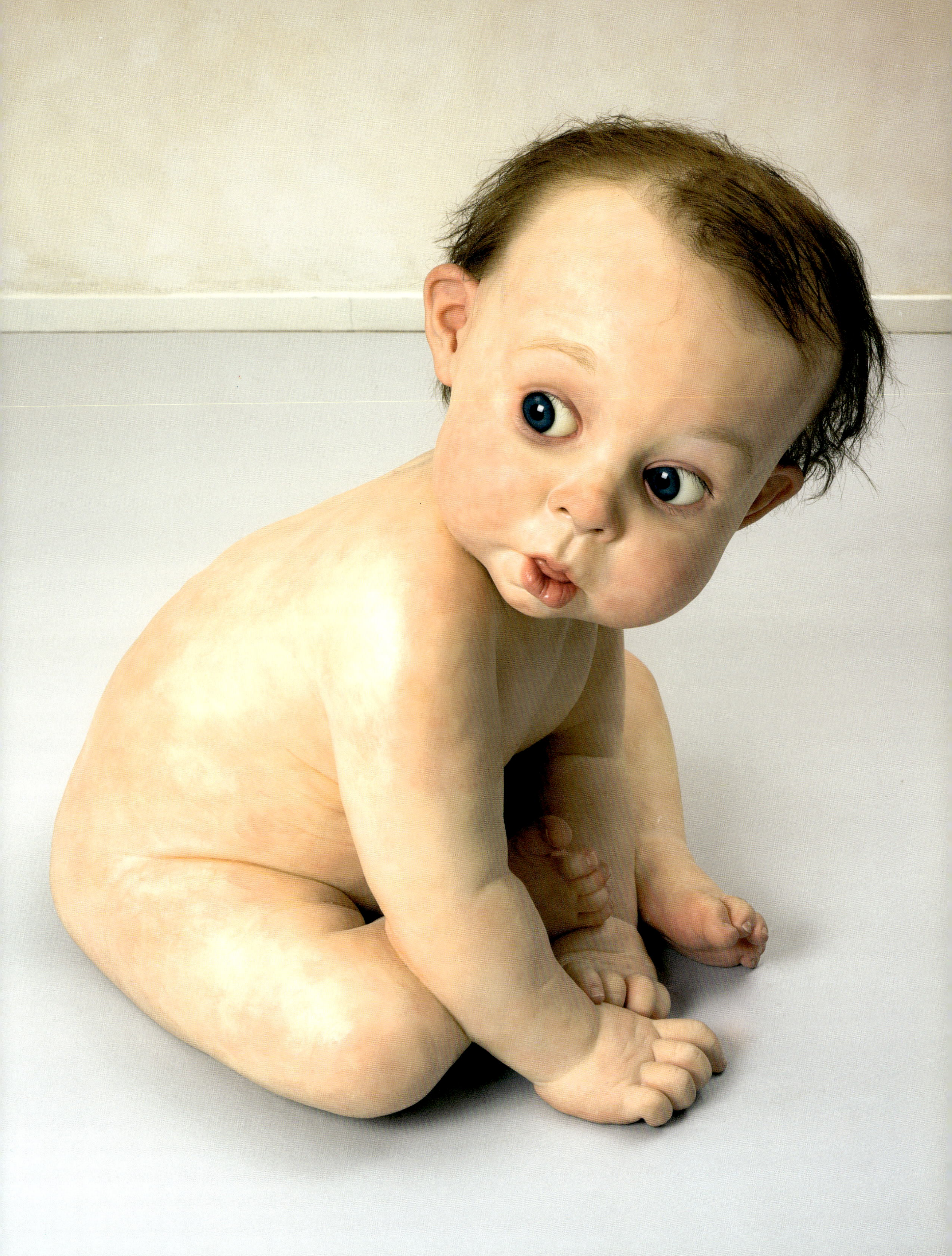

TIM NOBLE & SUE WEBSTER

Miss Understood and Mr Meanor 1997
rubbish, slide projector, wood, light sensor
140 x 70 x 60cm/55 x 27½ x 23½in

overleaf:
Toxic Schizophrenia 1997
516 UFO clamps, lamps and holders,
6mm foamex, vinyl, aerosol
260 x 200cm/102½ x 78¾in

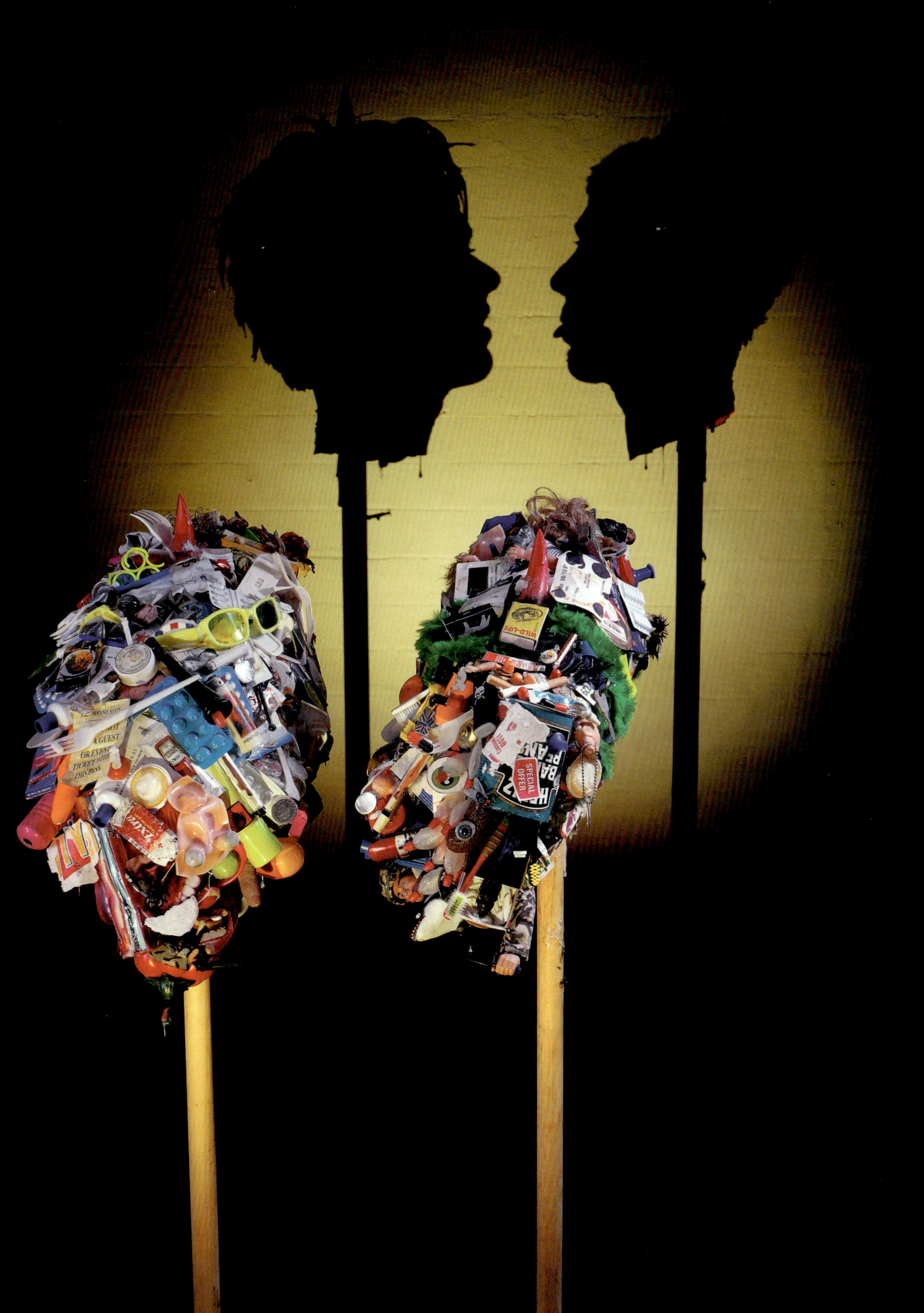

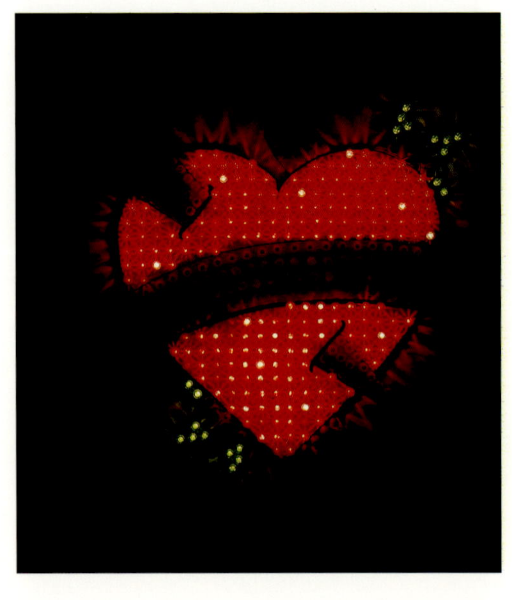 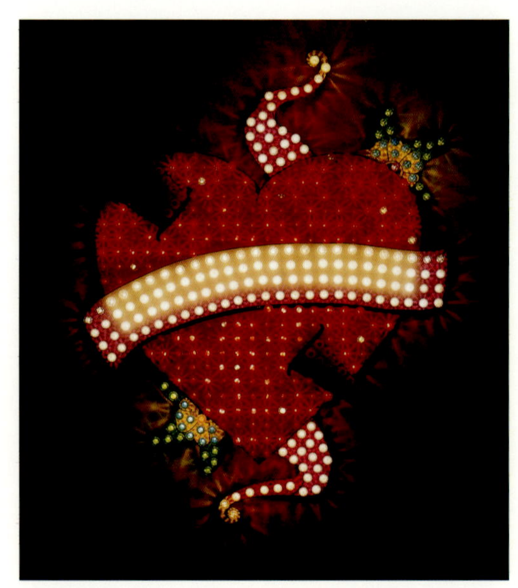

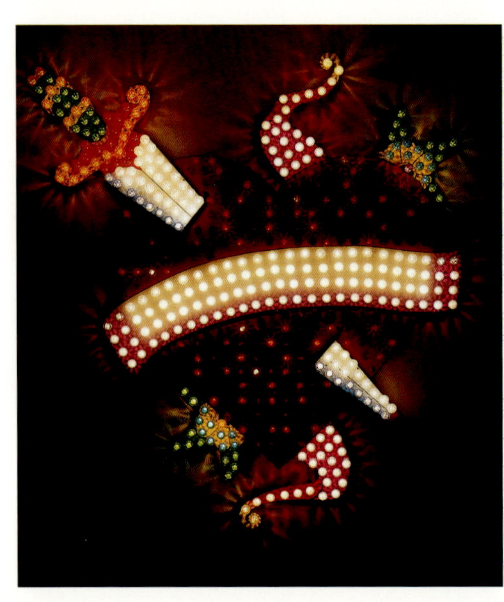 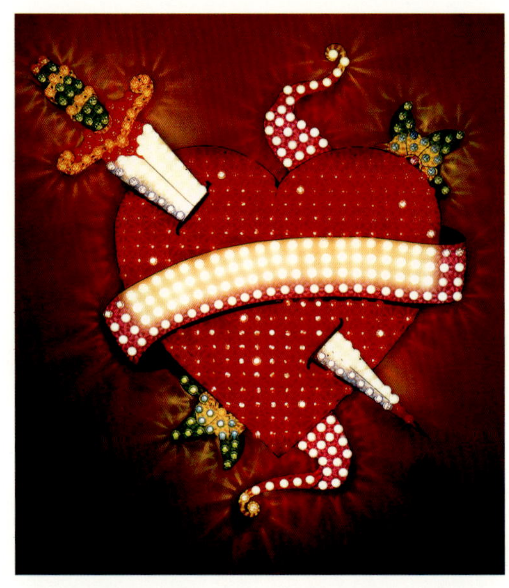

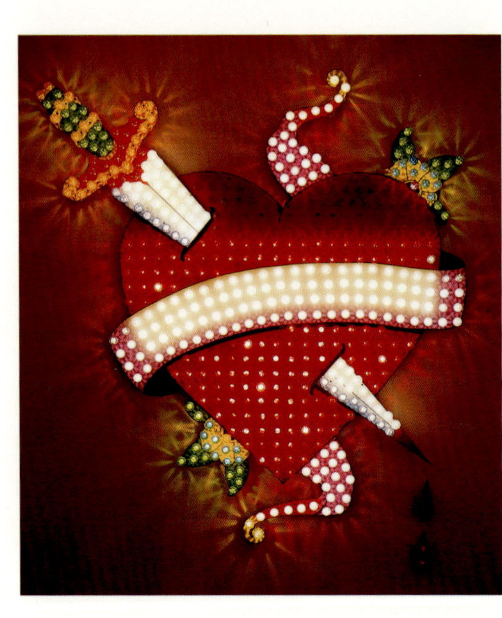 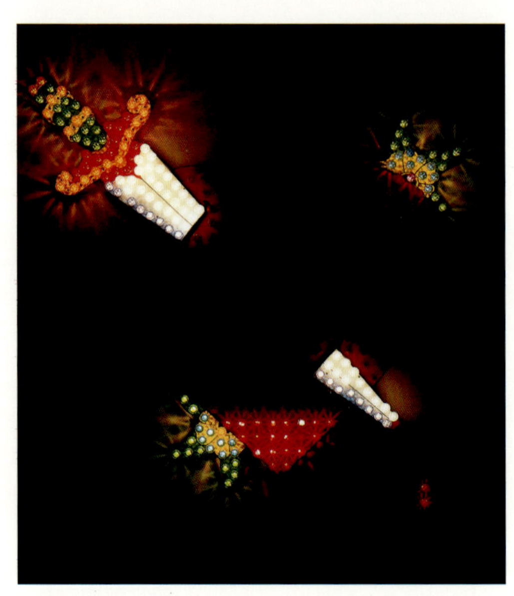

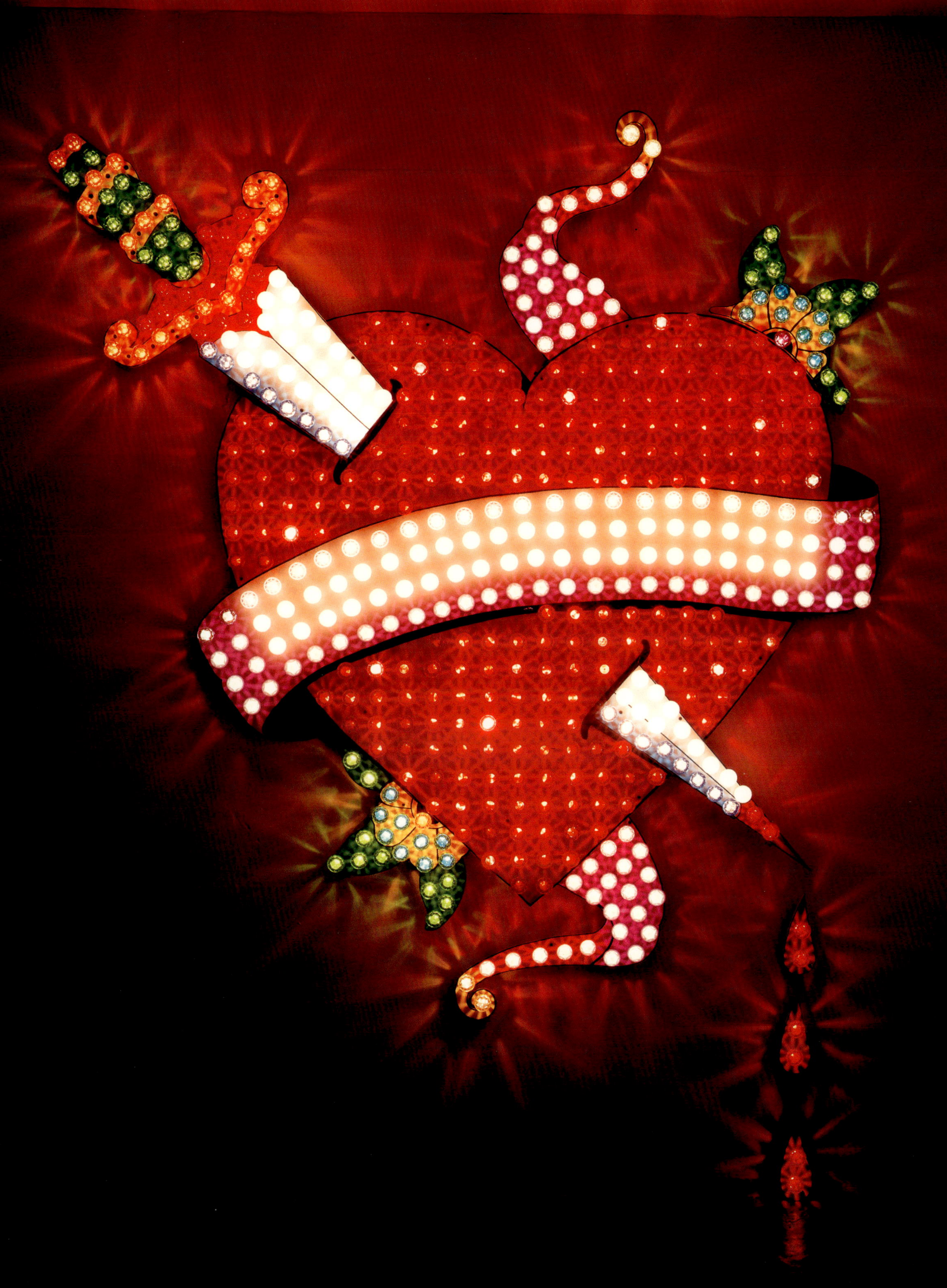

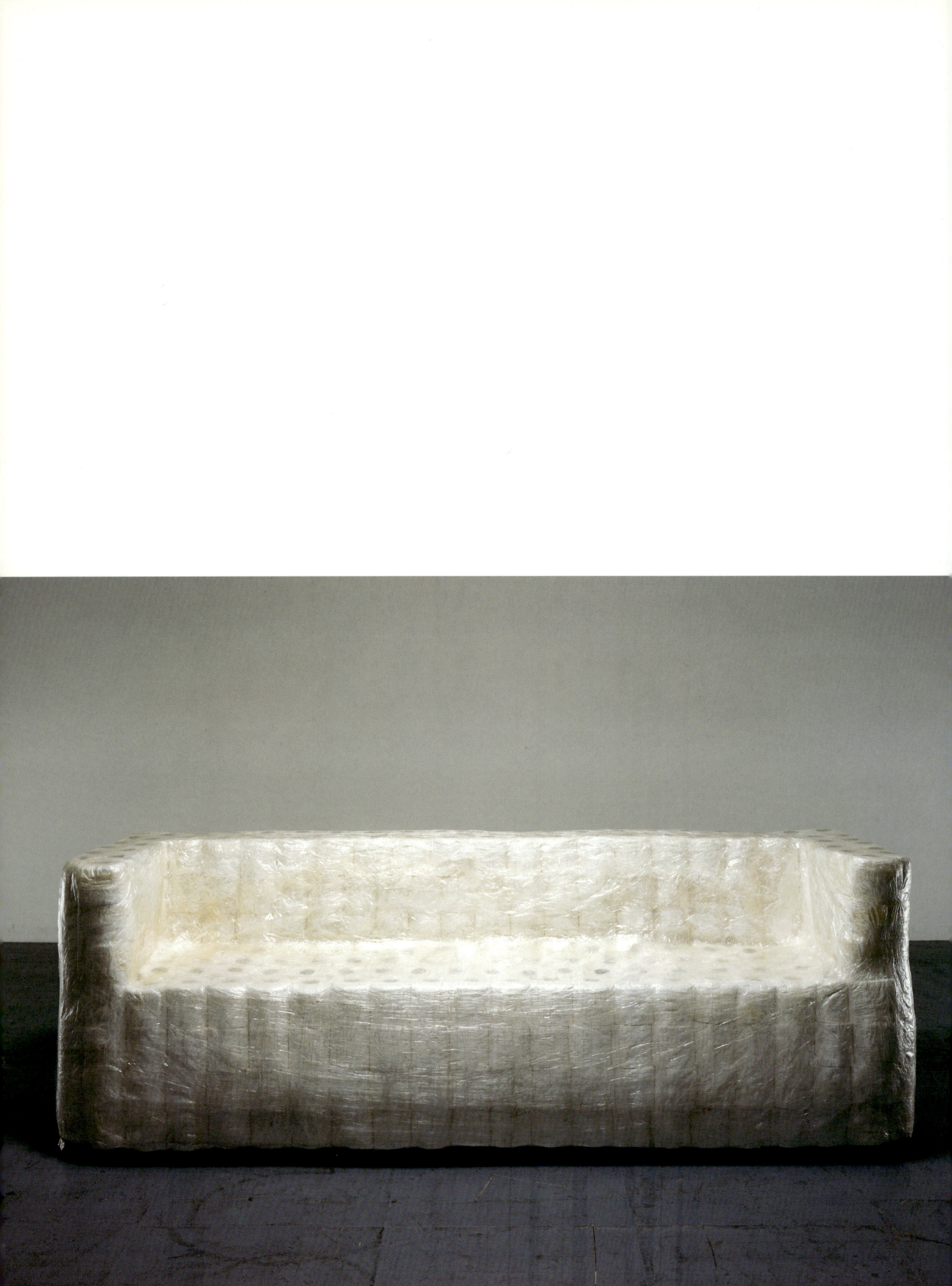

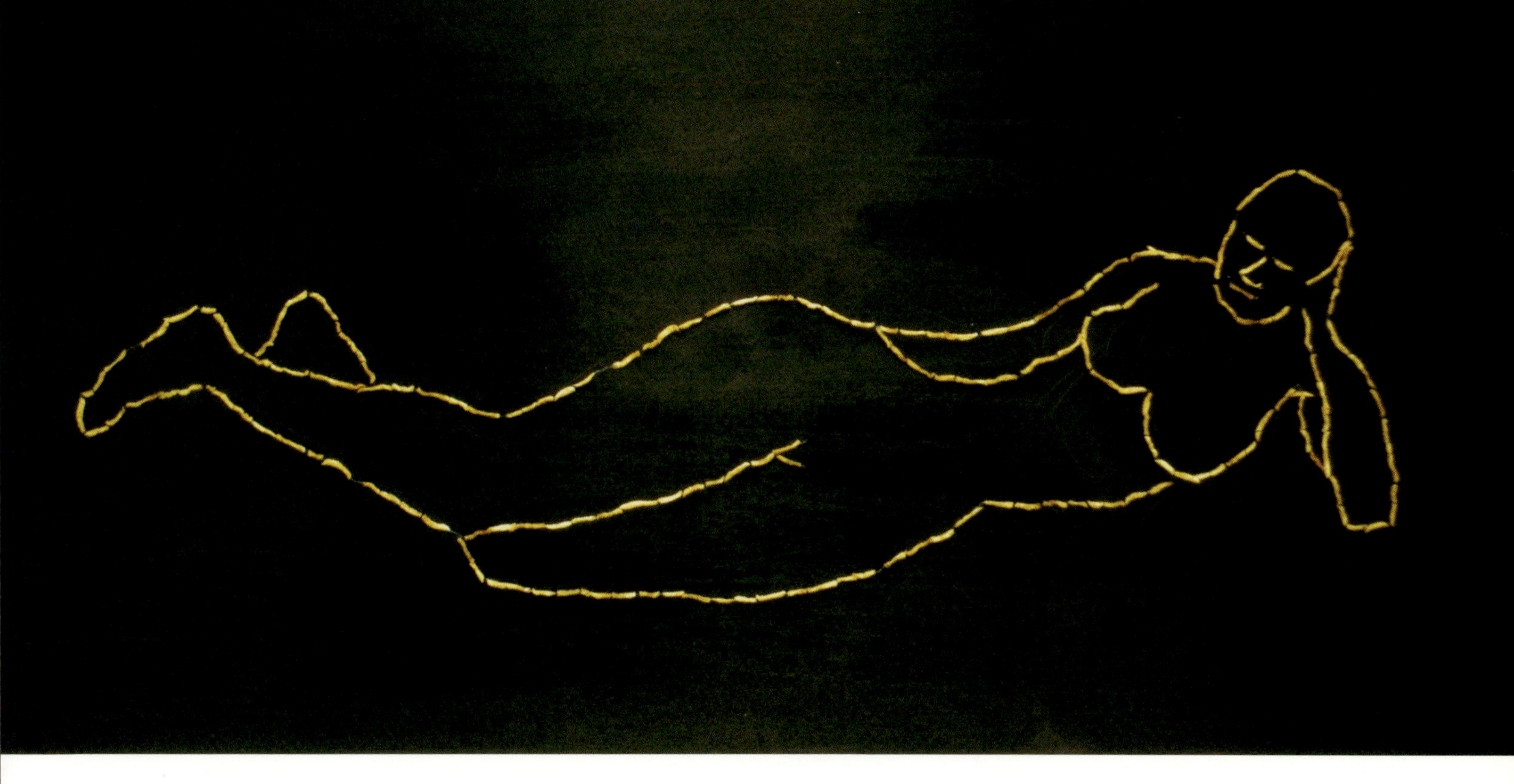

ANDREAS SCHLAEGEL

Chip Girl 1997
potato chips, wire, wood
152.5 x 305cm/60 x 120in

left:
Toiletpapersofa 1997
toilet paper, wooden framework, tape
82.5 x 240 x 66cm/32½ x 94½ x 26in

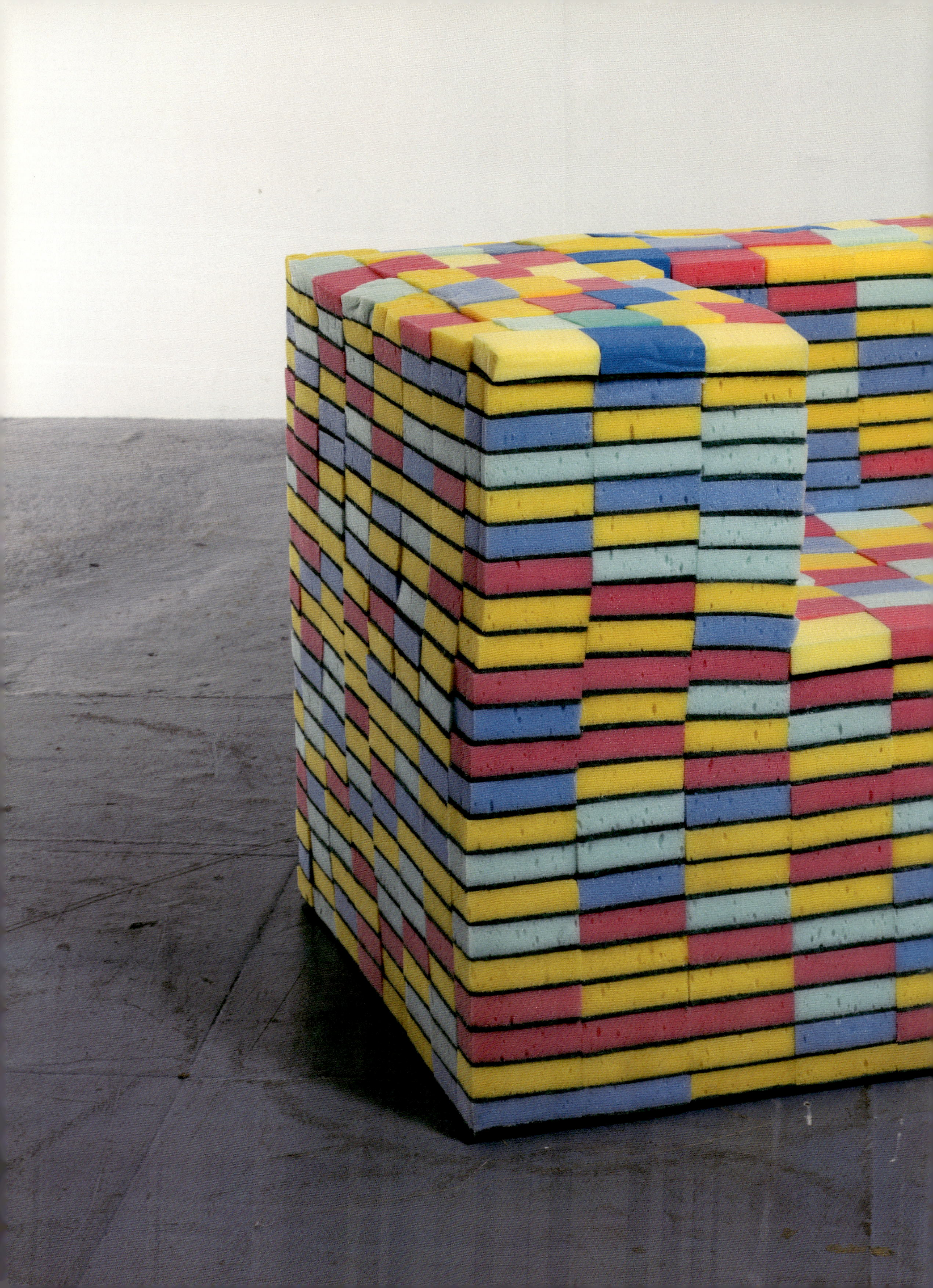

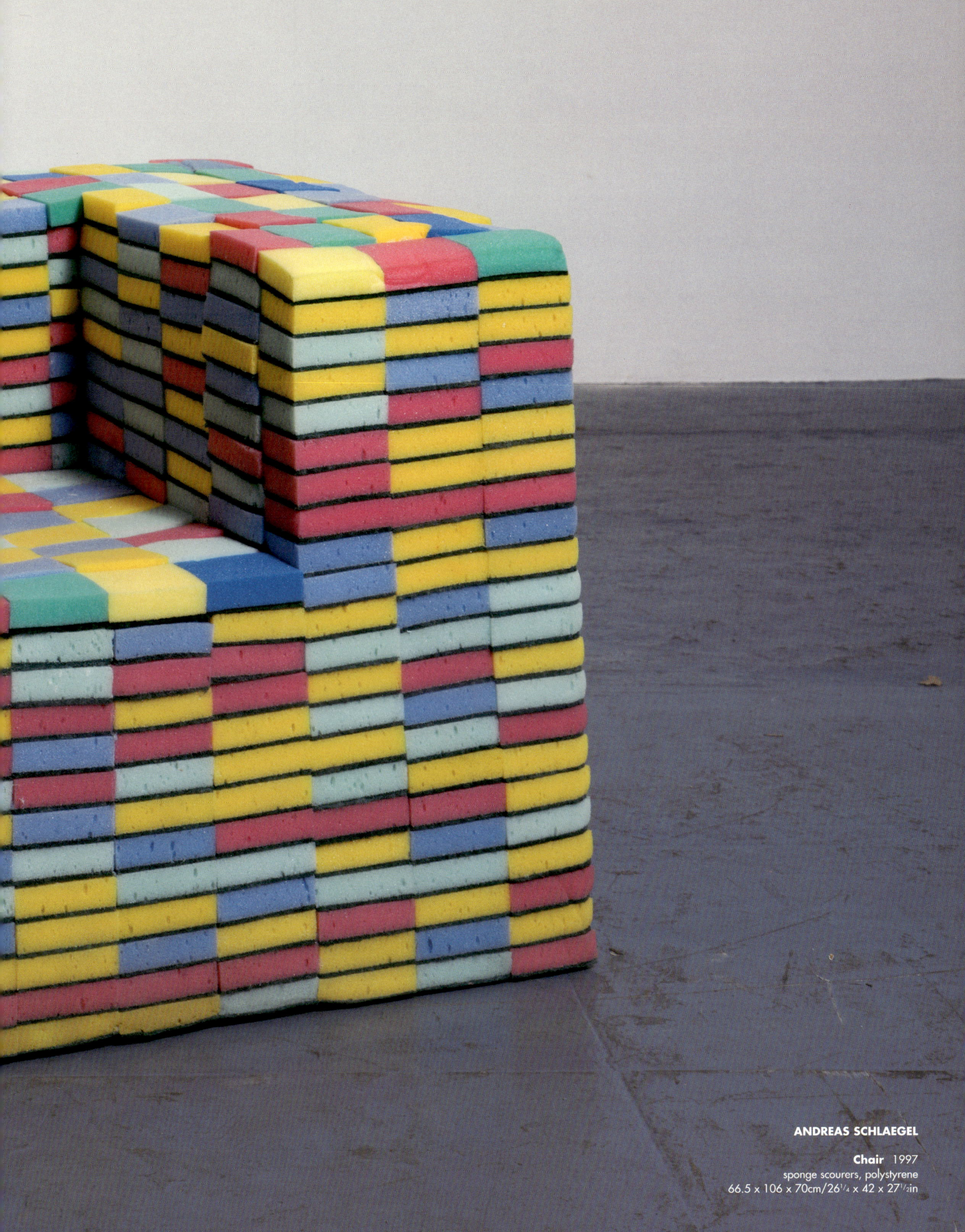

Chair 1997
sponge scourers, polystyrene
66.5 x 106 x 70cm/26¼ x 42 x 27½in

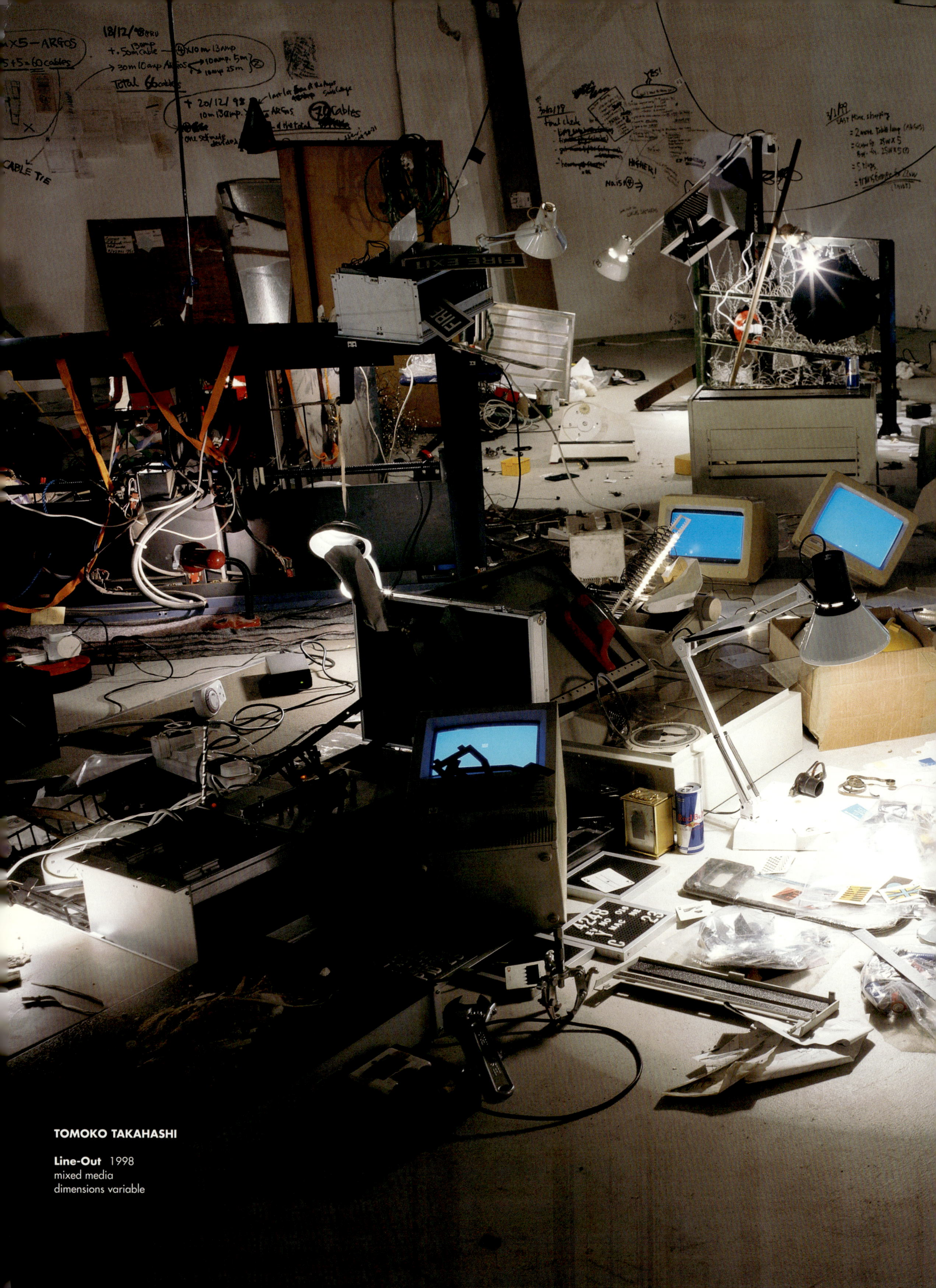

TOMOKO TAKAHASHI

Line-Out 1998
mixed media
dimensions variable

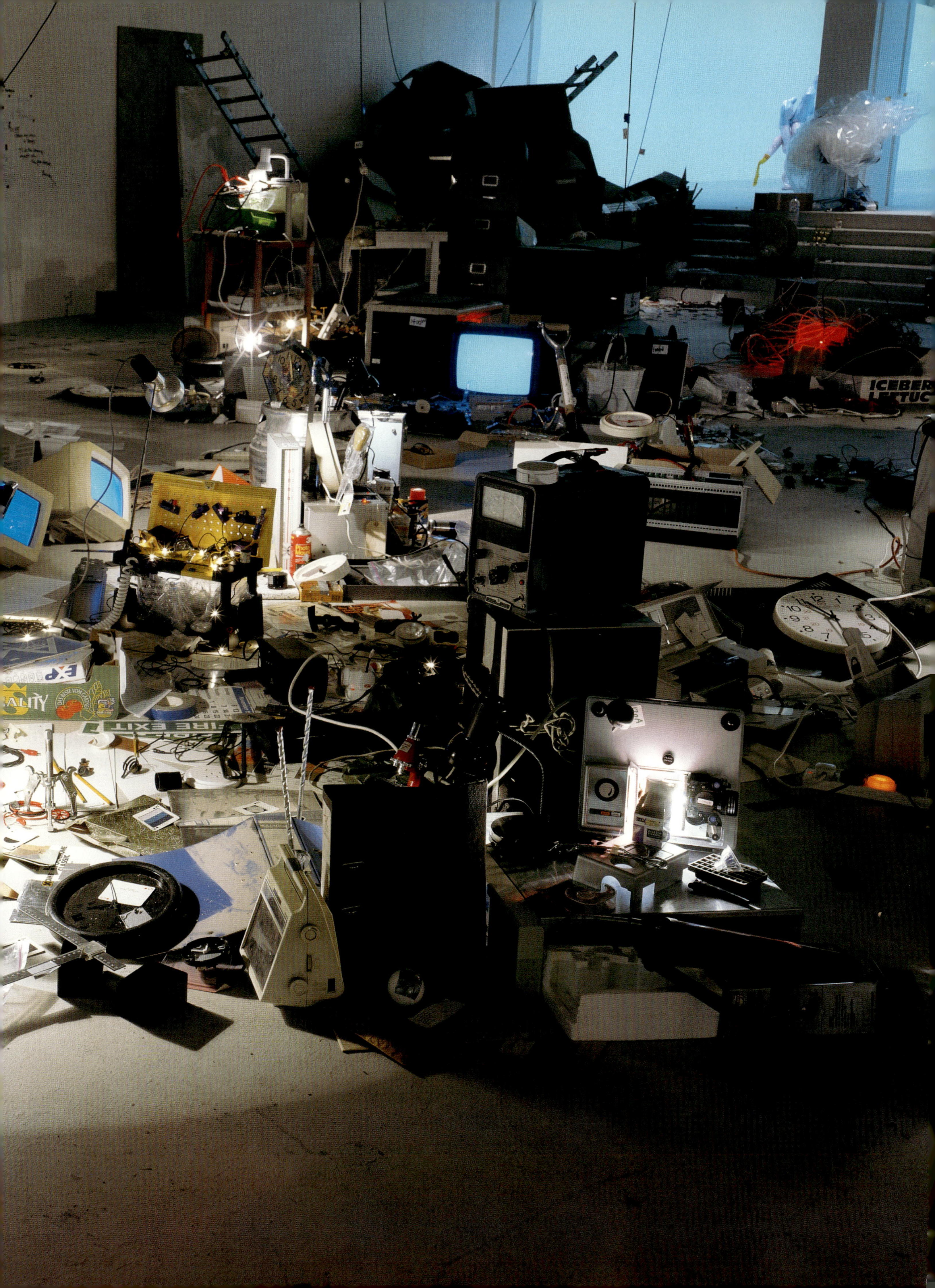

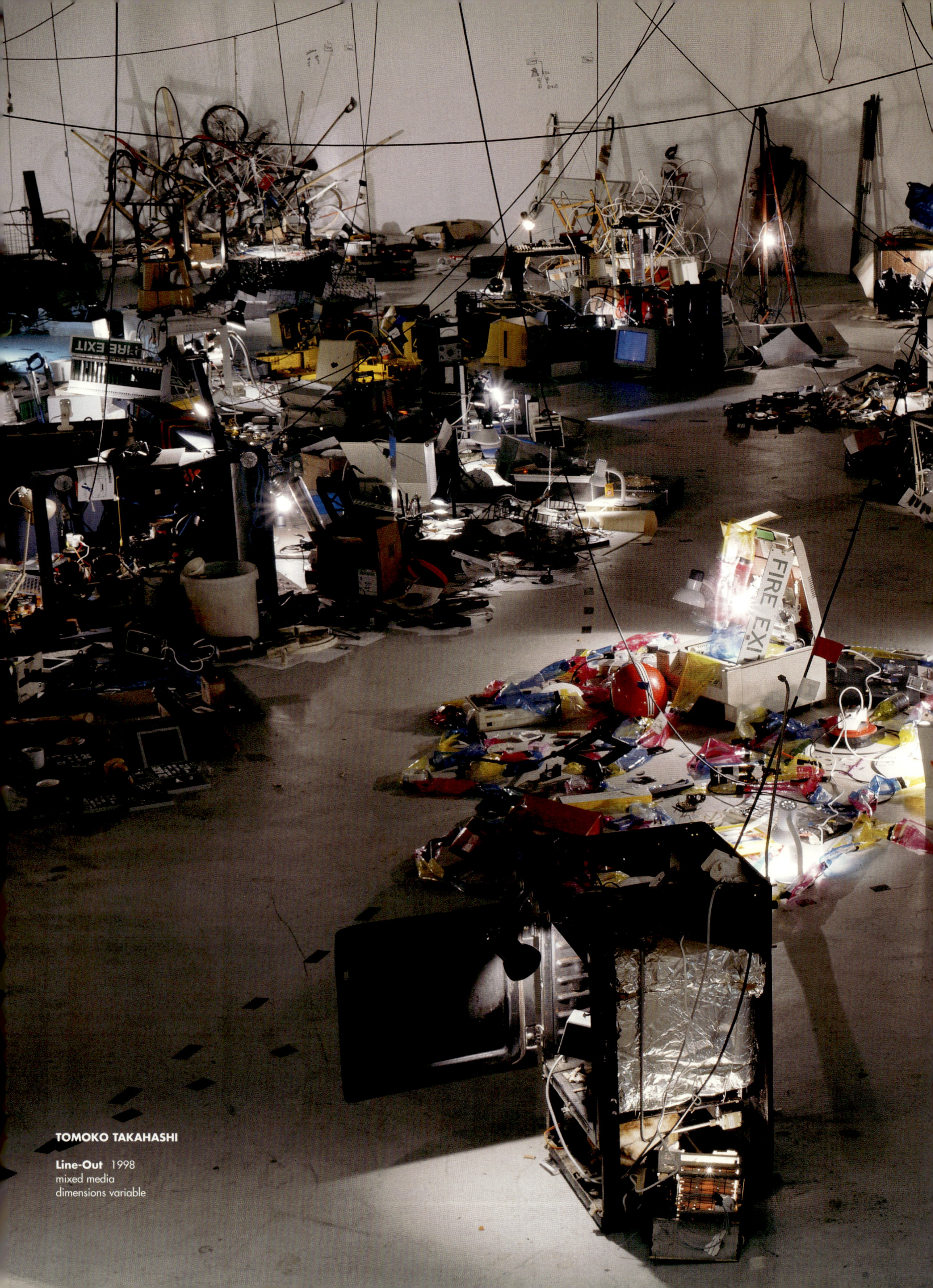

TOMOKO TAKAHASHI

Line-Out   1998
mixed media
dimensions variable

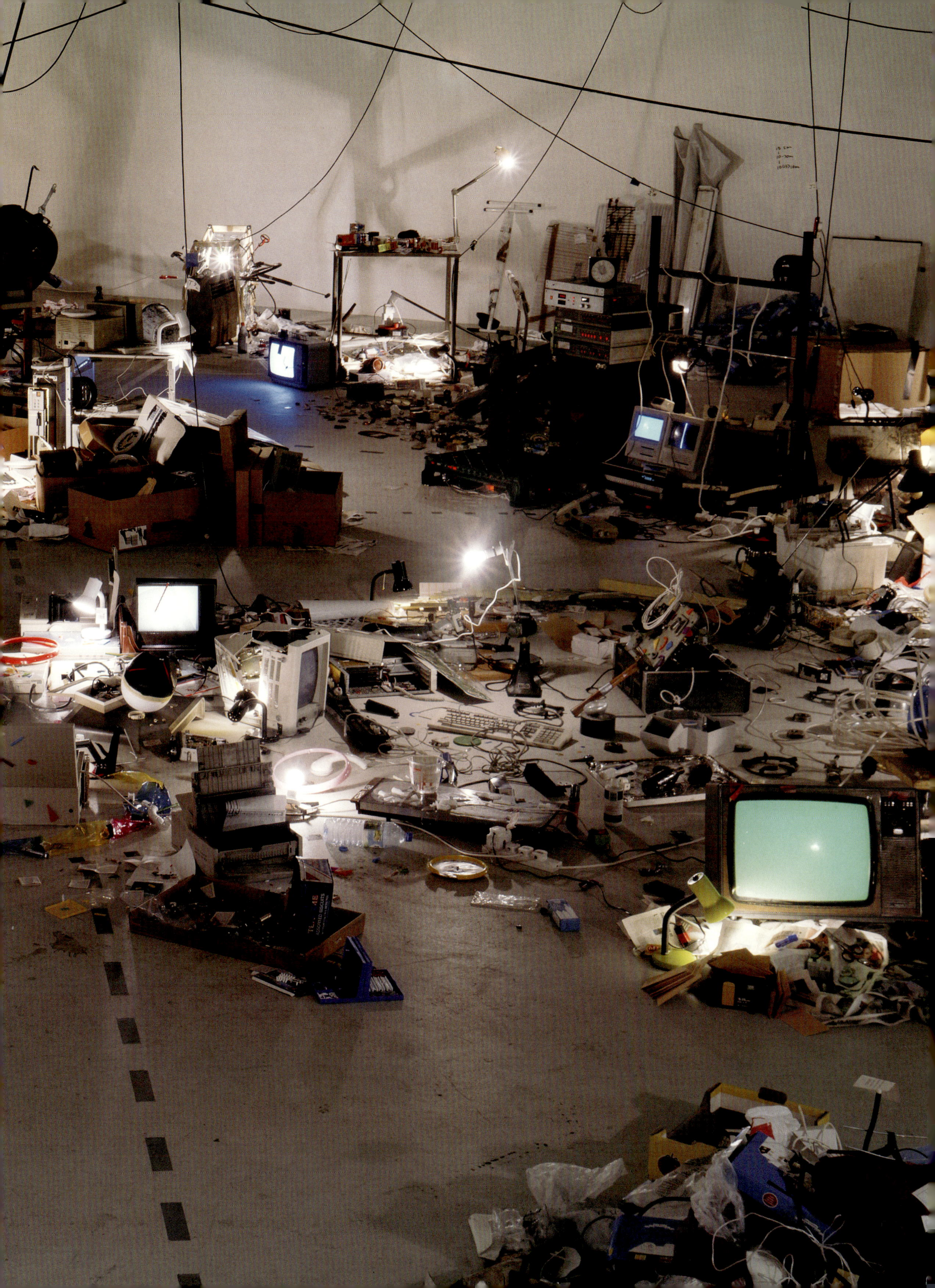

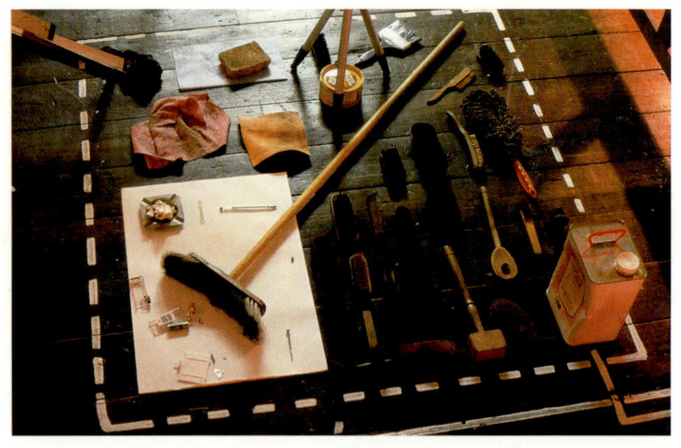
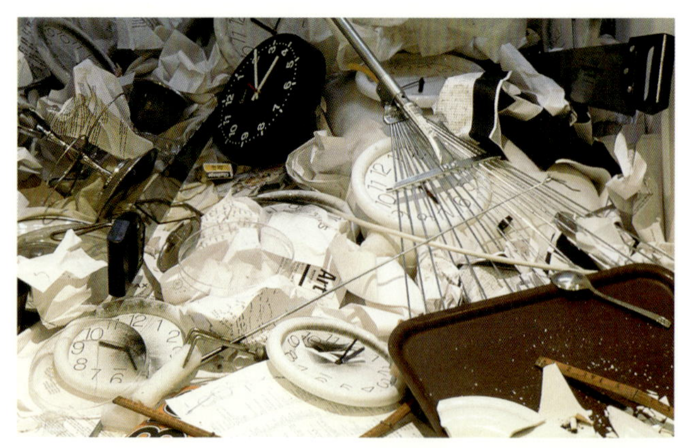
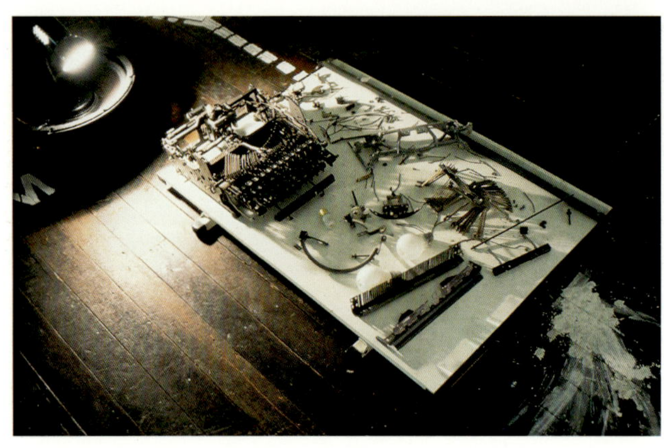
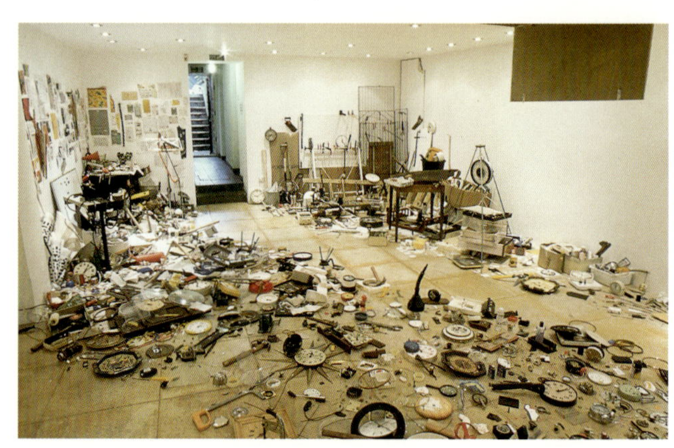
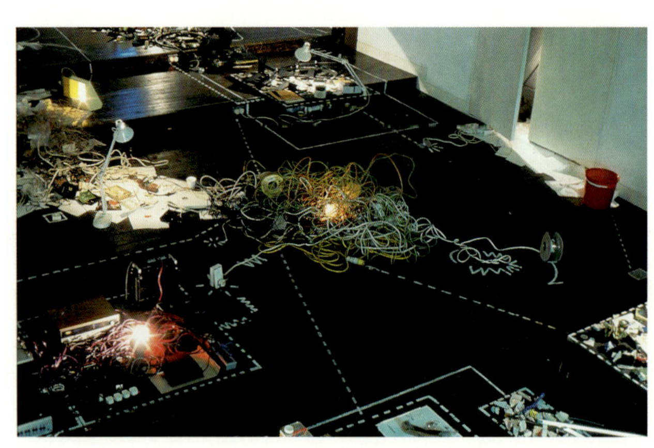
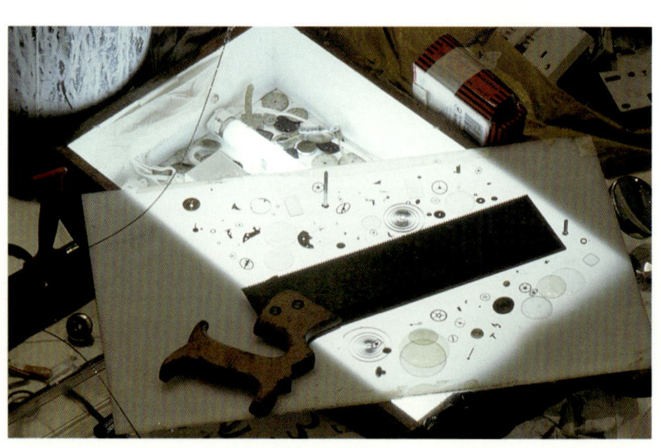
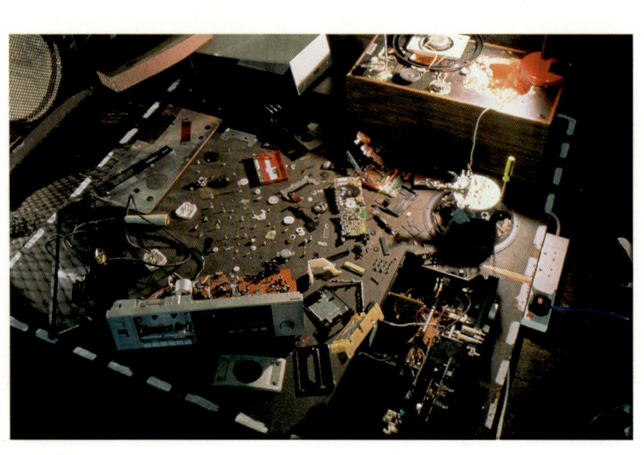
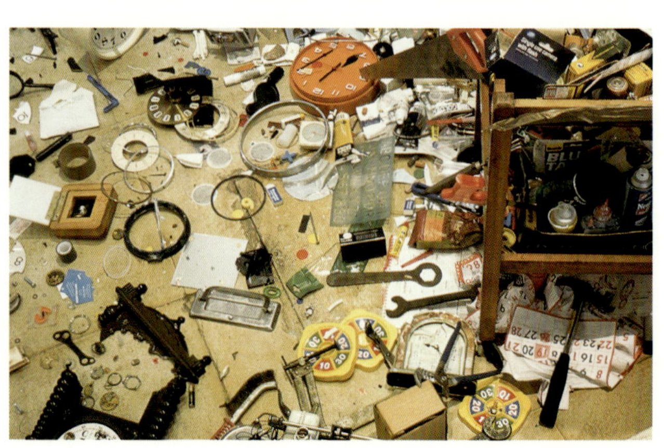

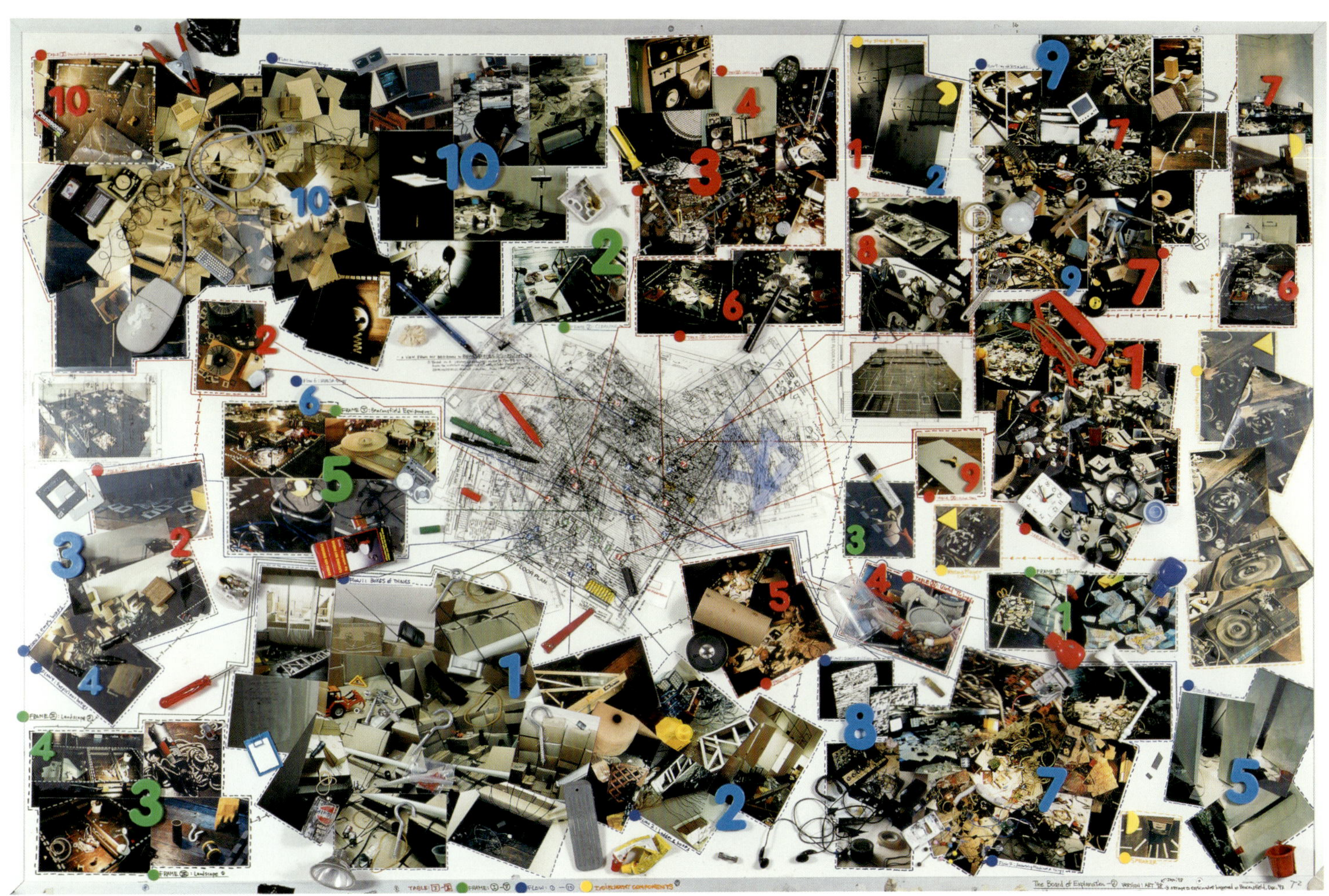

TOMOKO TAKAHASHI

Drawing for Beaconsfield 1997-98
photographs, acetates and mixed media
122 x 183cm/48 x 72in

far left:
Beaconsfield 1997 (details)
mixed media
dimensions variable

left:
Clockwork 1998 (details)
mixed media
dimensions variable

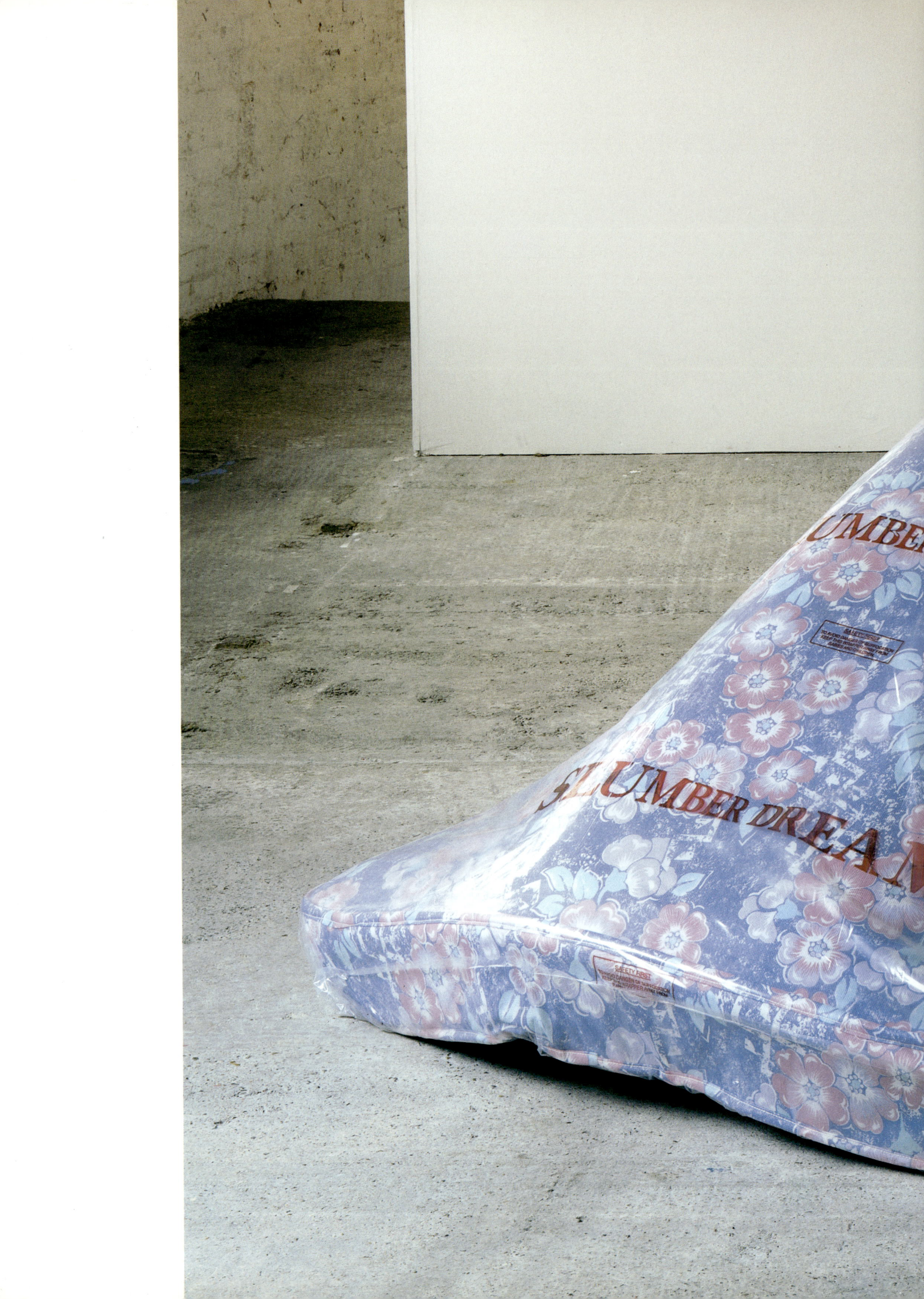
SLUMBER DREAM
SLUMBER DREAM
SAFETY FIRST

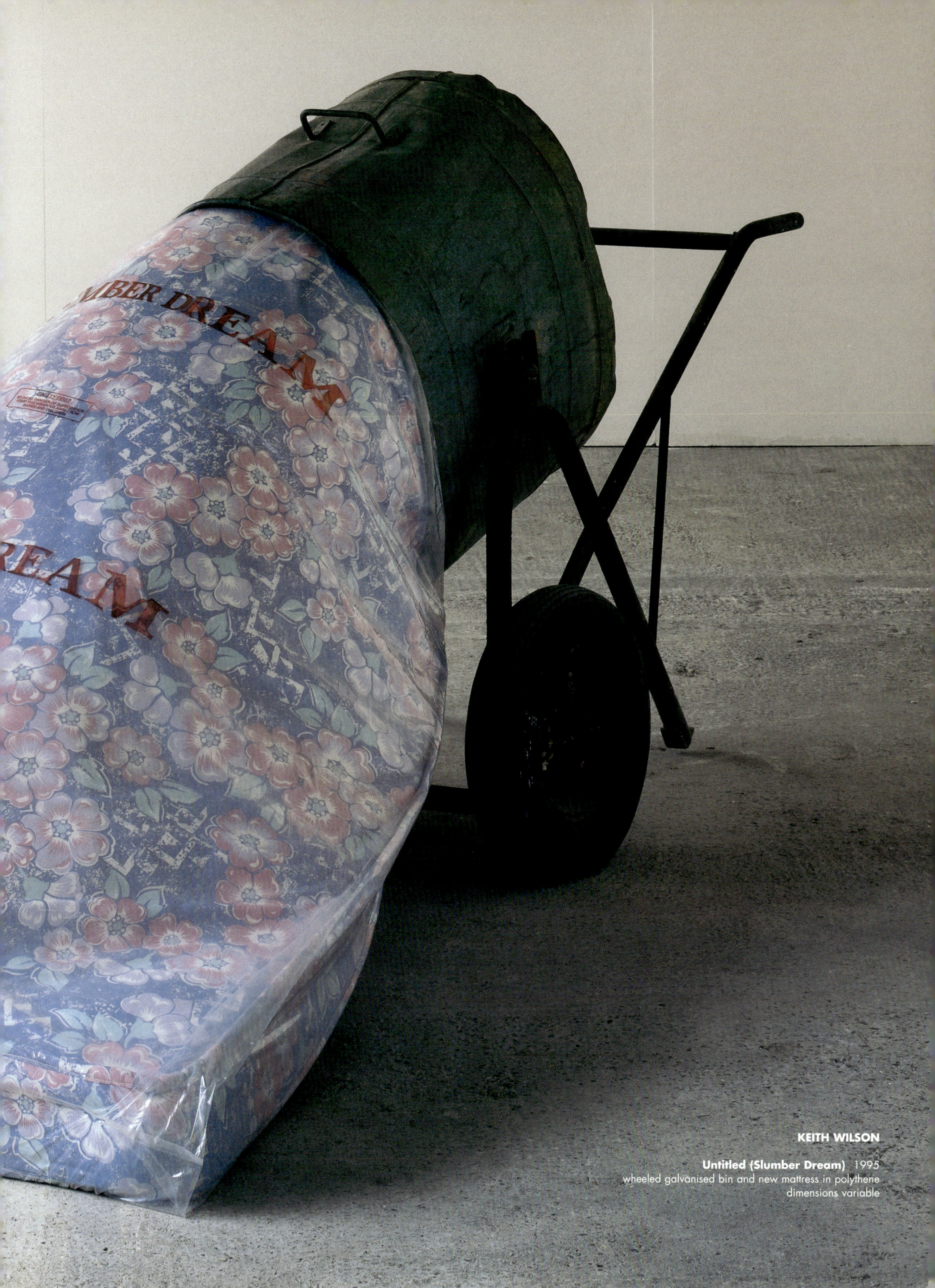

KEITH WILSON

Untitled (Slumber Dream) 1995
wheeled galvanised bin and new mattress in polythene
dimensions variable

P H o

G r

a

t O y p h

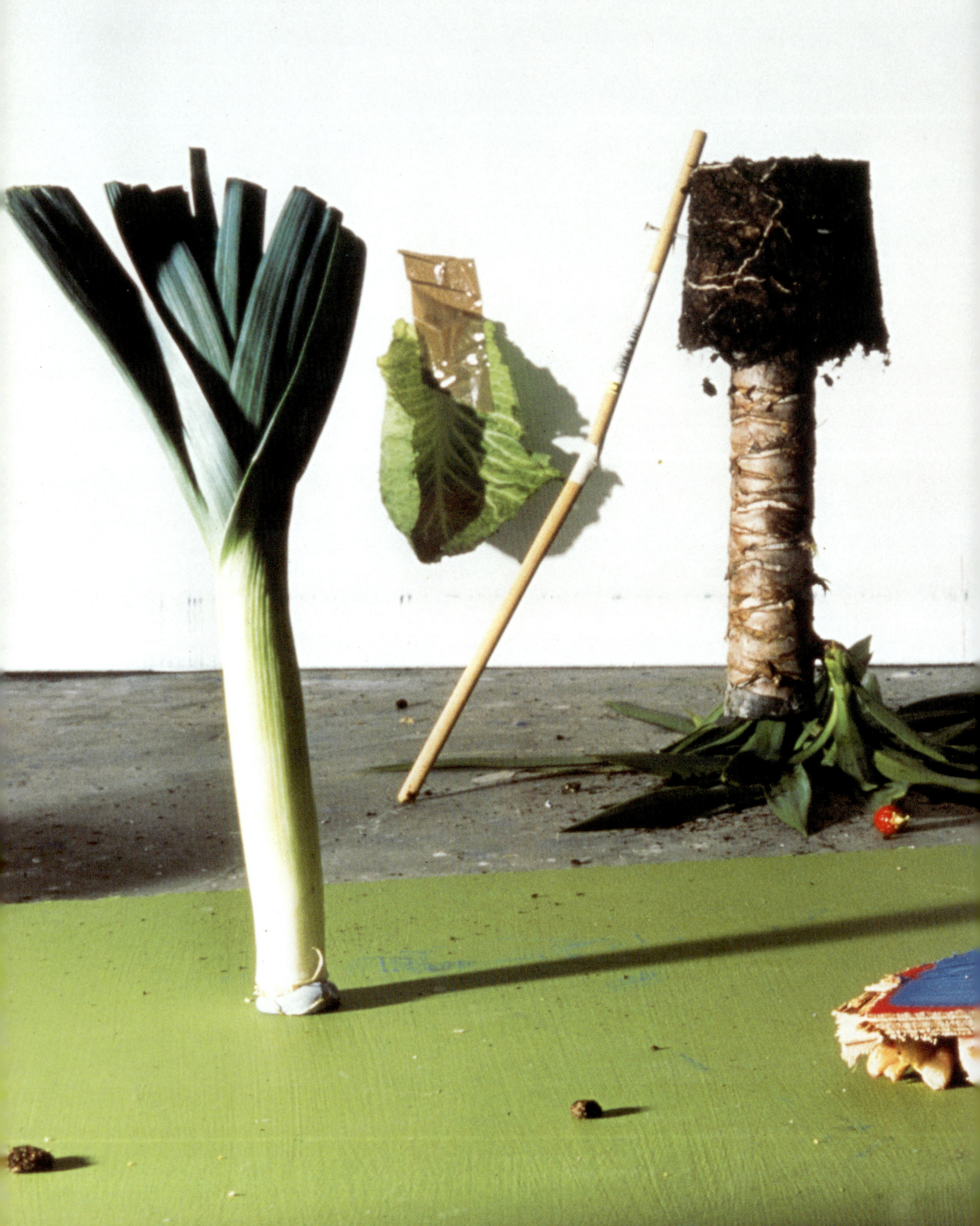

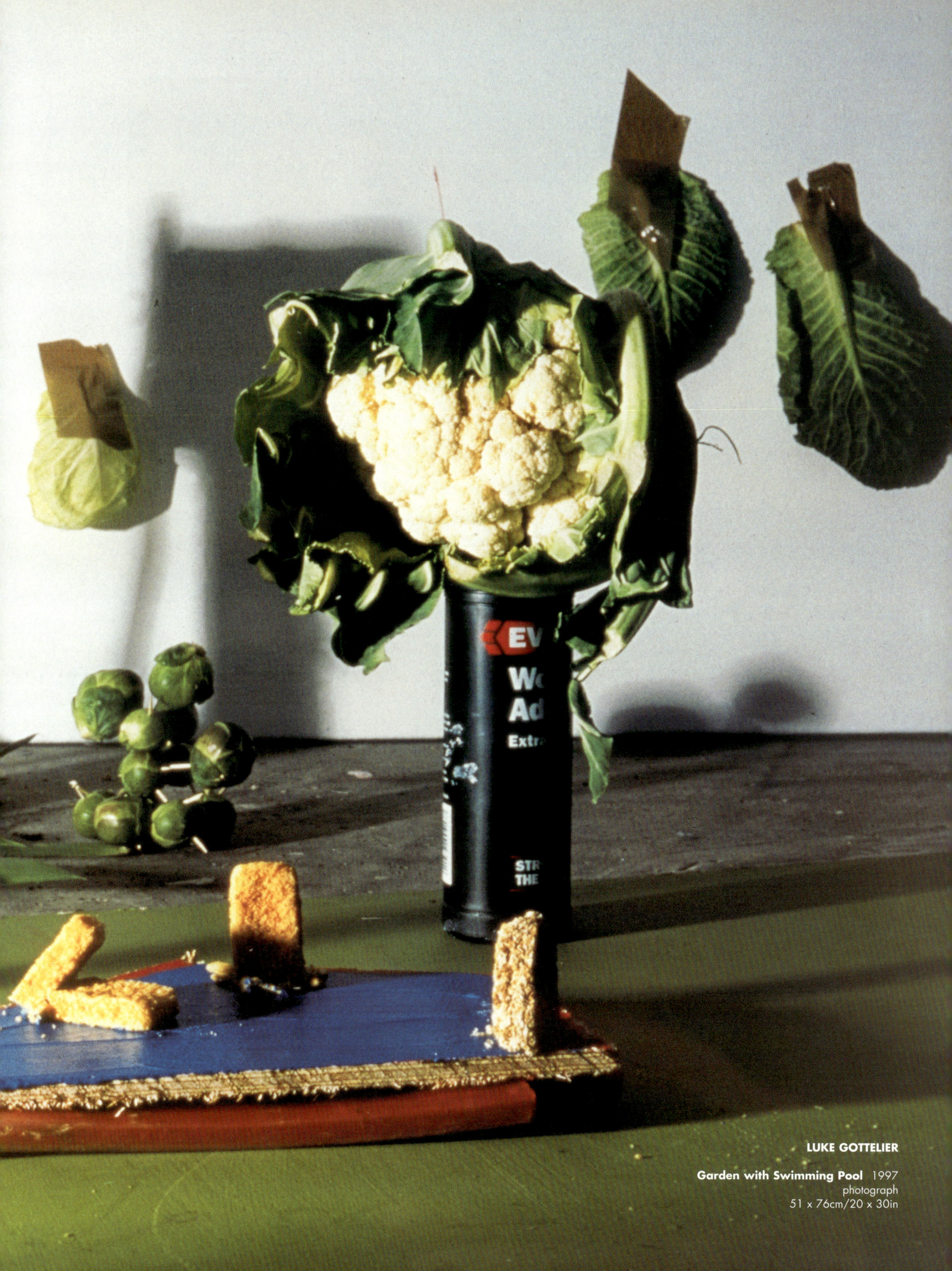

LUKE GOTTELIER

Garden with Swimming Pool 1997
photograph
51 x 76cm/20 x 30in

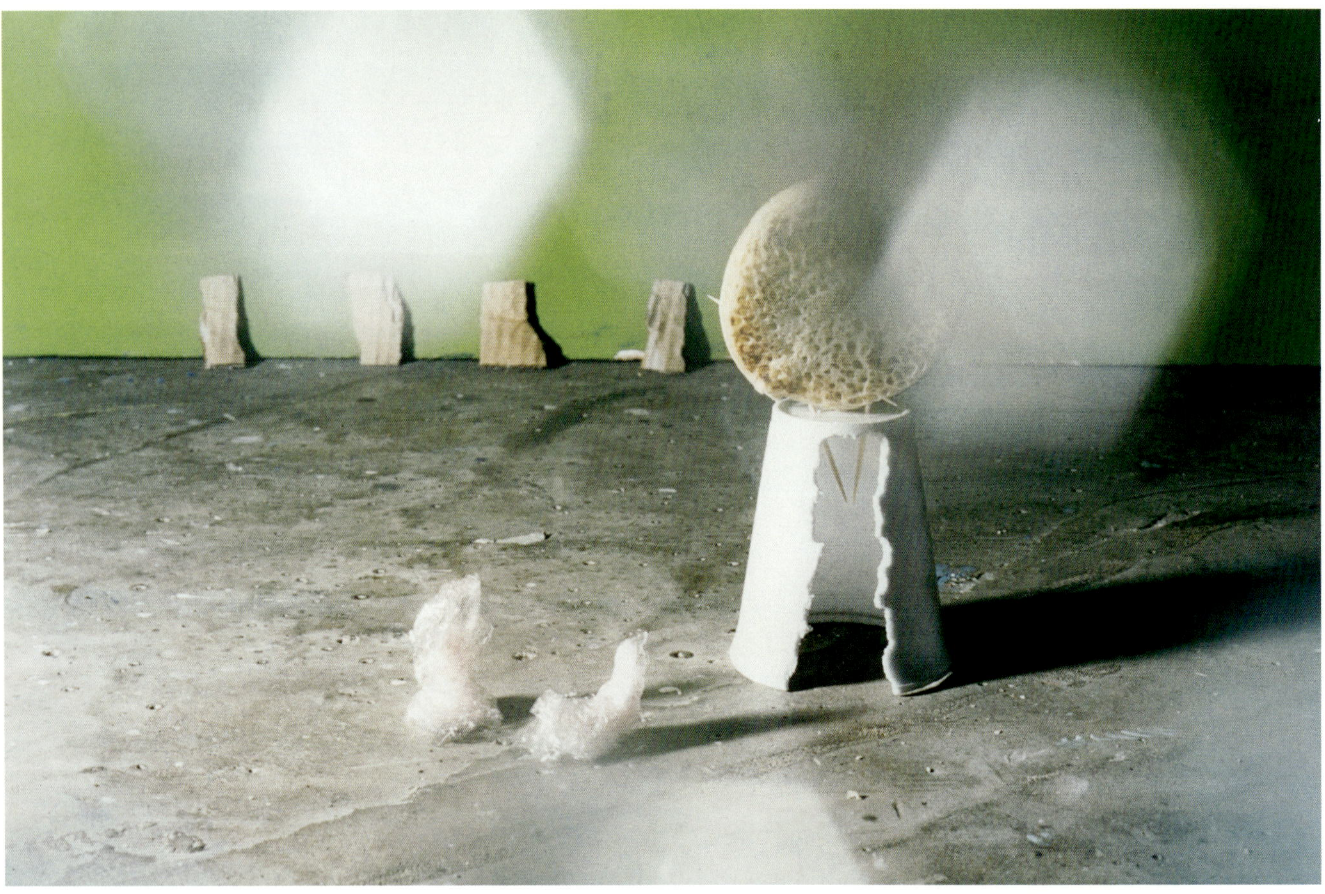

LUKE GOTTELIER A Garden 1997 photograph 67.5 x 102cm/26¹⁄₂ x 40in

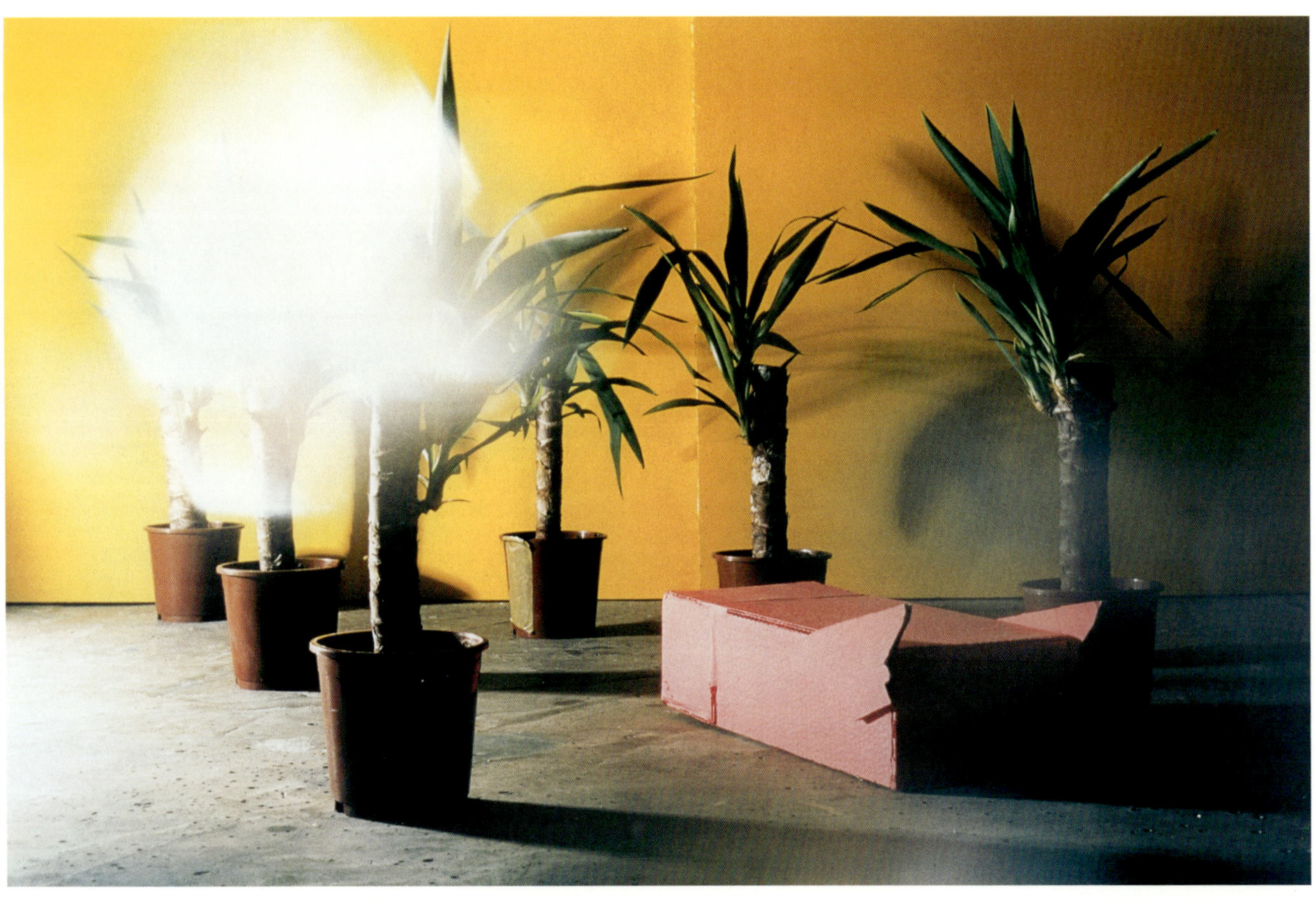

LUKE GOTTELIER California 1997 photograph 61 x 91.5cm/24 x 36in

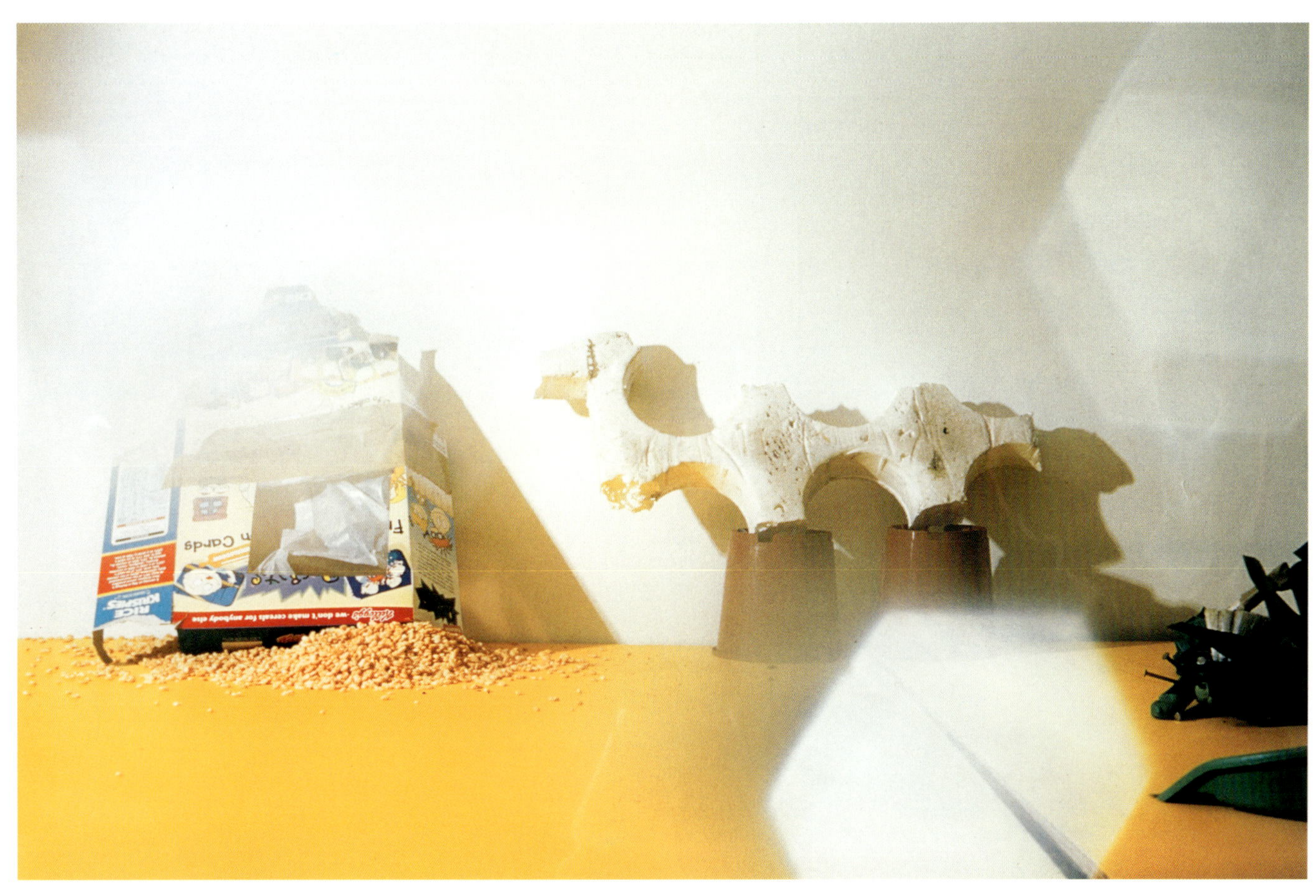

LUKE GOTTELIER Landscape with Camel 1997 photograph 50.8 x 76.2cm/20 x 30in

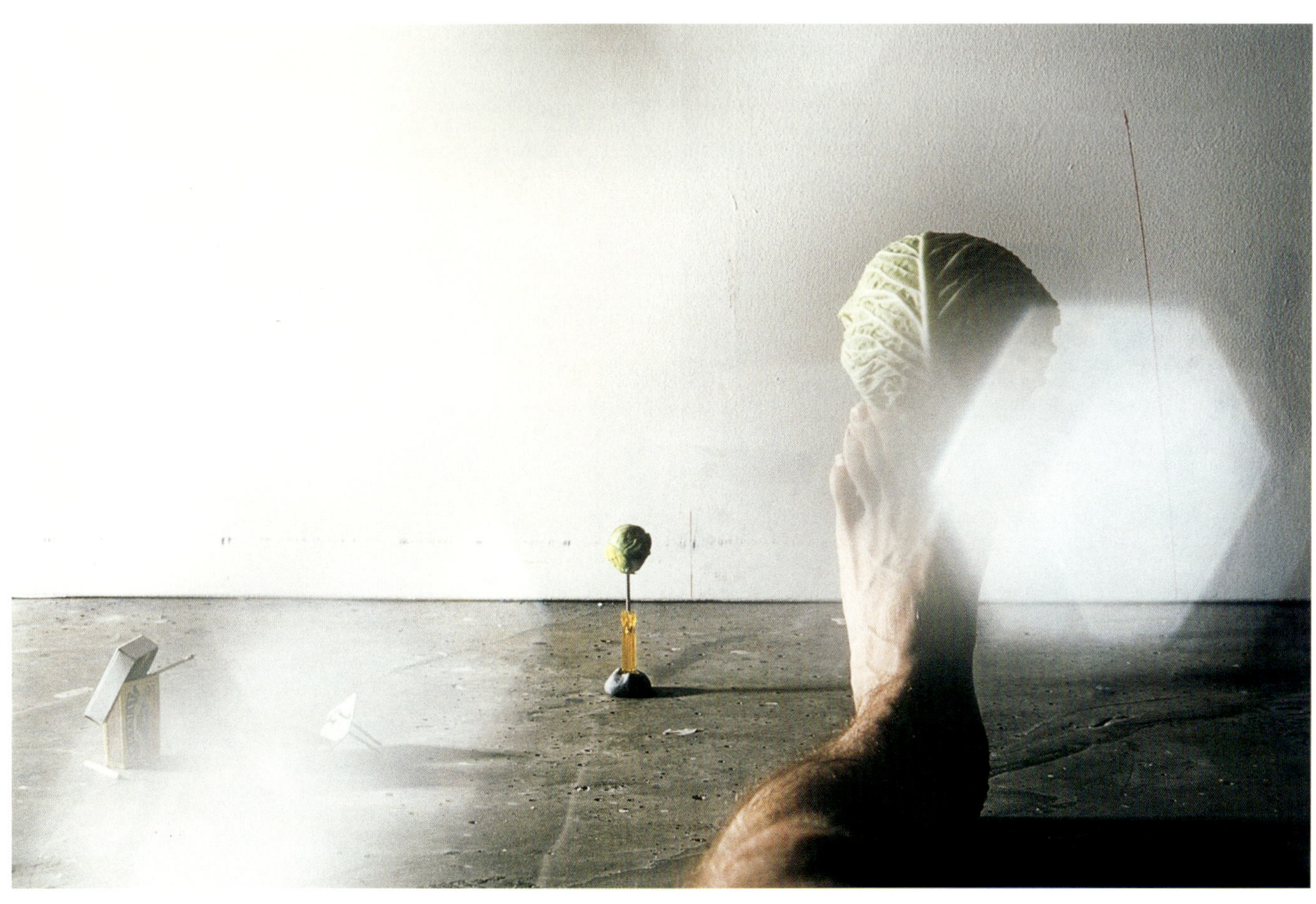

LUKE GOTTELIER A Garden 1997 photograph 50.8 x 76.2cm/20 x 30in

TOM HUNTER

Woman Reading Possession Order 1997
cibachrome print mounted on board
150 x 120cm/59 x 47in

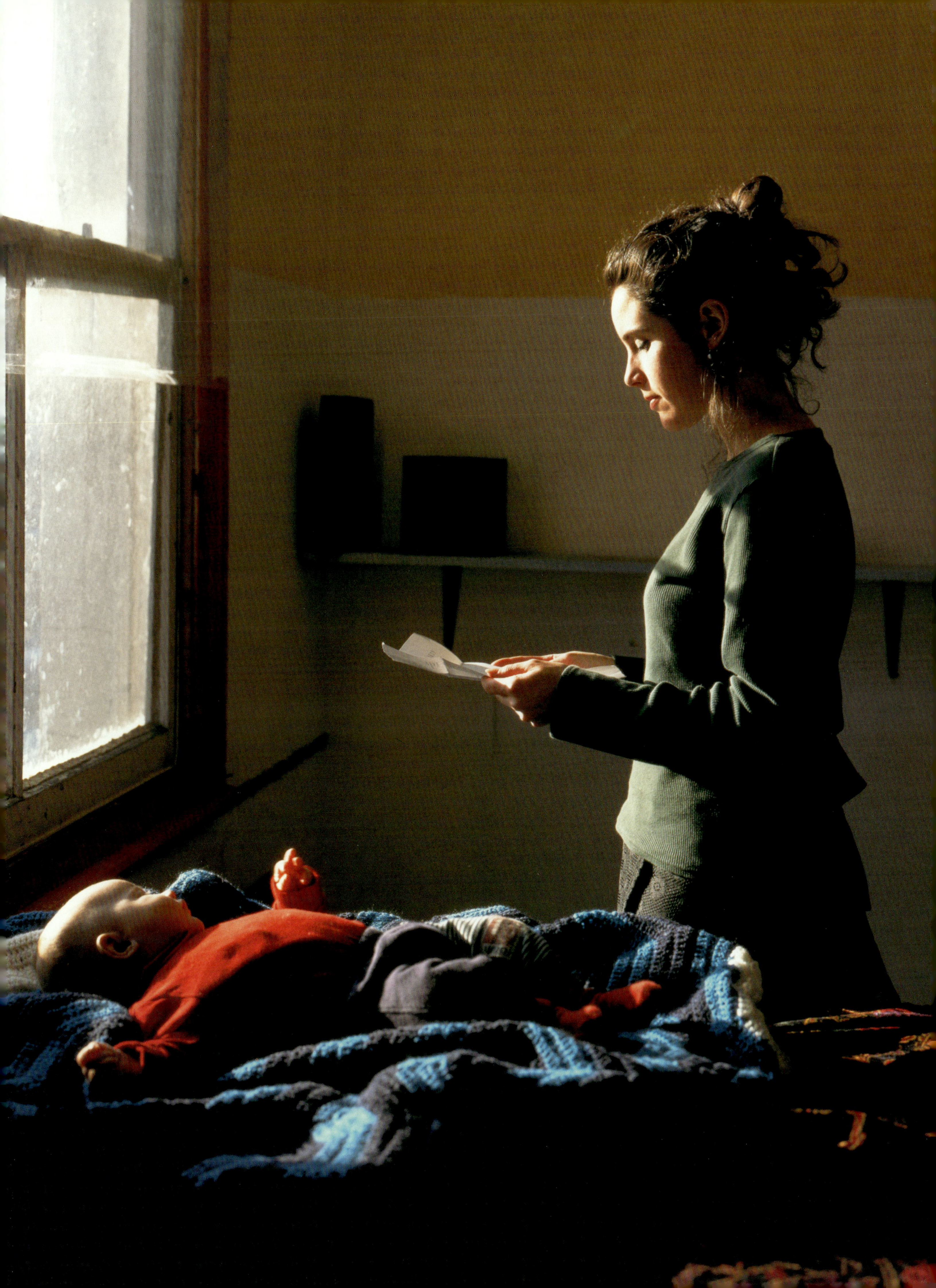

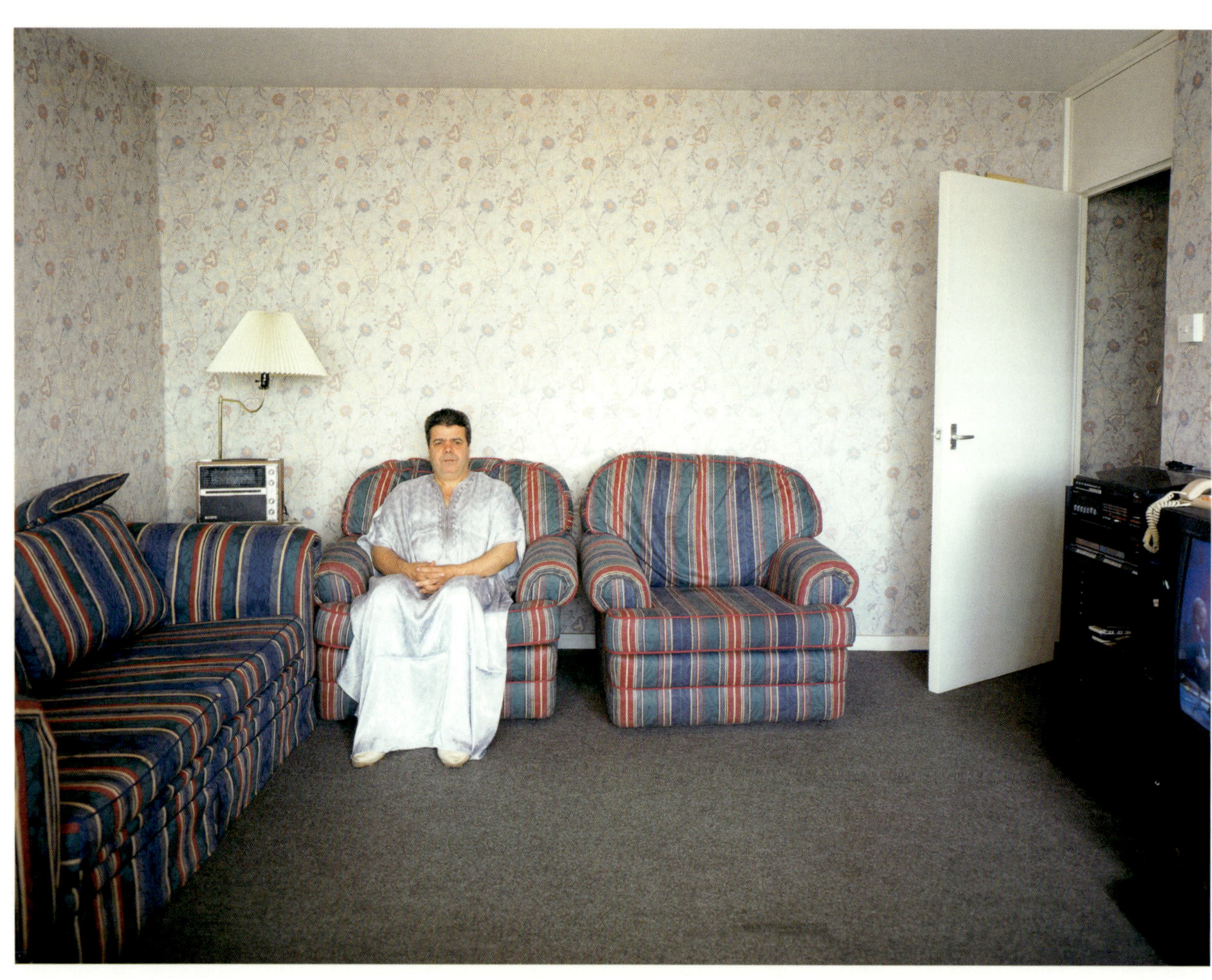

TOM HUNTER

**Holly Street Tower Block Project Series:
Residents of Cedar Court** 1997-98
c-type prints on foamex
243.8 x 304.8cm/96 x 120in

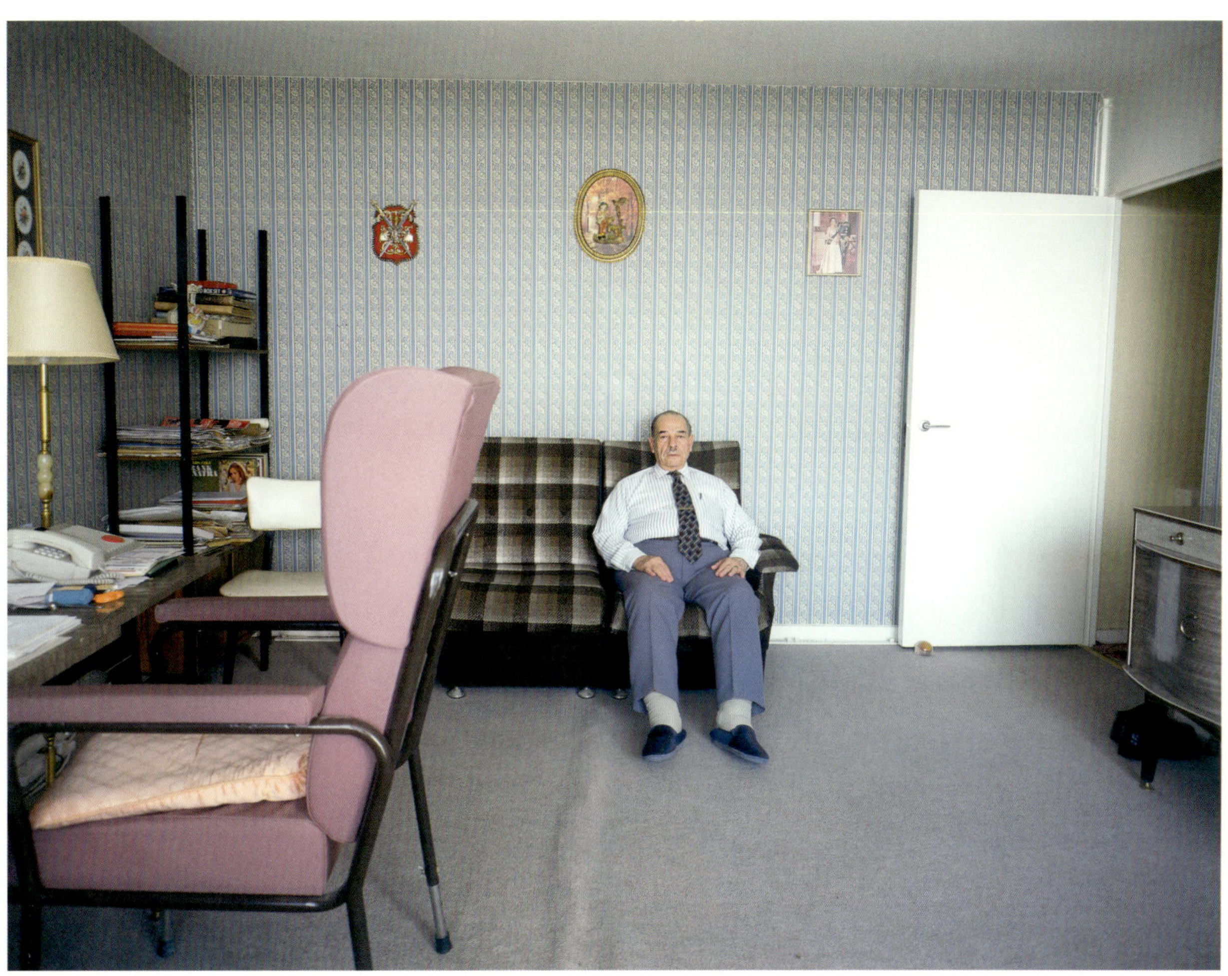

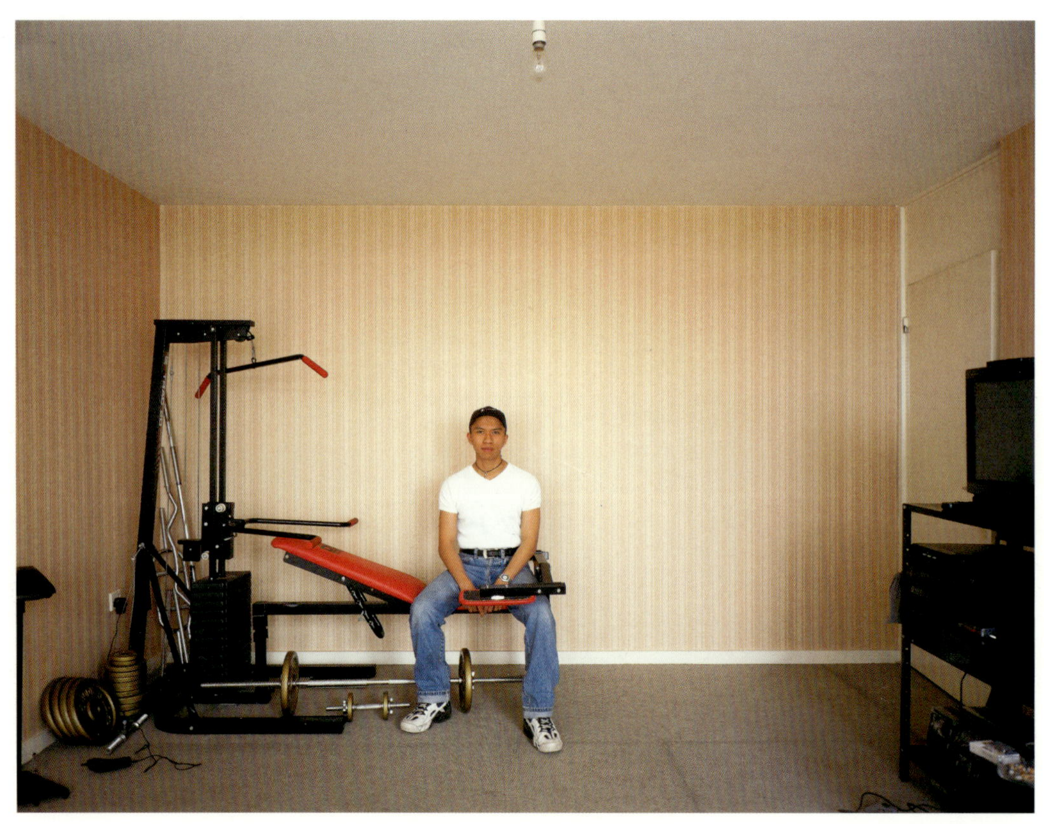

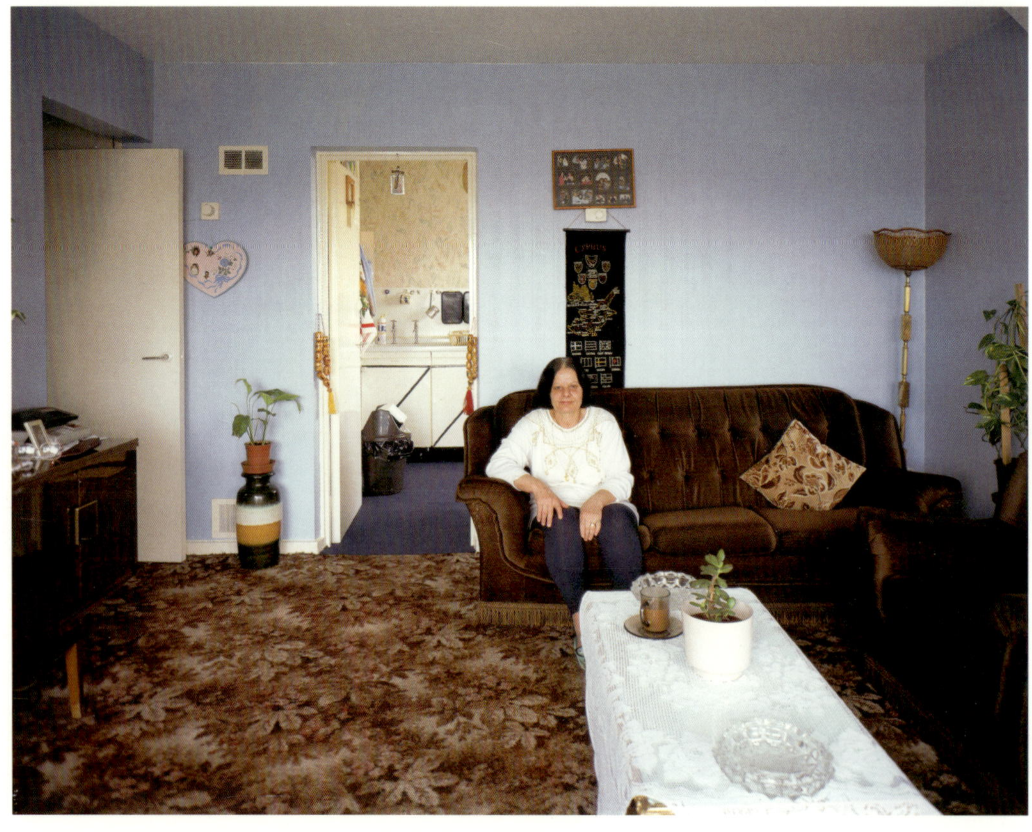

TOM HUNTER

**Holly Street Tower Block Project Series:
Residents of Cedar Court** 1997-98
c-type prints on foamex
243.8 x 304.8cm/96 x 120in

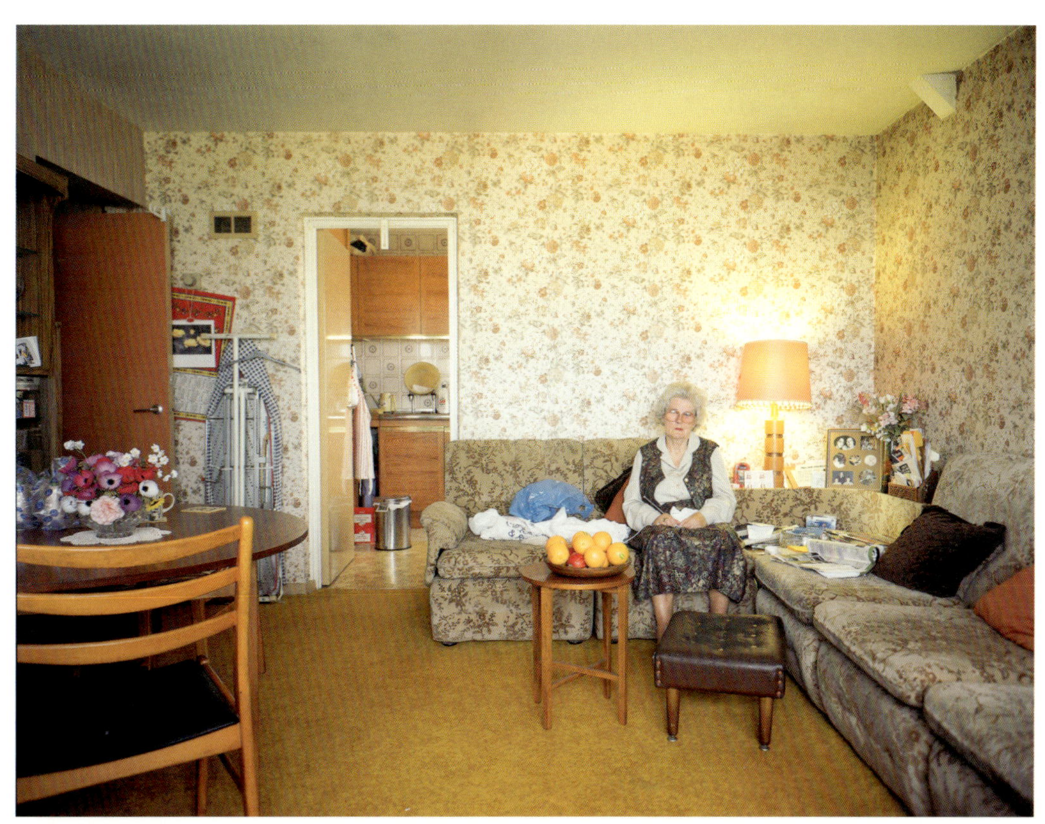

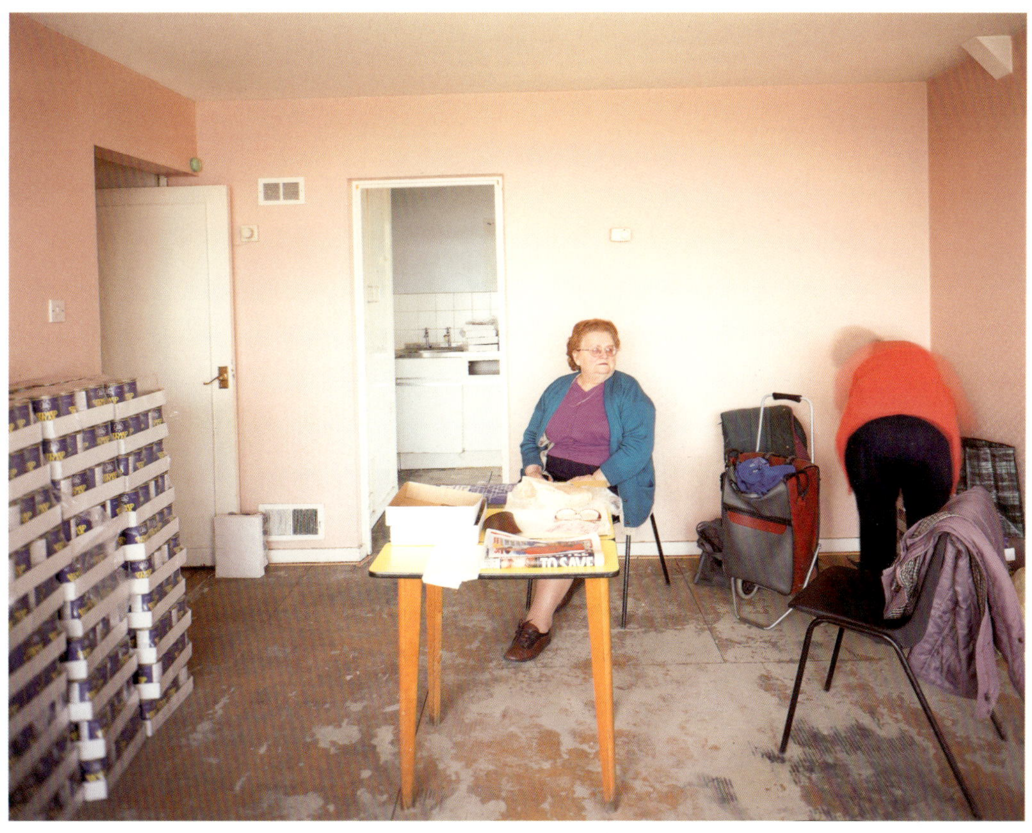

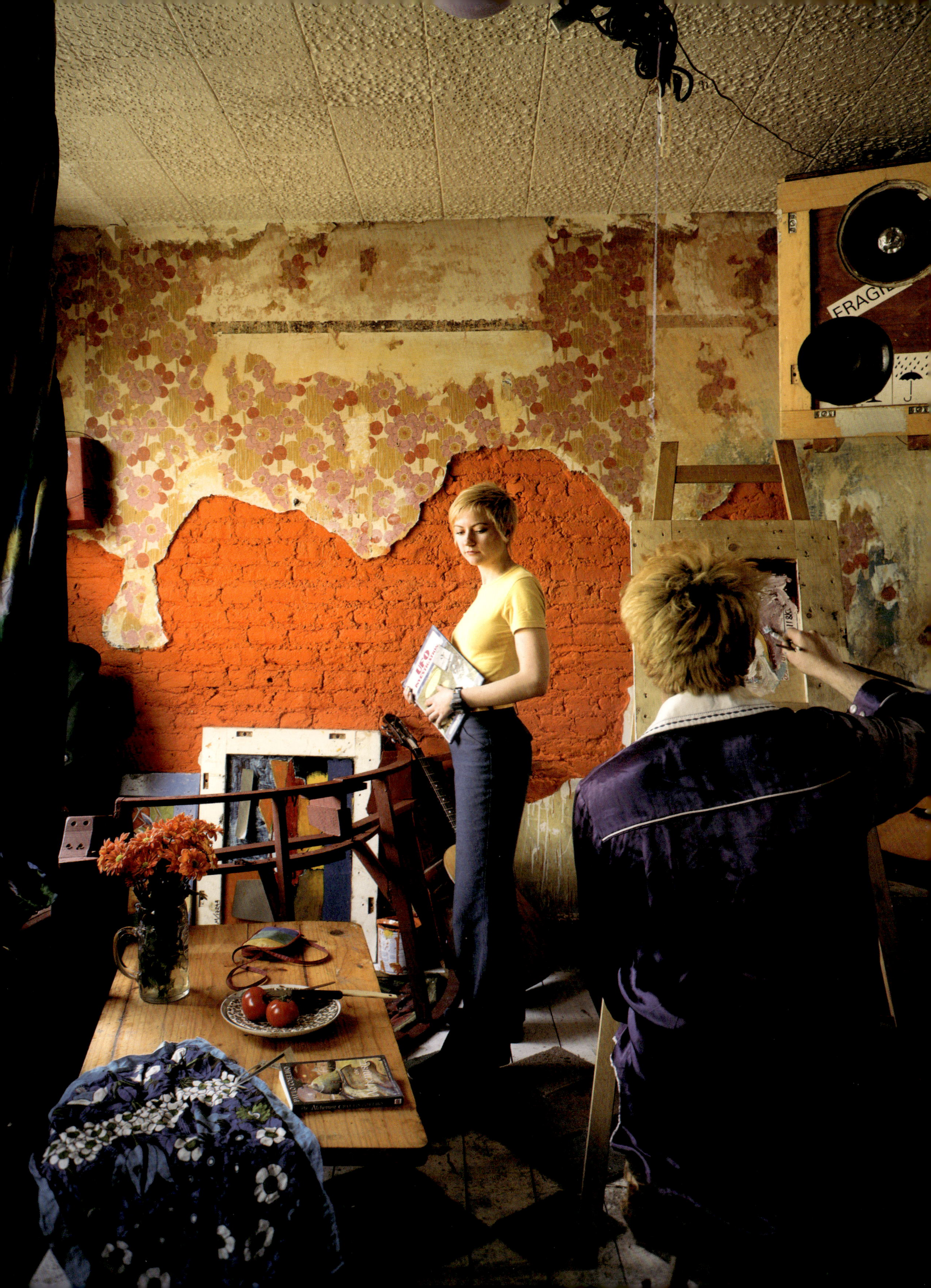

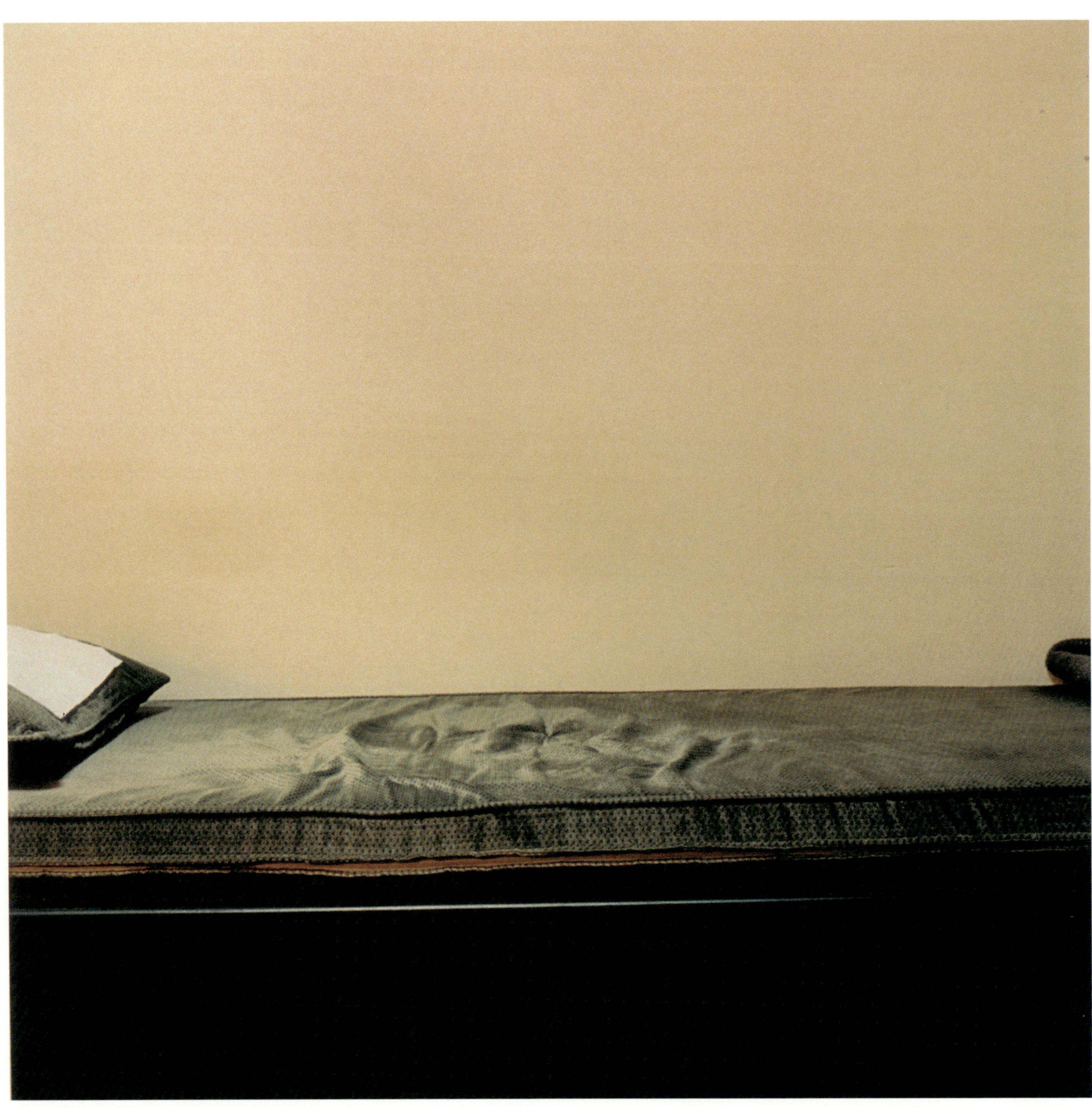

SARAH JONES

Consulting Room (Couch A) 1996
c-type photographic print, mounted on aluminium
152.4 x 152.4cm/60 x 60in

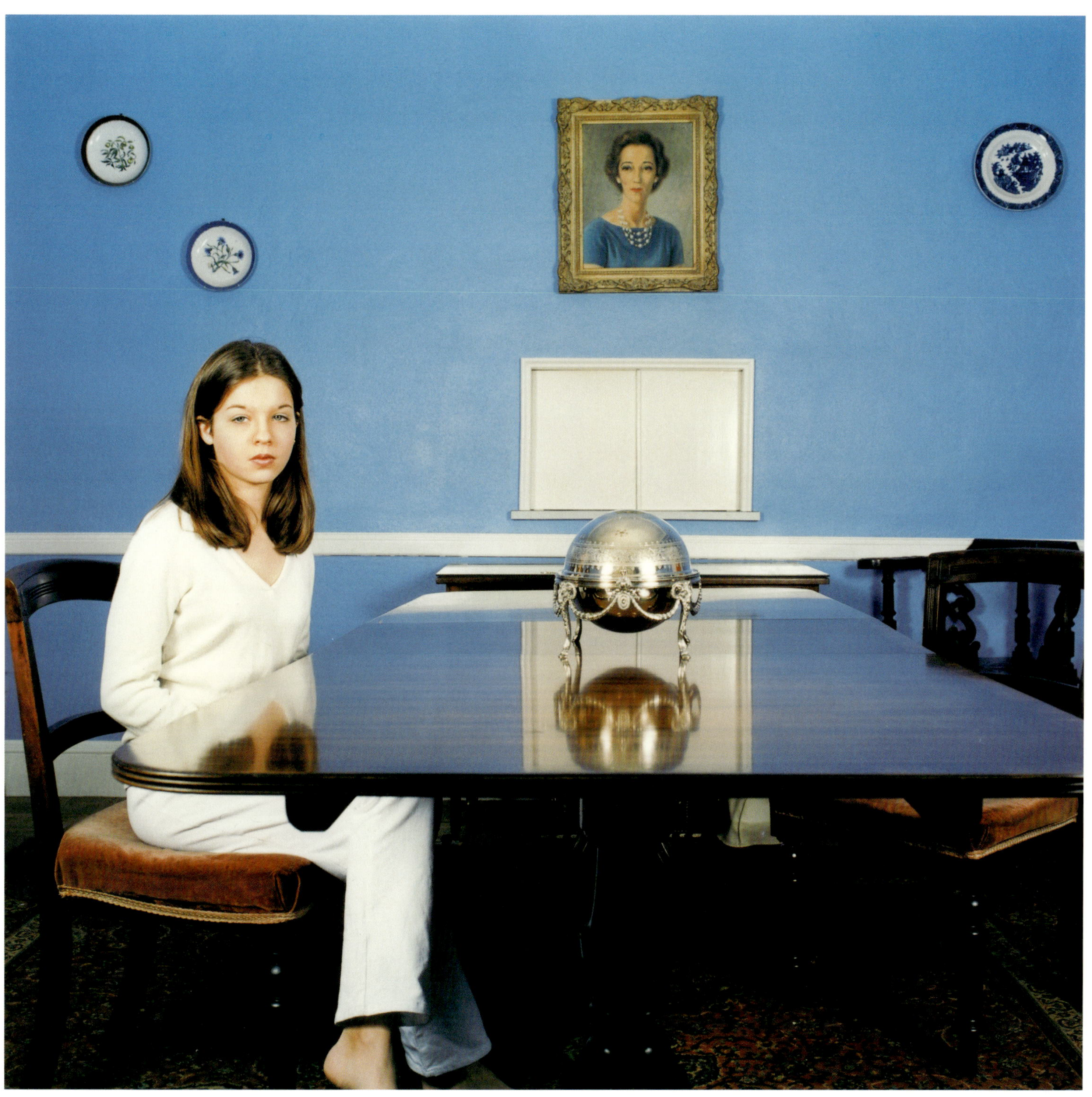

Dining Room (Francis Place) (III) 1997
c-type photographic print, mounted on aluminium
152.4 x 152.4cm/60 x 60in

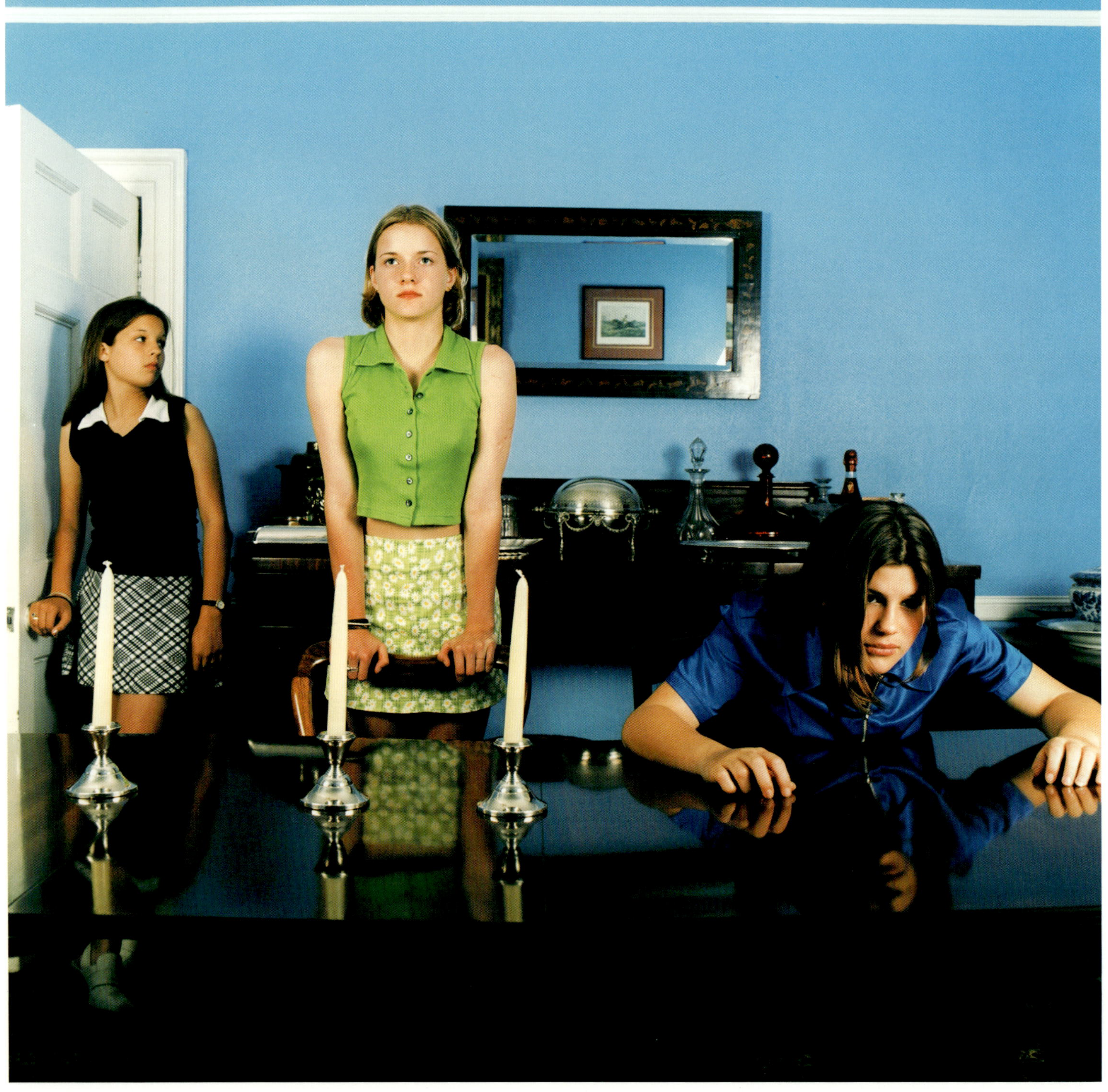

SARAH JONES

Dining Room (II) 1997 c-type photographic print, mounted on aluminium 152.4 x 152.4cm/60 x 60in

right above: **Dining Room (III)** 1997 c-type photographic print, mounted on aluminium 152.4 x 152.4cm/60 x 60in

right below: **Dining Room (I)** 1997 c-type photographic print, mounted on aluminium 152.4 x 152.4cm/60 x 60in

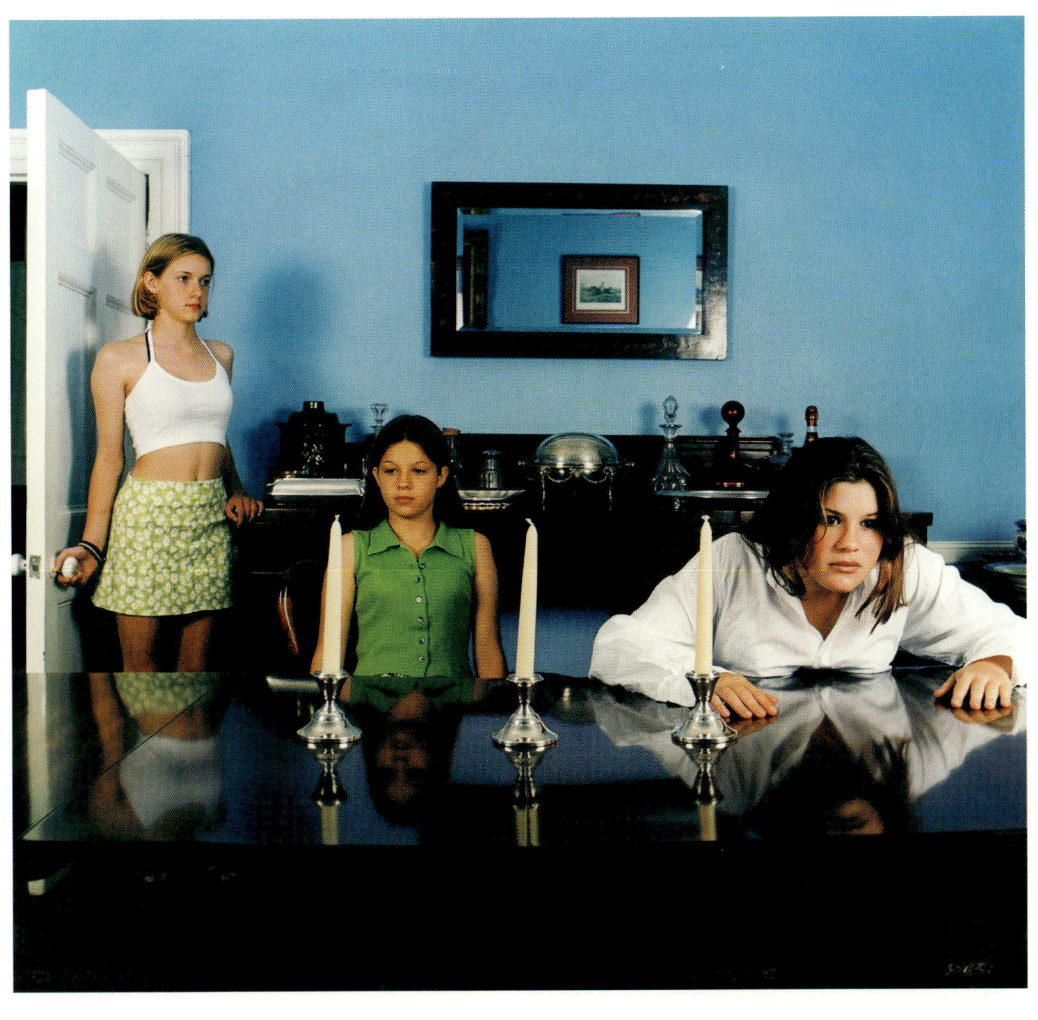

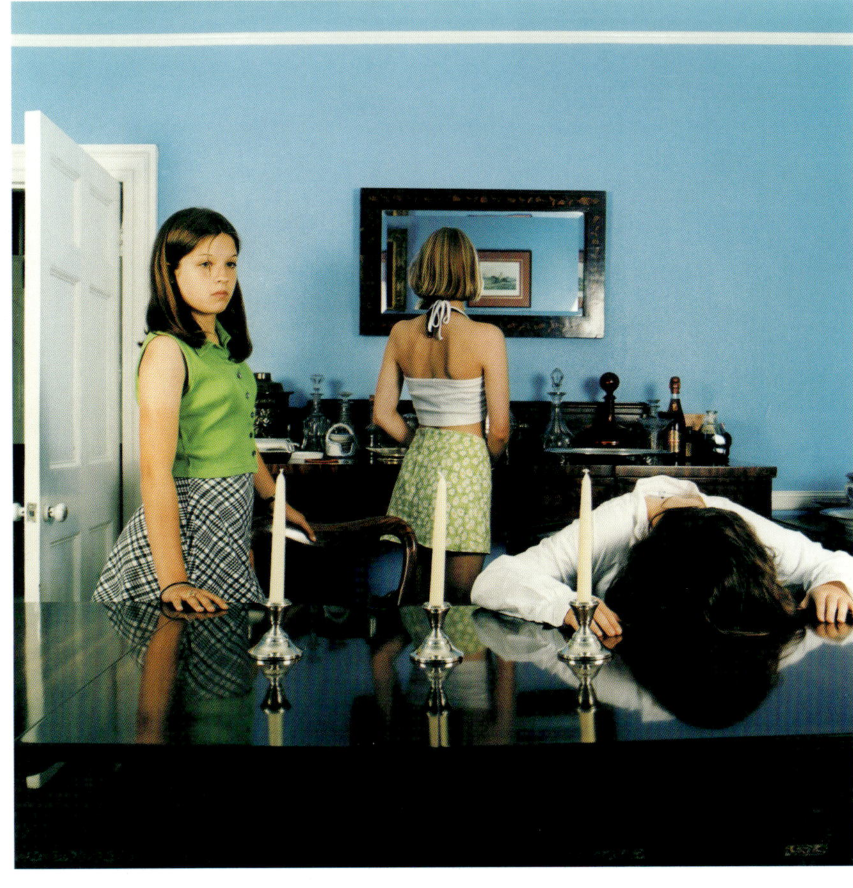

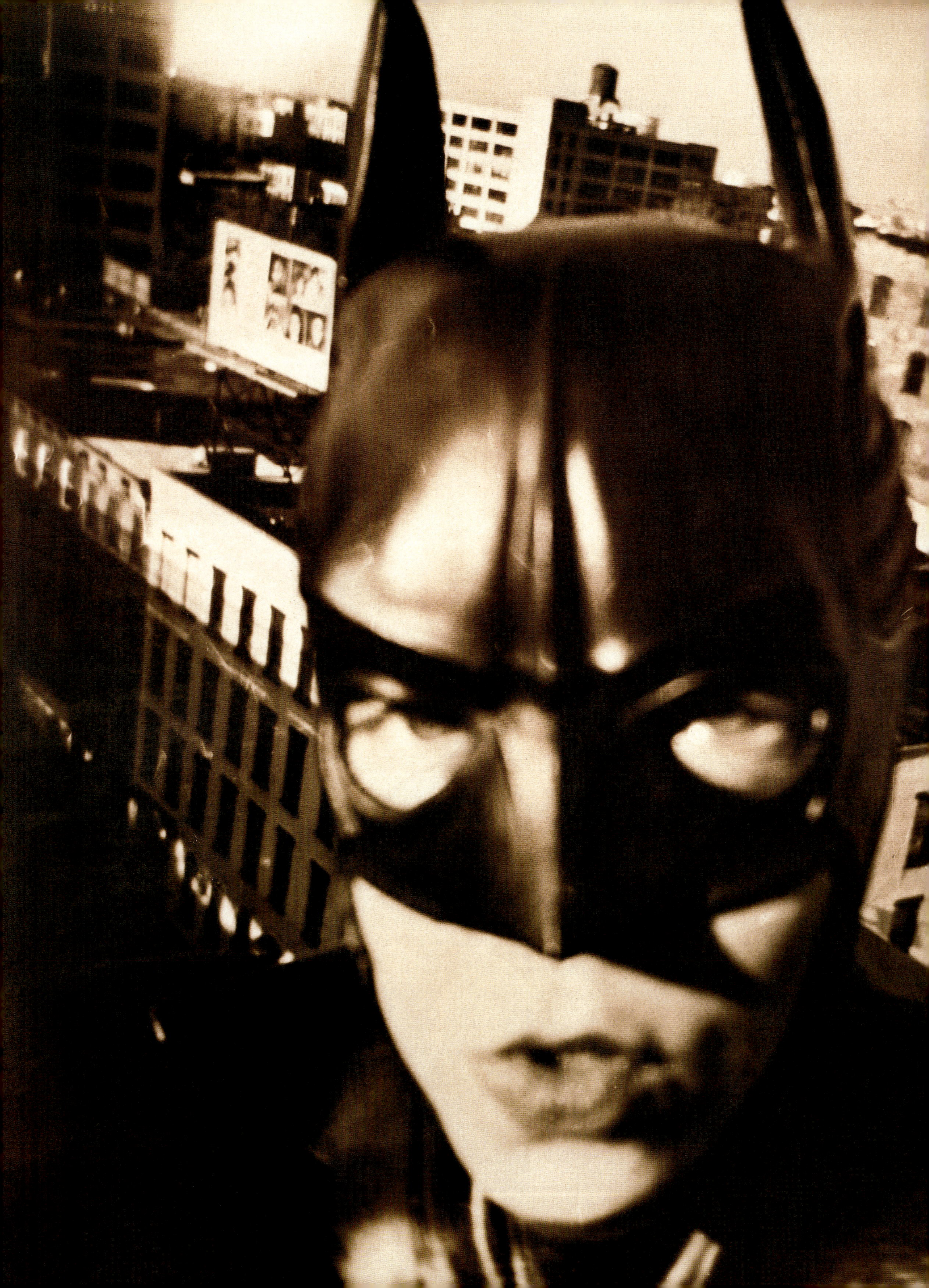

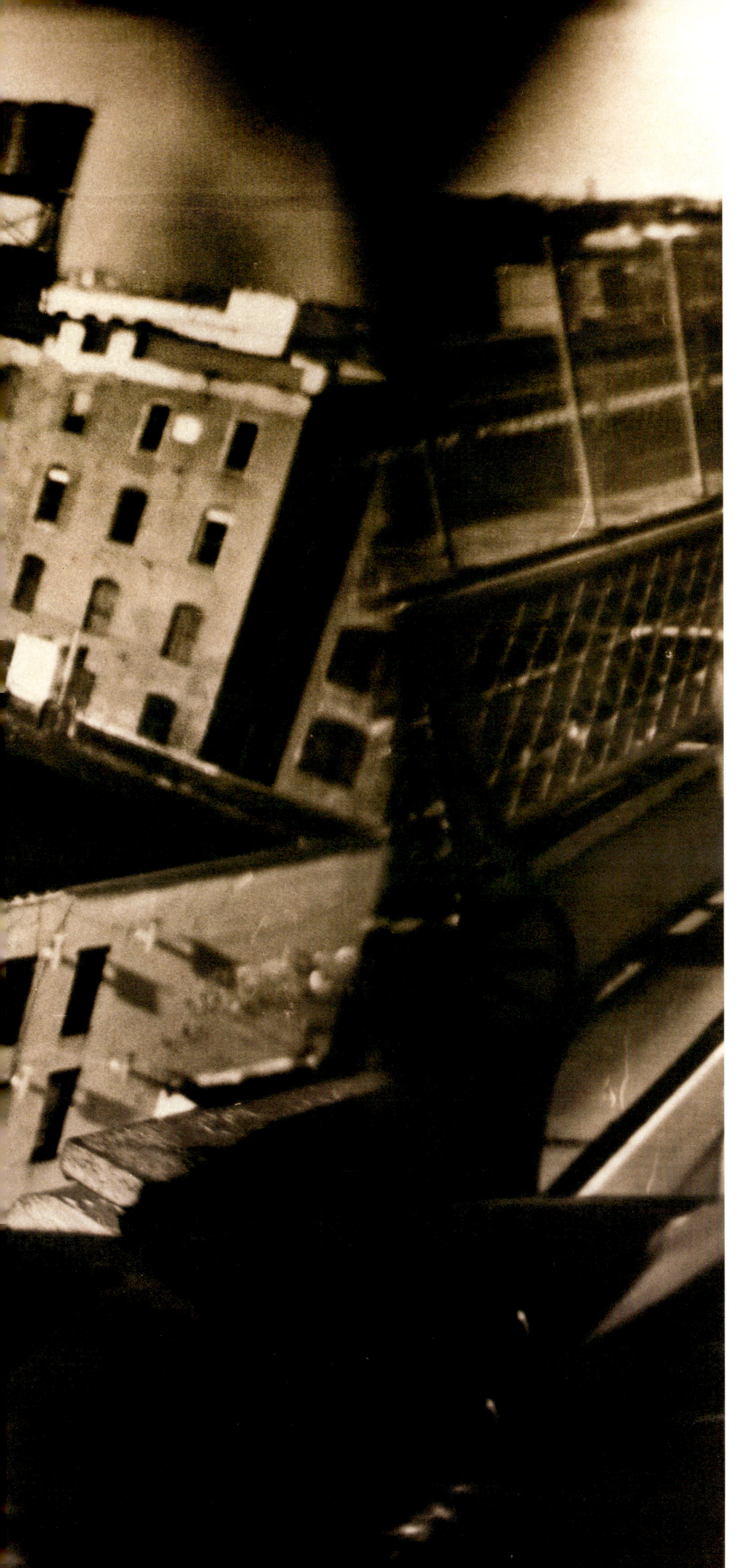

KATIA LIEBMANN

Gotham City 1997
series of 12 van dyke prints
76.2 x 62.2cm/30 x 24½in

and overleaf

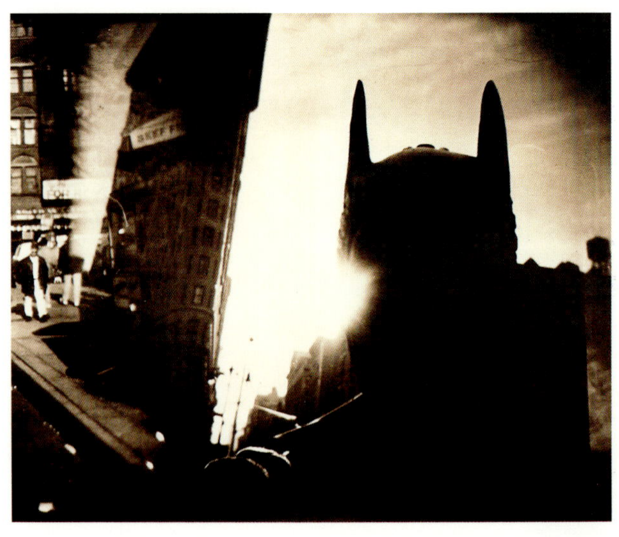
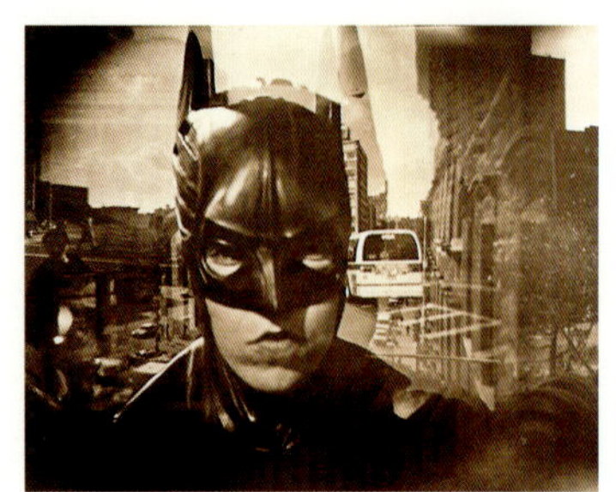
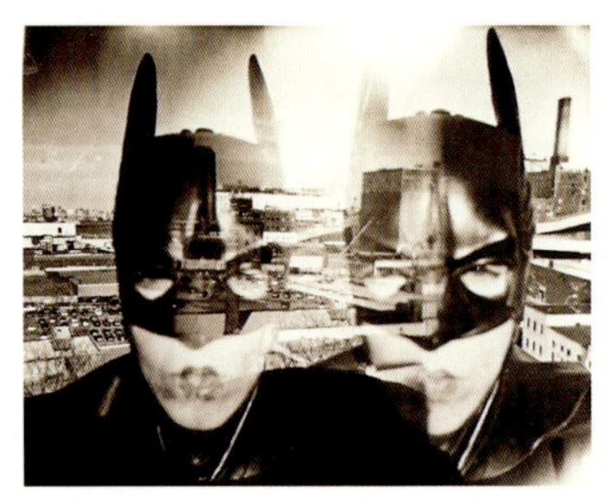
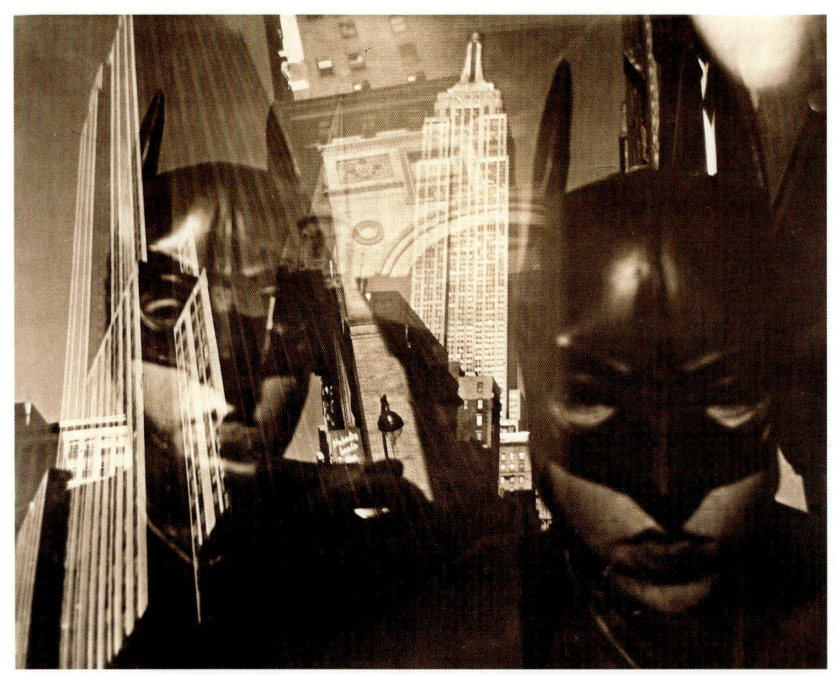
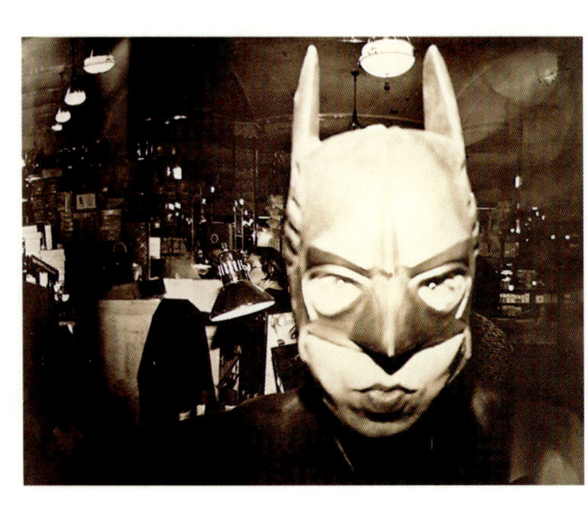
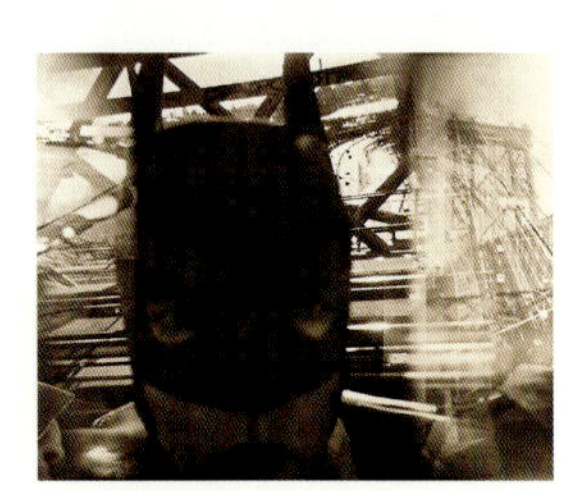
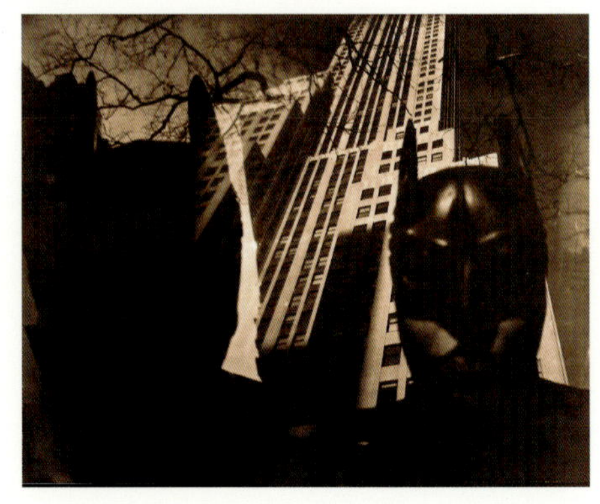

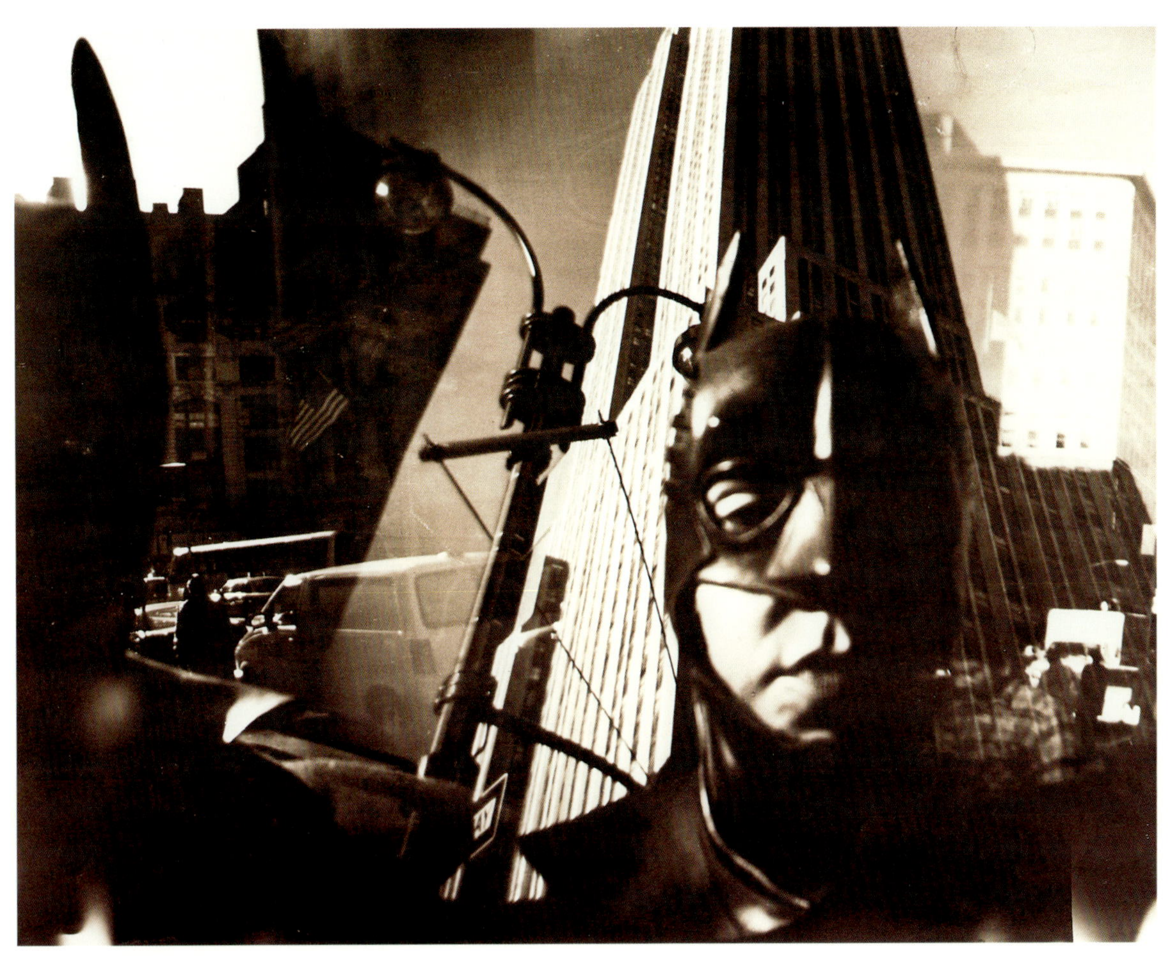

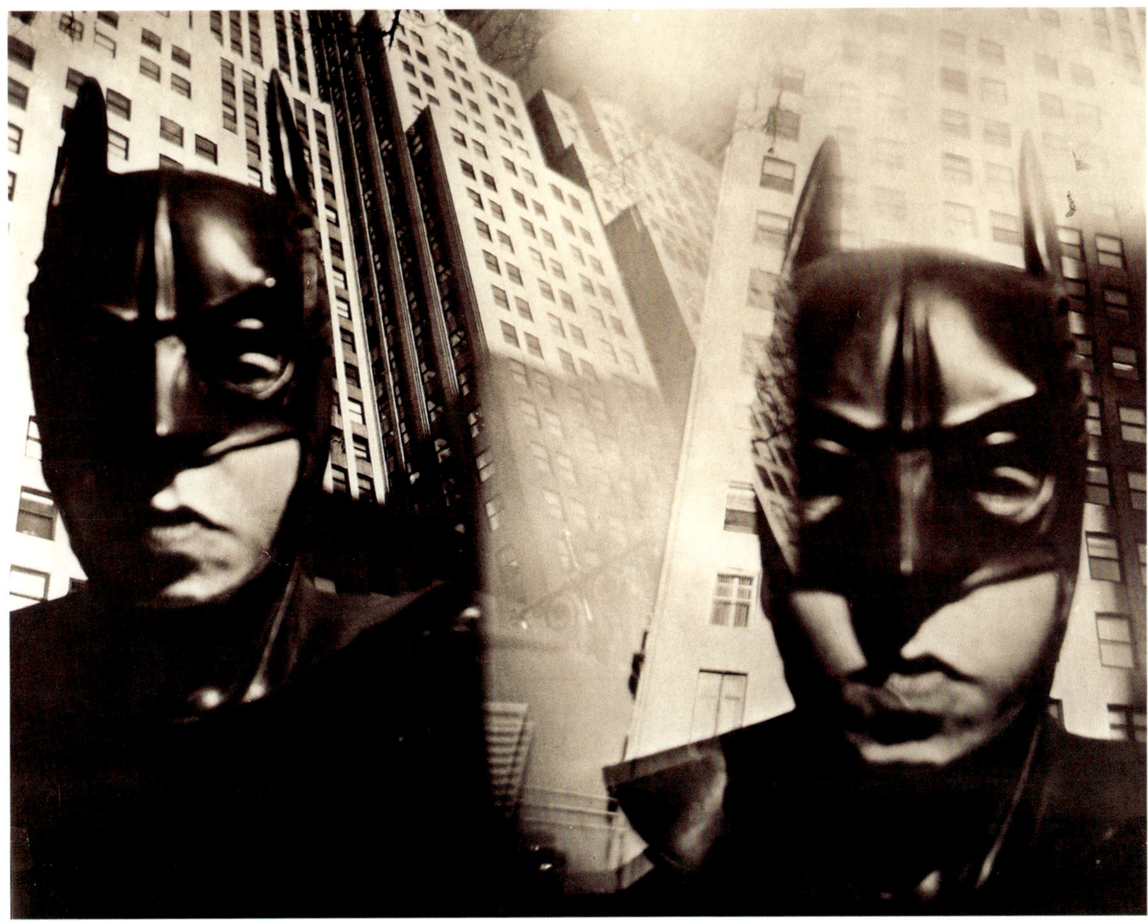

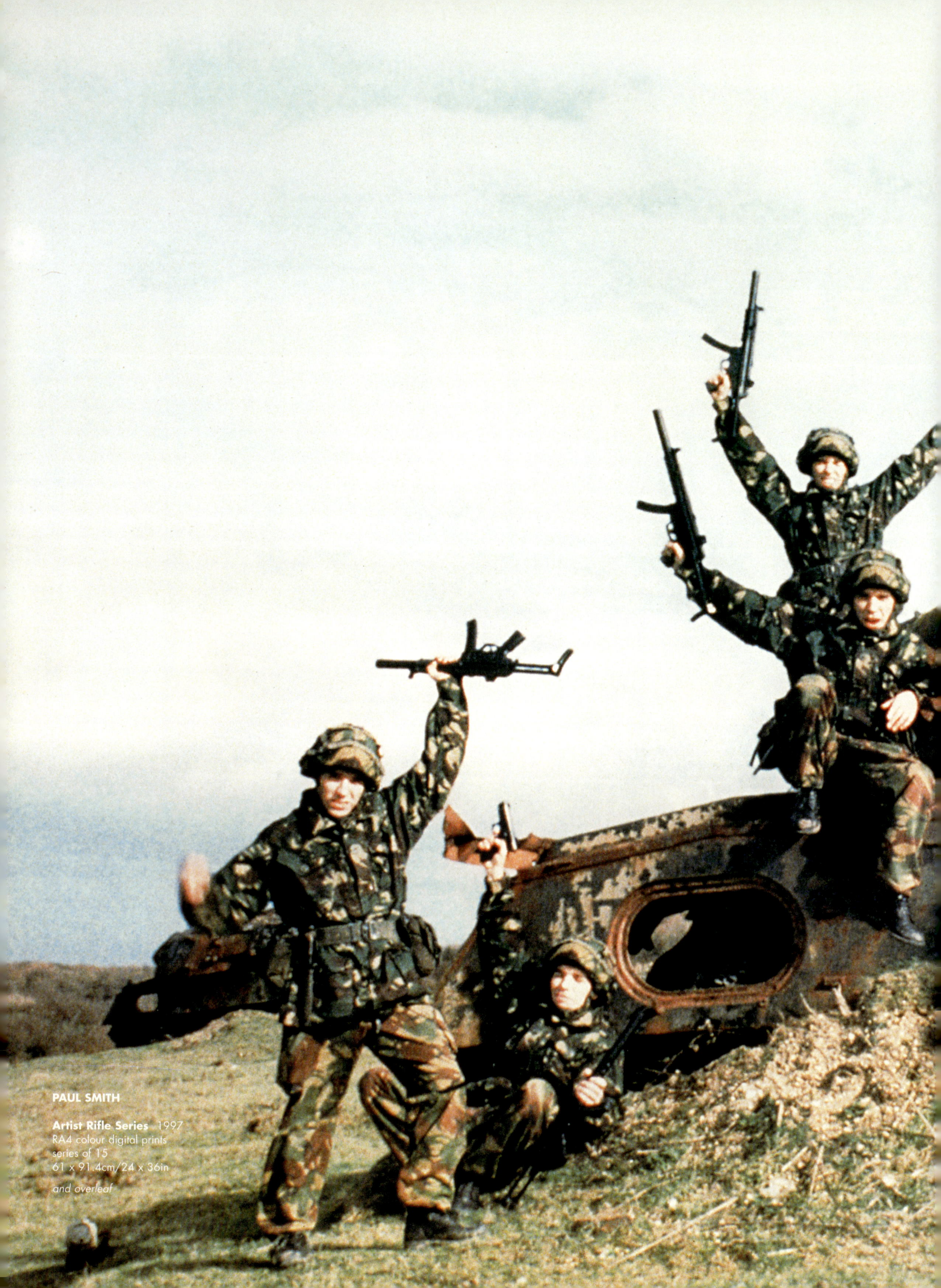

PAUL SMITH
Artist Rifle Series 1997
RA4 colour digital prints
series of 15
61 x 91.4cm/24 x 36in

and overleaf

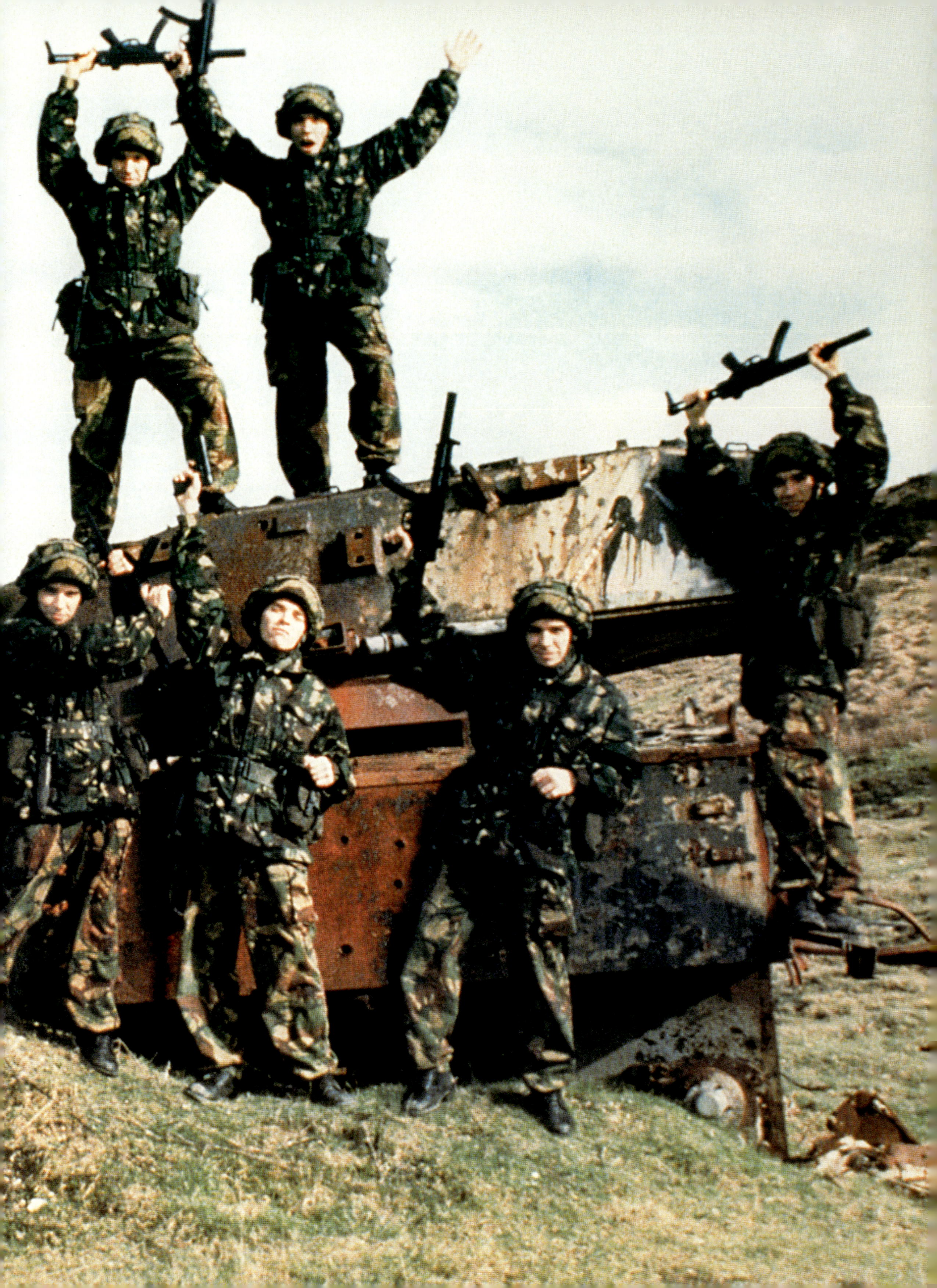

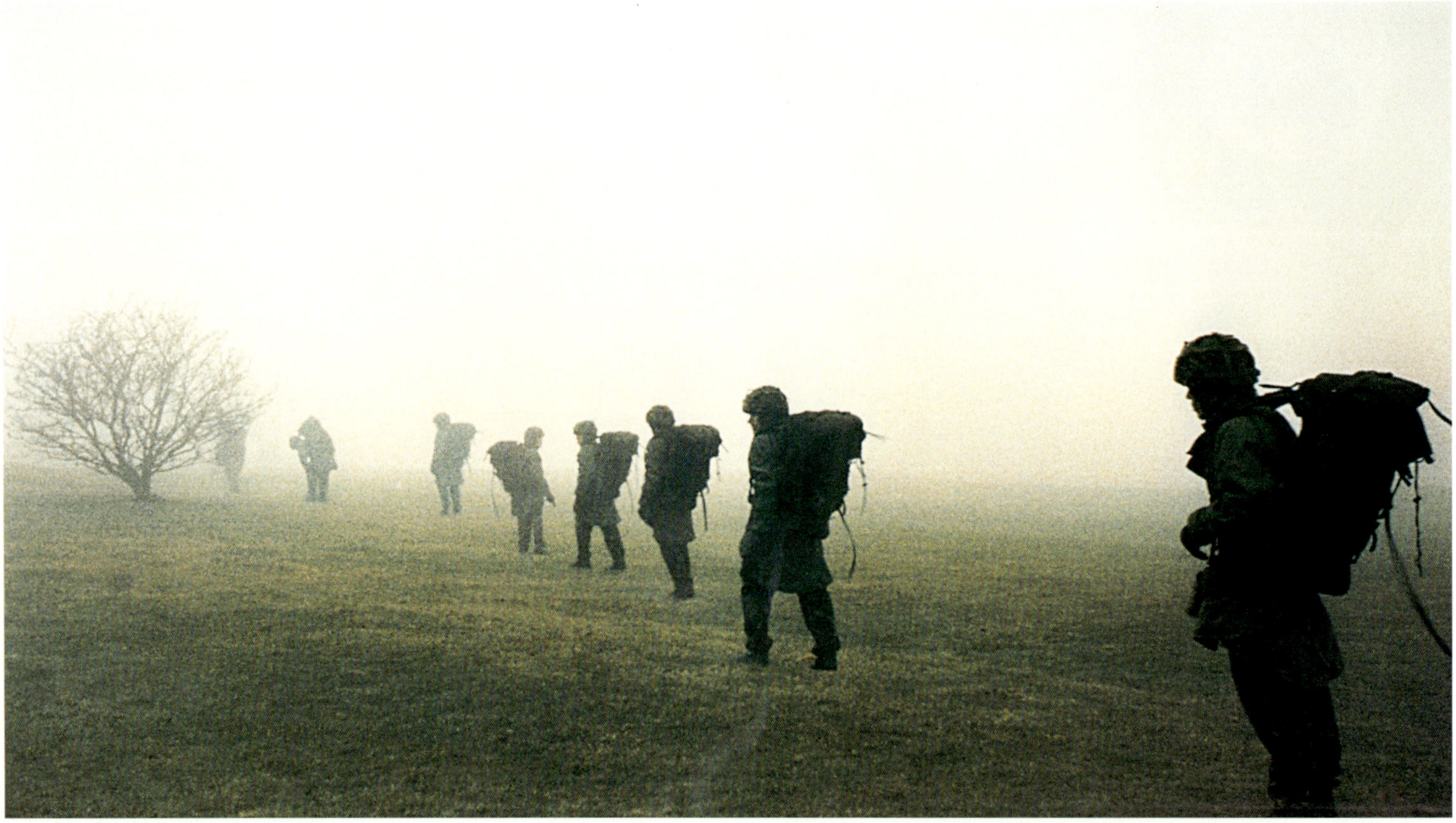

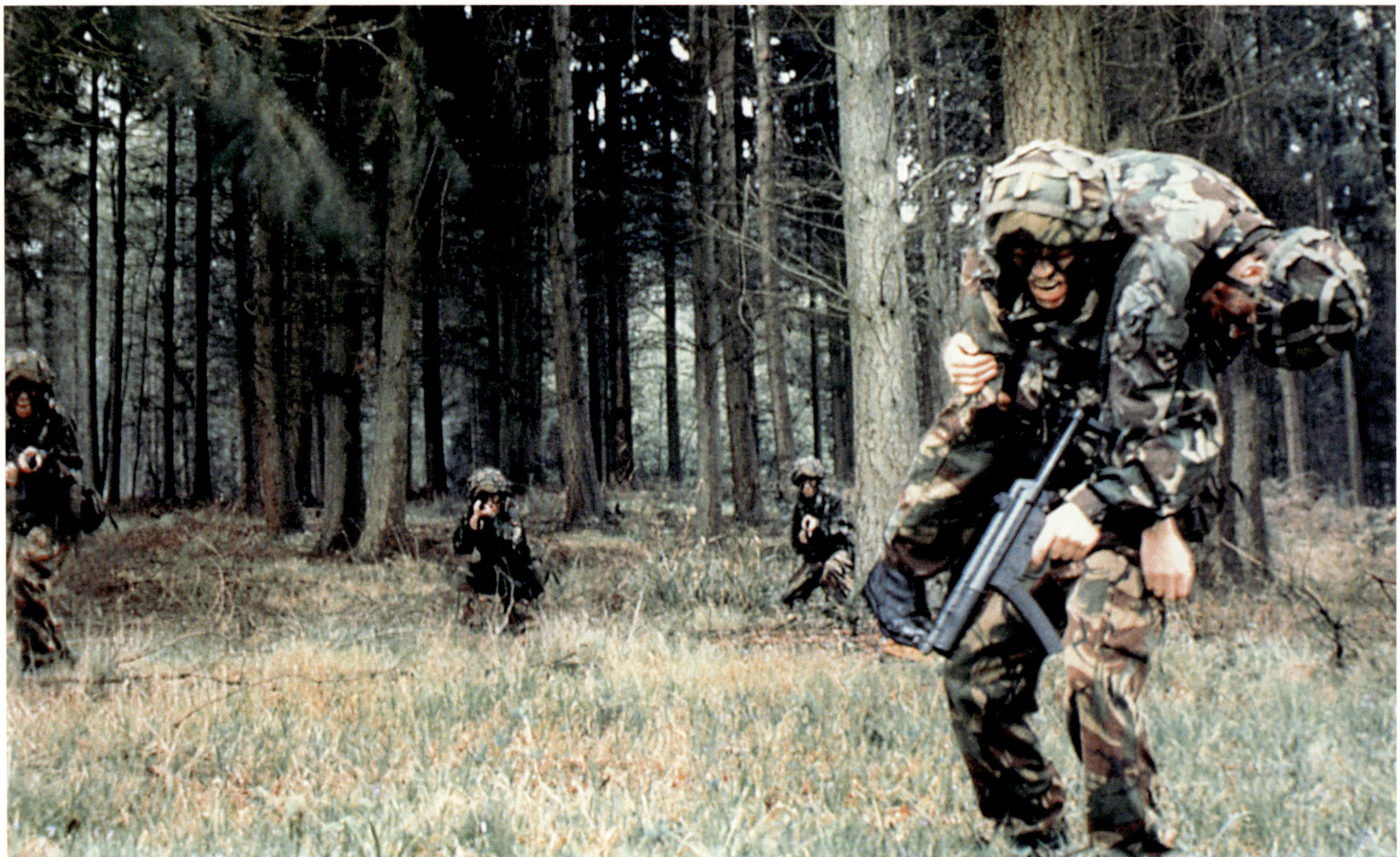

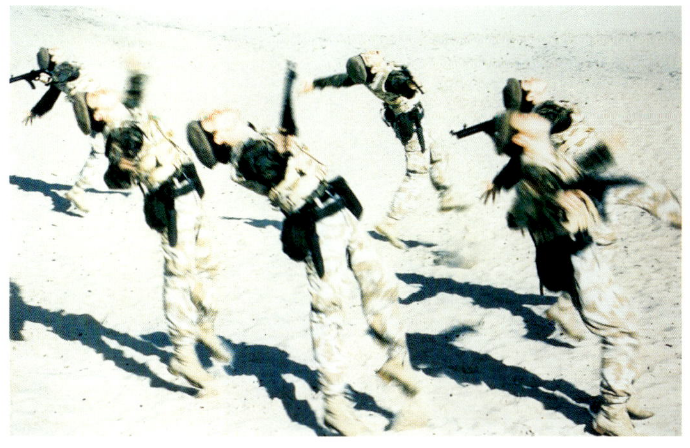
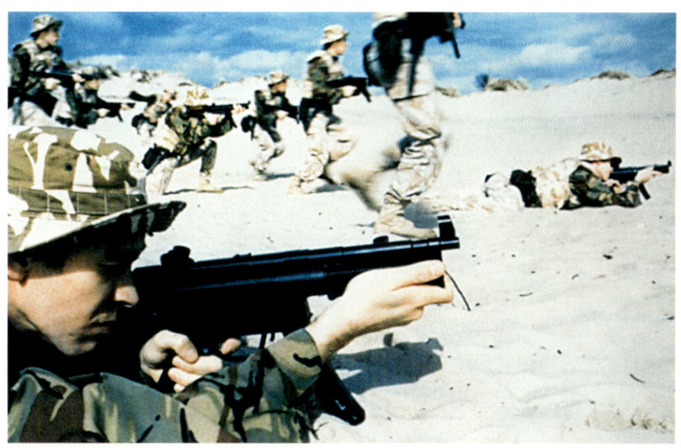
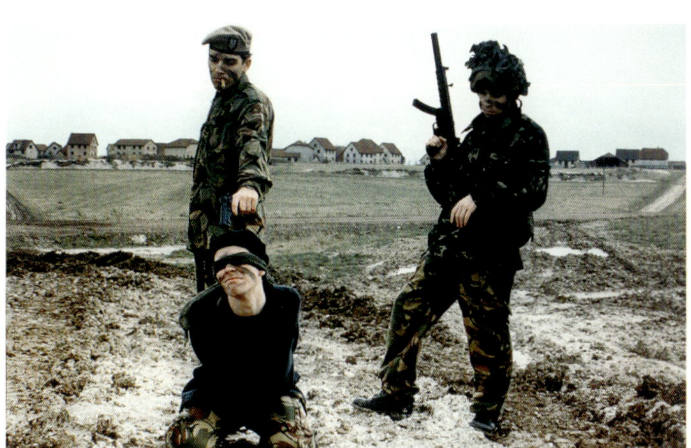
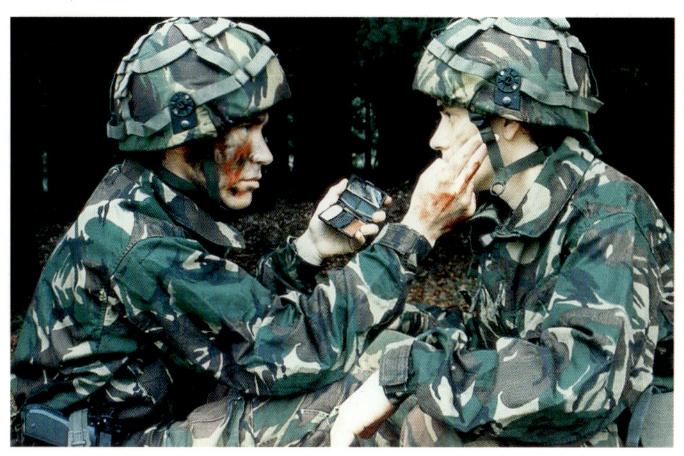
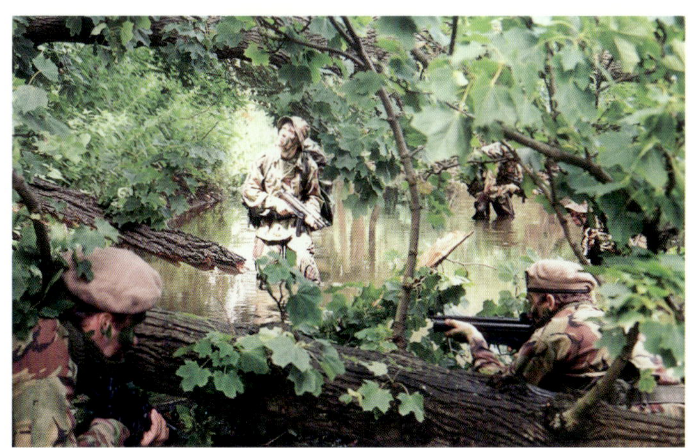
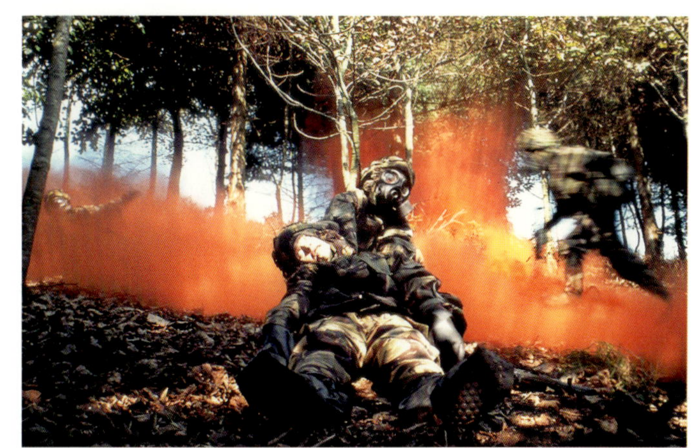
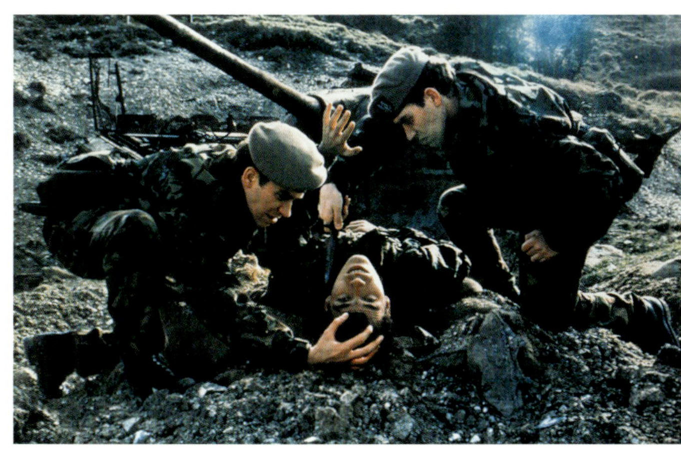
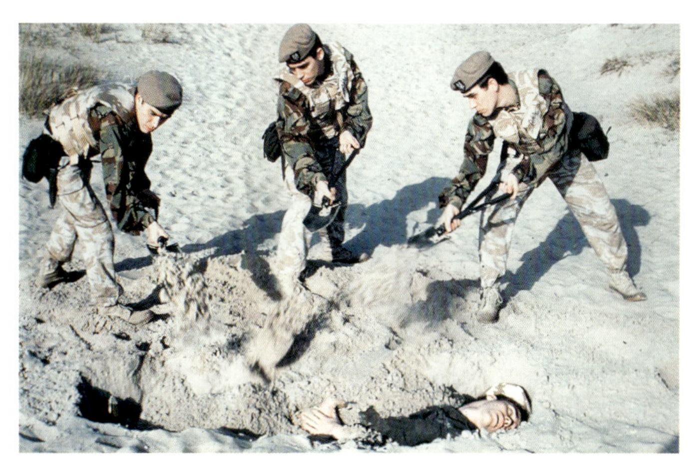

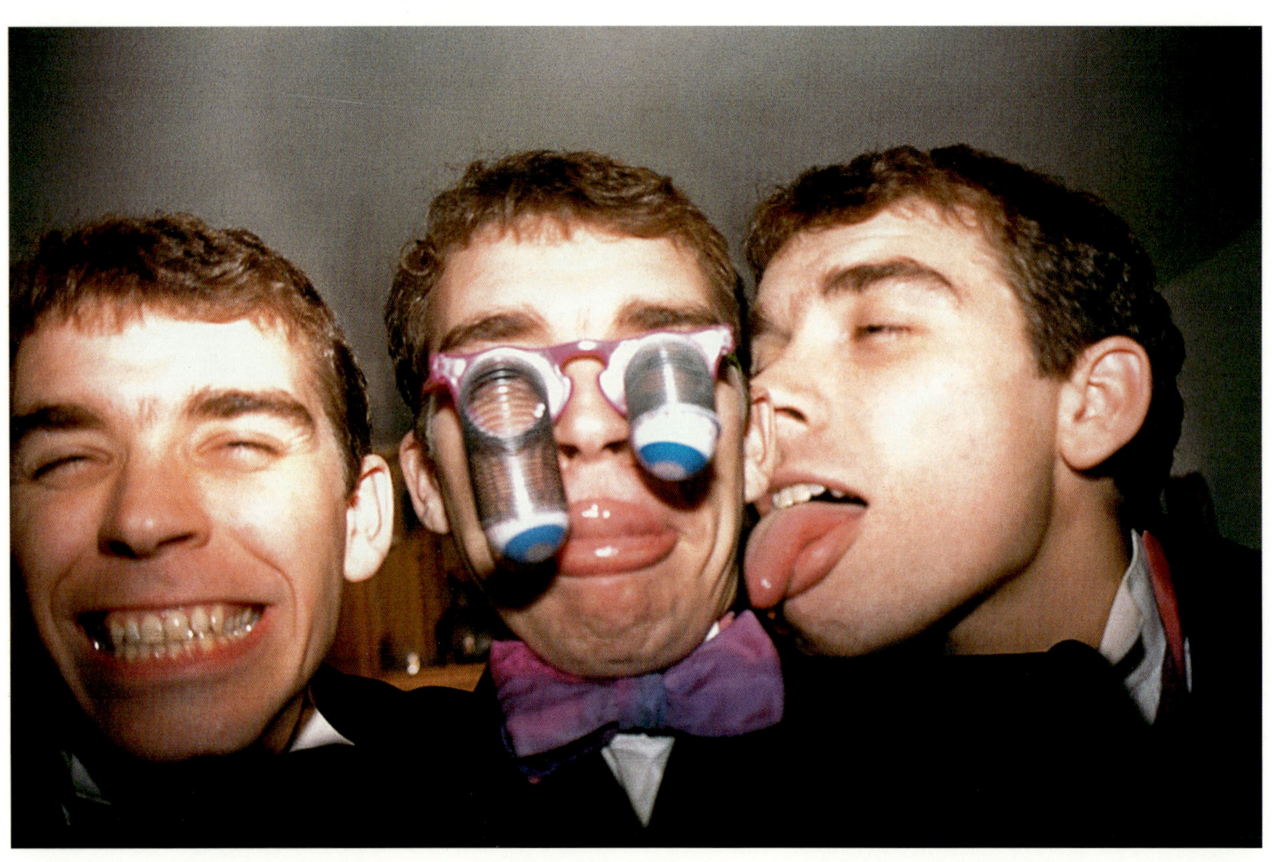

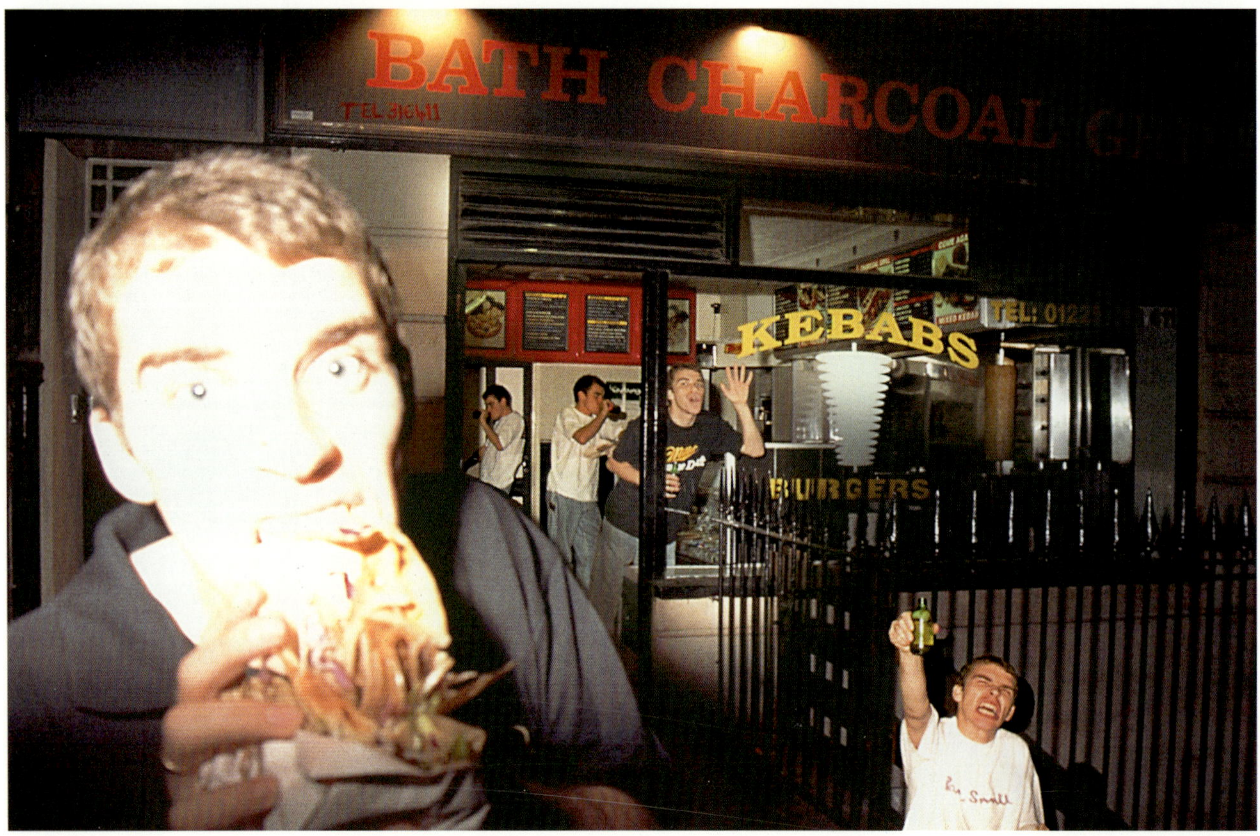
BATH CHARCOAL G
TEL 316411
KEBABS
TEL: 0122
BURGERS

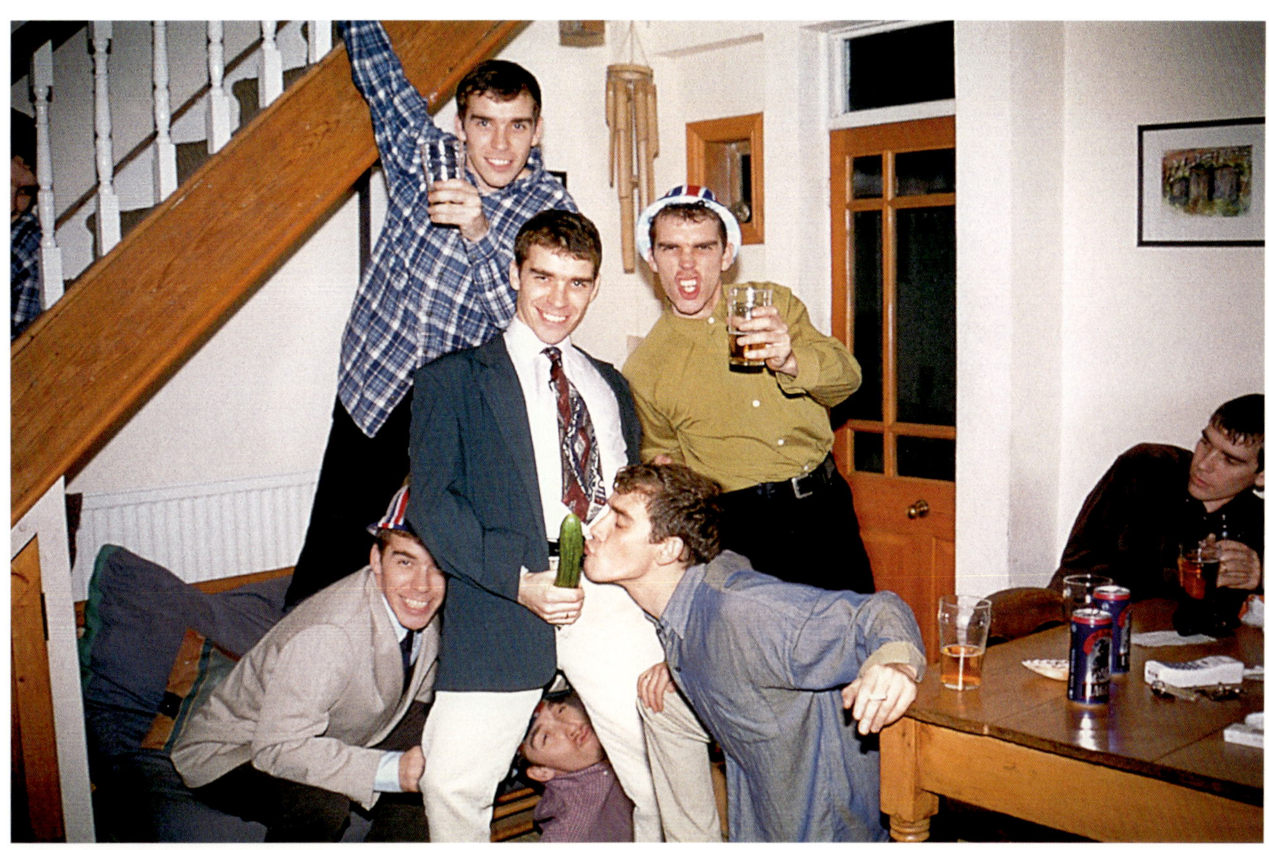

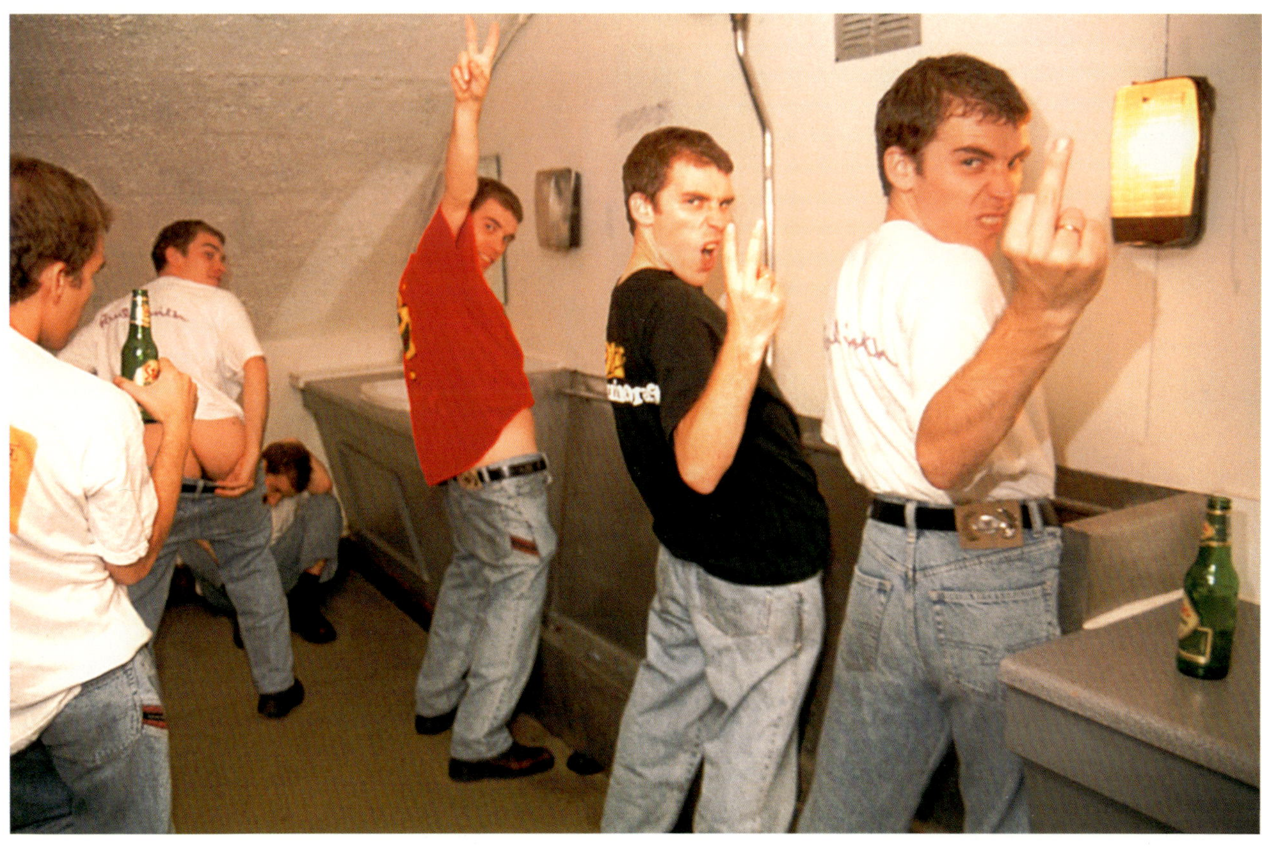

PAUL SMITH

Make My Night 1998
RA4 colour print, aluminium mounted
series of 12
71.1 x 101.6cm/28 x 40in *and overleaf*

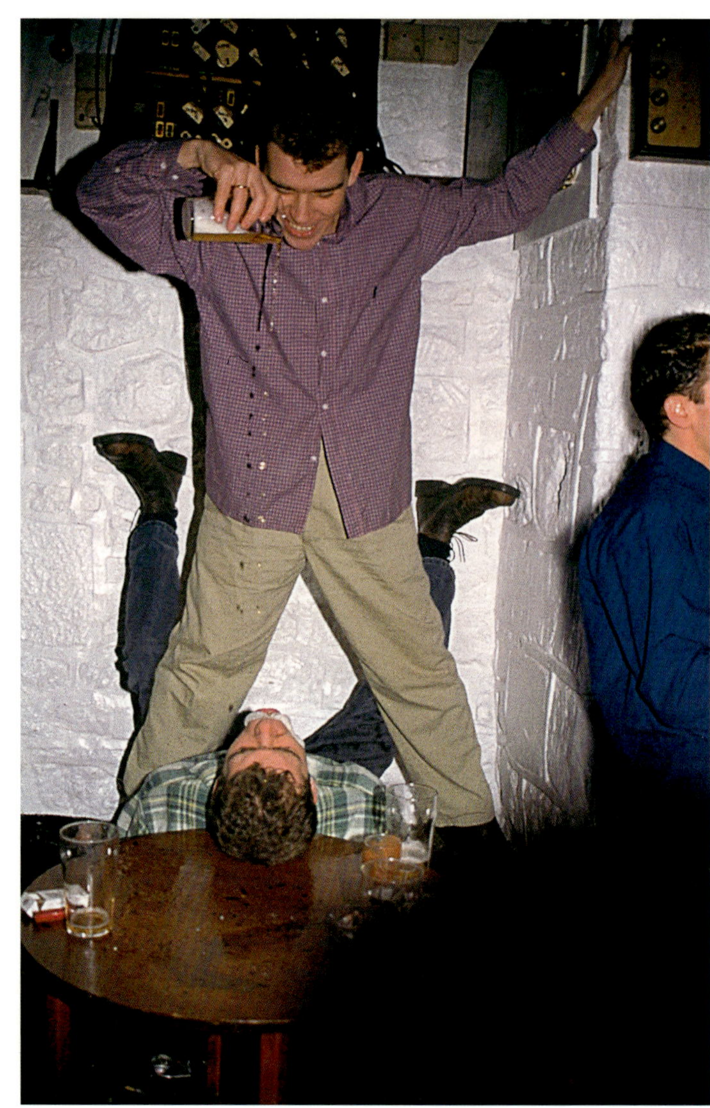

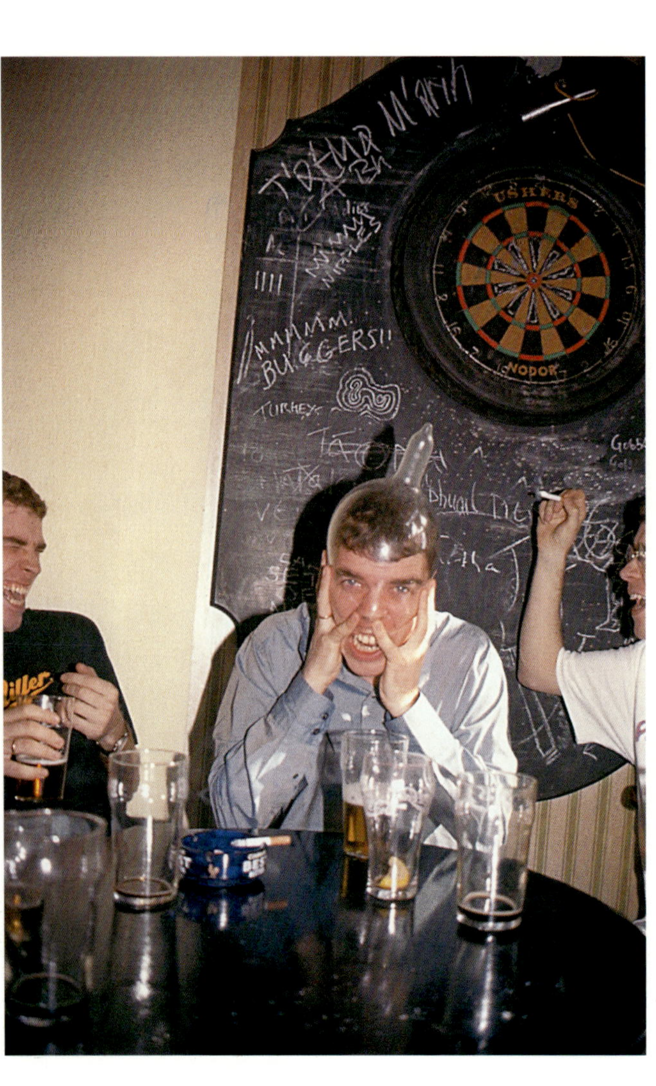

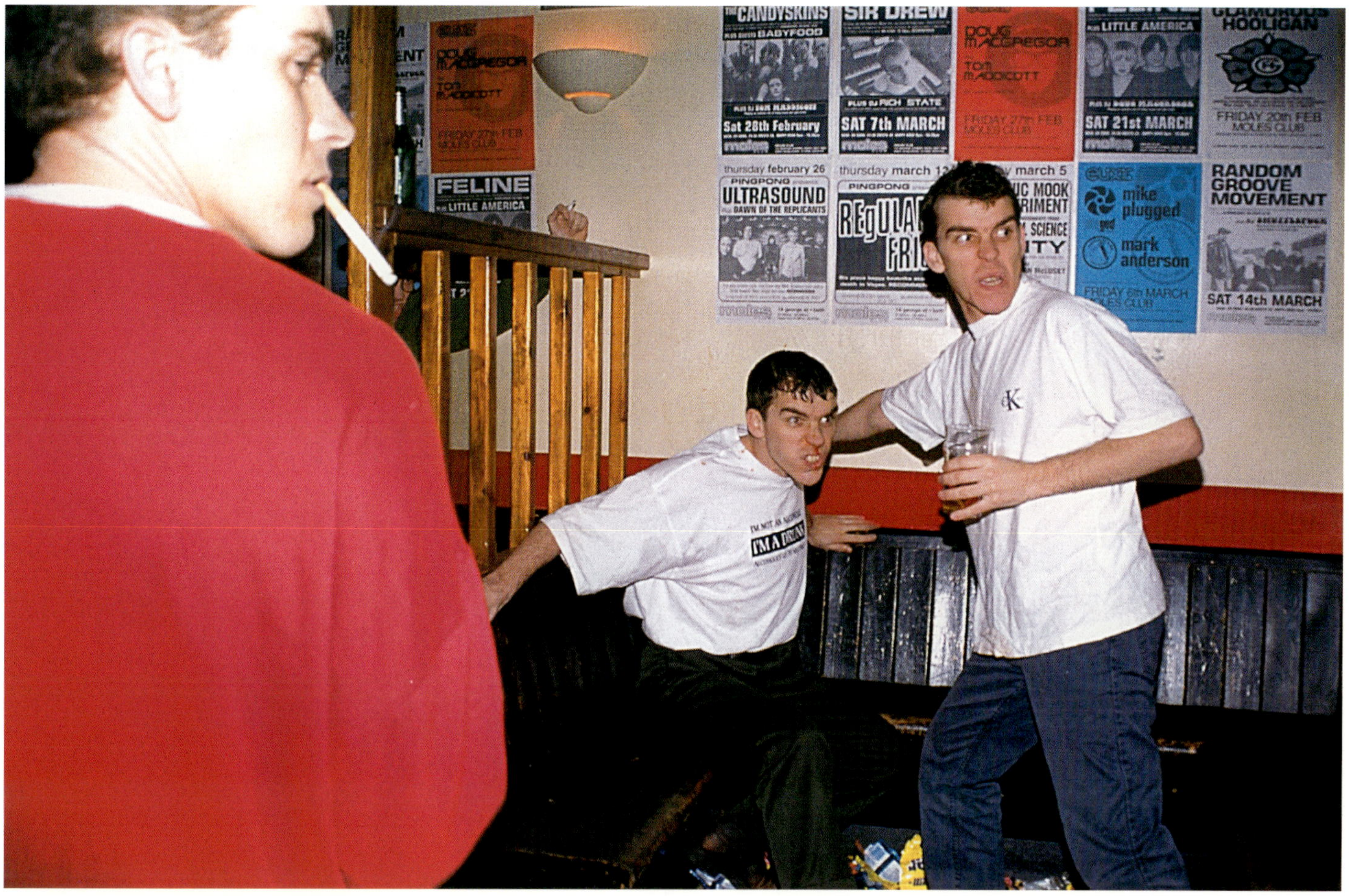

THE CANDYSKINS
PLUS BABYFOOD
SAT 28th February
FELINE
LITTLE AMERICA
SIR DREW
PLUS DJ RICH STATE
SAT 7th March
DOUG McGREGOR
TOM McADDICOTT
FRIDAY 27th FEB
LITTLE AMERICA
SAT 21st MARCH
GLAMOROUS HOOLIGAN
FRIDAY 20th FEB
MOLES CLUB
thursday february 26
ULTRASOUND
DAWN OF THE REPLICANTS
thursday march 12
REGULAR FRIE
RANDOM GROOVE MOVEMENT
mike plugged
mark anderson
FRIDAY 6th MARCH
SAT 14th MARCH

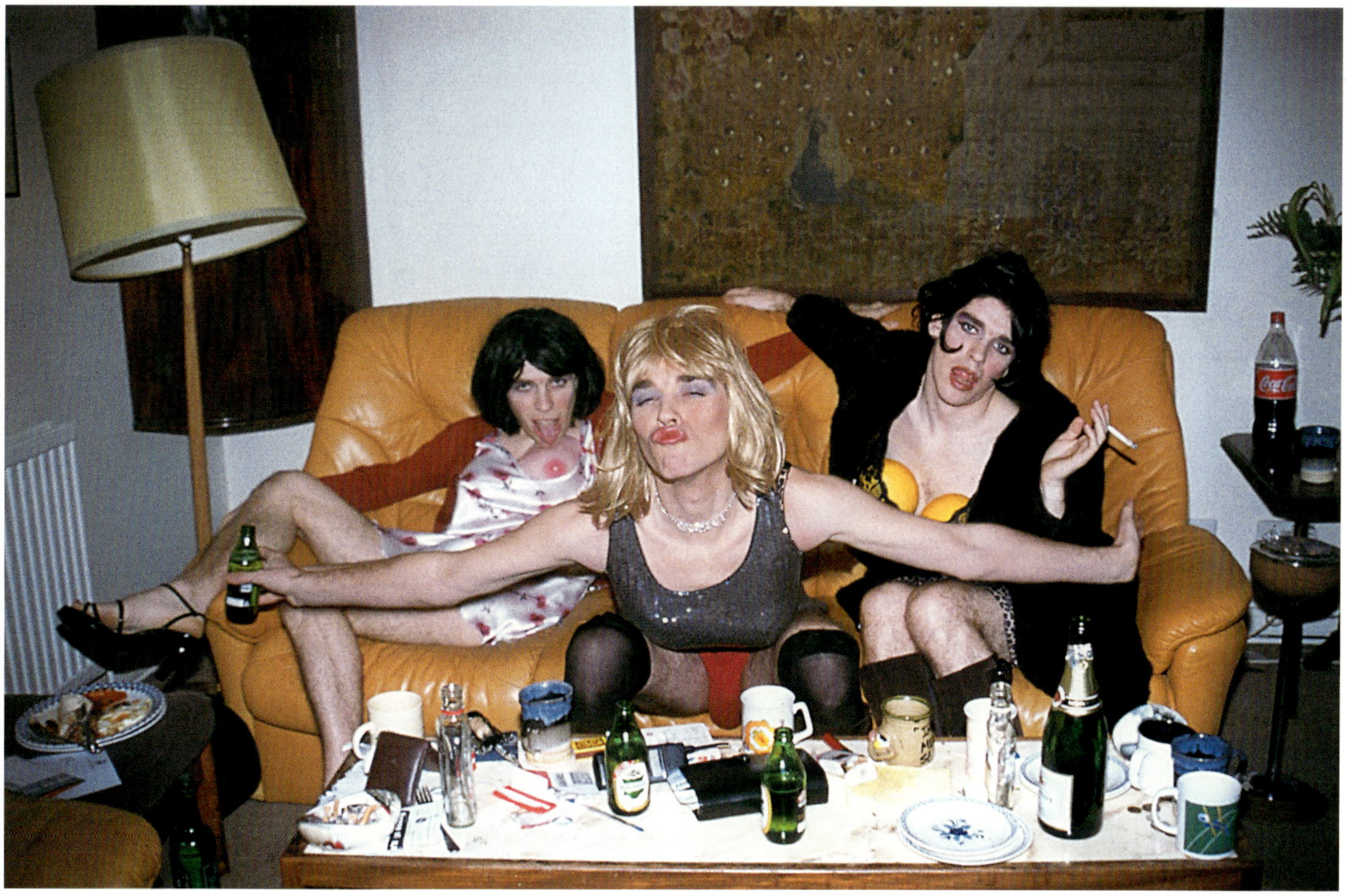

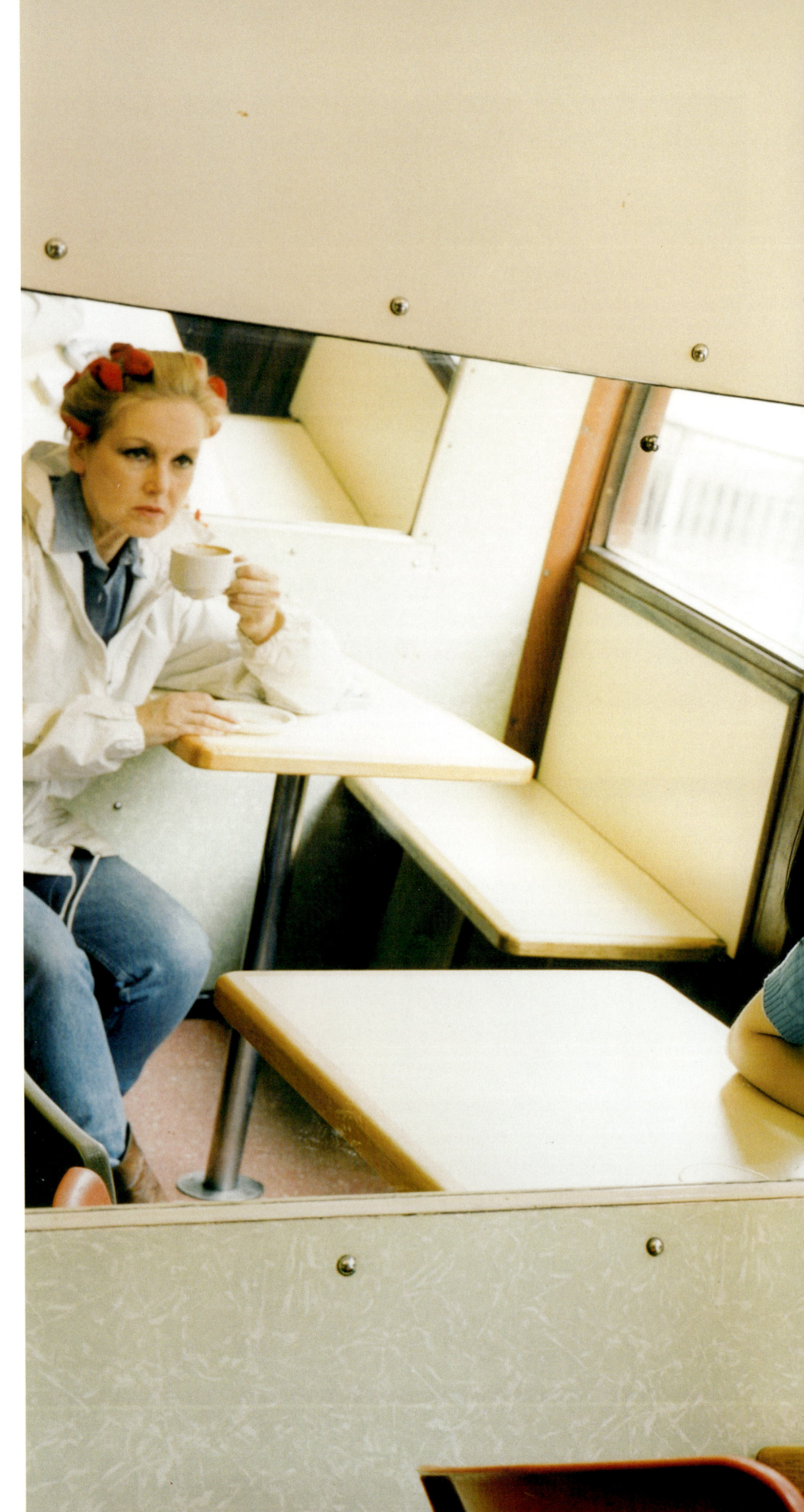

HANNAH STARKEY

Untitled – May 1997 (Cafe) 1997
c-type print
121.9 x 152.2cm/48 x 60in

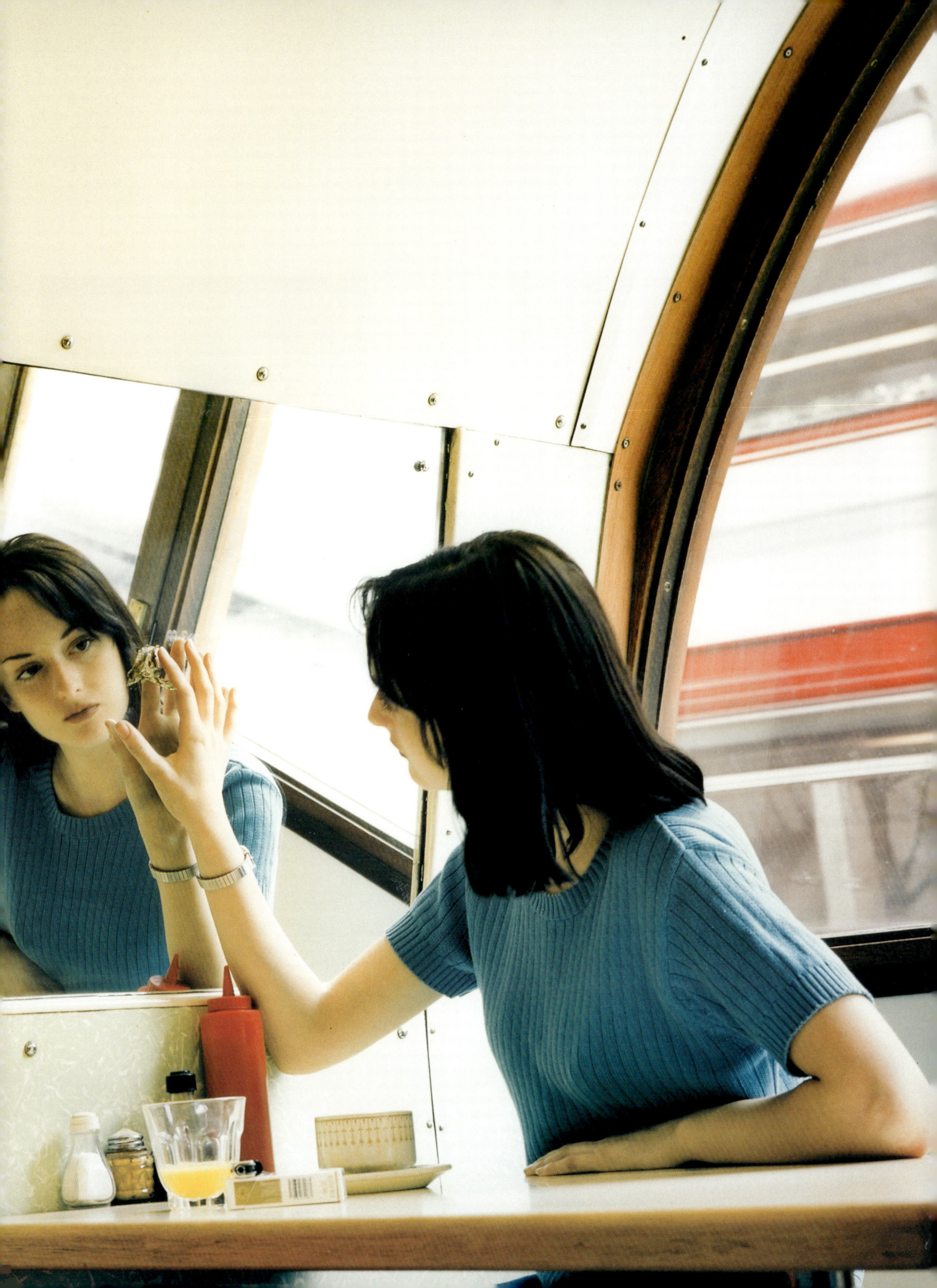

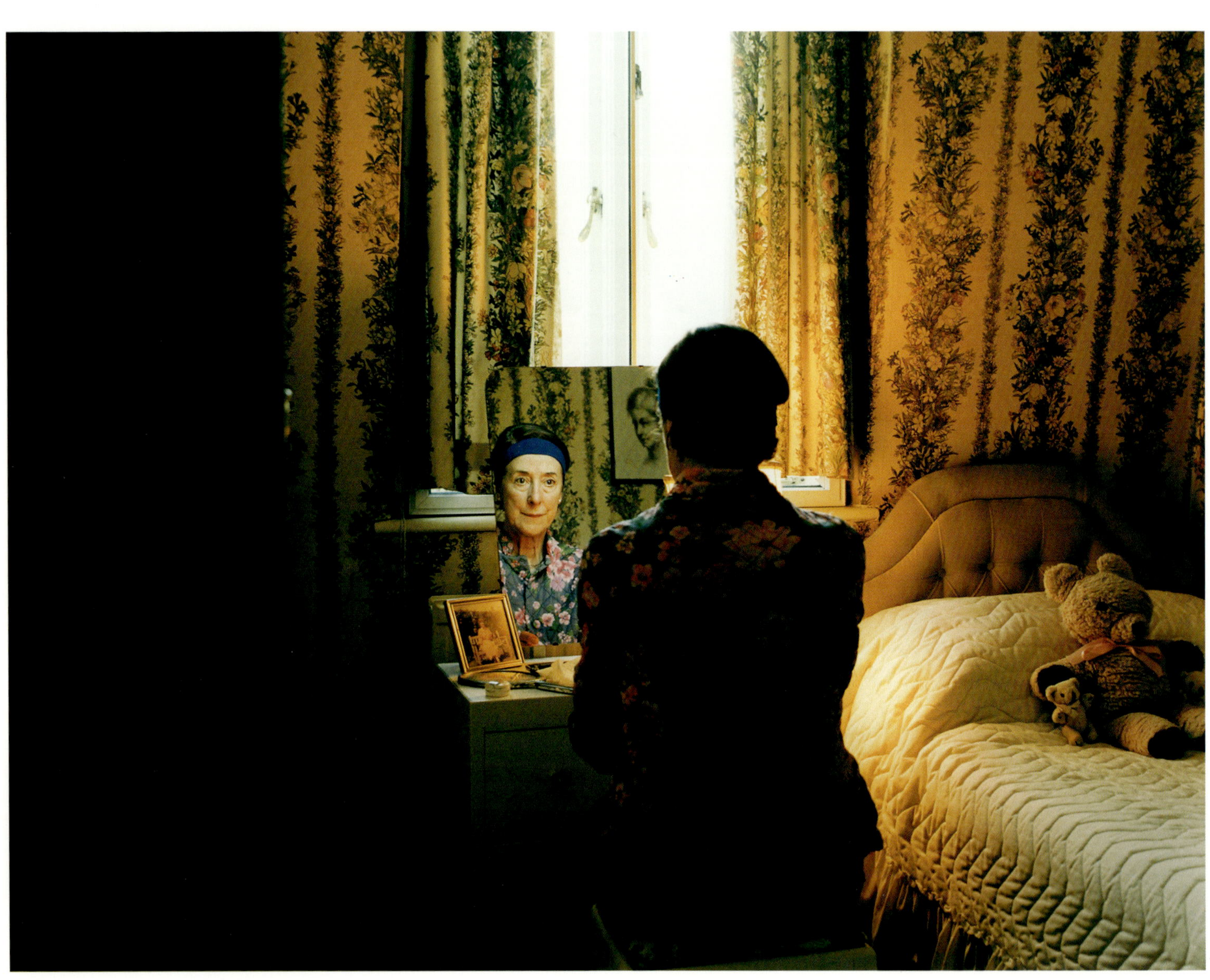

HANNAH STARKEY

Untitled – March 1997 (Room) 1997
c-type print
121.9 x 152.2cm/48 x 60in

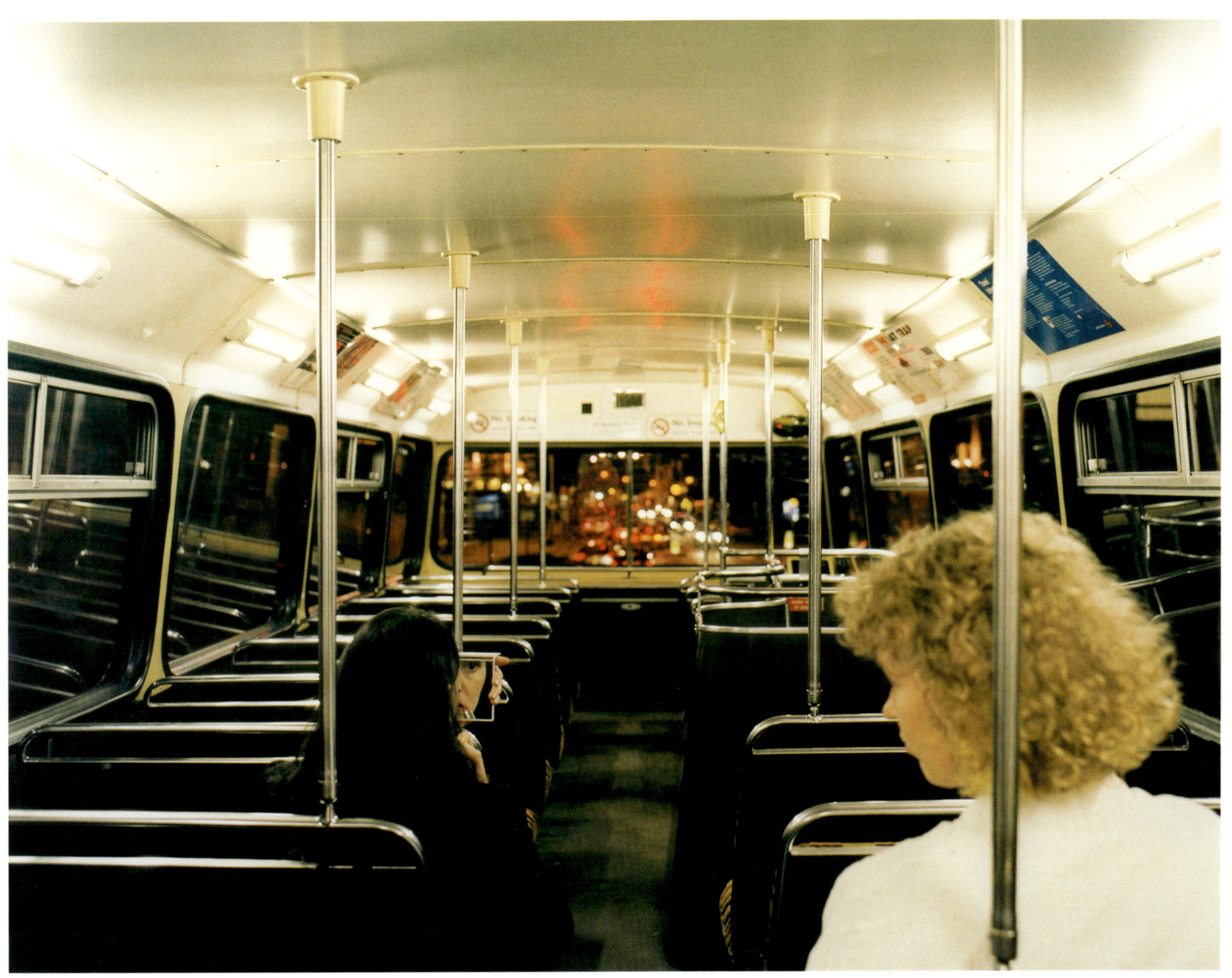

HANNAH STARKEY

Untitled – February 1997 (Bus) 1997
c-type print
121.9 x 152.2cm/48 x 60in

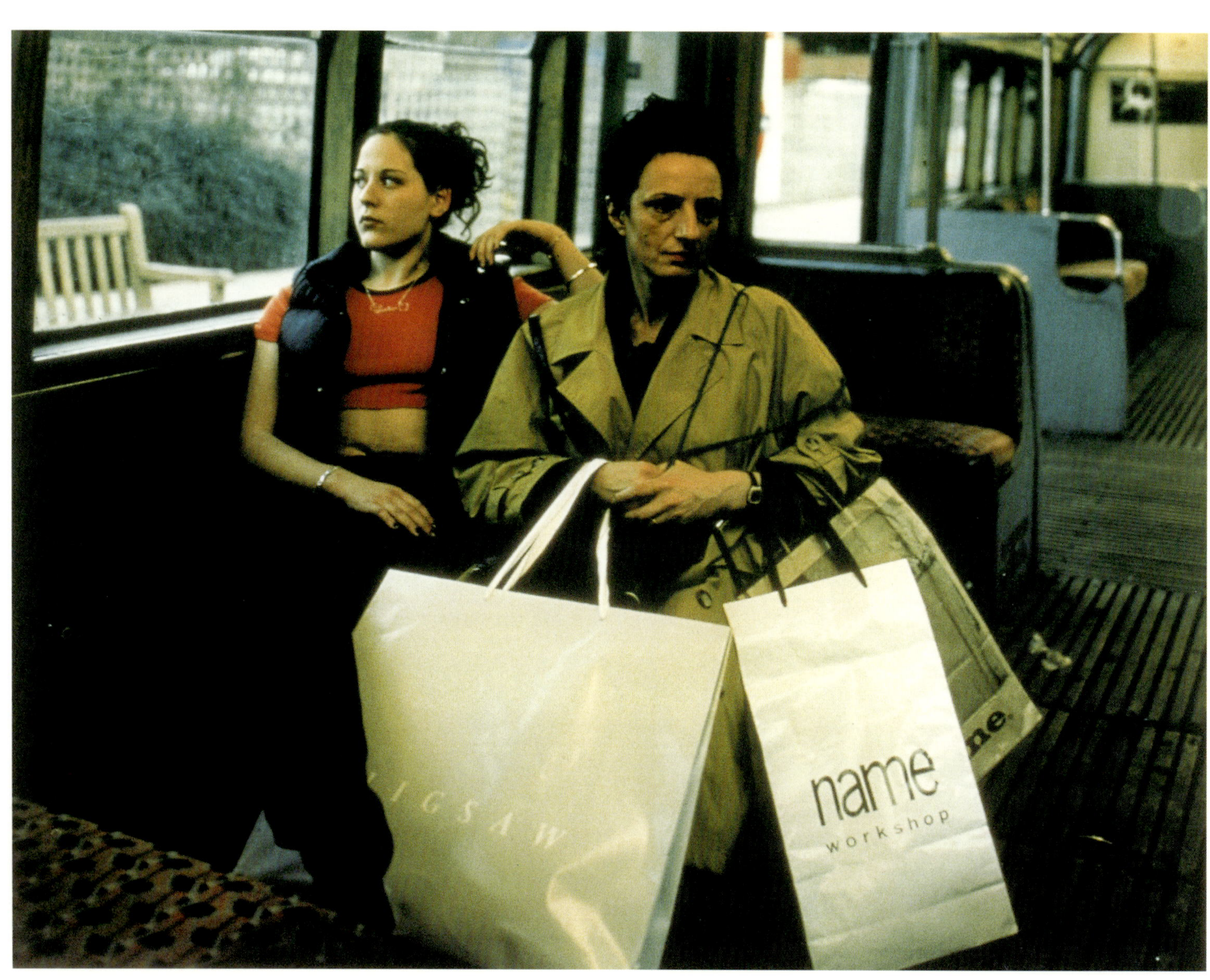

HANNAH STARKEY

Untitled – March 1997 (Tube) 1997
c-type print
121.9 x 152.2cm/48 x 60in

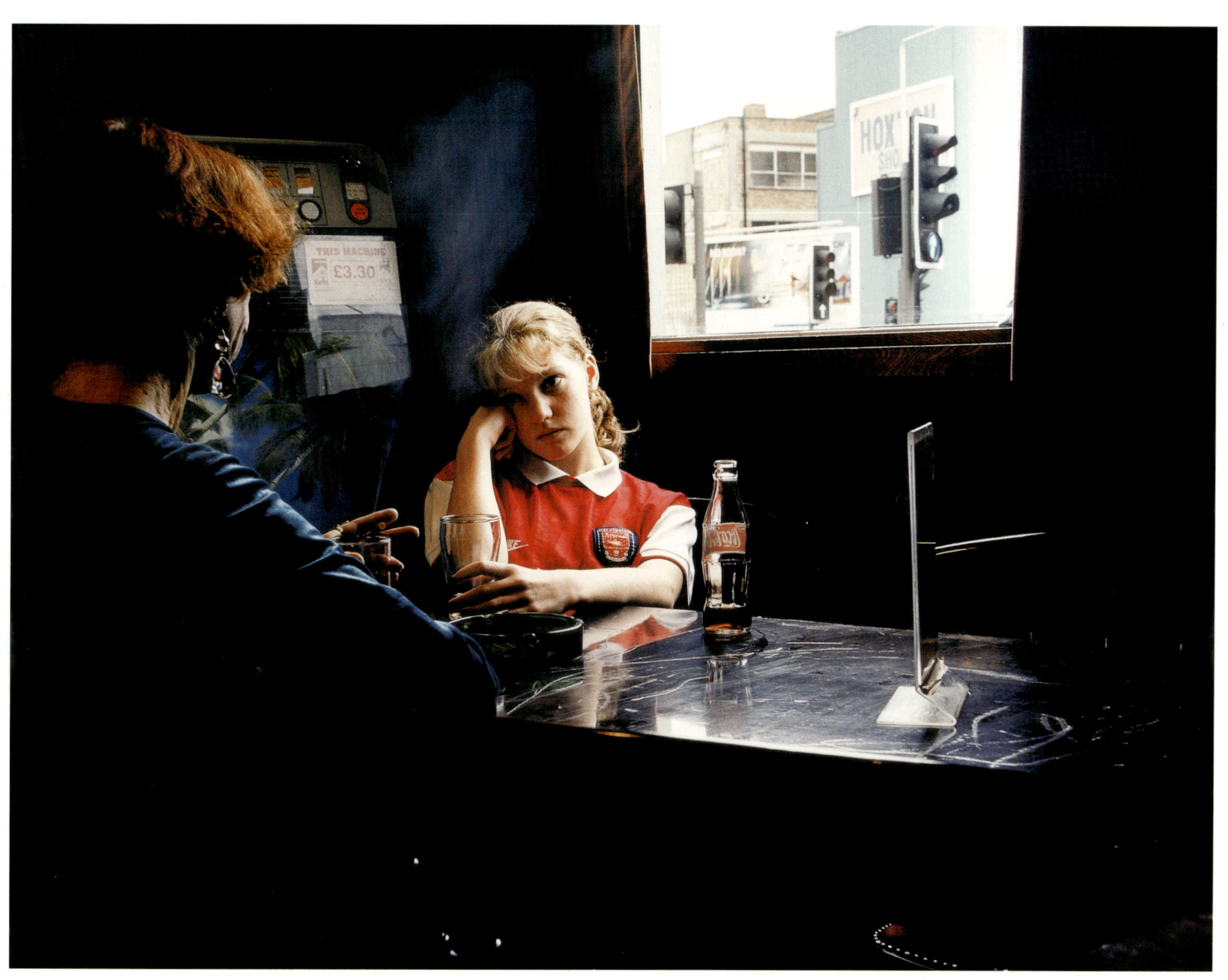

HANNAH STARKEY

October 1998 1998
c-type print
121.9 x 152.2cm/48 x 60in

Pai
i

n

t

N

G

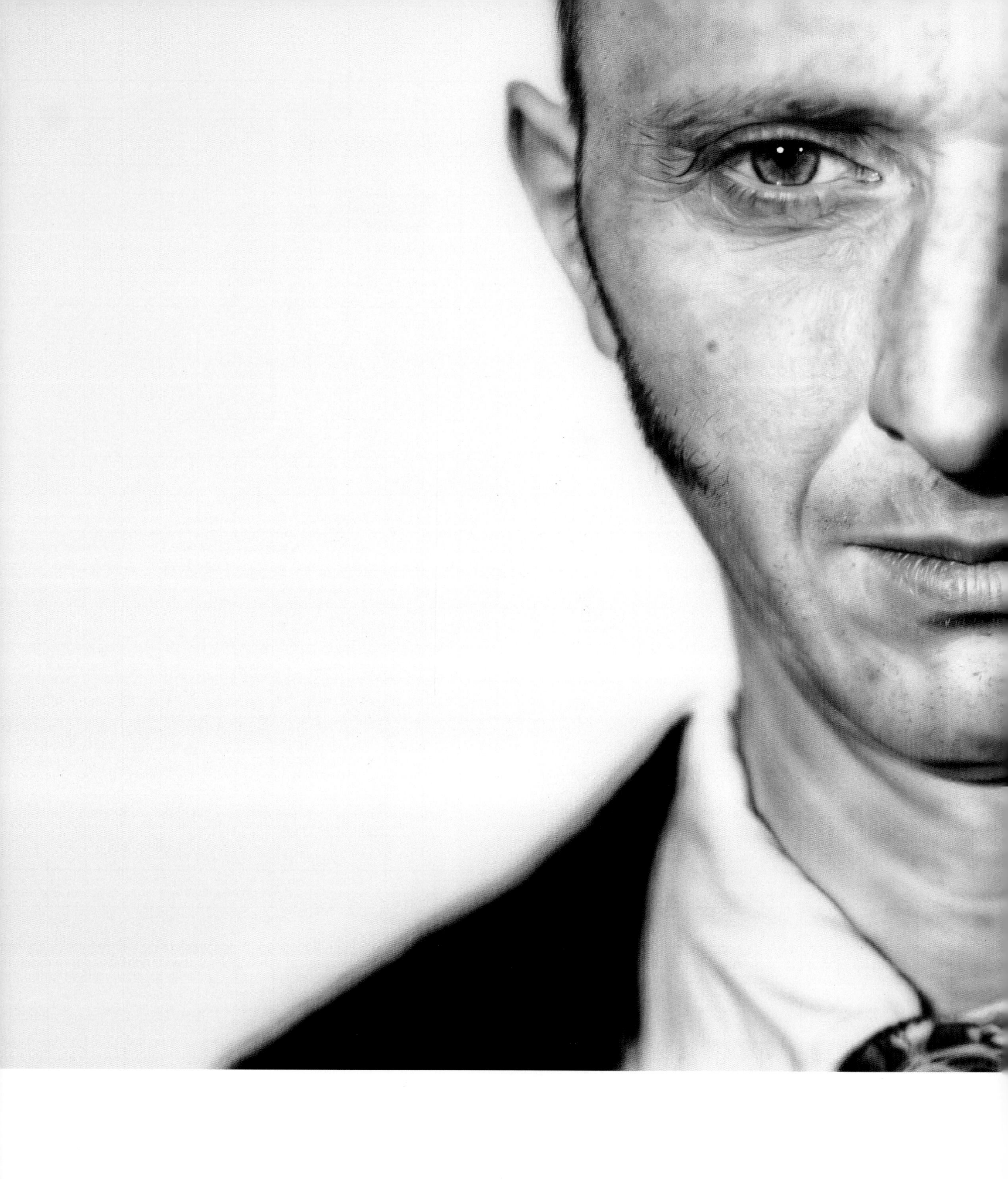

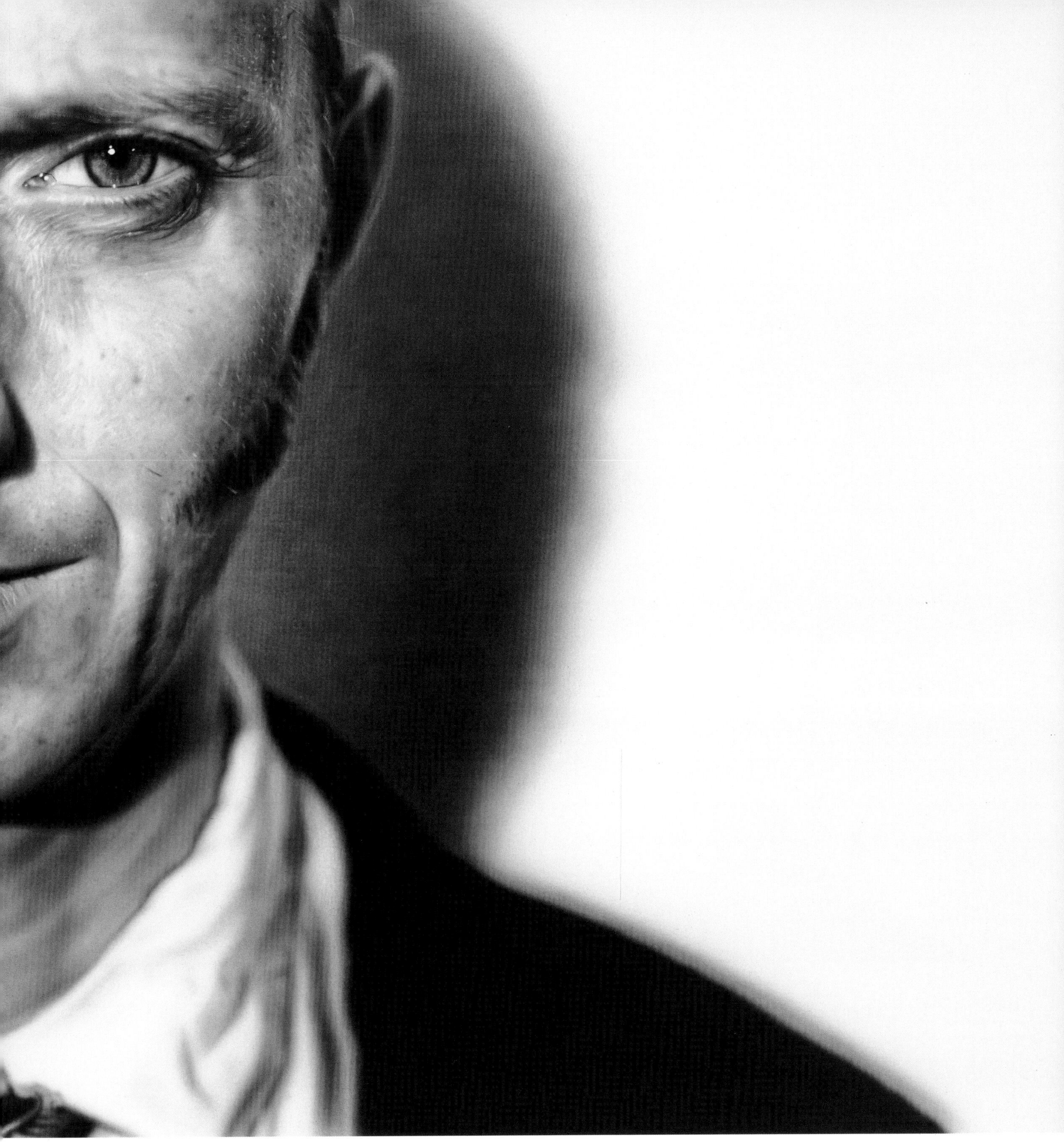

JASON BROOKS

Bob and Roberta 1997
acrylic on canvas
147 x 279cm/58 x 109³/₄in

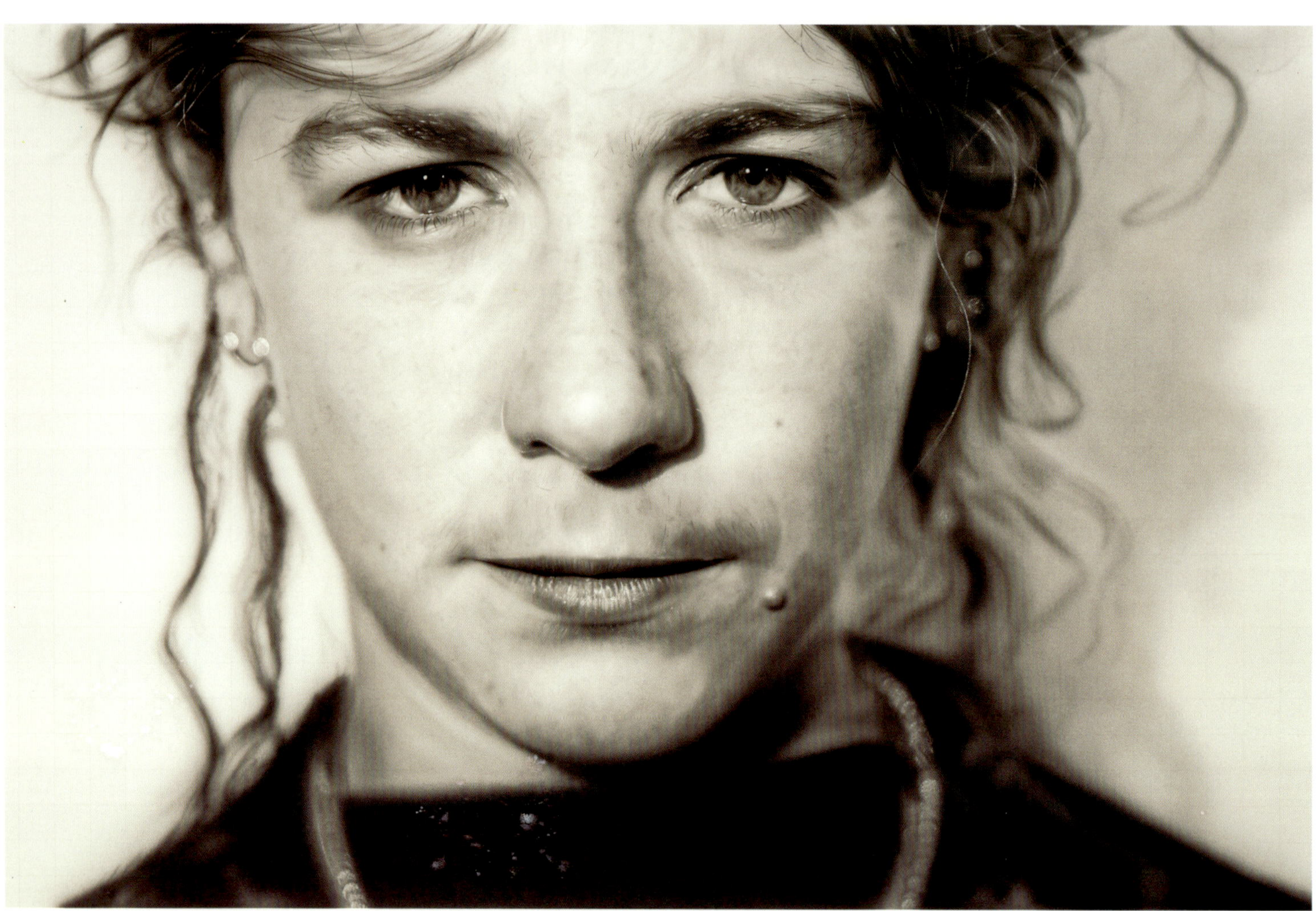

JASON BROOKS

Margarita 1997
acrylic on paper
122 x 152cm/48 x 59³/₄in

right:
Sassy 1997
acrylic on linen
244 x 153cm/96 x 60¹/₄in

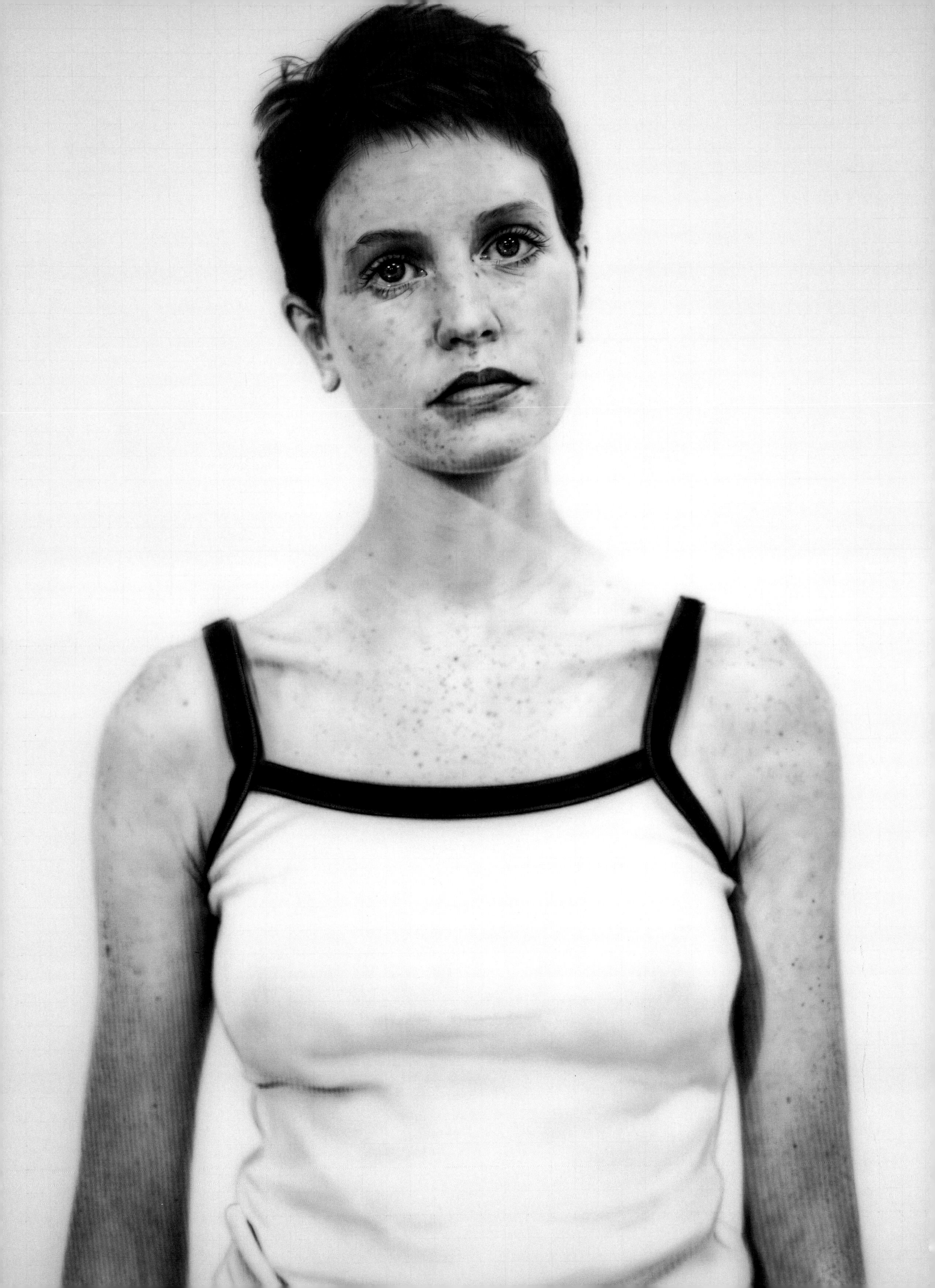

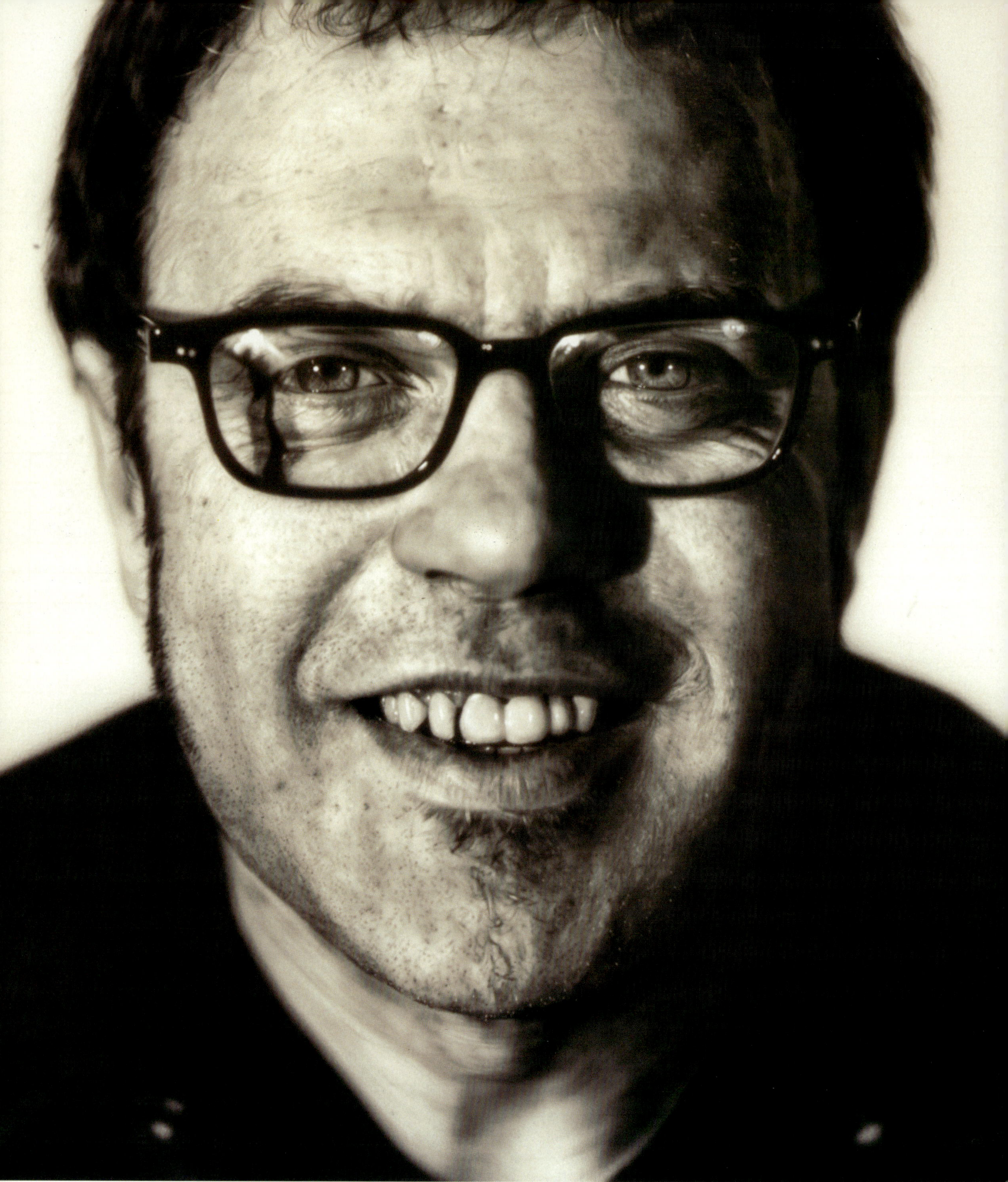

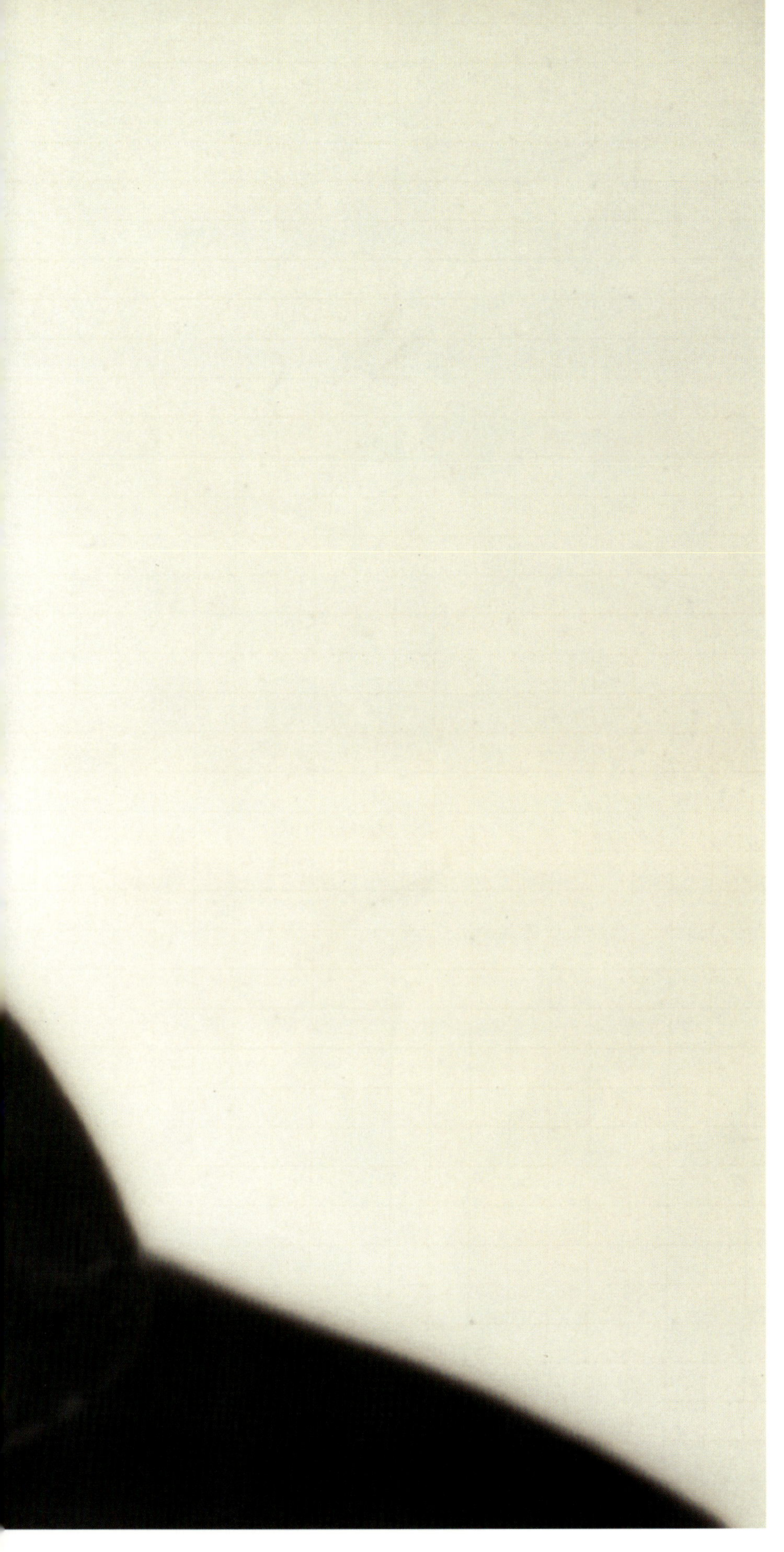

JASON BROOKS

Matthew (detail) 1998
acrylic on linen
147 x 365cm/57.9 x 143.7in

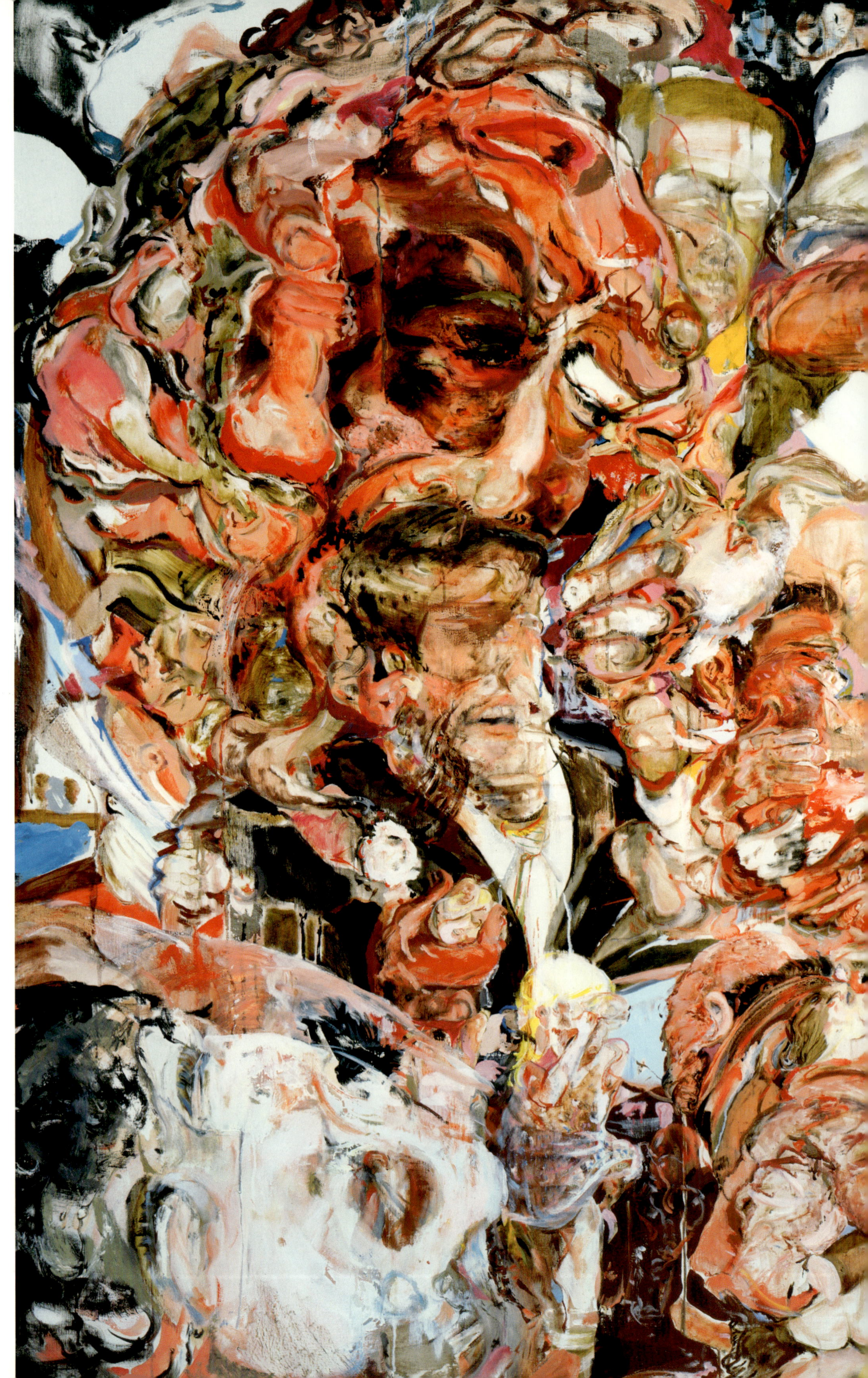

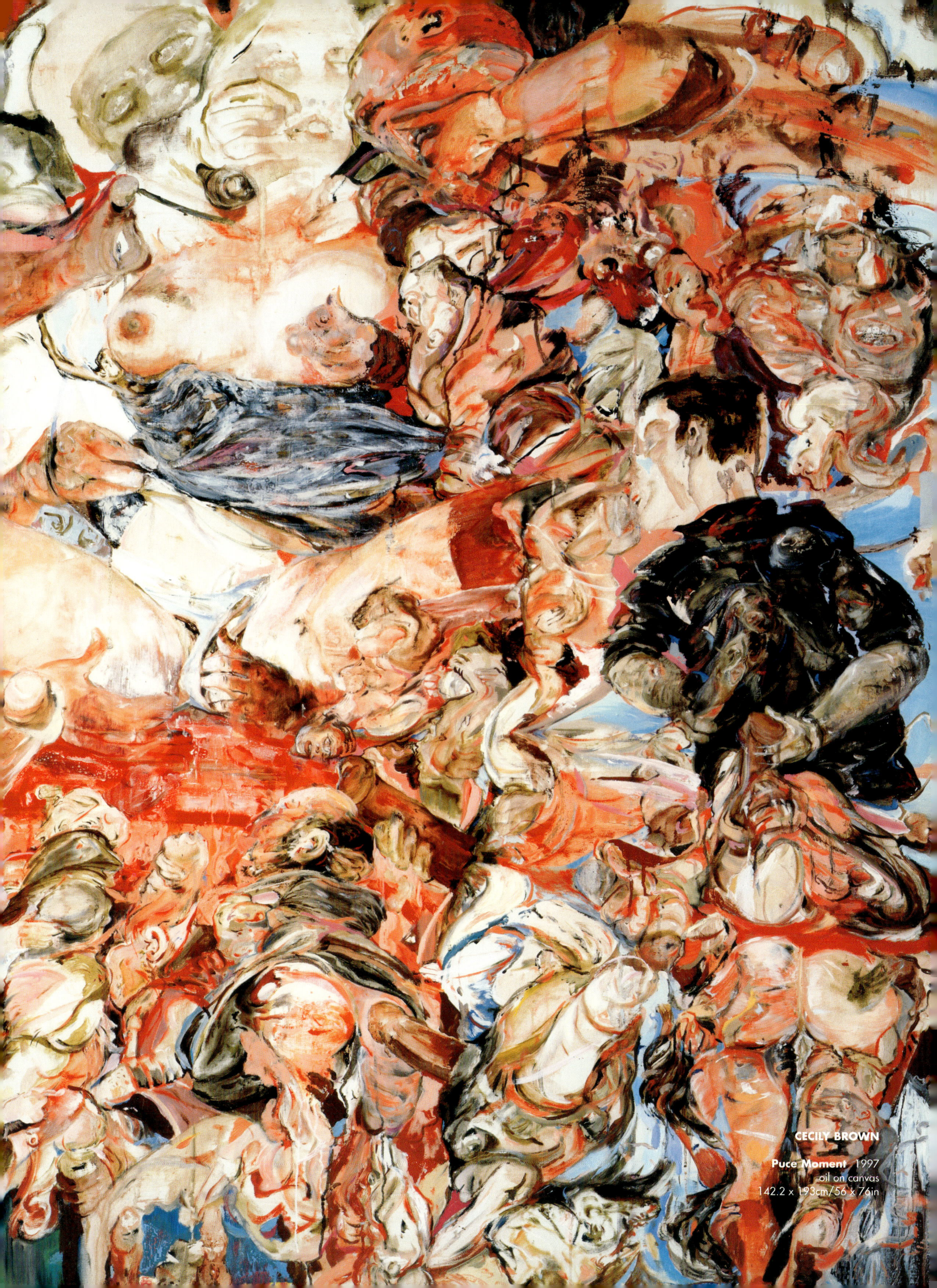

CECILY BROWN
Puce Moment 1997
oil on canvas
142.2 x 193cm/56 x 76in

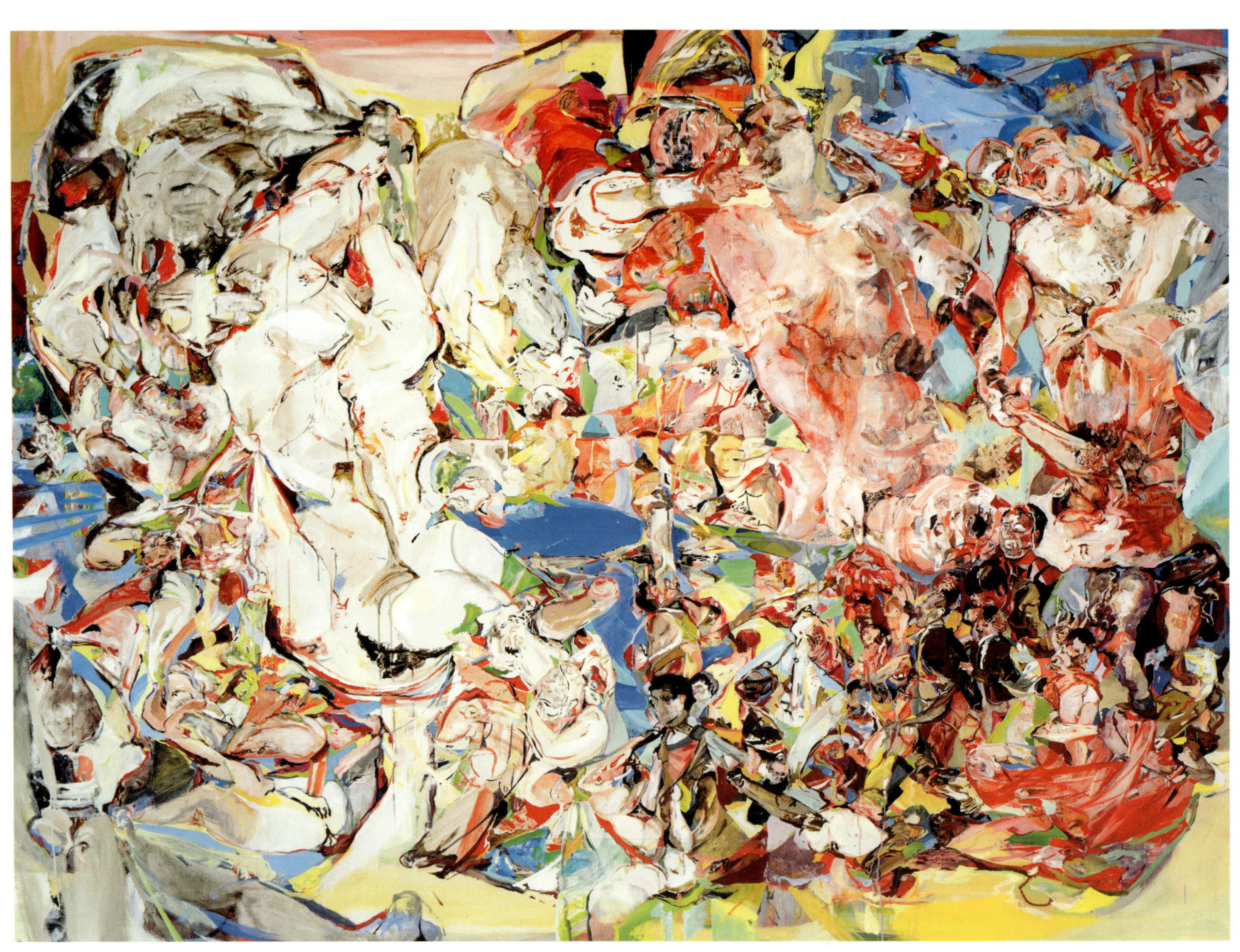

CECILY BROWN

High Society 1998
oil on linen
193 x 248.9cm/76 x 98in

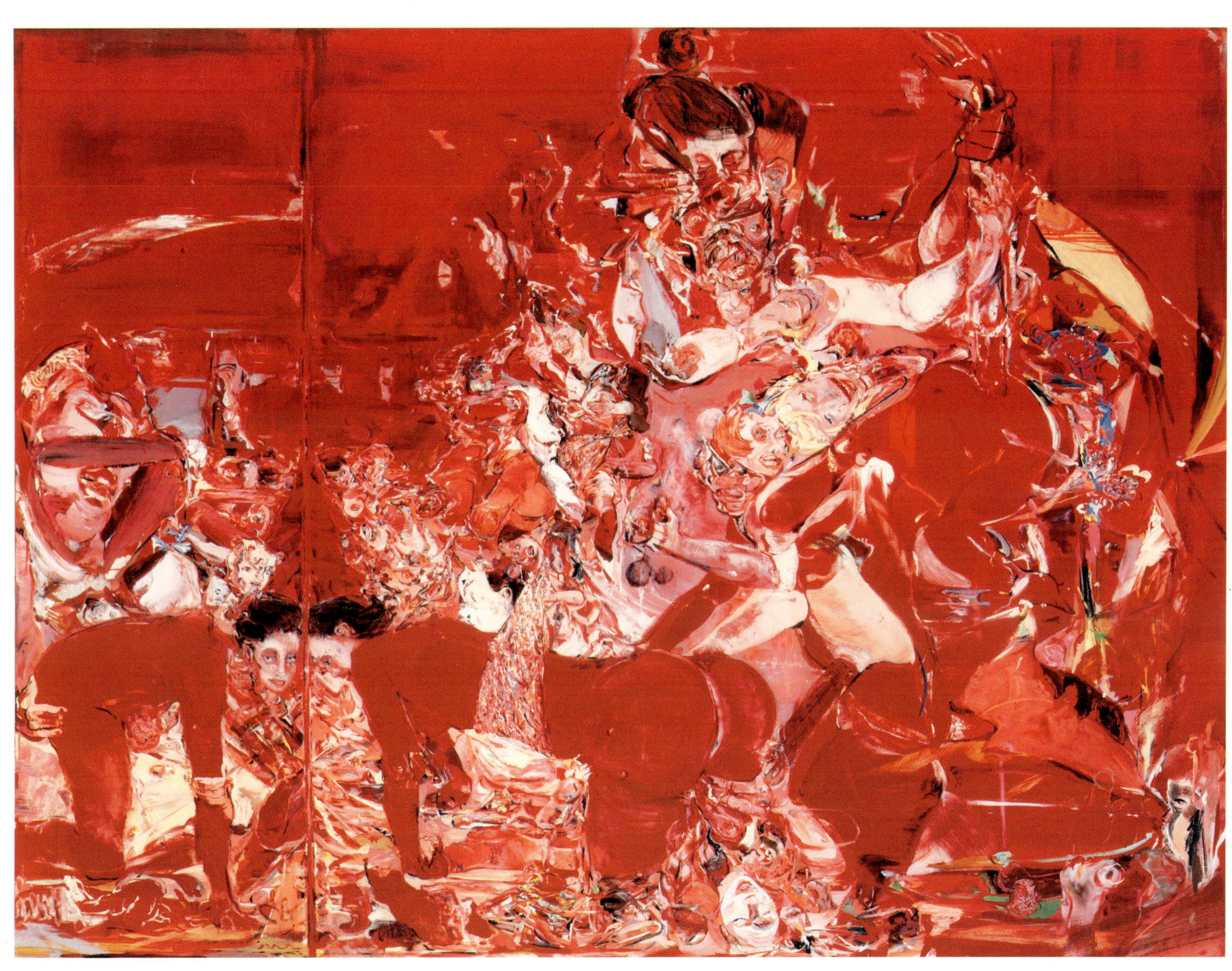

CECILY BROWN

Pyjama Game 1998
oil on linen
193 x 248.9cm/76 x 98in

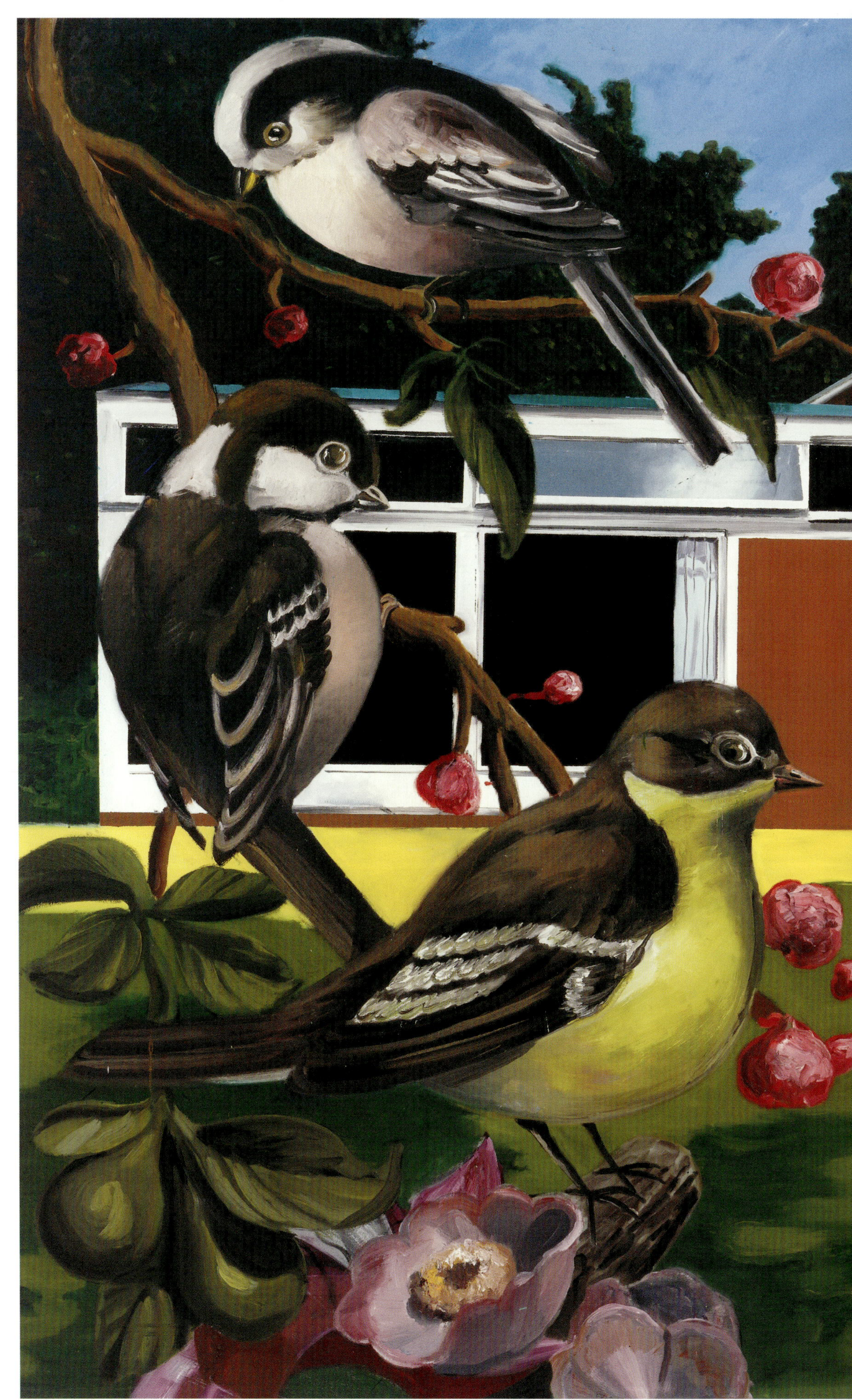

DANIEL COOMBS

97 Lexden Road 1995
oil on canvas
228.6 x 304cm/90 x 120in

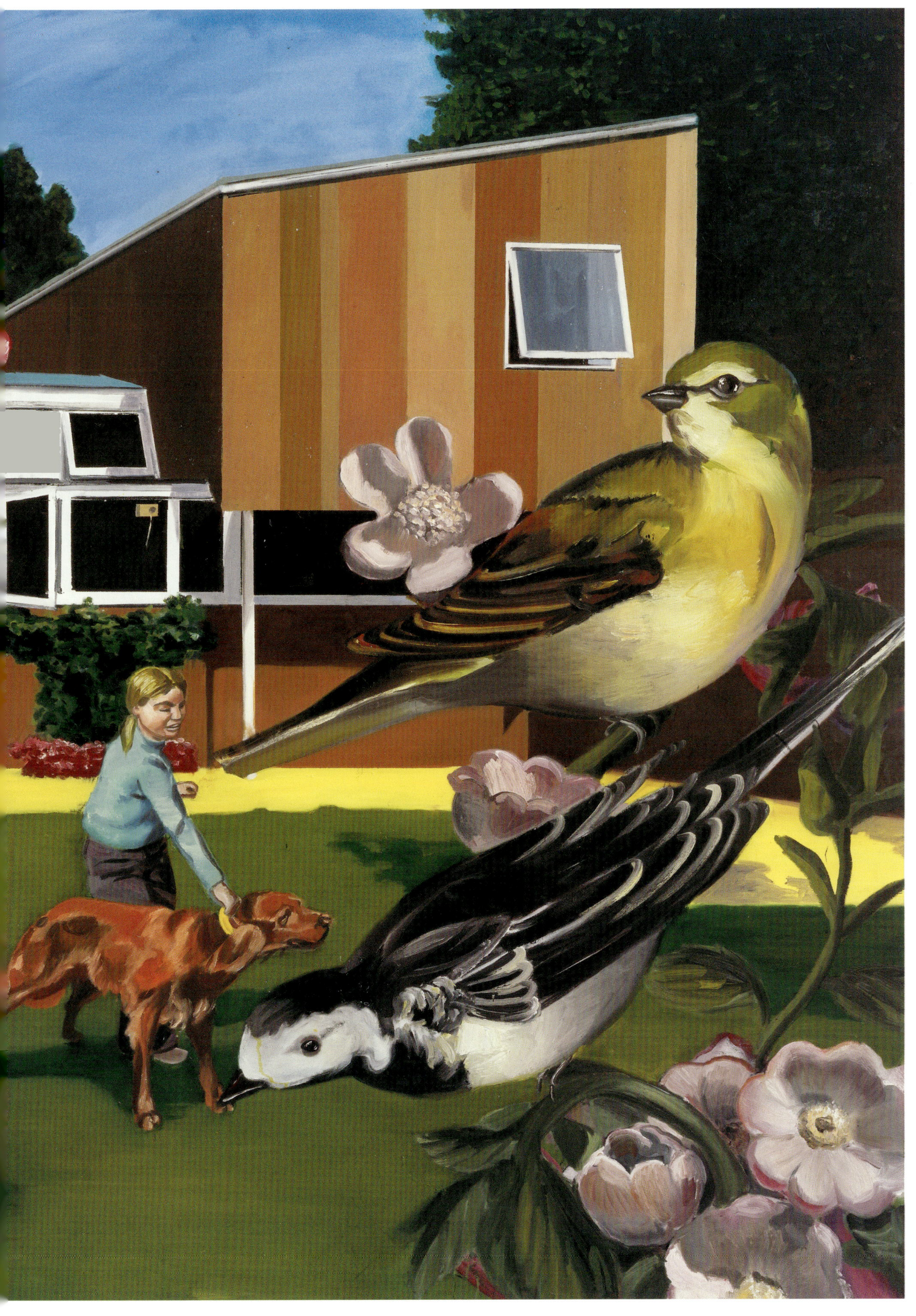

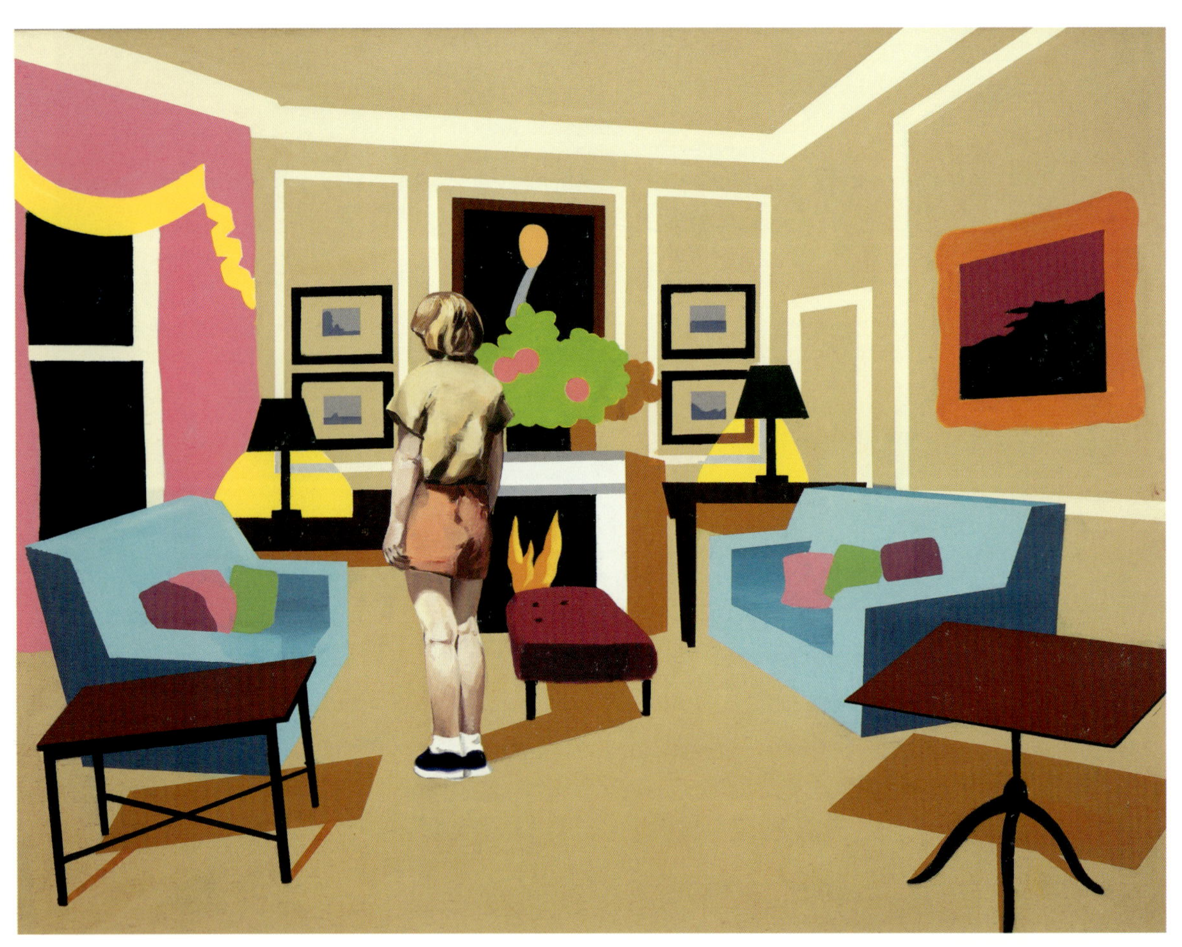

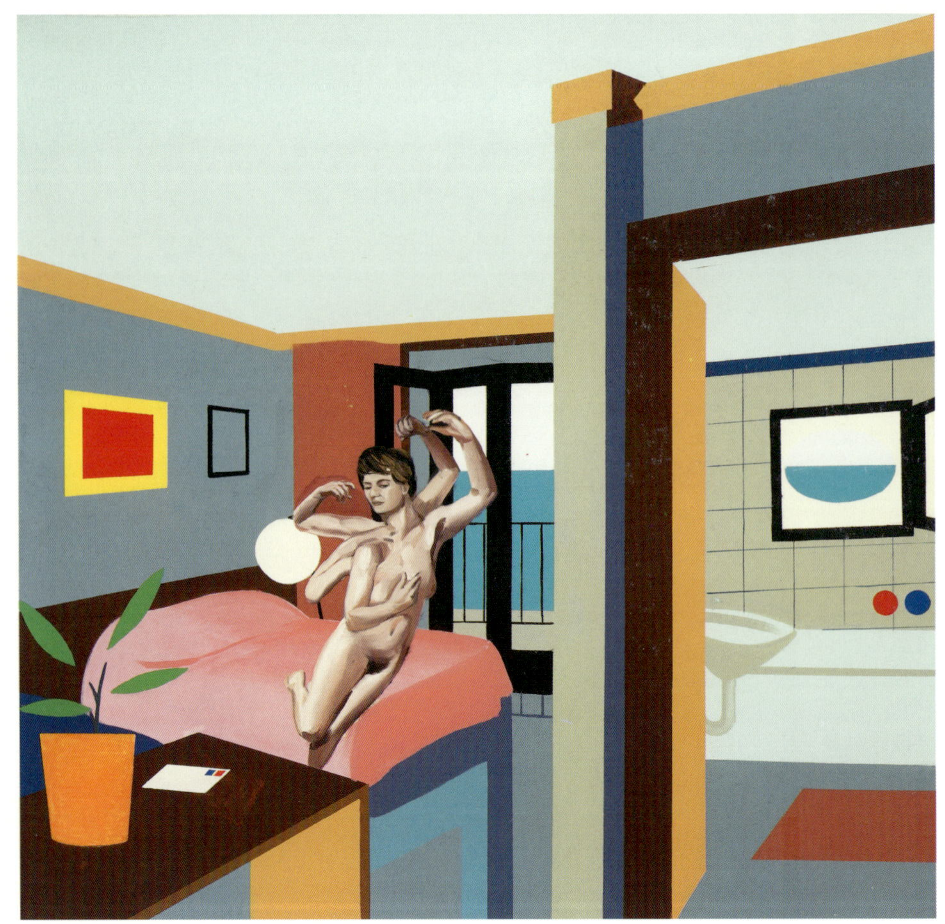

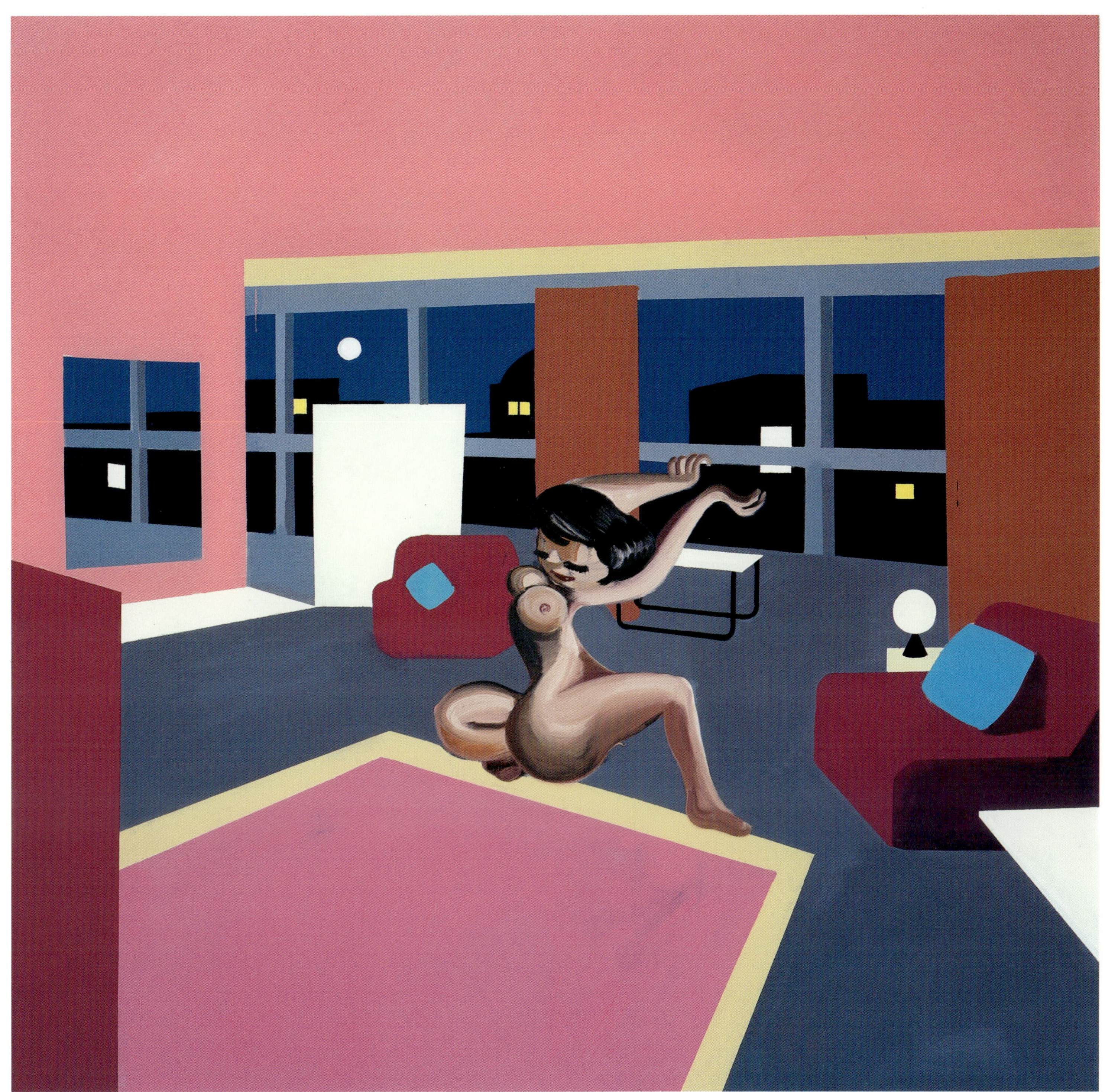

DANIEL COOMBS

Room III (Naked) 1995
oil and acrylic on canvas
200 x 200cm/78³/₄ x 78³/₄in

left above:
Room I (Waiting) 1995
oil and acrylic on canvas
200 x 250cm/78³/₄ x 98¹/₂in

left below:
Room II (Falling) 1995
oil and acrylic on canvas
200 x 200cm/78³/₄ x 78³/₄in

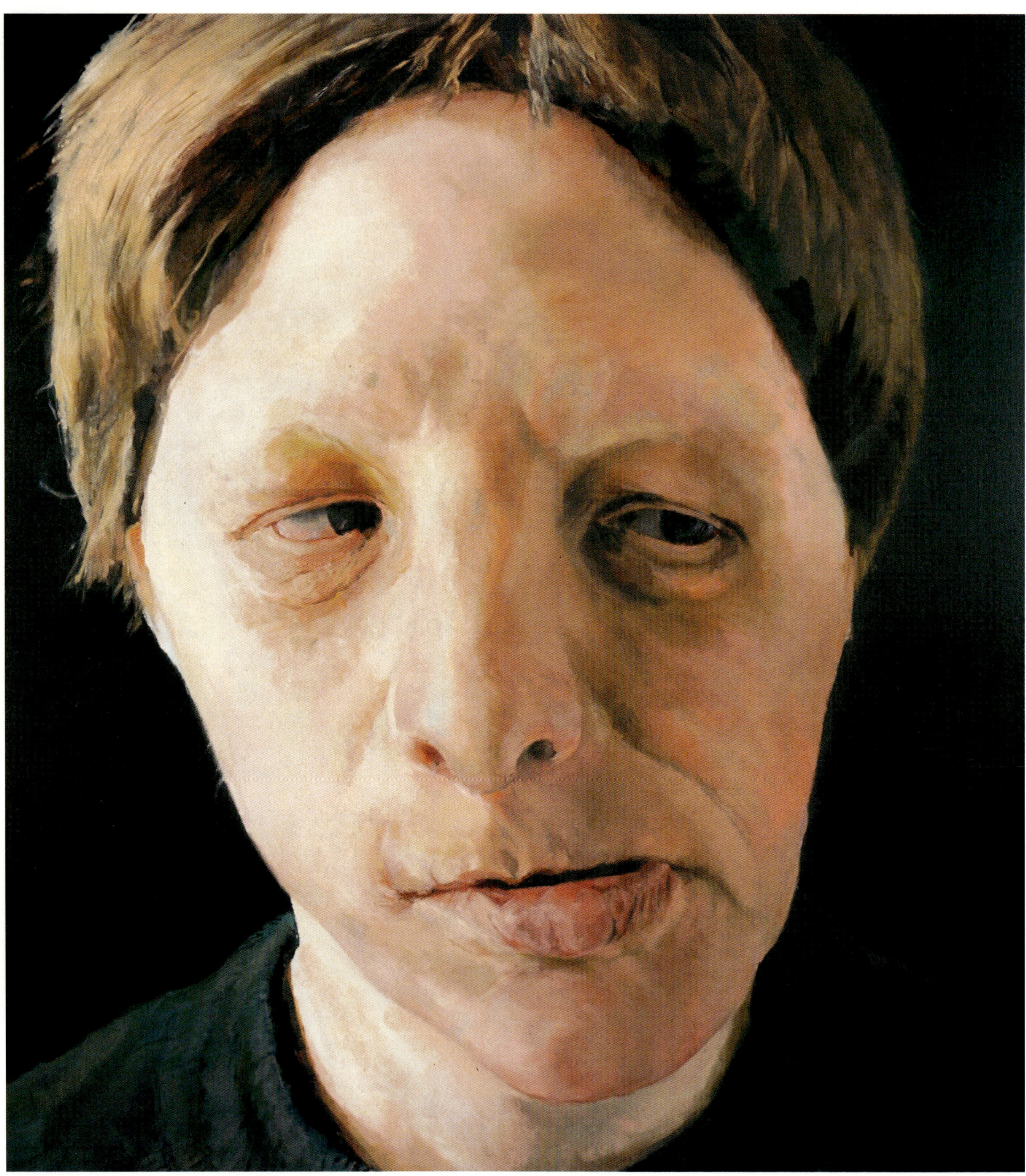

VICTORIA CHALMERS

Charlotte (1-4) 1997
oil on canvas
166.4 x 147.3cm/65½ x 58in

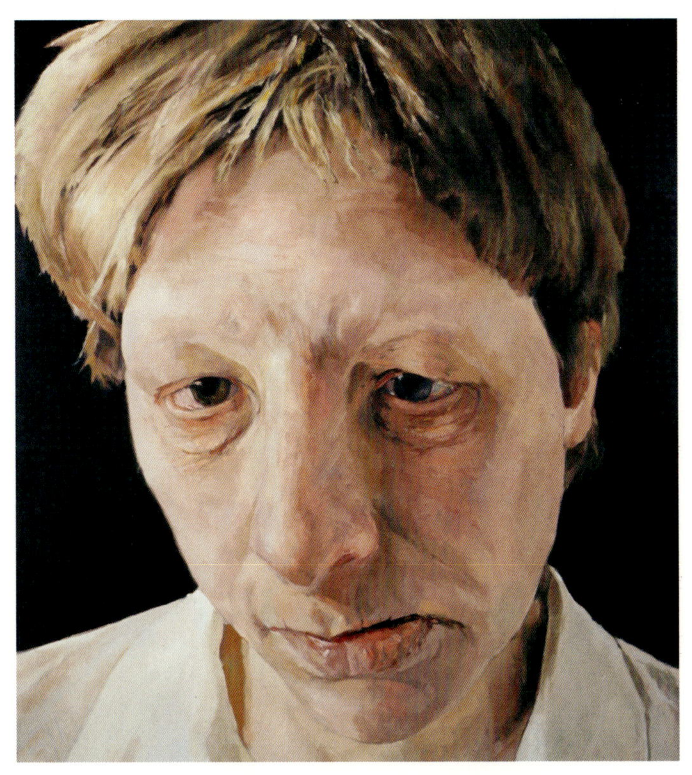

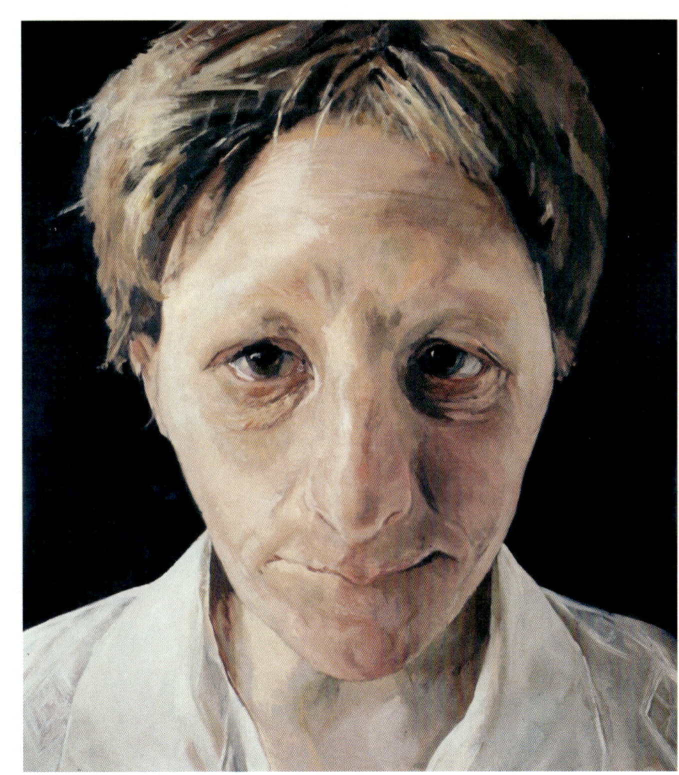

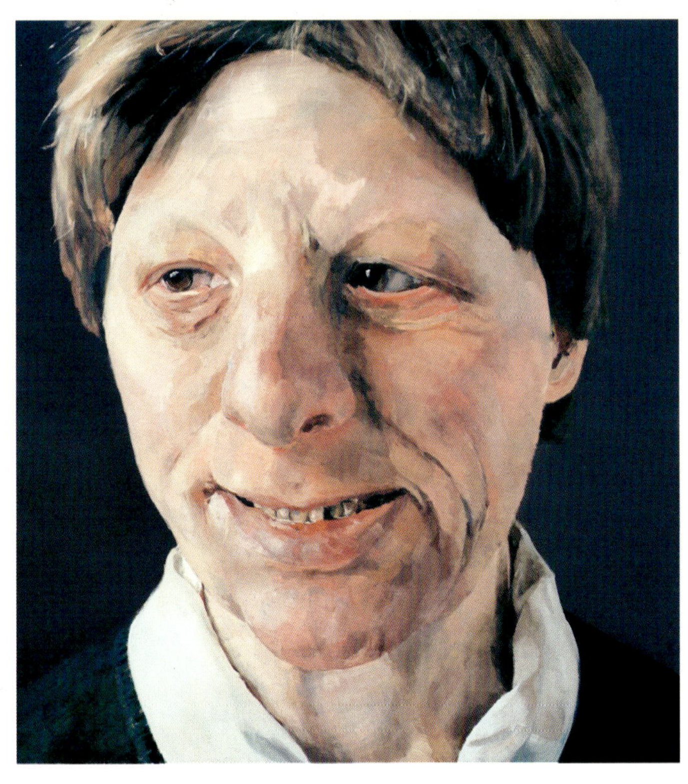

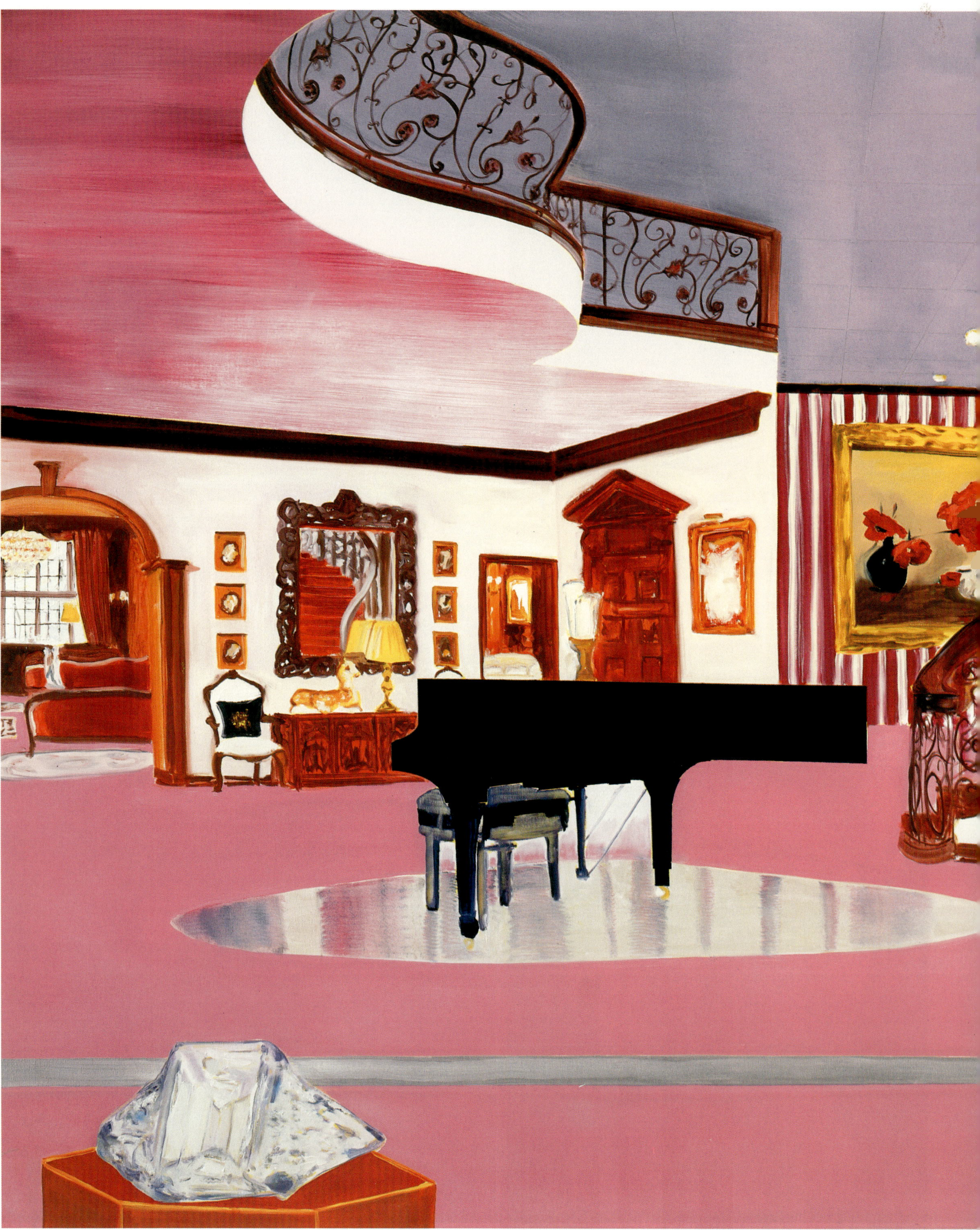

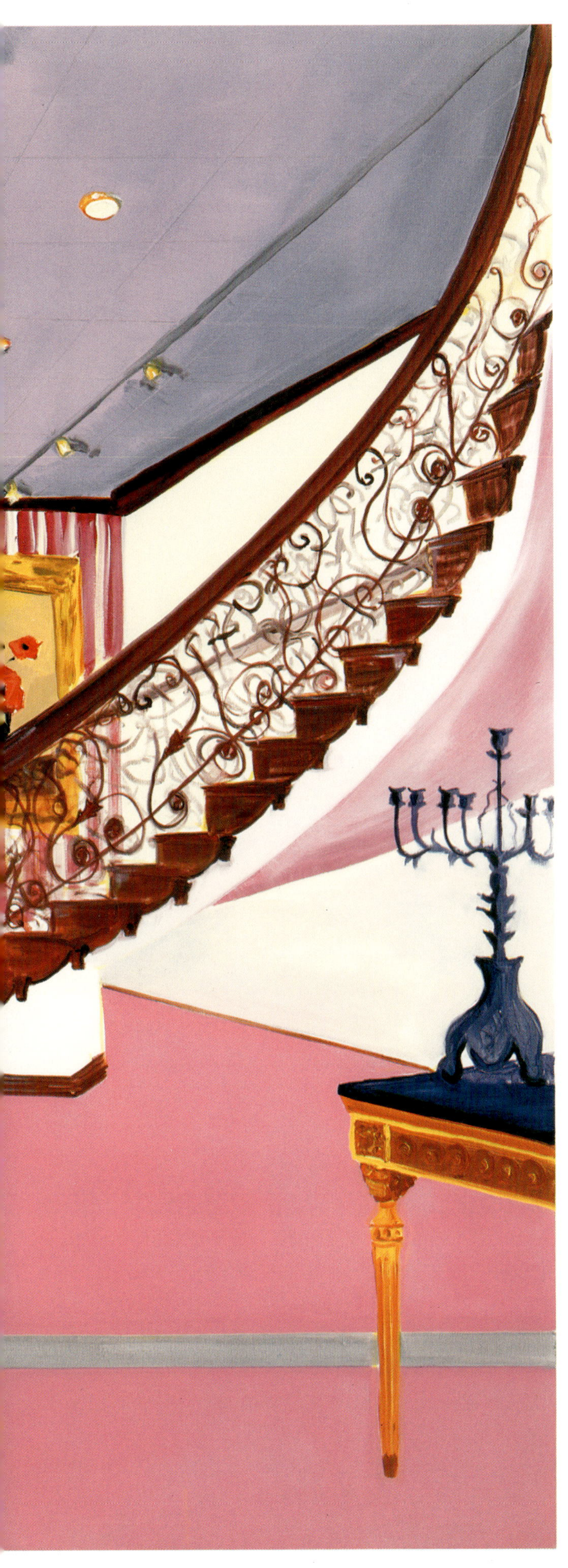

DEXTER DALWOOD

The Liberace Museum 1998
oil on canvas
152.4 x 183cm/60 x 72in

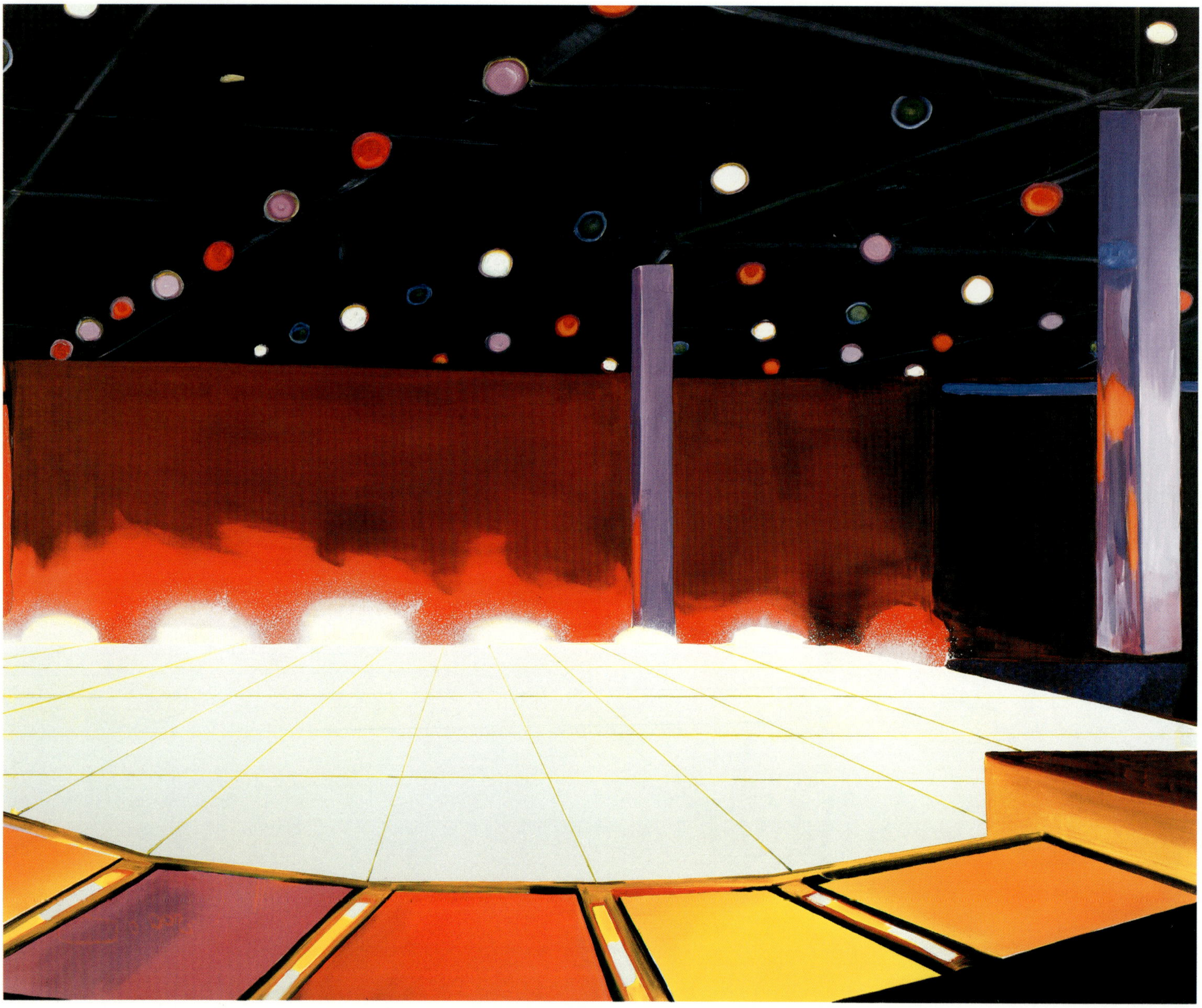

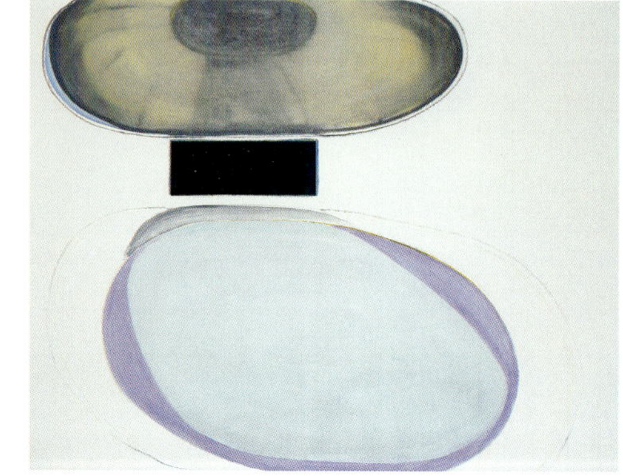

DEXTER DALWOOD

Studio 54 1998
oil on canvas
152.4 x 183cm/60 x 72in

Bridge of the Enterprise 1998
oil on canvas
121.9 x 152.4cm/48 x 60in

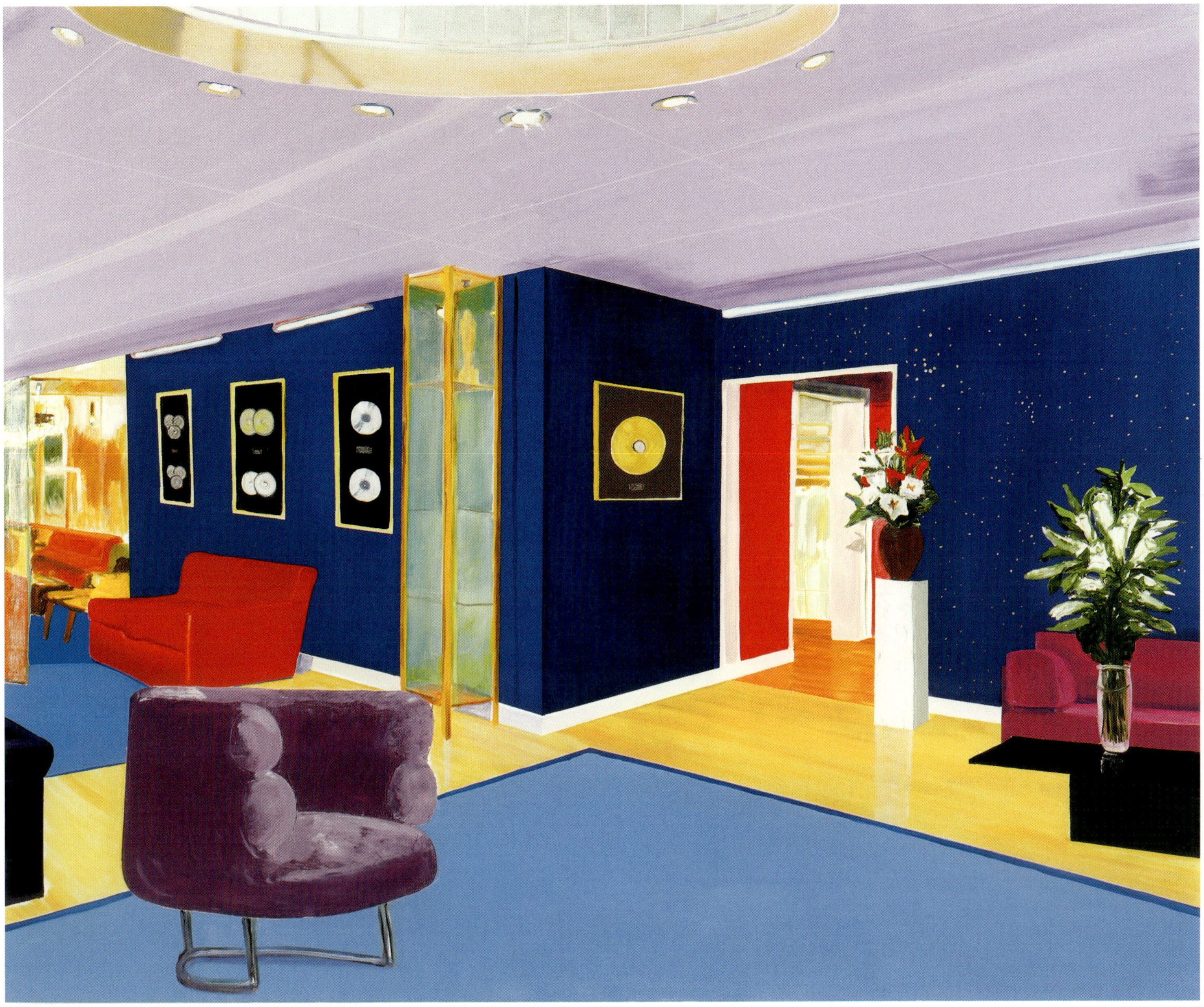

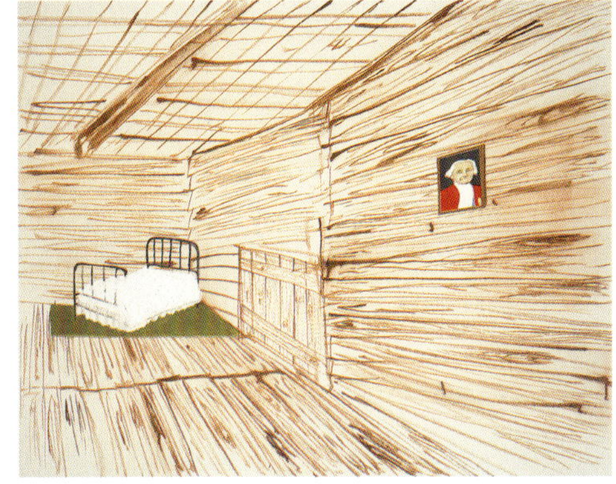

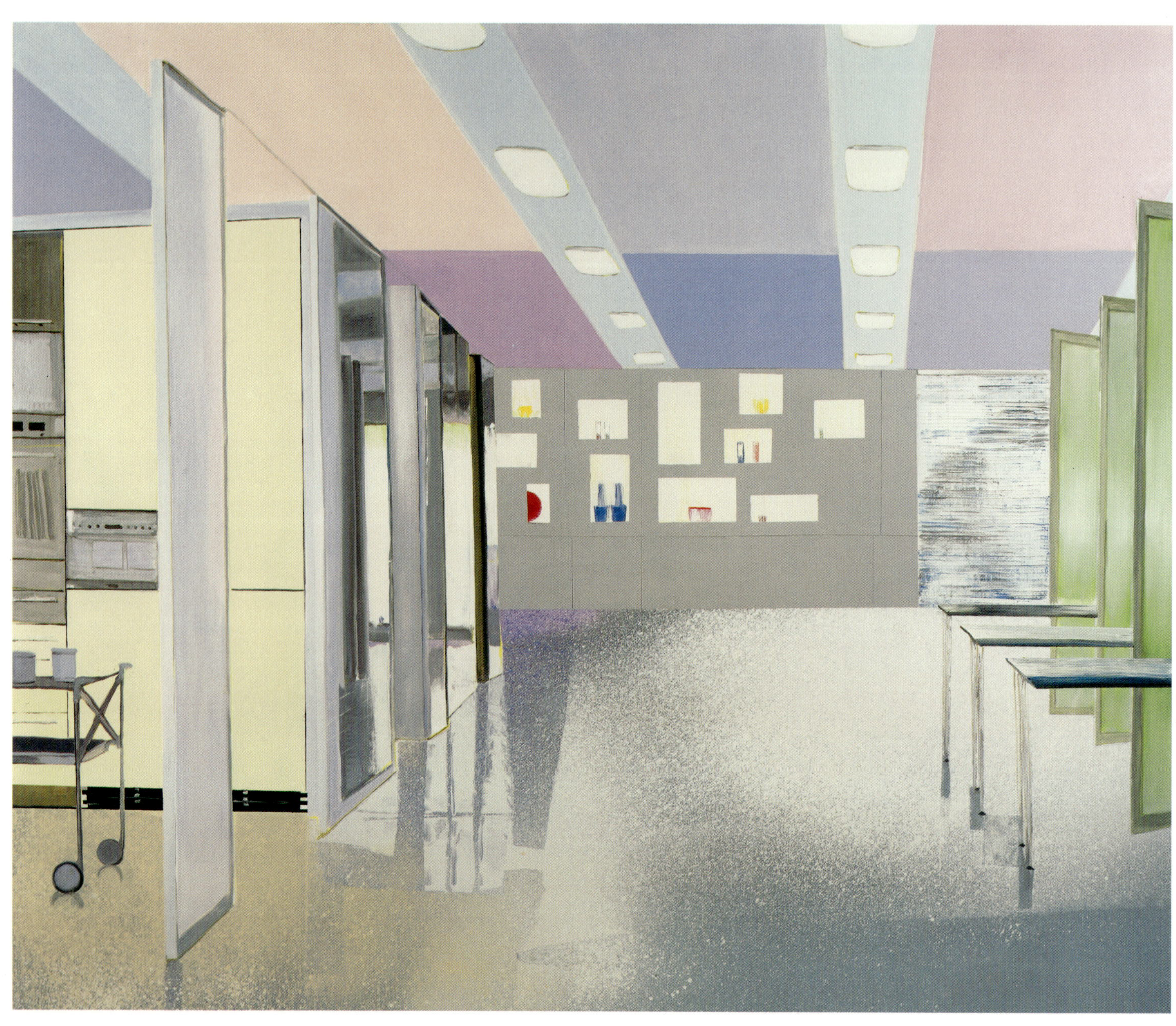

DEXTER DALWOOD

Laboratoire Garnier 1998
oil on canvas
183 x 235cm/72 x 92½in

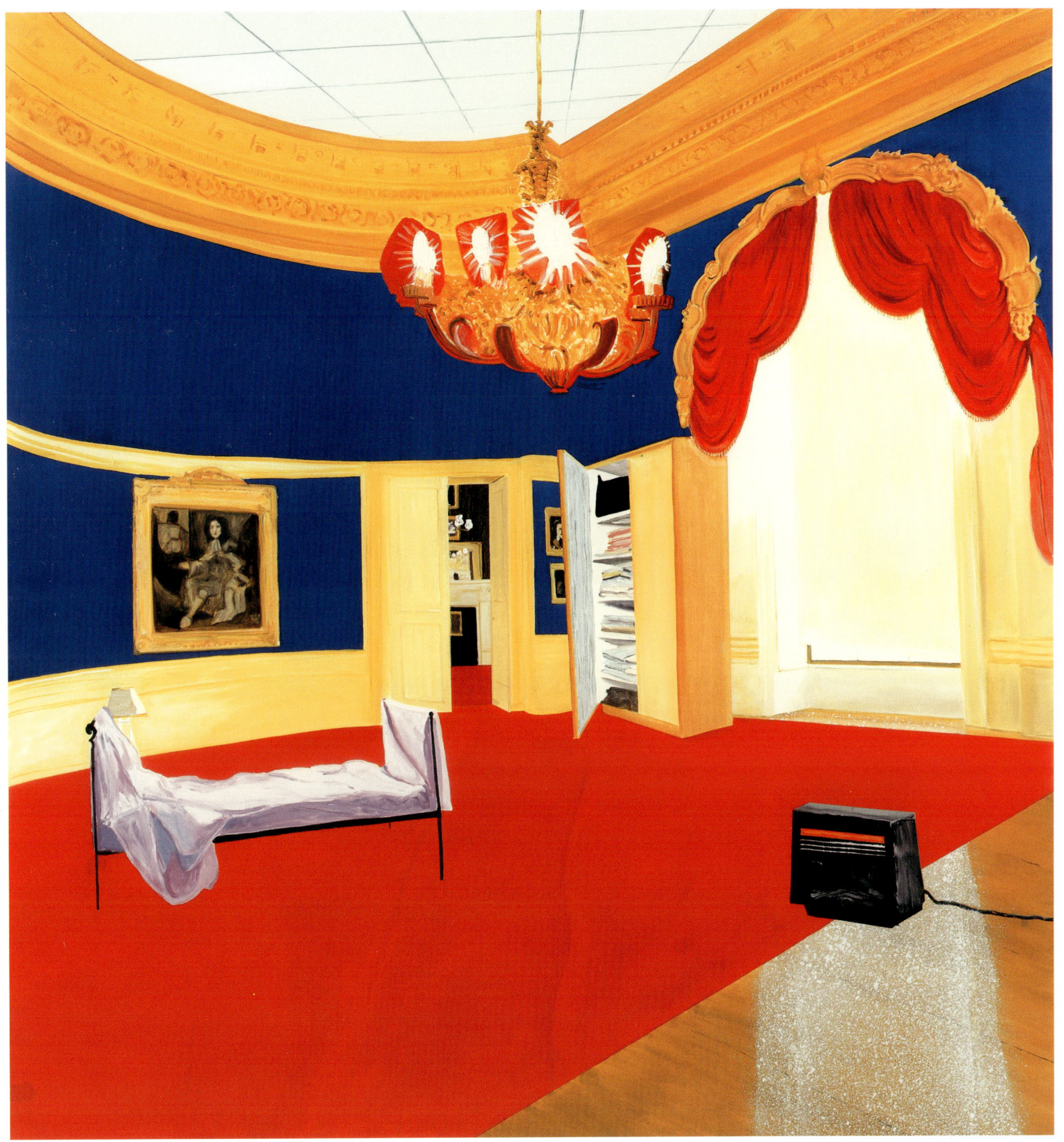

DEXTER DALWOOD

The Queen's Bedroom 1998
oil on canvas
193 x 183cm/76 x 72in

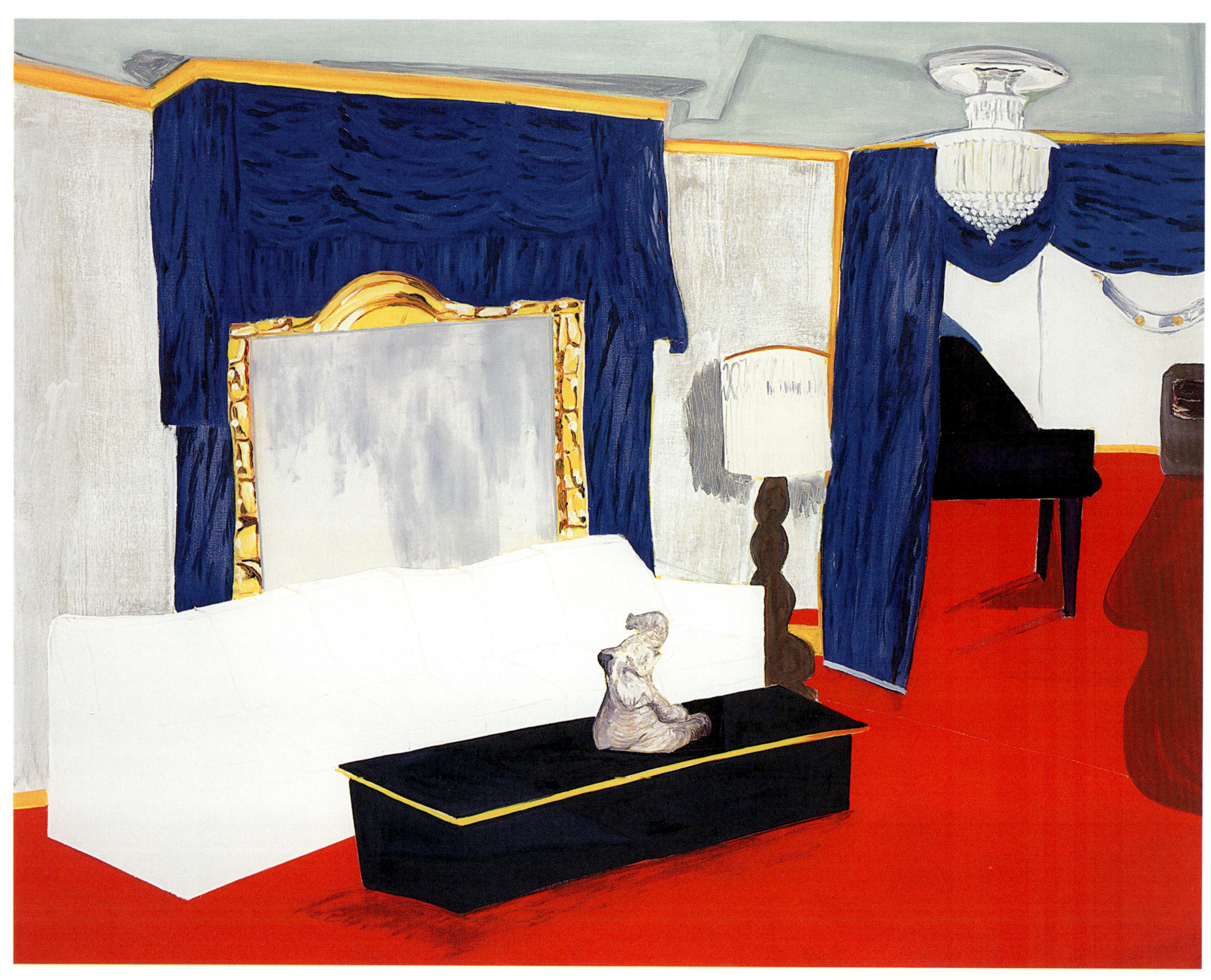

DEXTER DALWOOD

Graceland 1998
oil on canvas
121.9 x 152.4cm/48 x 60in

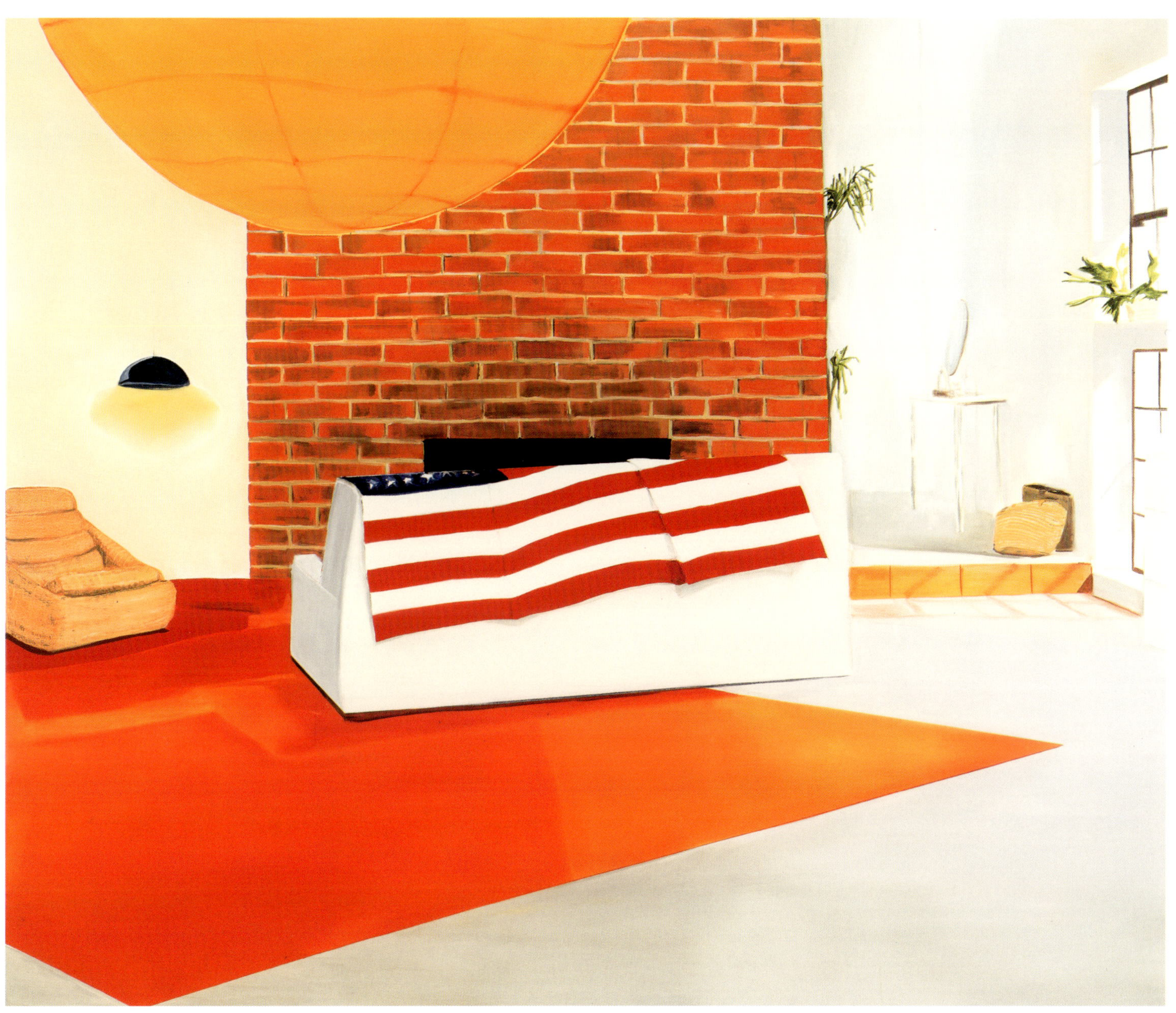

DEXTER DALWOOD

Sharon Tate's House 1998
oil on canvas
183 x 235cm/72 x 92½in

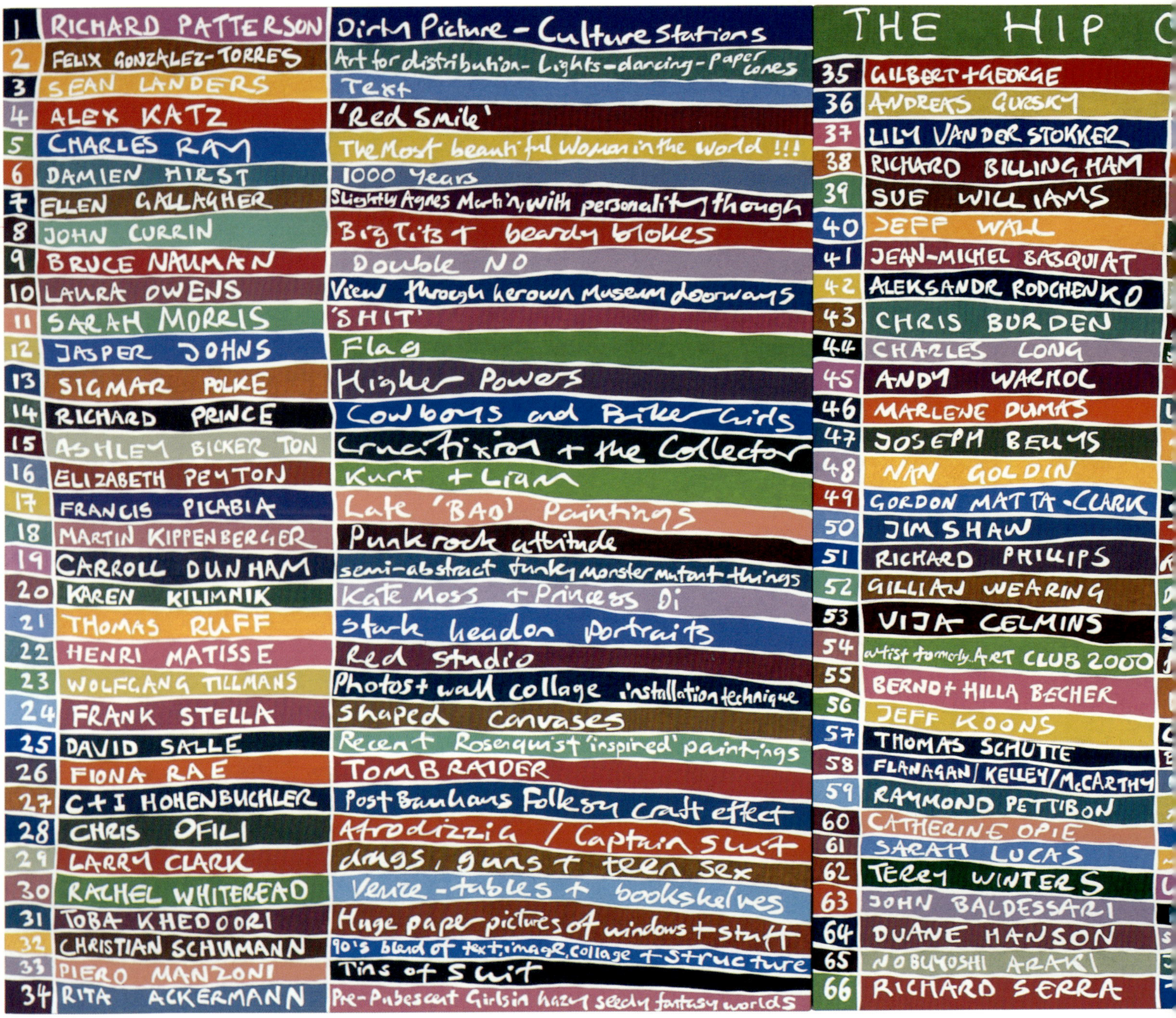

PETER DAVIES

The Hip One Hundred 1998
acrylic on canvas
254 x 609.6cm/100 x 240in

overleaf:
The Hot One Hundred 1997
oil on canvas
254 x 203.2cm/100 x 80in

Fun With the Animals:
Joseph Beuys Text Painting 1998
acrylic on canvas
396.2 x 243.8cm/156 x 96in

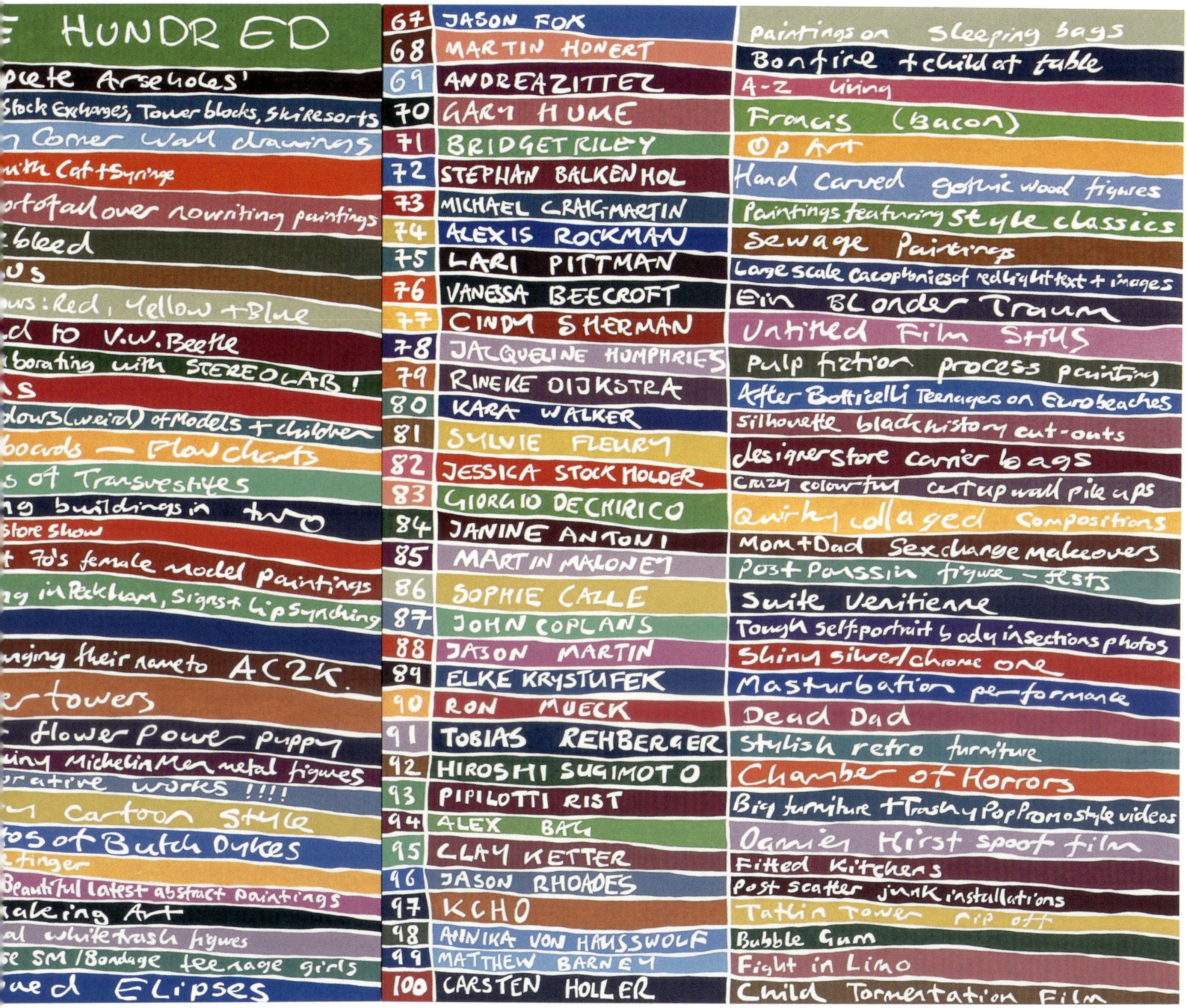

HUNDRED

(left column, cut off at page edge — partial fragments)

...pete Arseholes'
...Stock Exchanges, Tower blocks, Ski resorts
...n Corner Wall drawings
...with Cat + Syringe
...ort of all over nowriting paintings
...bleed
...us
...ours: Red, Yellow + Blue
...d to V.W. Beetle
...borating with STEREOLAB!
...s
...lours (weird) of Models + children
...boards — Flow charts
...s of Transvestites
...ng buildings in two
store show
...t 70's female model paintings
...ng in Peckham, Signs + Lip Synching
...nging their name to AC2K.
...r towers
...flower Powe puppy
...iny Michelin Men metal figures
...rative works !!!!
...y cartoon style
...tos of Butch Dykes
...stinger
...Beautiful latest abstract paintings
...aking Art
...al white trash figures
...se SM/Bondage teenage girls
...ued Elipses

No.	Artist	Work
67	JASON FOX	paintings on sleeping bags
68	MARTIN HONERT	Bonfire + child at table
69	ANDREA ZITTEL	A-Z living
70	GARY HUME	Francis (Bacon)
71	BRIDGET RILEY	Op Art
72	STEPHAN BALKENHOL	Hand carved gothic wood figures
73	MICHAEL CRAIG-MARTIN	Paintings featuring style classics
74	ALEXIS ROCKMAN	Sewage Paintings
75	LARI PITTMAN	Large scale cacophonies of red light text + images
76	VANESSA BEECROFT	Ein Blonder Traum
77	CINDY SHERMAN	Untitled Film Stills
78	JACQUELINE HUMPHRIES	Pulp fiction process painting
79	RINEKE DIJKSTRA	After Botticelli Teenagers on Euro beaches
80	KARA WALKER	Silhouette black history cut-outs
81	SYLVIE FLEURY	designer store carrier bags
82	JESSICA STOCKHOLDER	Crazy colourful cut up wall pile ups
83	GIORGIO DE CHIRICO	Quirky collaged compositions
84	JANINE ANTONI	Mom + Dad Sex change makeovers
85	MARTIN MALONEY	Post Poussin figure — fests
86	SOPHIE CALLE	Suite Venitienne
87	JOHN COPLANS	Tough self-portrait body in sections photos
88	JASON MARTIN	Shiny silver/chrome one
89	ELKE KRYSTUFEK	Masturbation performance
90	RON MUECK	Dead Dad
91	TOBIAS REHBERGER	Stylish retro furniture
92	HIROSHI SUGIMOTO	Chamber of Horrors
93	PIPILOTTI RIST	Big furniture + Trashy Pop Promo style videos
94	ALEX BAG	Damien Hirst spoof film
95	CLAY KETTER	Fitted Kitchens
96	JASON RHOADES	Post scatter junk installations
97	KCHO	Tatlin Tower rip off
98	ANNIKA VON HAUSSWOLF	Bubble Gum
99	MATTHEW BARNEY	Fight in Limo
100	CARSTEN HOLLER	Child Tormentation Film

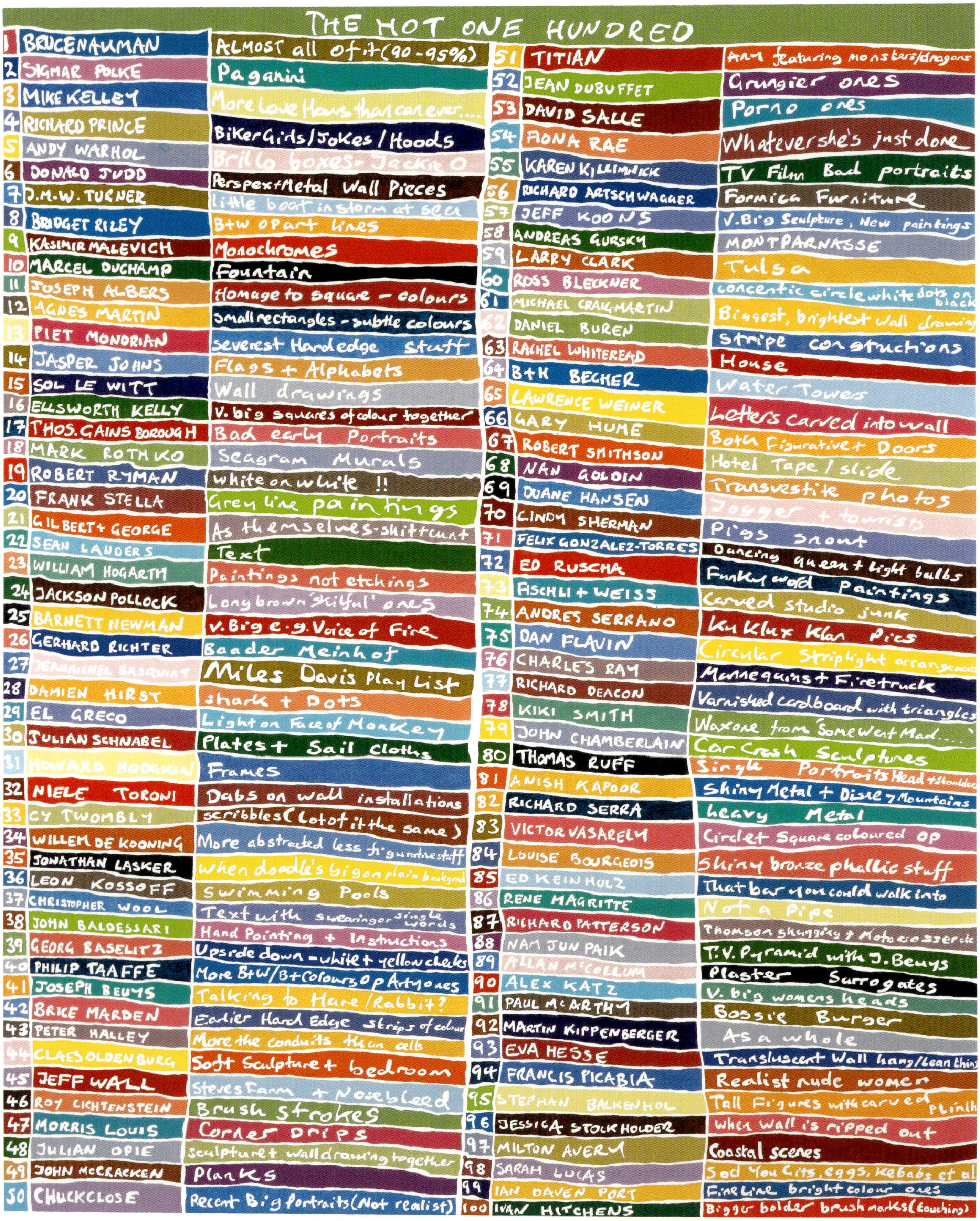

THE HOT ONE HUNDRED

#	Artist	Work
1	BRUCE NAUMAN	ALMOST all of it (90-95%)
2	SIGMAR POLKE	Paganini
3	MIKE KELLEY	More Love Hours than can ever....
4	RICHARD PRINCE	Biker Girls / Jokes / Hoods
5	ANDY WARHOL	Brillo boxes - Jackie O
6	DONALD JUDD	Perspex + Metal Wall Pieces
7	J.M.W. TURNER	little boat in storm at sea
8	BRIDGET RILEY	B+W Op Art lines
9	KASIMIR MALEVICH	Monochromes
10	MARCEL DUCHAMP	Fountain
11	JOSEPH ALBERS	Homage to square - colours
12	AGNES MARTIN	Small rectangles - subtle colours
13	PIET MONDRIAN	severest Hard edge Stuff
14	JASPER JOHNS	Flags + Alphabets
15	SOL LE WITT	Wall drawings
16	ELLSWORTH KELLY	V. big squares of colour together
17	THOS. GAINSBOROUGH	Bad early Portraits
18	MARK ROTHKO	Seagram Murals
19	ROBERT RYMAN	white on white !!
20	FRANK STELLA	Grey line paintings
21	GILBERT + GEORGE	As themselves - shit cunt +
22	SEAN LANDERS	Text
23	WILLIAM HOGARTH	Paintings not etchings
24	JACKSON POLLOCK	Long brown 'skilful' ones
25	BARNETT NEWMAN	V. Big e.g. Voice of Fire
26	GERHARD RICHTER	Baader Meinhof
27	JEAN-MICHEL BASQUIAT	Miles Davis Play List
28	DAMIEN HIRST	shark + Dots
29	EL GRECO	Light on Face of Monkey
30	JULIAN SCHNABEL	Plates + Sail Cloths
31	HOWARD HODGKIN	Frames
32	NIELE TORONI	Dabs on wall installations
33	CY TWOMBLY	scribbles (Lot of it the same)
34	WILLEM DE KOONING	More abstracted less figurative stuff
35	JONATHAN LASKER	When doodle's big on plain background
36	LEON KOSSOFF	Swimming Pools
37	CHRISTOPHER WOOL	Text with swearing or single words
38	JOHN BALDESSARI	Hand Pointing + Instructions
39	GEORG BASELITZ	Upside down - white + yellow checks
40	PHILIP TAAFFE	More B+W / B+ Colours Op Art ones
41	JOSEPH BEUYS	Talking to Hare / Rabbit?
42	BRICE MARDEN	Earlier Hard Edge strips of colour
43	PETER HALLEY	More the conduits than cells
44	CLAES OLDENBURG	Soft Sculpture + bedroom
45	JEFF WALL	Steves Farm + Nosebleed
46	ROY LICHTENSTEIN	Brush Strokes
47	MORRIS LOUIS	Corner Drips
48	JULIAN OPIE	sculpture + wall drawing together
49	JOHN McCRACKEN	Planks
50	CHUCK CLOSE	Recent Big portraits (Not realist)
51	TITIAN	Any featuring monsters/dragons
52	JEAN DUBUFFET	Grungier ones
53	DAVID SALLE	Porno ones
54	FIONA RAE	Whatever she's just done
55	KAREN KILIMNICK	TV Film Bad portraits
56	RICHARD ARTSCHWAGGER	Formica Furniture
57	JEFF KOONS	V. Big Sculpture, New paintings
58	ANDREAS GURSKY	MONTPARNASSE
59	LARRY CLARK	Tulsa
60	ROSS BLECKNER	concentic circle white dots on black
61	MICHAEL CRAIG-MARTIN	Biggest, brightest Wall drawing
62	DANIEL BUREN	stripe constructions
63	RACHEL WHITEREAD	House
64	B+H BECHER	Water Towers
65	LAWRENCE WEINER	Letters carved into wall
66	GARY HUME	Both Figurative + Doors
67	ROBERT SMITHSON	Hotel Tape / slide
68	NAN GOLDIN	Transvestite photos
69	DUANE HANSEN	Jogger + tourist
70	CINDY SHERMAN	Pigs snout
71	FELIX GONZALEZ-TORRES	Dancing queen + light bulbs
72	ED RUSCHA	Funky word Paintings
73	FISCHLI + WEISS	Carved studio junk
74	ANDRES SERRANO	Ku Klux Klan Pics
75	DAN FLAVIN	Circular Striplight arrangements
76	CHARLES RAY	Mannequins + Firetruck
77	RICHARD DEACON	Varnished cardboard with triangles
78	KIKI SMITH	Wax one from 'Some Went Mad....'
79	JOHN CHAMBERLAIN	Car Crash Sculptures
80	THOMAS RUFF	Single Portraits Head + shoulders
81	ANISH KAPOOR	Shiny Metal + Disney Mountains
82	RICHARD SERRA	heavy Metal
83	VICTOR VASARELY	Circle + Square coloured op
84	LOUISE BOURGEOIS	Shiny bronze phallic stuff
85	ED KEINHOLZ	That bar you could walk into
86	RENE MAGRITTE	Not a Pipe
87	RICHARD PATTERSON	Thomson shagging + Motocrosser etc
88	NAM JUN PAIK	T.V. Pyramid with J. Beuys
89	ALLAN McCOLLUM	Plaster Surrogates
90	ALEX KATZ	V. big womens heads
91	PAUL McARTHY	Bossie Burger
92	MARTIN KIPPENBERGER	As a whole
93	EVA HESSE	Transluscent Wall hang/Lean thing
94	FRANCIS PICABIA	Realist nude women
95	STEPHAN BALKENHOL	Tall Figures with carved plinth
96	JESSICA STOCKHOLDER	When Wall is ripped out
97	MILTON AVERY	Coastal scenes
98	SARAH LUCAS	Sod You Cits, eggs, kebabs et al
99	IAN DAVENPORT	Fine Line bright colour ones
100	IVAN HITCHENS	Bigger bolder brush marks (touching)

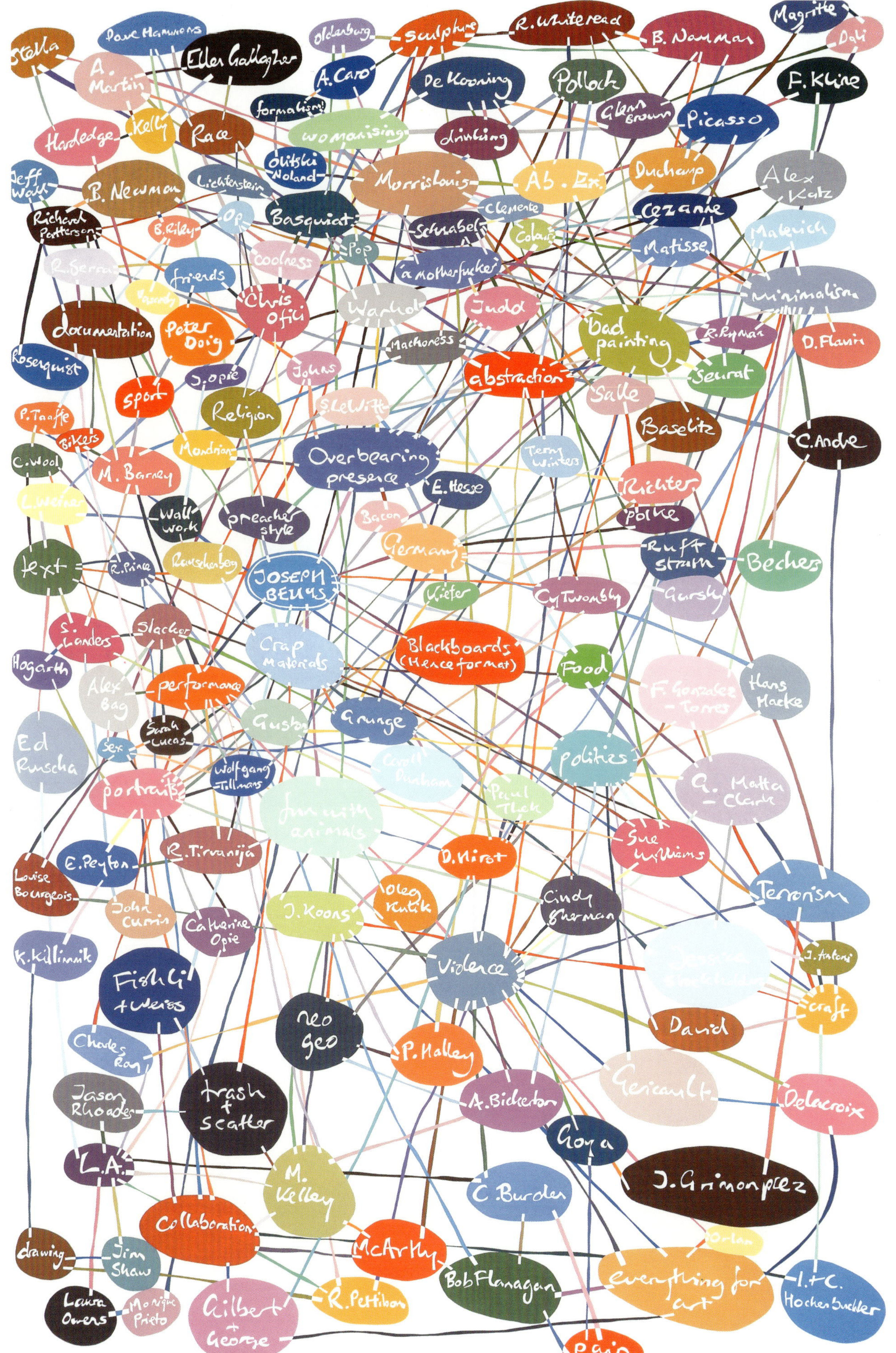

Stella
Dave Hammons
Ellen Gallagher
Oldenburg
Sculpture
R. Whiteread
B. Nauman
Magritte
Dali
A. Martin
A. Caro
De Kooning
Pollock
F. Kline
formalism?
Kelly
Race
womanising
drinking
Glenn Brown
Picasso
Hardedge
Olitski Noland
Morris Louis
Ab. Ex.
Duchamp
Alex Katz
Jeff Wall
B. Newman
Lichtenstein
Clemente
Cezanne
Richard Patterson
B. Riley
Op
Basquiat
Schnabel
Colour
Matisse
Malevich
R. Serra
Coolness
Pop
a motherfucker
friends
Minimalism
Chris Ofili
Warhol
Judd
bad painting
R. Ryman
D. Flavin
documentation
Peter Doig
Machoness
Rosenquist
Johns
abstraction
Seurat
J. Opie
Sport
Salle
P. Taaffe
Religion
S. LeWitt
Baselitz
C. Andre
Bikers
Mondrian
Overbearing presence
Terry Winters
C. Wool
M. Barney
E. Hesse
Richter
L. Weiner
Wall work
preacher style
Bacon
Polke
Germany
Ruff Struth
Bechers
text
R. Prince
Rauschenberg
JOSEPH BEUYS
Kiefer
Cy Twombly
Gursky
S. Landers
Slacker
Crap materials
Blackboards (Hence format)
Food
Hogarth
Alex Bag
performance
F. Gonzalez-Torres
Hans Haacke
Ed Ruscha
Sarah Lucas
Guston
Grunge
Sex
politics
Carroll Dunham
Wolfgang Tillmans
portraits
Fun with animals
Paul Thek
G. Matta-Clark
R. Tiravanija
Sue Williams
E. Peyton
D. Hirst
Louise Bourgeois
Oleg Kulik
Cindy Sherman
Terrorism
John Currin
Catherine Opie
J. Koons
K. Killimnik
Violence
J. Antoni
Fischli + Weiss
neo geo
craft
David
Charles Ray
P. Halley
Gericault
Jason Rhoades
trash + scatter
A. Bickerton
Delacroix
Goya
L.A.
M. Kelley
C. Burden
J. Grimonprez
Collaboration
Orlan
drawing
Jim Shaw
McArthy
Bob Flanagan
everything for art
I+C. Hochenbuchler
Laura Owens
Monique Prieto
Gilbert + George
R. Pettibon
pain

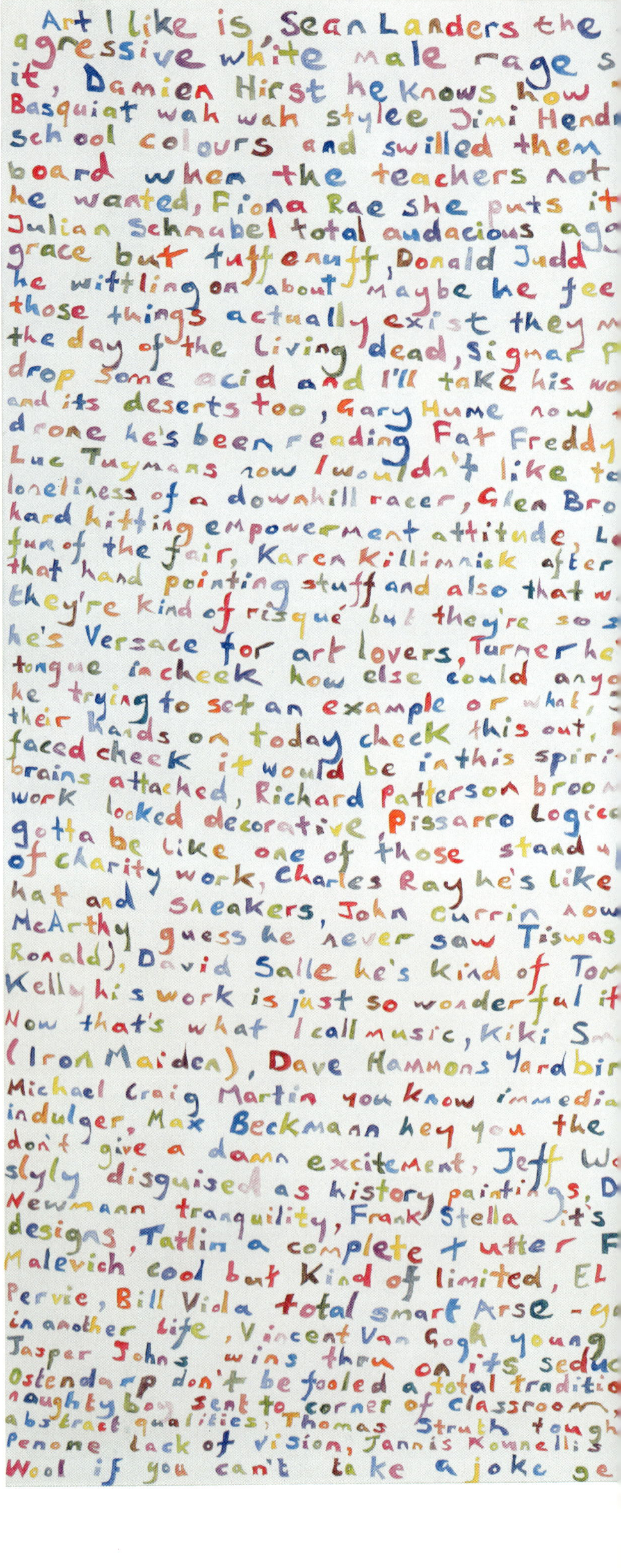

PETER DAVIES

Text Painting 1998
acrylic on canvas
203 x 254cm/80 x 100in

t important artist of his generation, Bruce Nauman all that
f, Mike Kelley he does everything so trashy but we love
state the obvious big time with such panache, Jean Michel
air guitar, Willem de Kooning like you spilt all your nursery
and beautiful, Cy Twombly then you scribbled on the black
king + tried to rub it out, Picasso he just did whatever the fuck
together, Bridget Riley so complicated but such eloquent funky results,
ion yes please, Rachel Whiteread in contrast such tranquility and
ted to take over the world don't we all, Peter Halley just what is
imprisoned or something, Caroll Dunham what a dude I can't believe
so much to me, Brice Marden scary monster, Gerhard Richter
super trooper up yours he's in total control, Joseph Beuys just
for it more like Bugs Bunny, Agnes Martin now that is total terrorvision
for dessert blancmange meets Haagen-Daz, Jason Fox megaphone
Kat, Alex Katz its kind of timeless but oh those night scenes,
et him down a dark alley, Peter Doig ellesse super cool the
oh when the saints come marching in repro classics, Sarah Lucas her
e Bourgeois tough tits she'll rip you to bits, Bernard Cohen kind of all the
k sheer black magic, Lily Van der Stoker Mutha Fucka, John Baldessari
g he's like Bruce Springsteen - the boss, Gilbert + George now people say
e, Antony Caro now he really is one mean badass M.F. S.O.B, Velasquez
ike some Byron/Shelley opium high, Sherrie Levine now that's got to be
be bothered to do that shit, Andy Warhol my fucking headmaster now was
f Albers totally up to date if you want the funkiest thing Gucci could get
rd Prince now this really is the greatest thing if ever there was bare
ee the Blue Lagoon), Meg Cranston L.A. style funk + sexiness only with the
room, Matisse he had no problems with some fucker telling him his
ogression but I say this guy is totally radical, Jenny Holzer she's
medians who always manages to keep a straight face + does loads
fucking spoilt brat with his giant dolls + trucks + Run DMC style
ever anyone turned a love for Metallica to their advantage, Paul
he must've seen Texas chainsaw whilst eating a McDonalds (hello
es of the art world but I dug that stuff it was really clever, Ellsworth
ves me speechless but then I always liked kites, William Tucker
"Maybe when your life is close at hand, maybe then you'll understand"
ite ain't that neat, Ashley Bickerton word up Cameo meets Ray Petri,
what he's on about, Richard Deacon, another space case trip
steady crew, Larry Clark now that's what I call stream of consciousness
he's got an eye for detail look at those fashion statements
Graham spiel spiel house + gardens meets Lawnmower man, Barnett
House, Constable total memorabilia, Juan Miro kind of tasteful rug
nutcase, Aleksandr Rodchenko kind of art director over design,
sitsky cool got better angles more Star Wars, Beat Streuli kind of
hand it to him, Oskar Kokoshka d'ya think he'd hang with Schnabel
rebel, Claes Oldenburg combine harvester a bit of an alien life form,
ness, Mitja Tusek kind of the wicked witch of the west, Carl
Kenny Scharf downright groovy, Chris Burden black humour, Vito Acconci
istian Schumann adolescent sniggering meets P.funk, Andreas Gursky kind of
Bernard Frize left over 60's hippy sentiments with 90's technology, Giuseppe
animals, Thomas Grunfeld dead animals, Meyer Vaisman fake animals, Christophe
e fuck out of my house, Phillip Taaffe control freak, Marina Abramovic

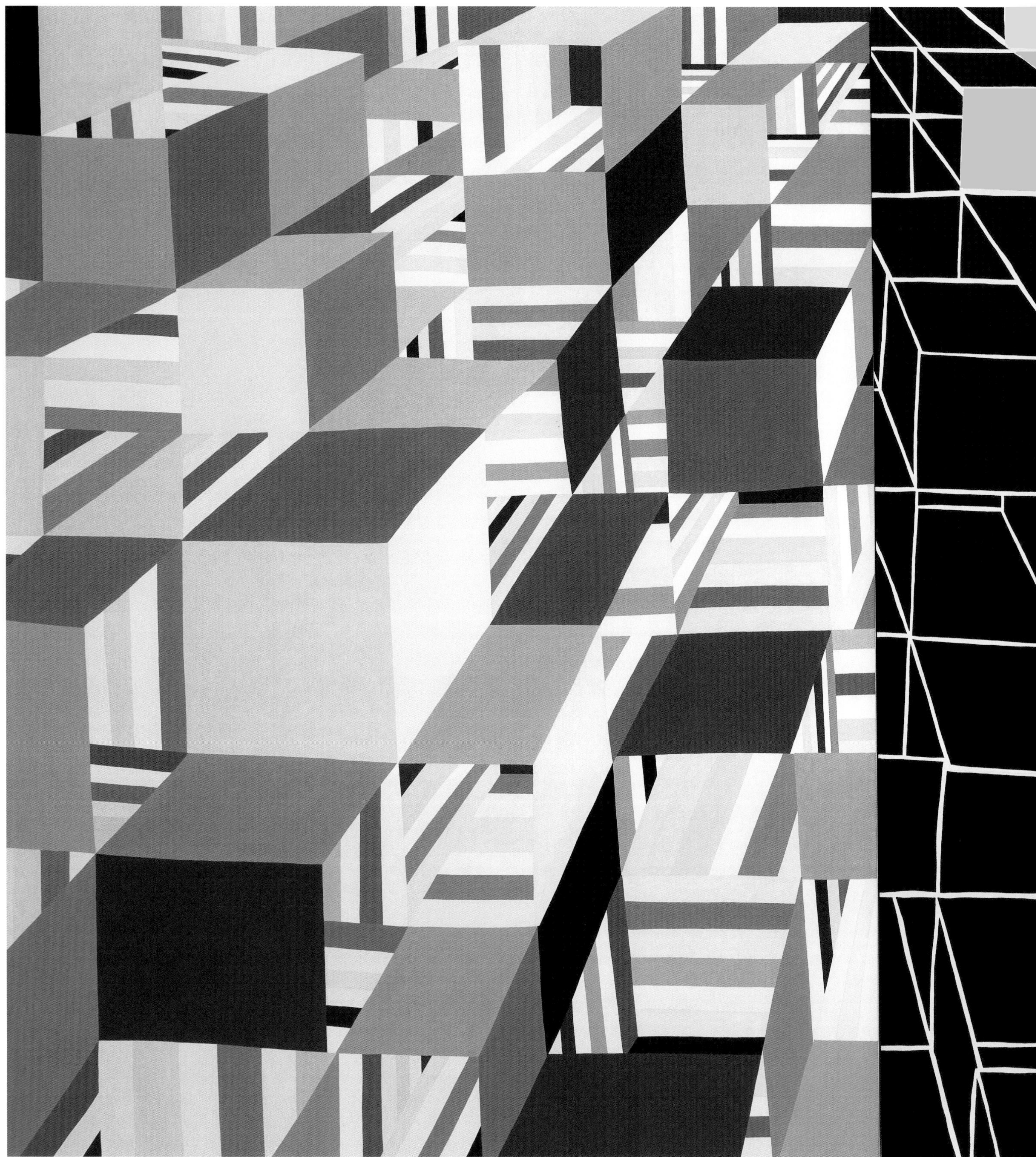

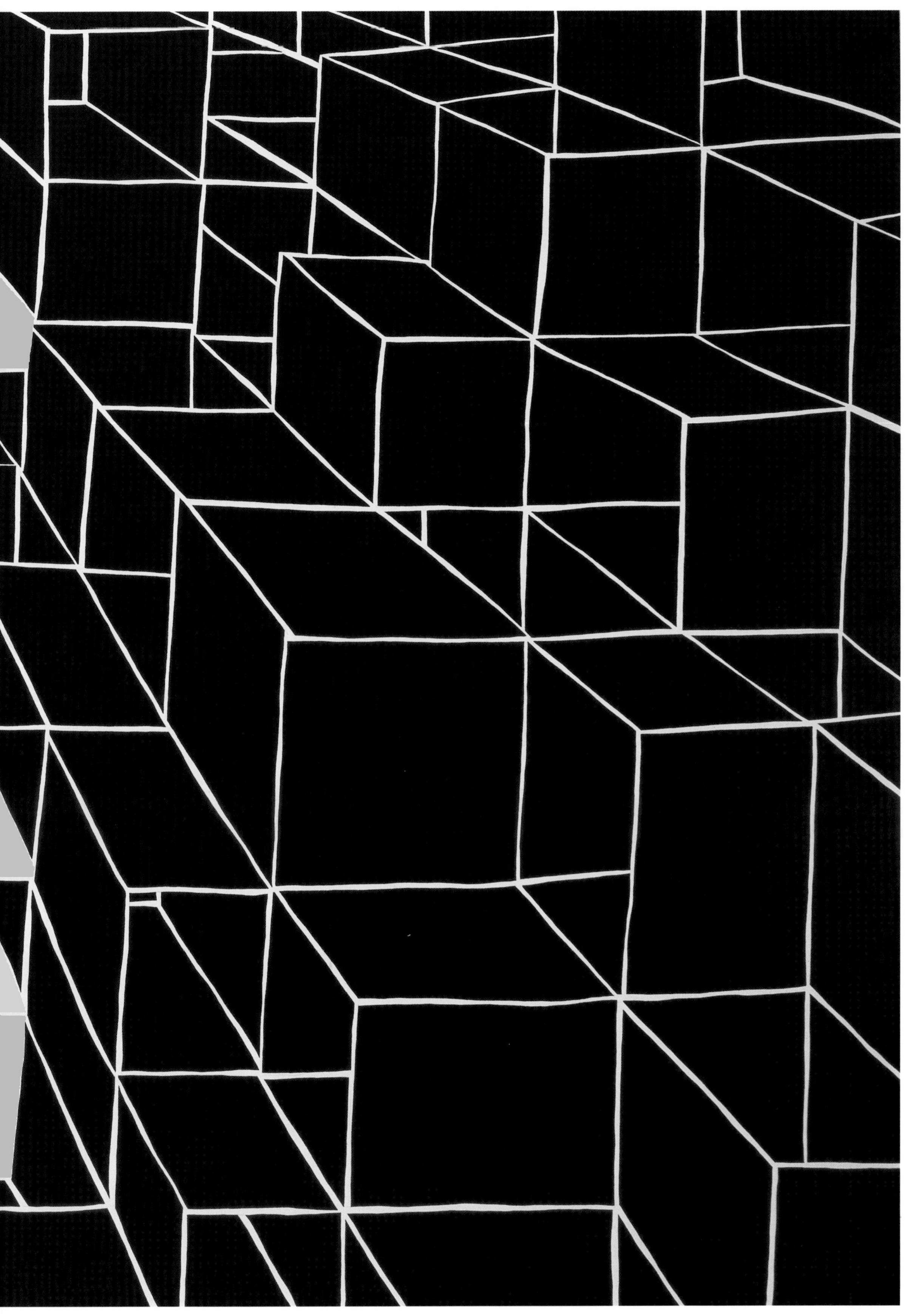

PETER DAVIES

Black and Grey Perspective Cubes Painting 1998
acrylic on canvas
213.4 x 335.3cm/84 x 132in

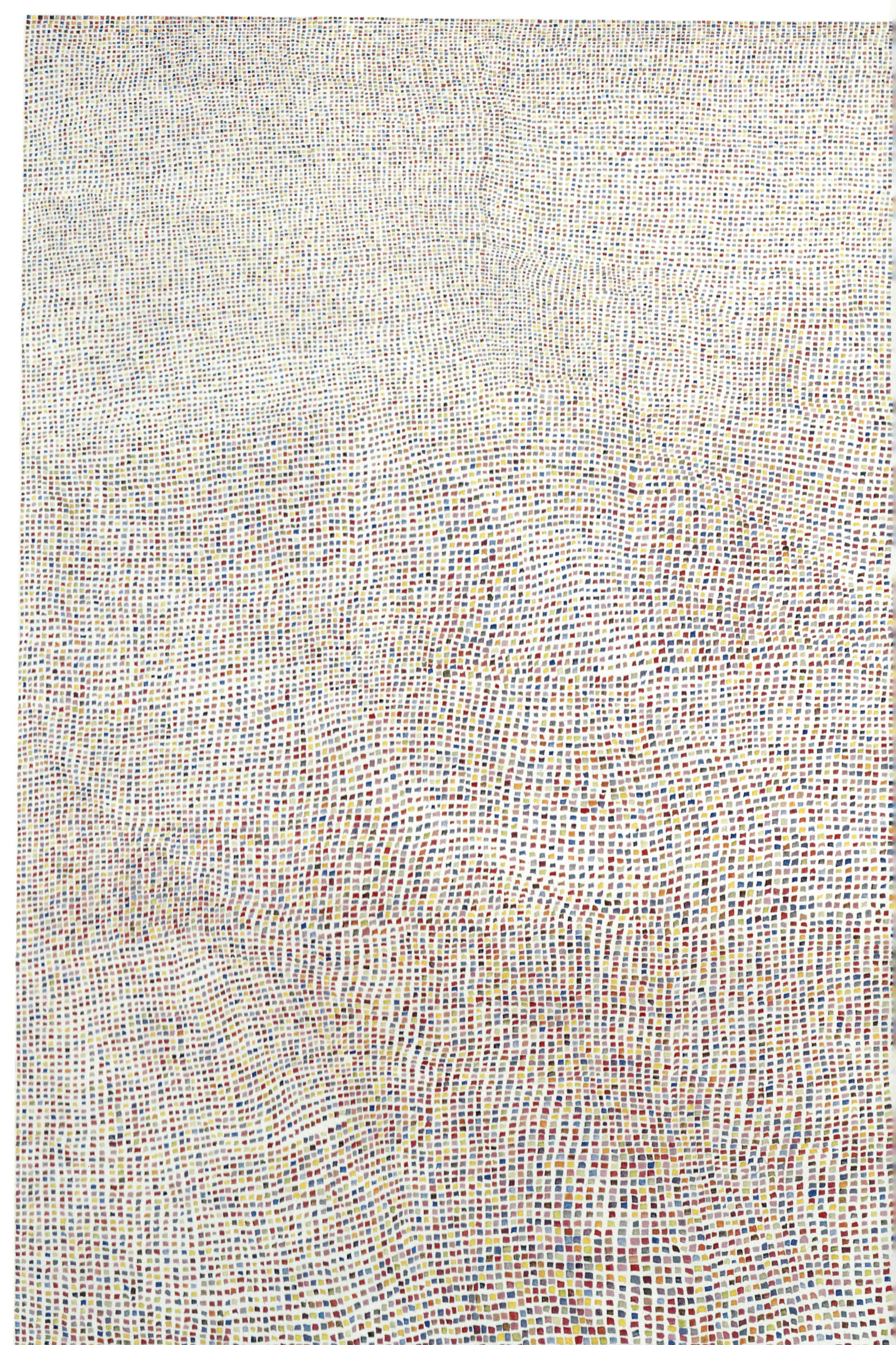

PETER DAVIES

Small Squares Painting 1996
acrylic on canvas
238.8 x 365.8cm/94 x 144in

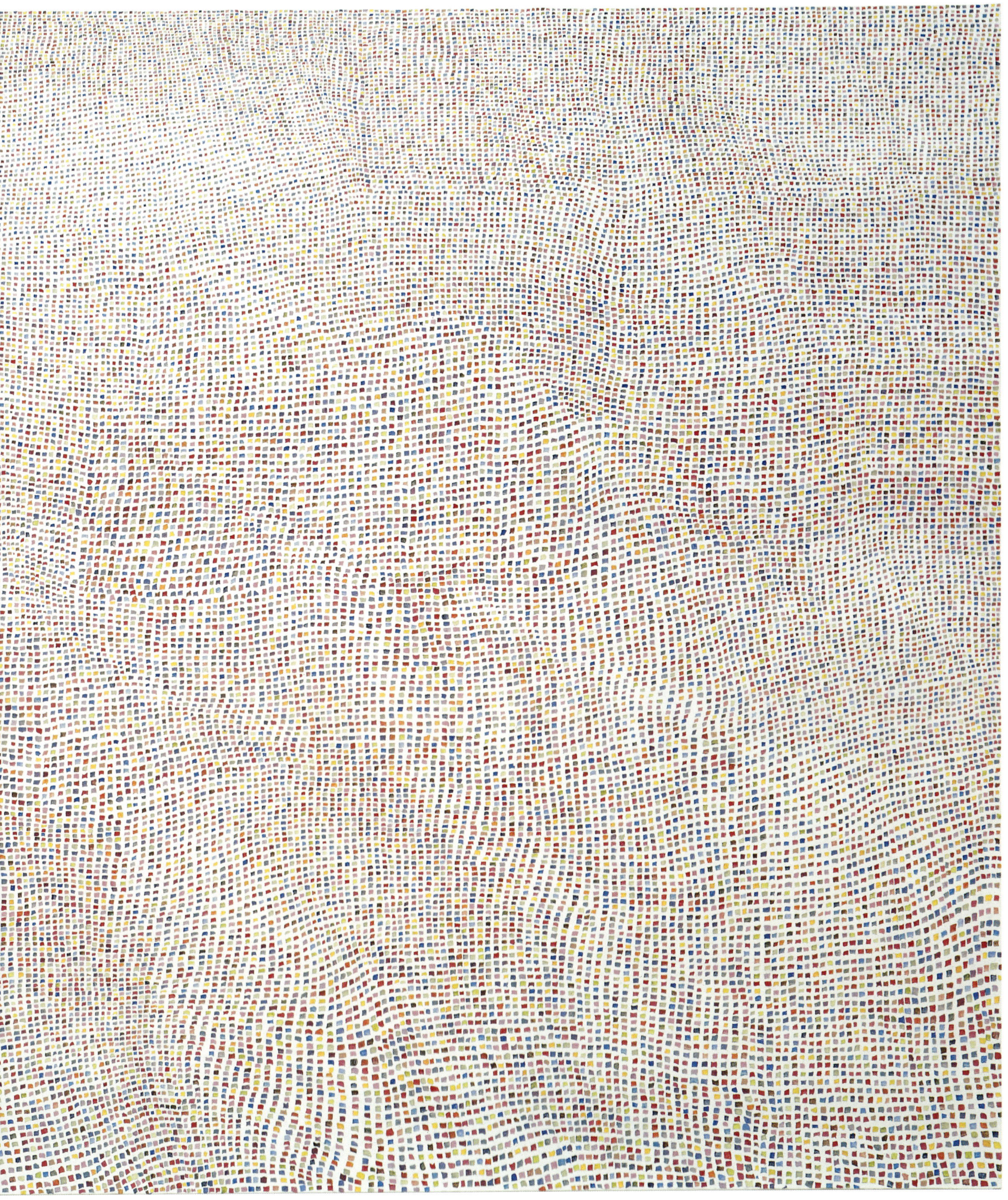

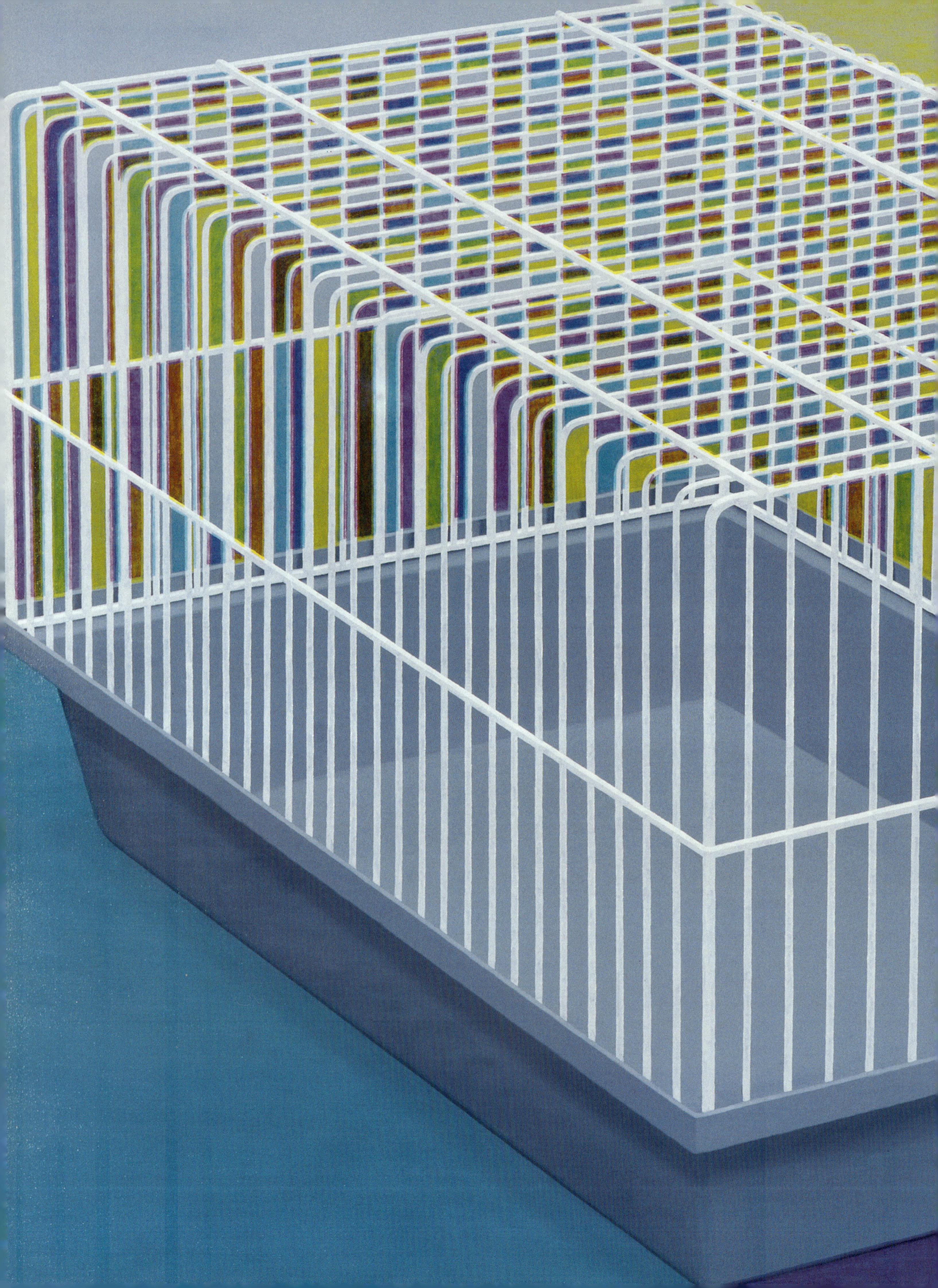

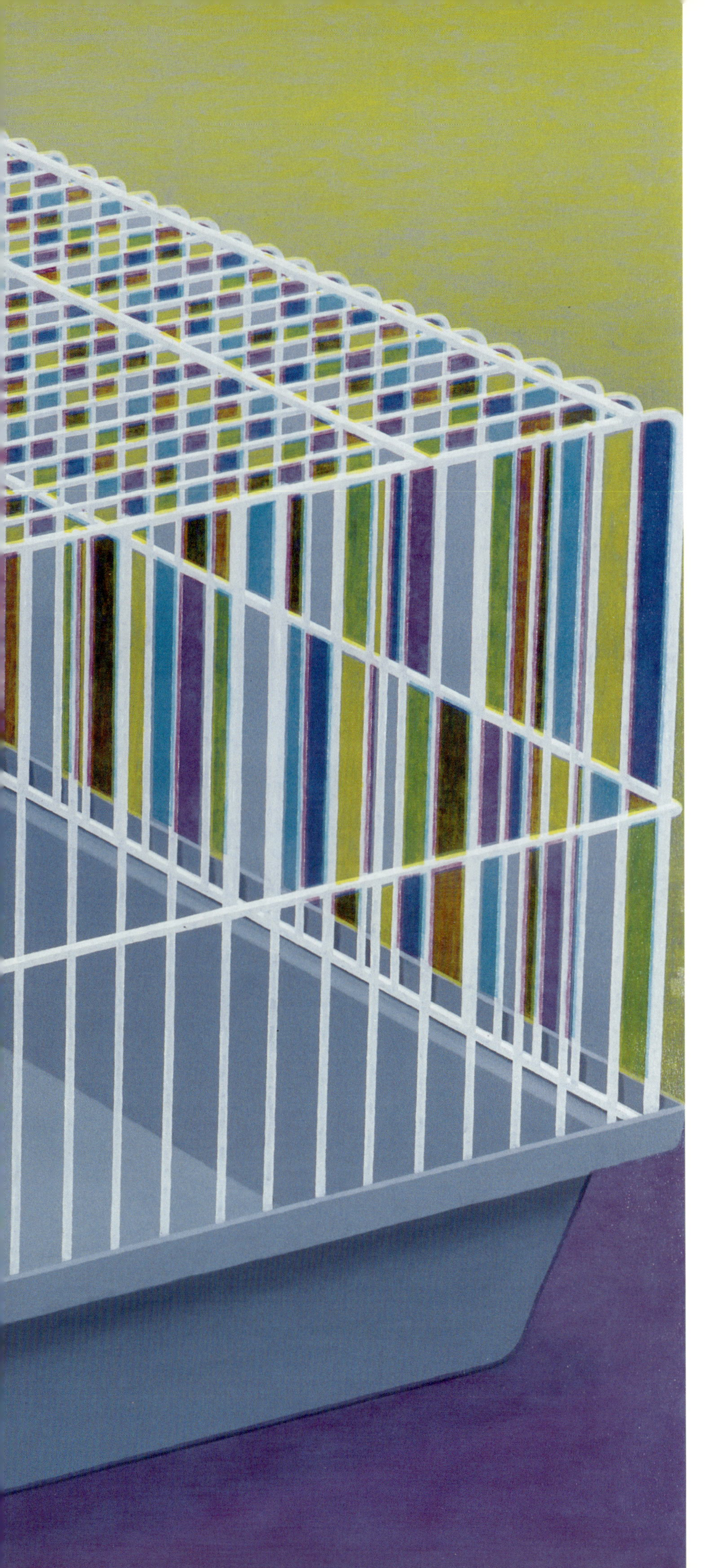

DAN HAYS

Separation 1998
oil on canvas
168 x 168cm/66 x 66in

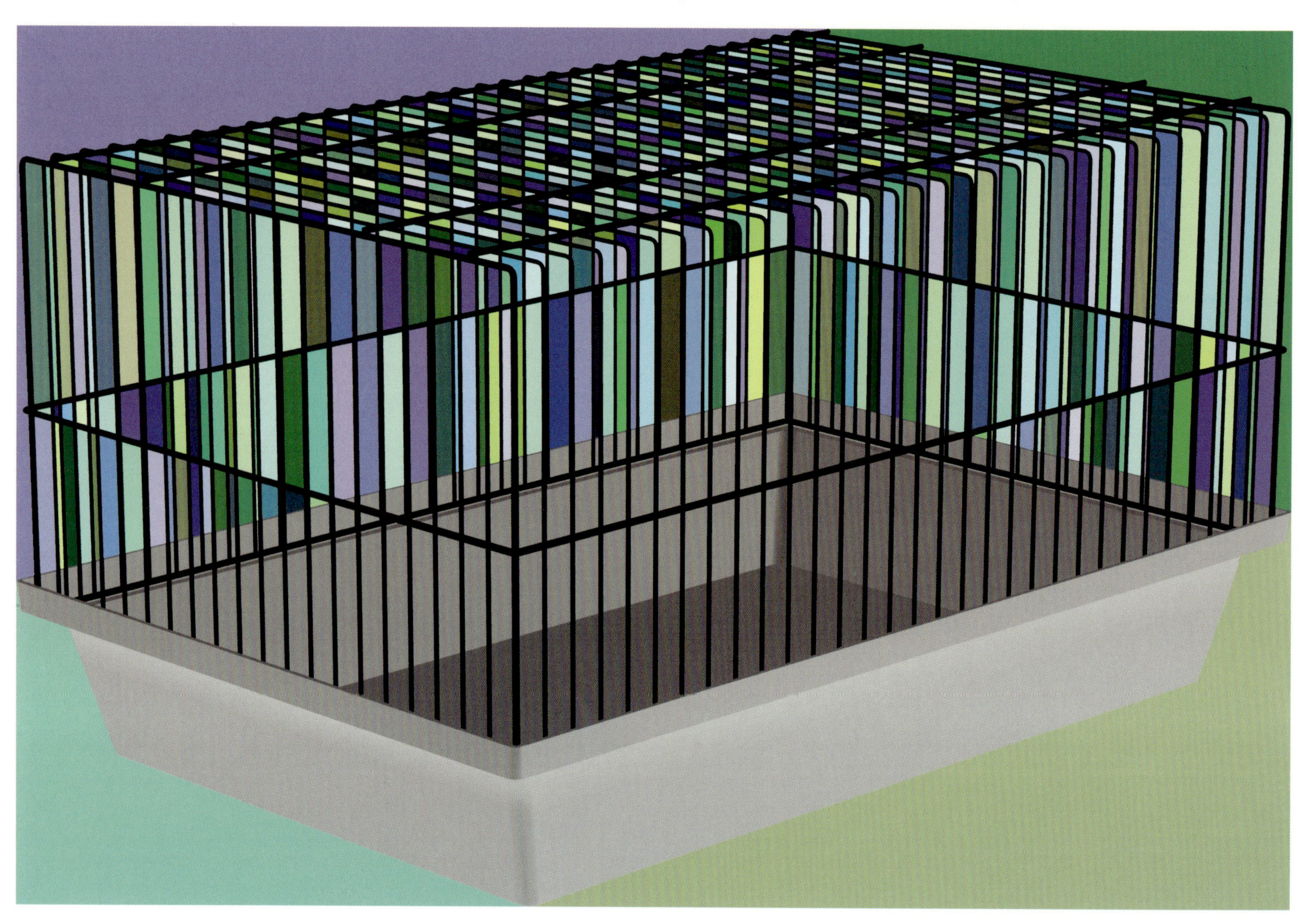

DAN HAYS

Mutual Understanding (Black & White) 1998
oil on canvas
diptych: 200 x 288cm/78³/₄ x 113¹/₂in each panel

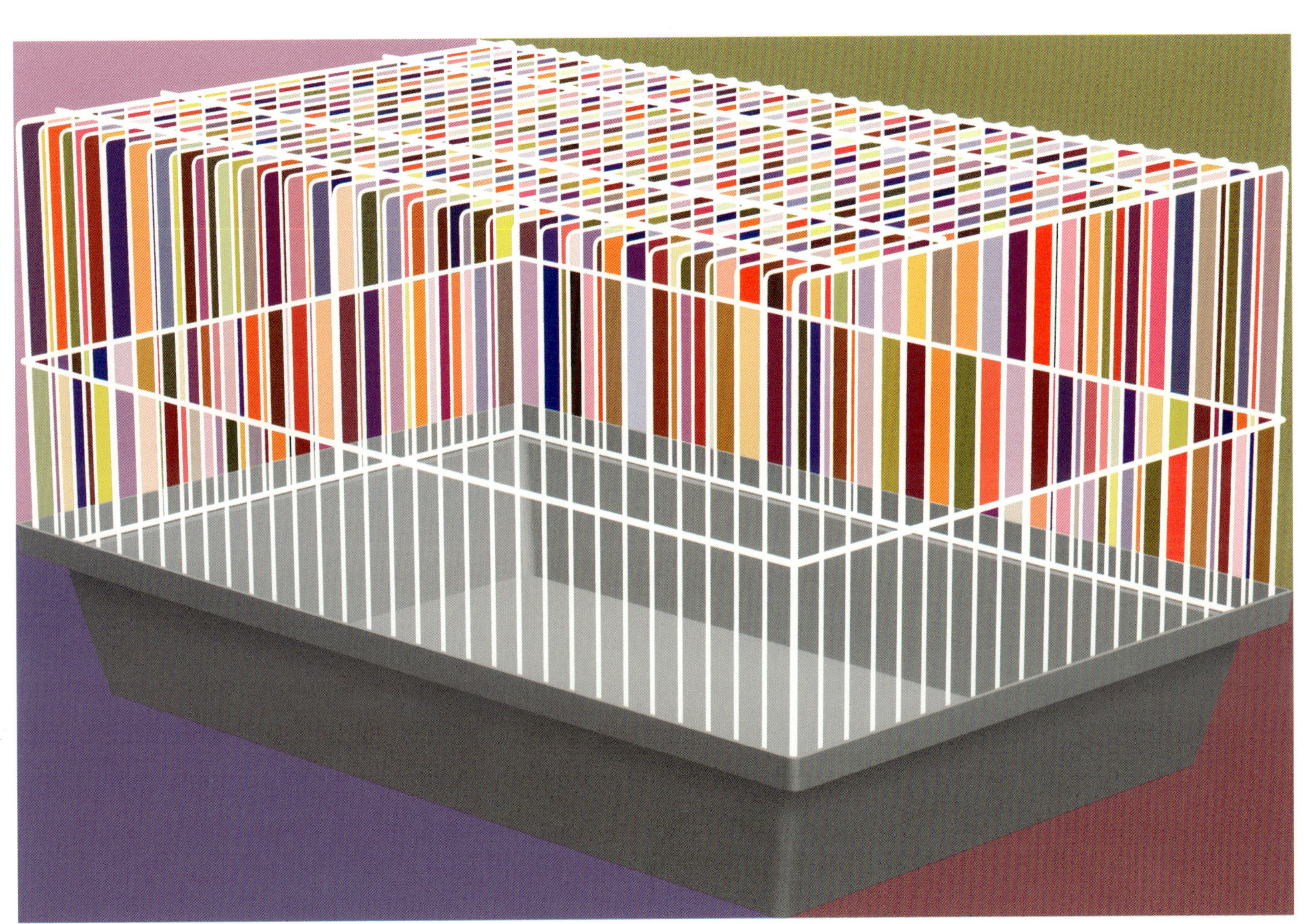

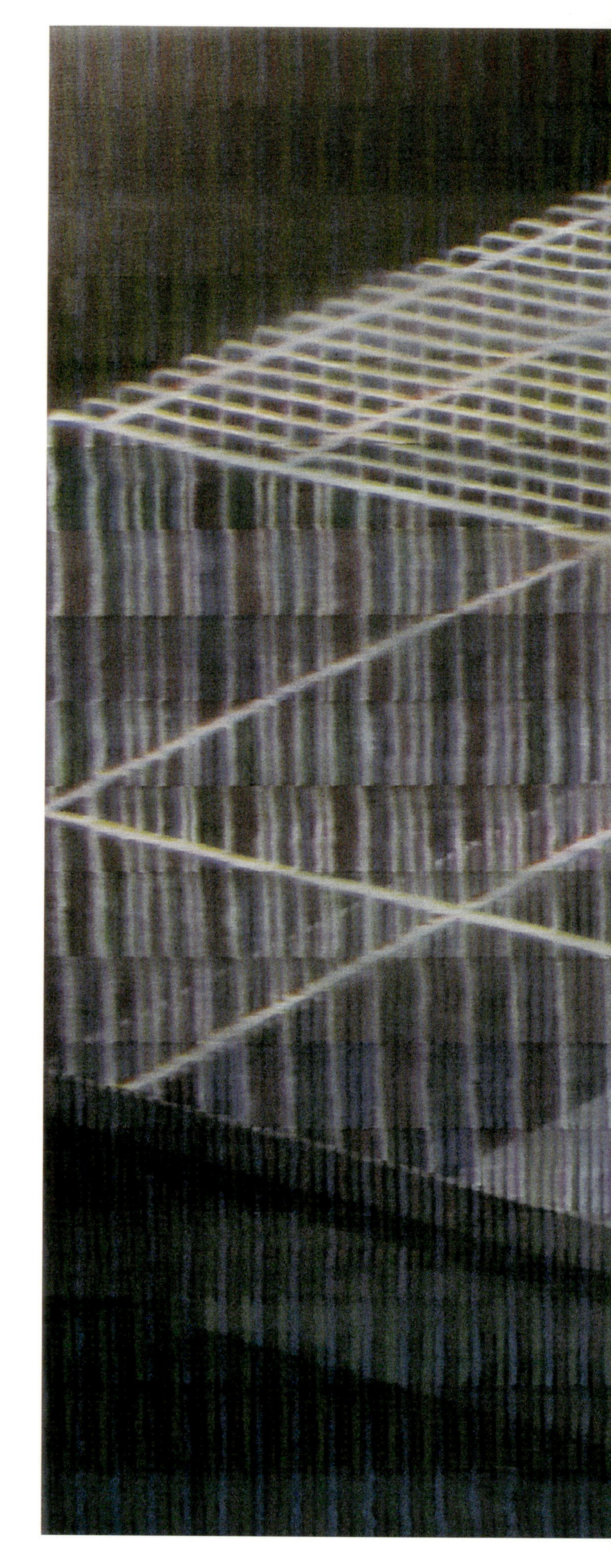

DAN HAYS

Dissolve 1998
oil on canvas
190 x 230cm/74³/₄ x 90¹/₂in

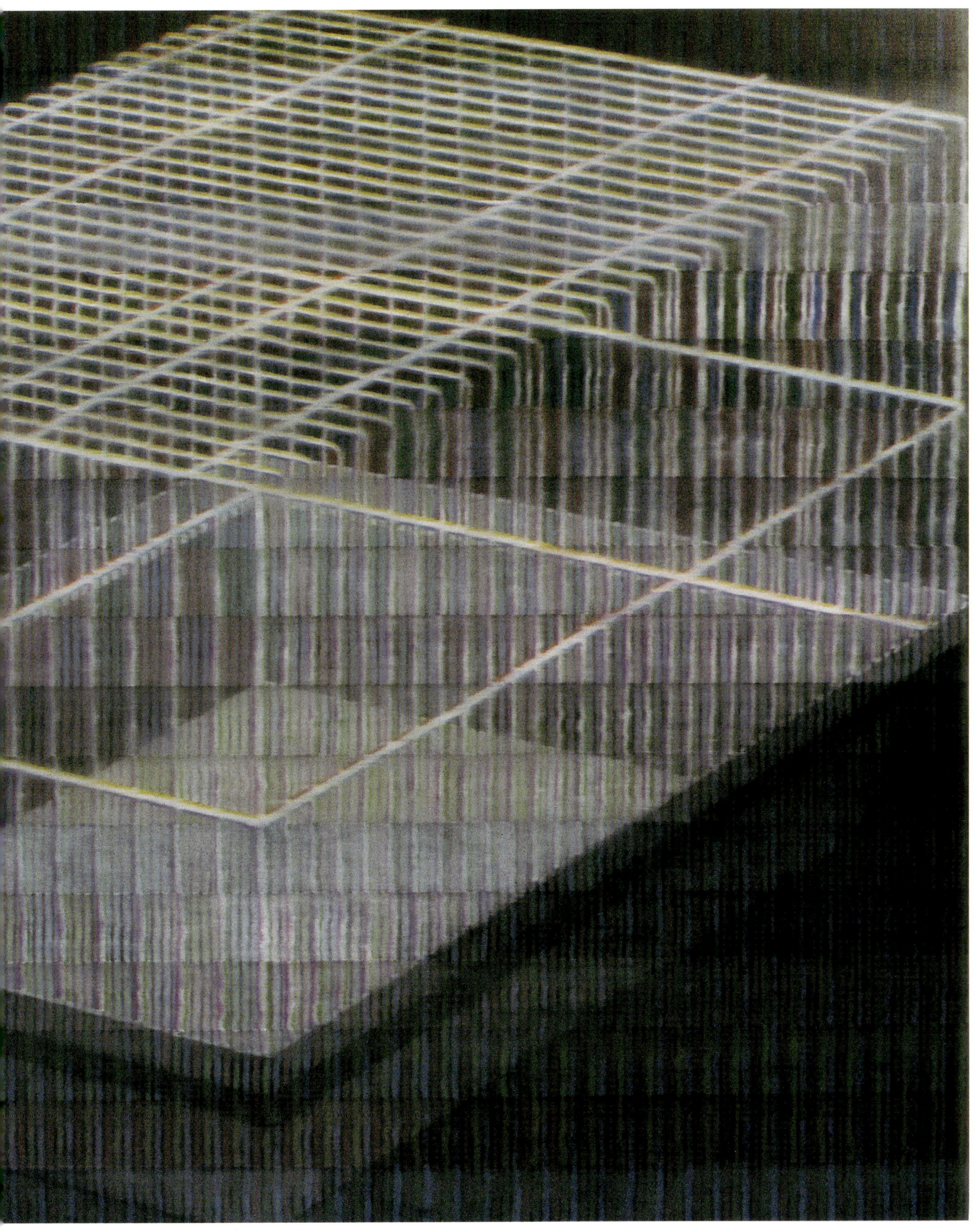

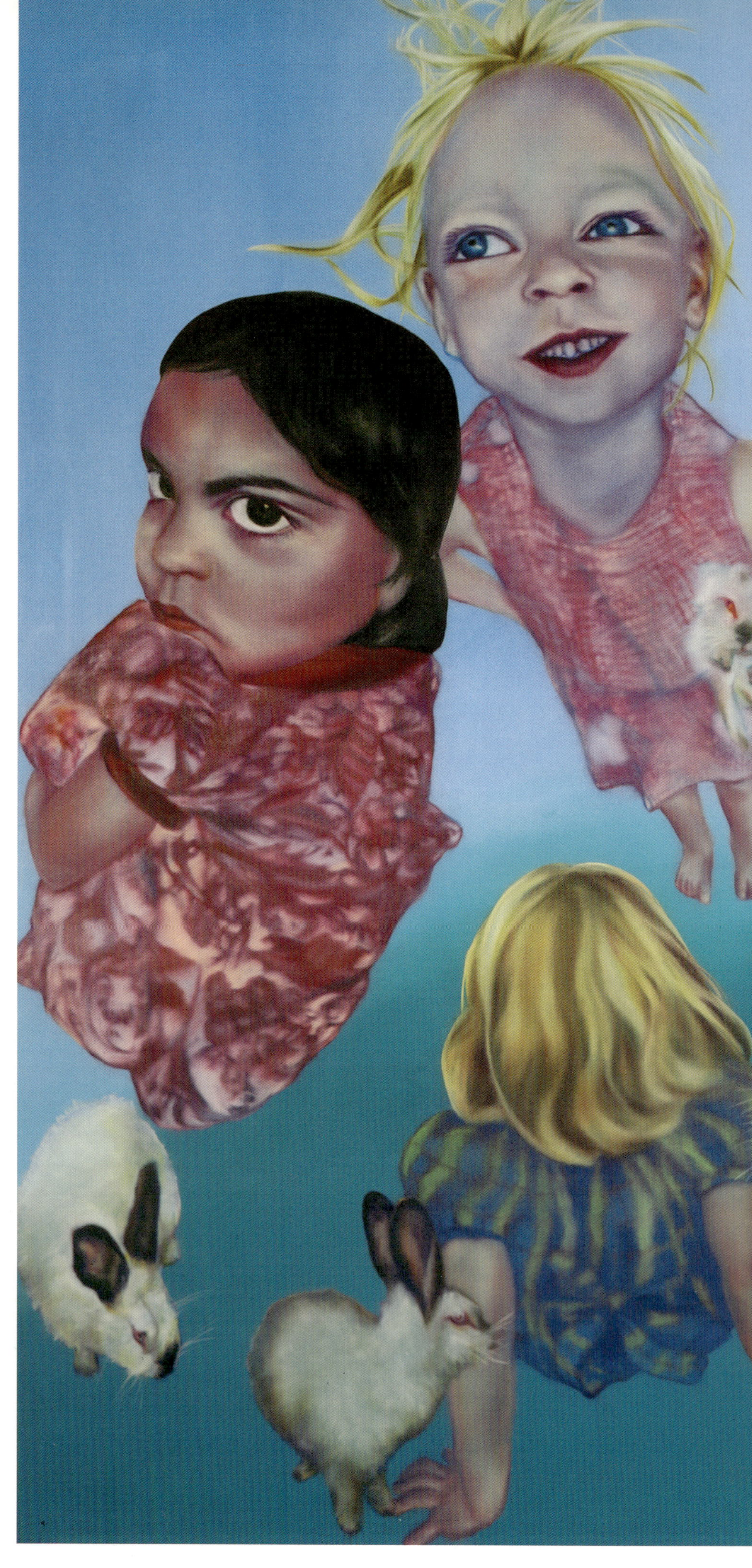

NICKY HOBERMAN

Honeybun 1997
oil on canvas
213 x 275cm/83¾ x 108¼in

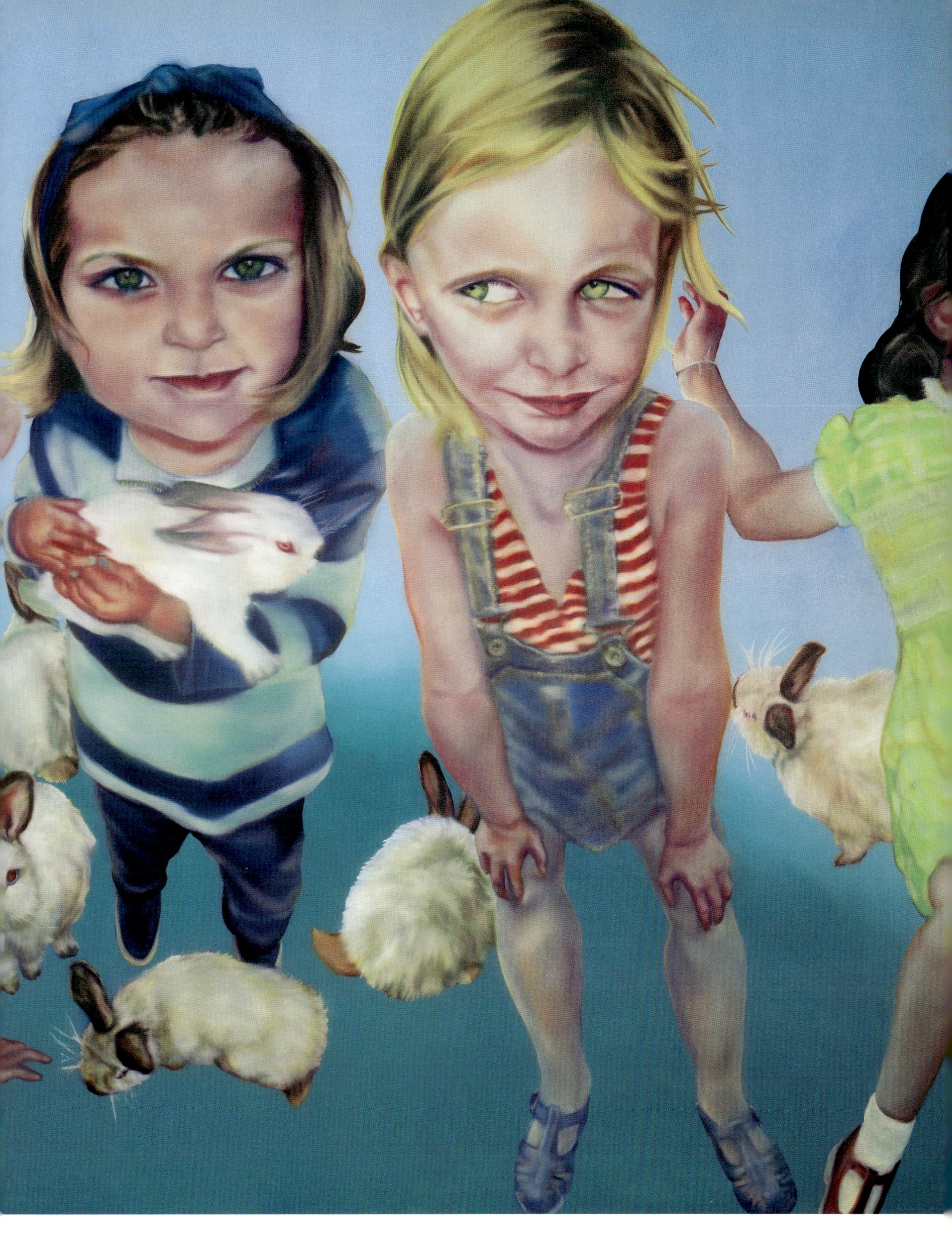

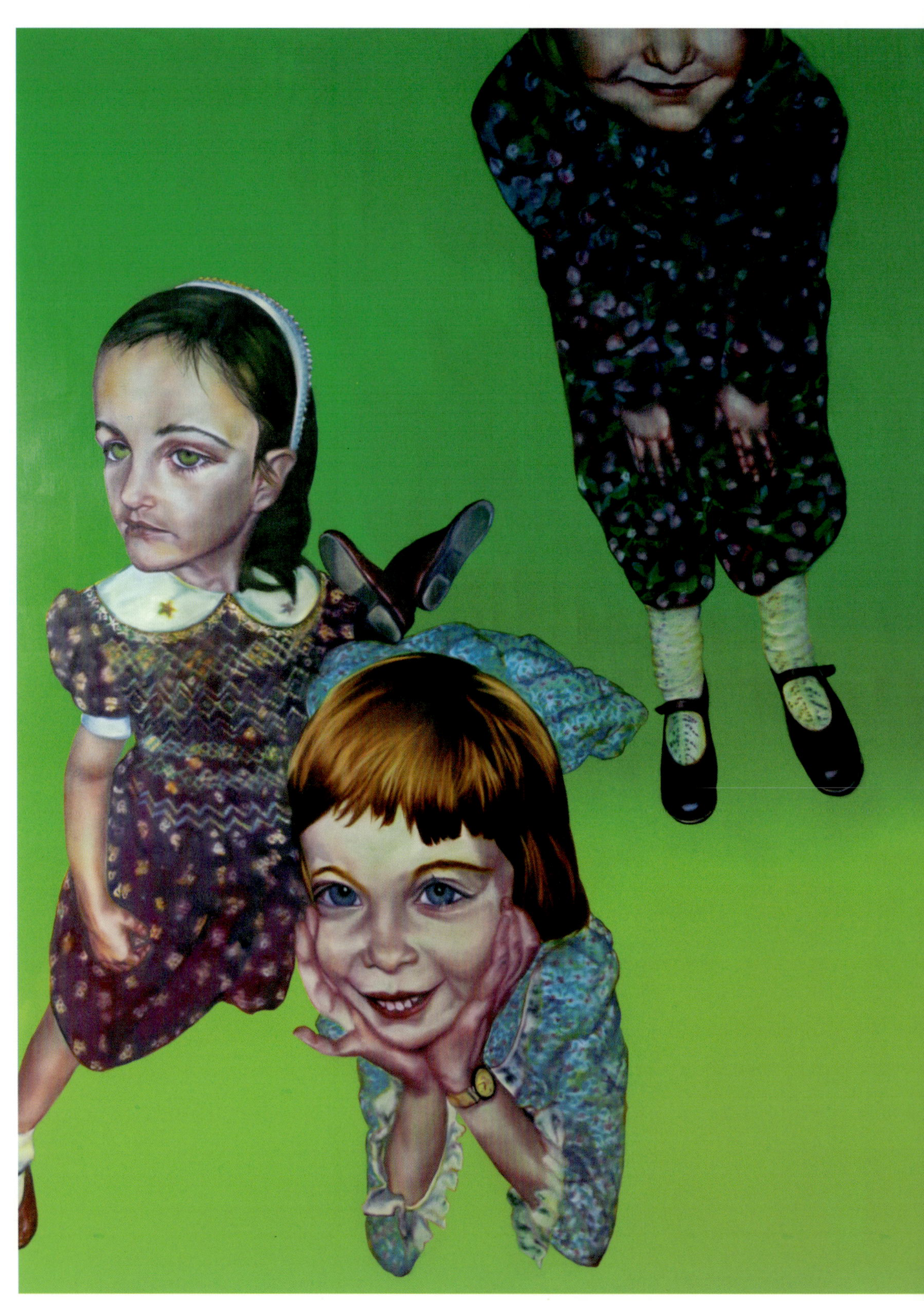

NICKY HOBERMAN

Hide and Seek 1997
oil on canvas
244 x 350cm/96 x 137³/₄in

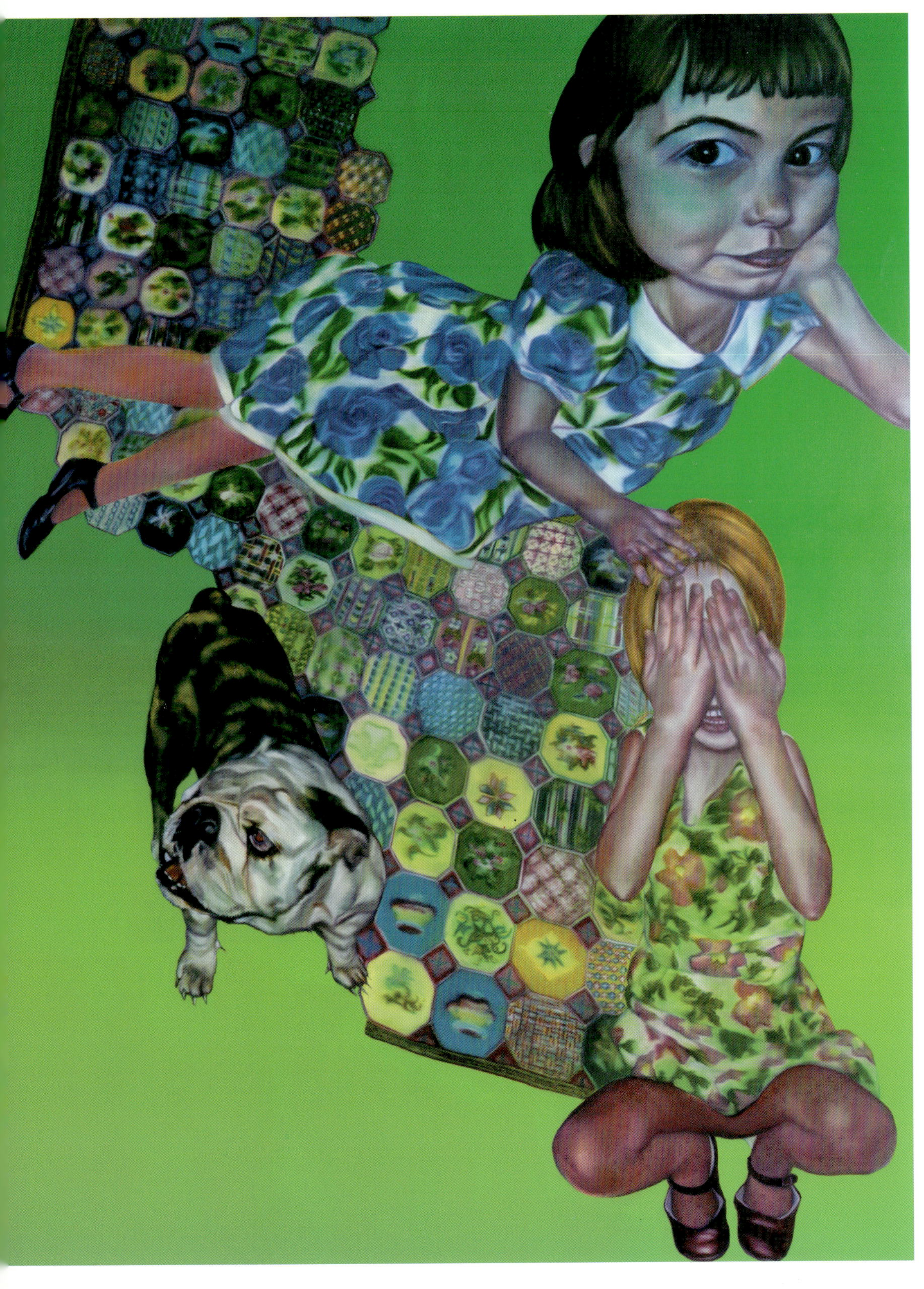

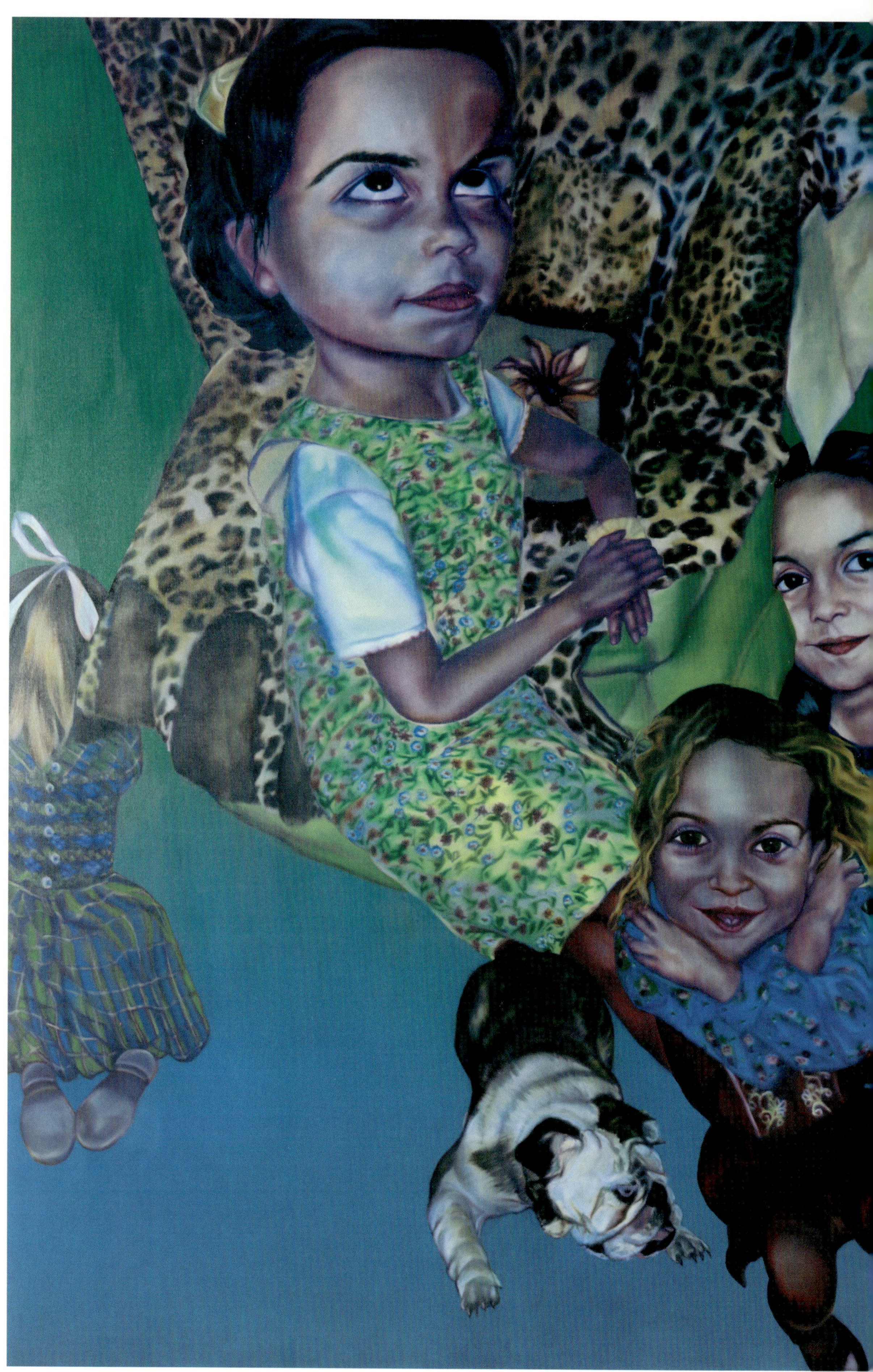

NICKY HOBERMAN

Camouflage 1998
oil on canvas
244 x 350cm/96 x 137³/₄in

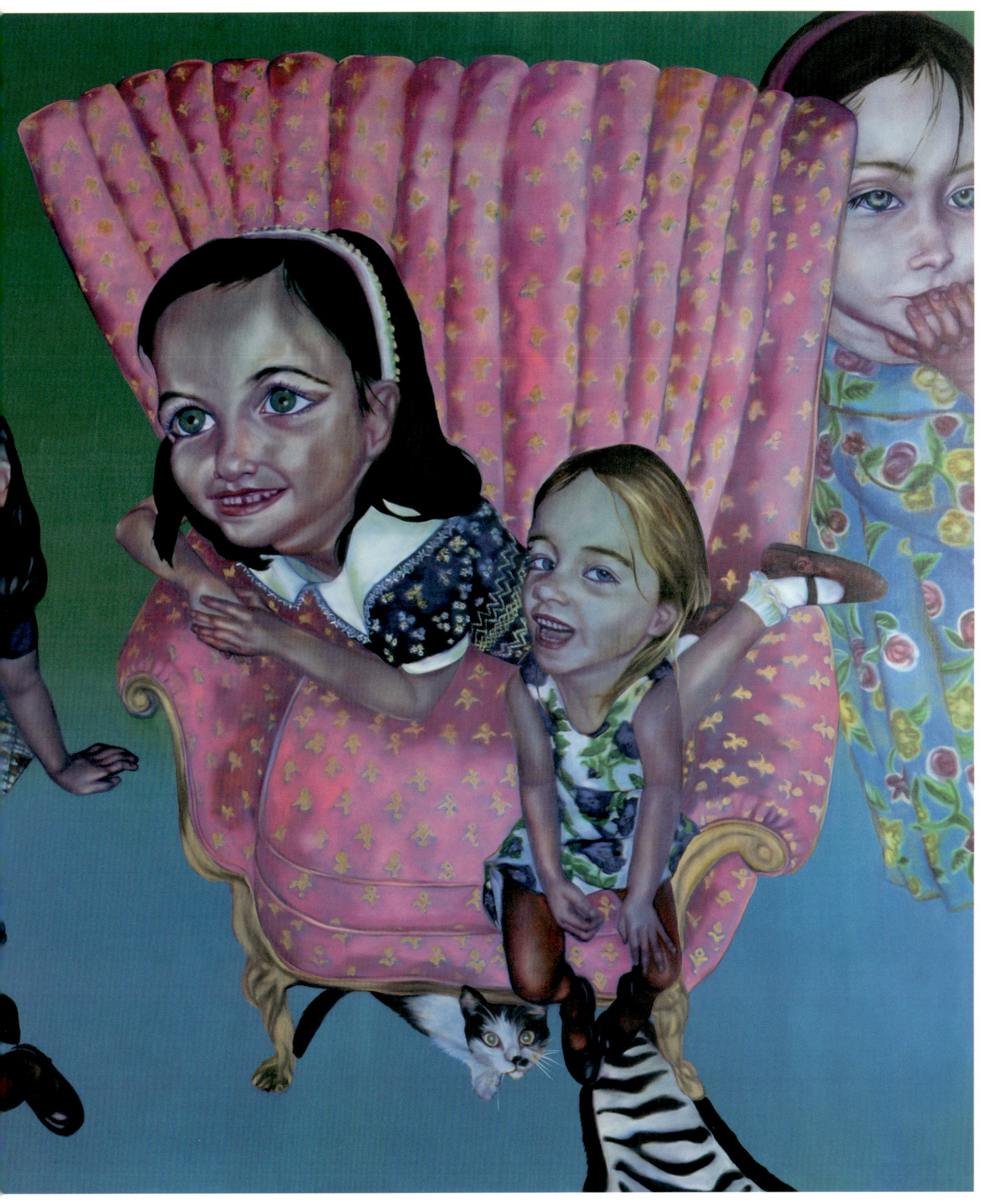

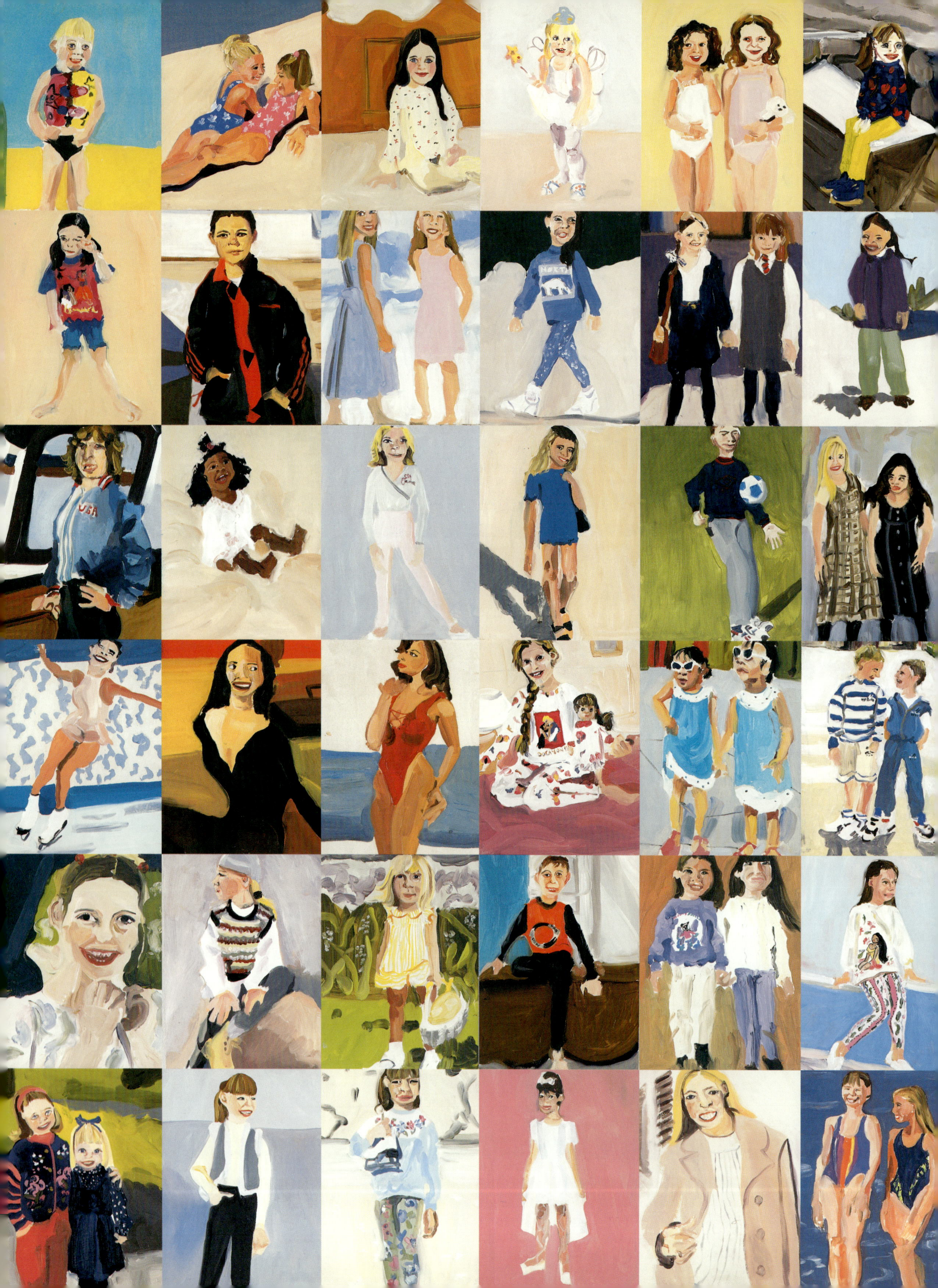

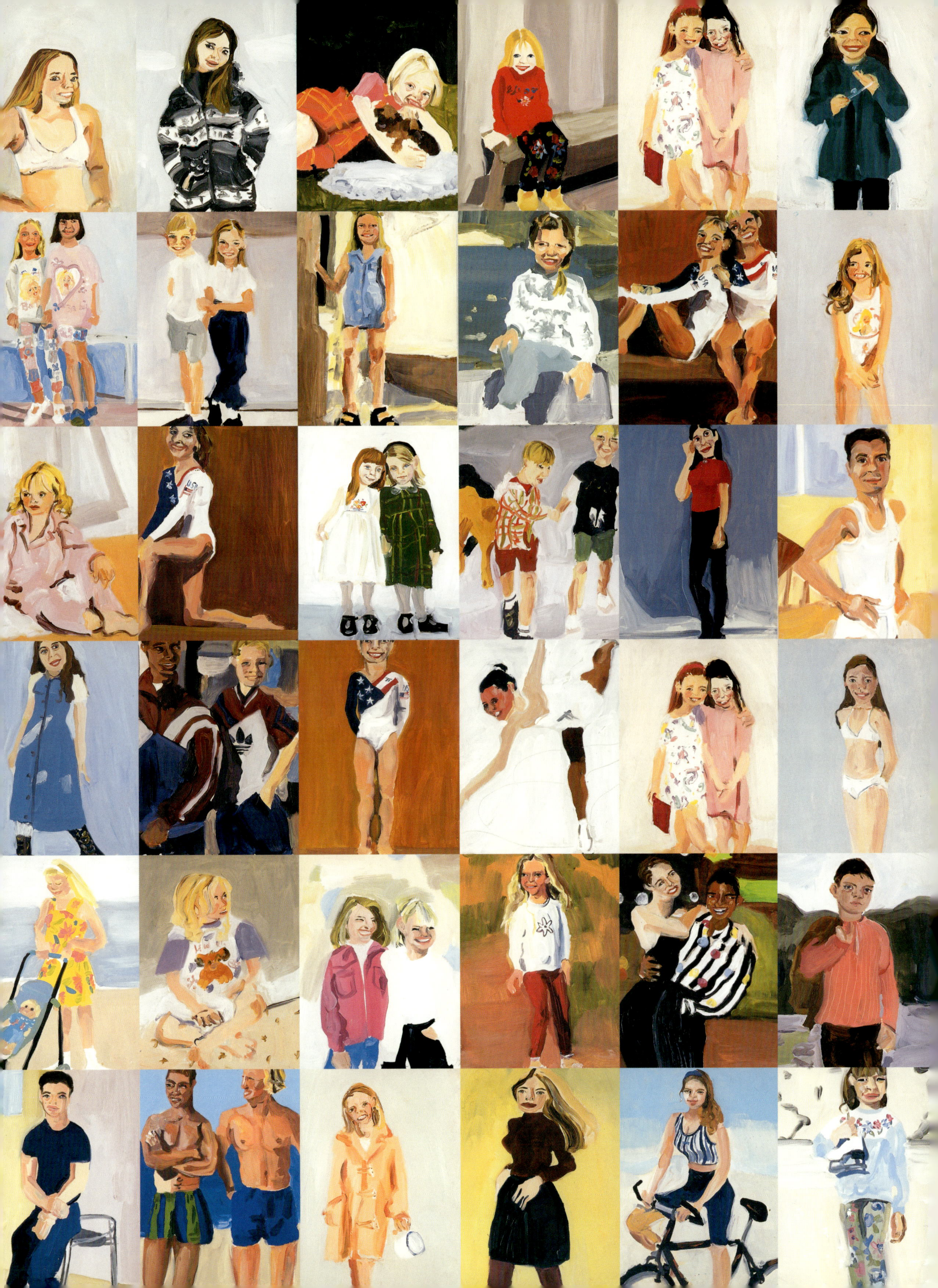

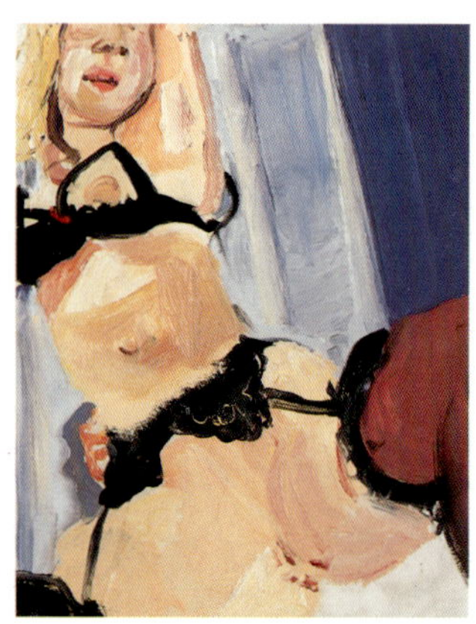
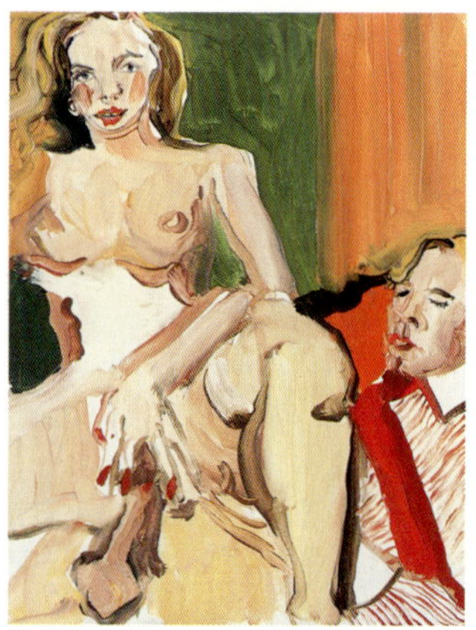
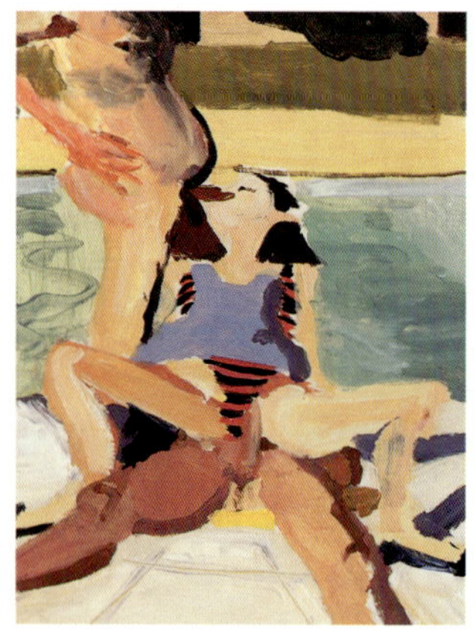
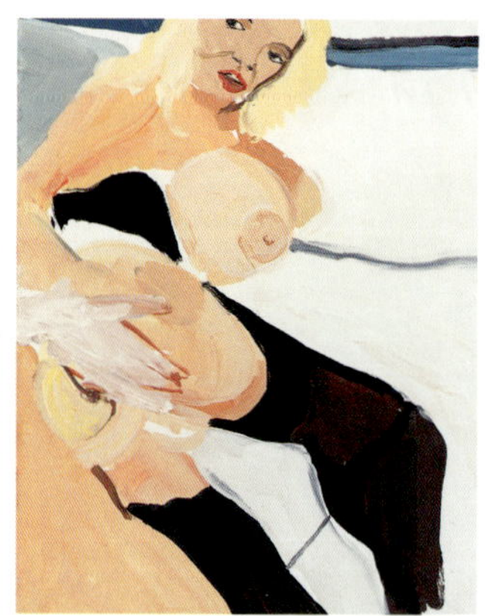

CHANTAL JOFFE

Untitled (8 paintings)1995-96
oil on gesso on board
29.2 x 21.6cm/11^{1}/$_{2}$ x 8^{1}/$_{2}$in

previous page:
Untitled (72 paintings)1995-96
oil on gesso on board
29.2 x 21.6cm/11^{1}/$_{2}$ x 8^{1}/$_{2}$in

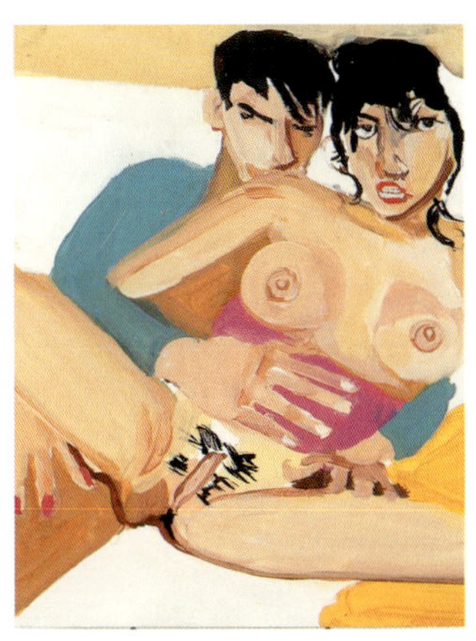
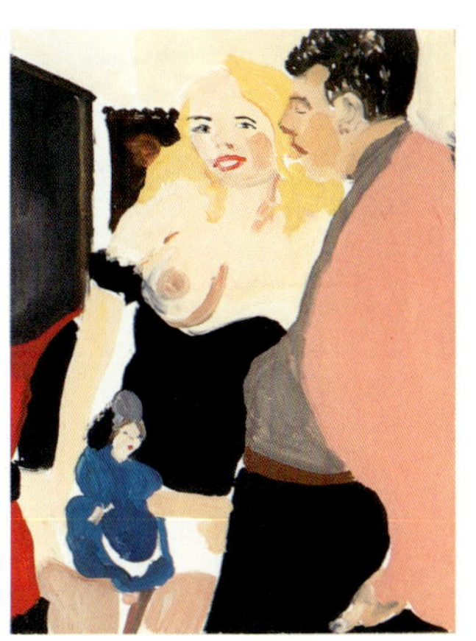
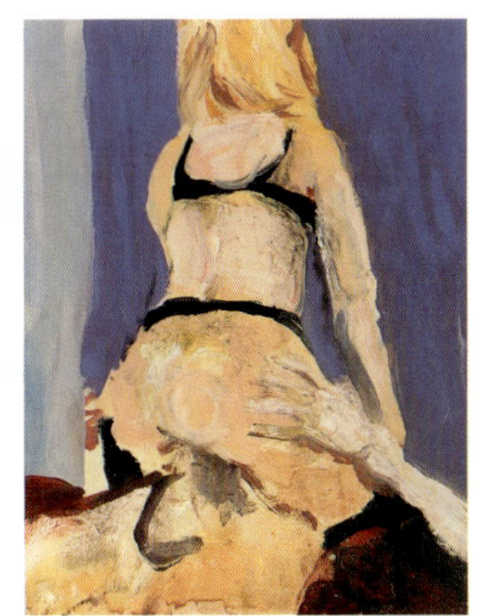
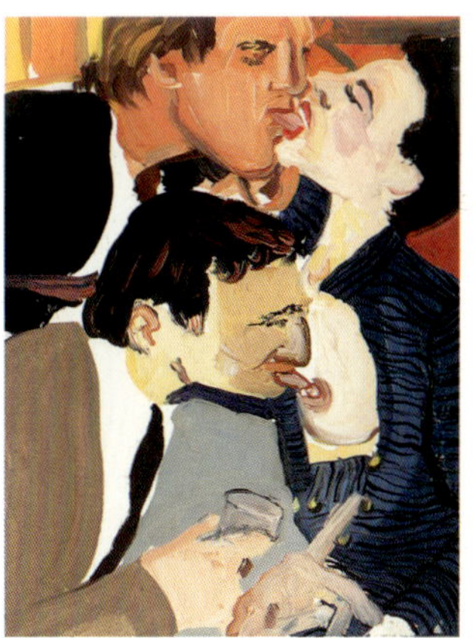

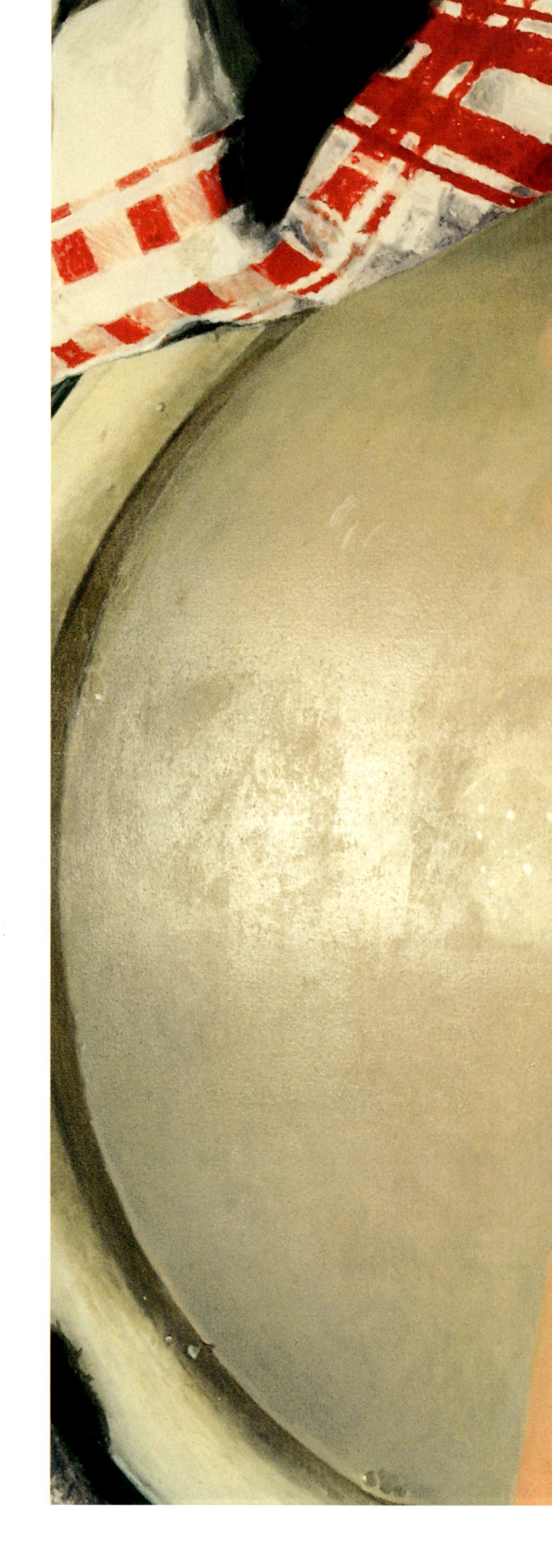

FELICIA LARSSON

Washing My Hands Clean 1995
oil on canvas
213.4 x 243.8cm/84 x 96in

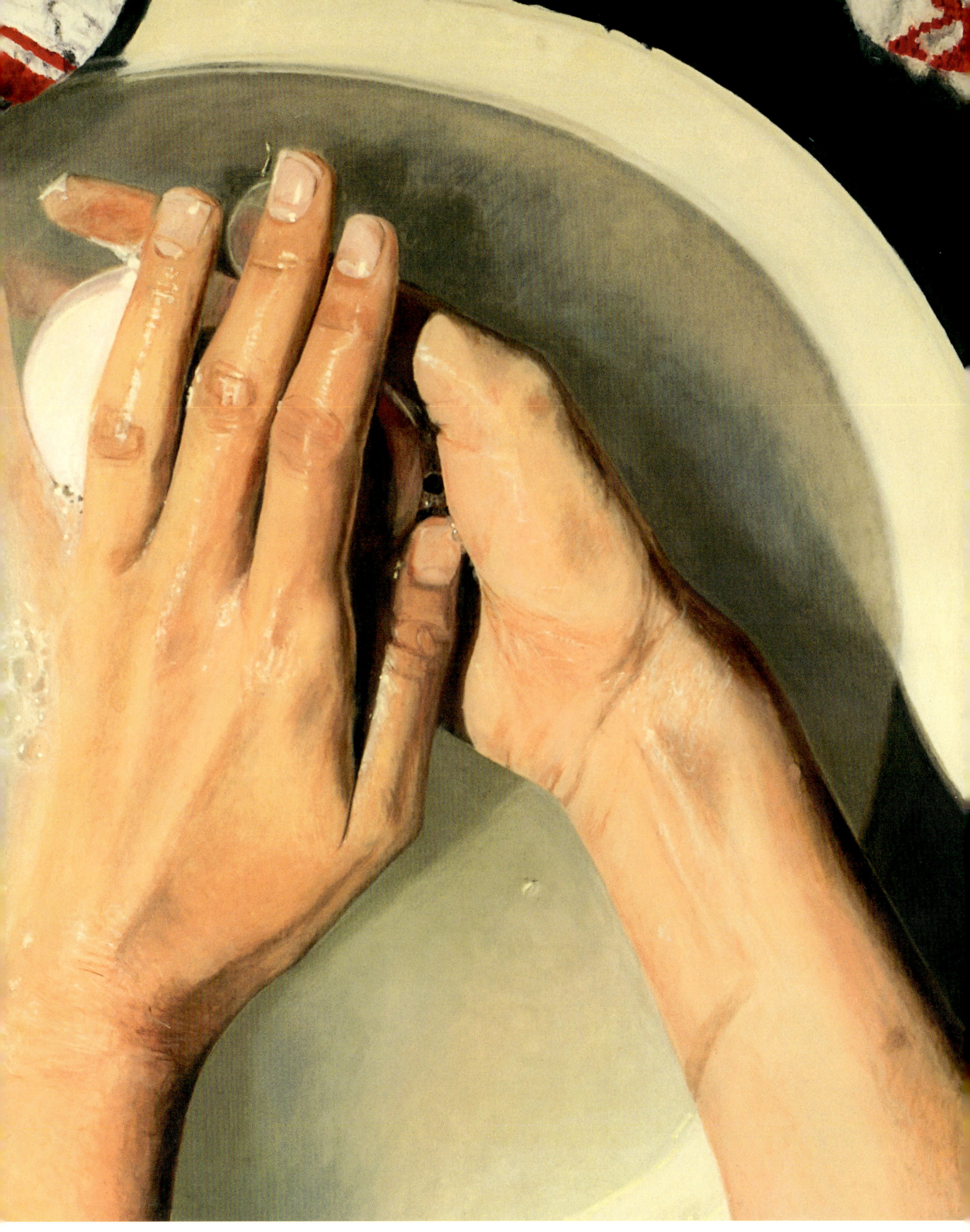

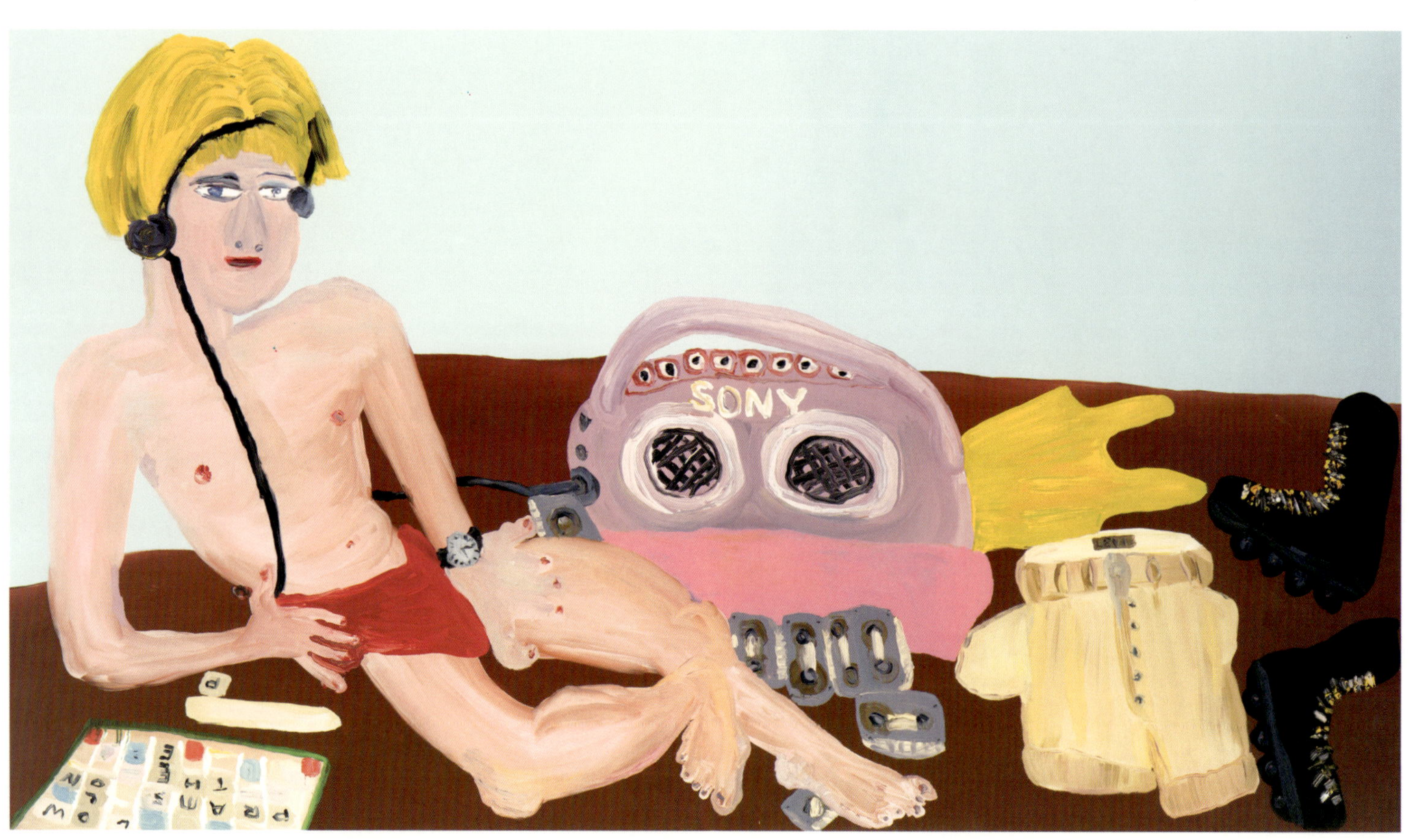

MARTIN MALONEY

Sony Levi 1997
oil on canvas
173.5 x 298cm/68¹/₄ x 117¹/₄in

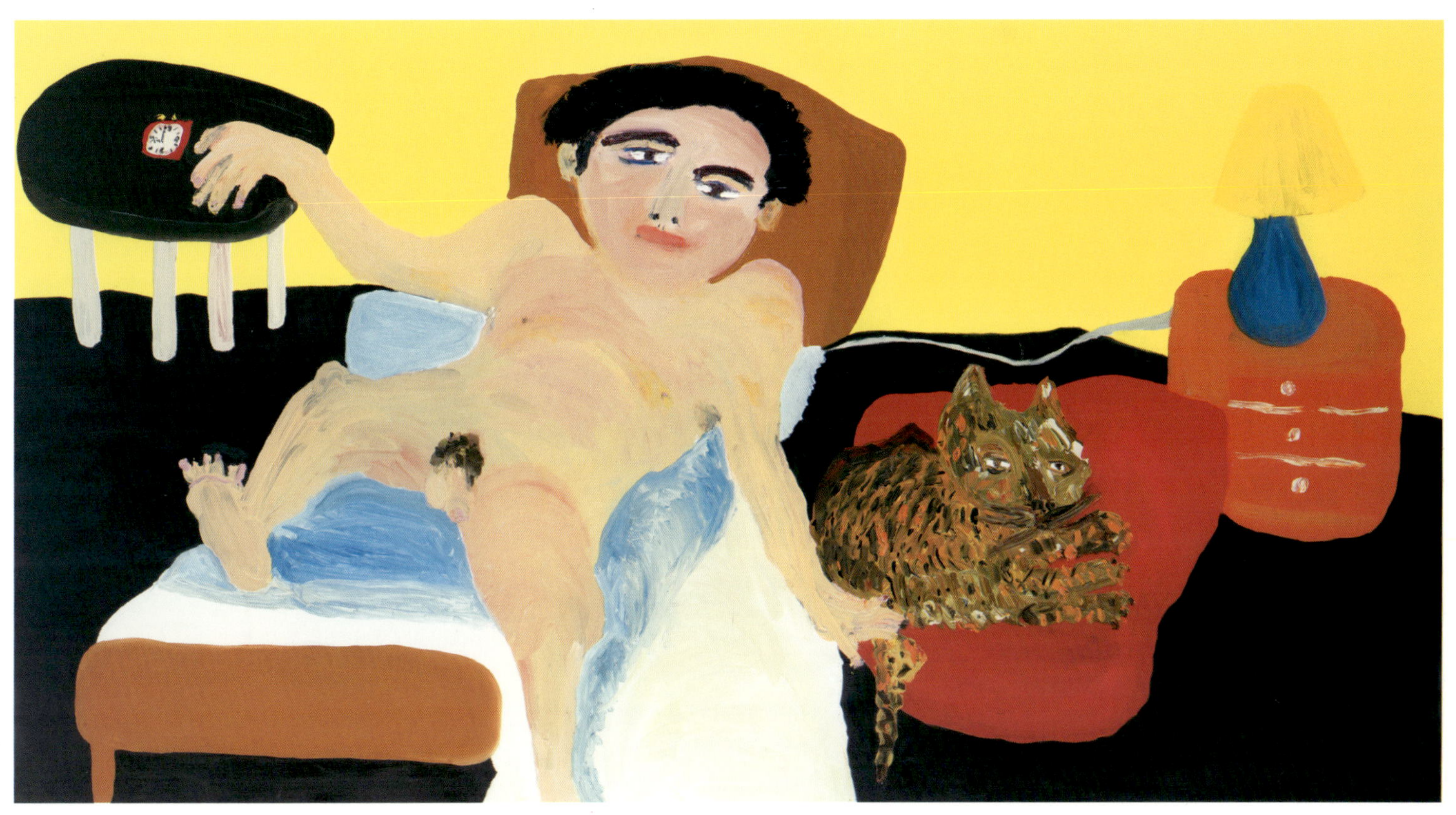

MARTIN MALONEY

Sleeping Arrangements 1997
oil on canvas
167.5 x 297cm/66 x 117in

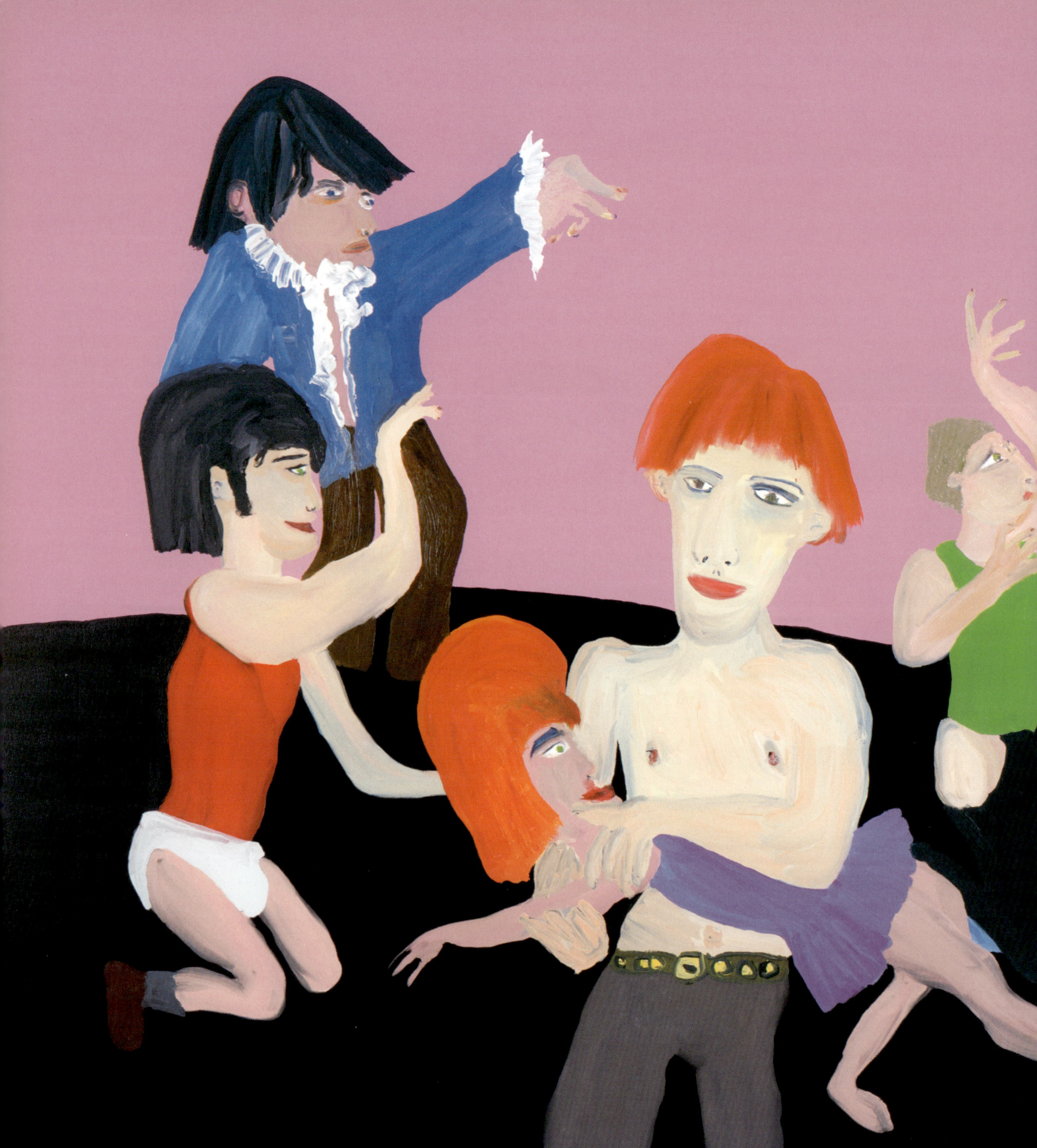

MARTIN MALONEY

Rave (After Poussin's Triumph of Pan) 1997
oil on canvas
244 x 457cm/96 x 180in

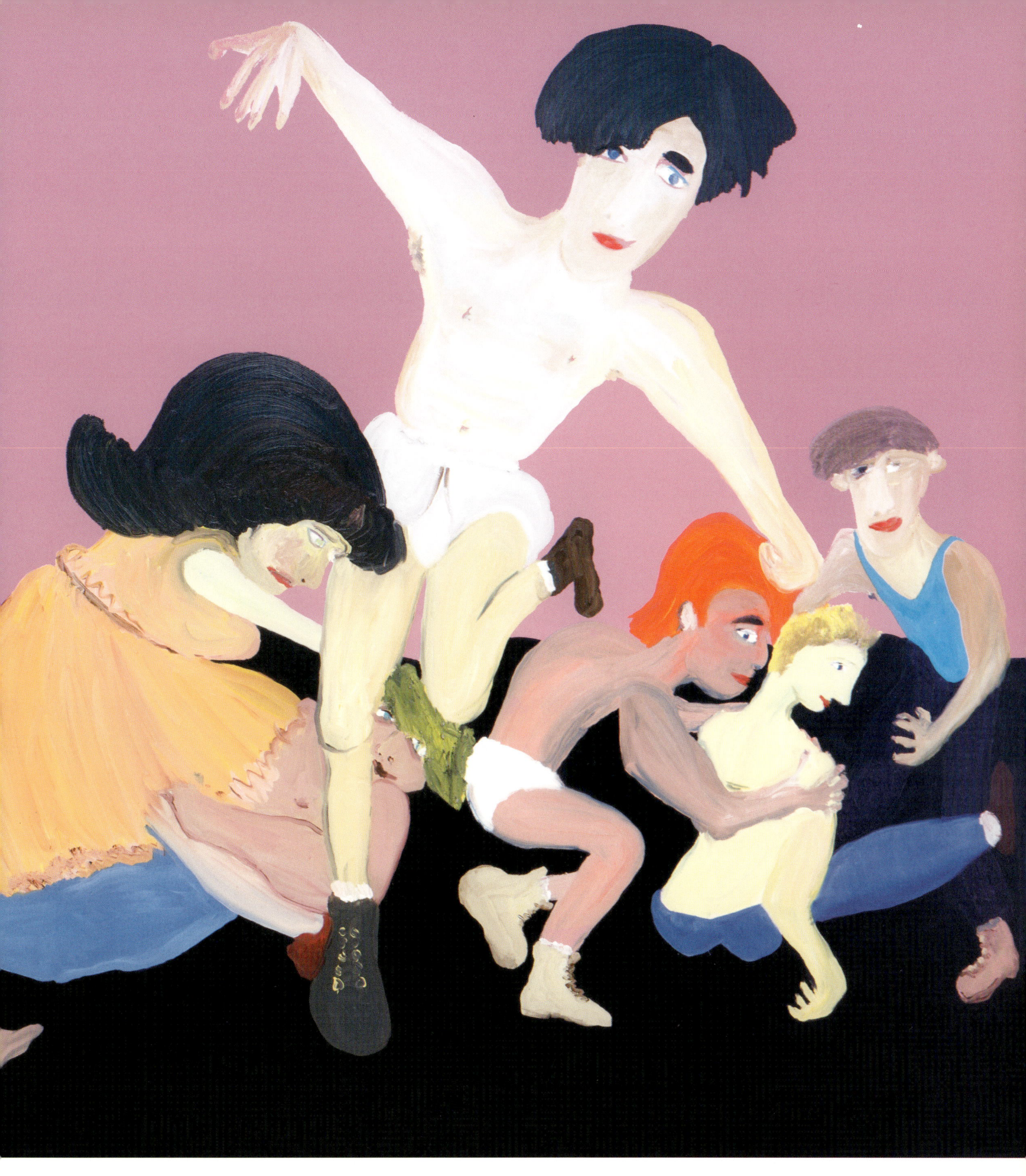

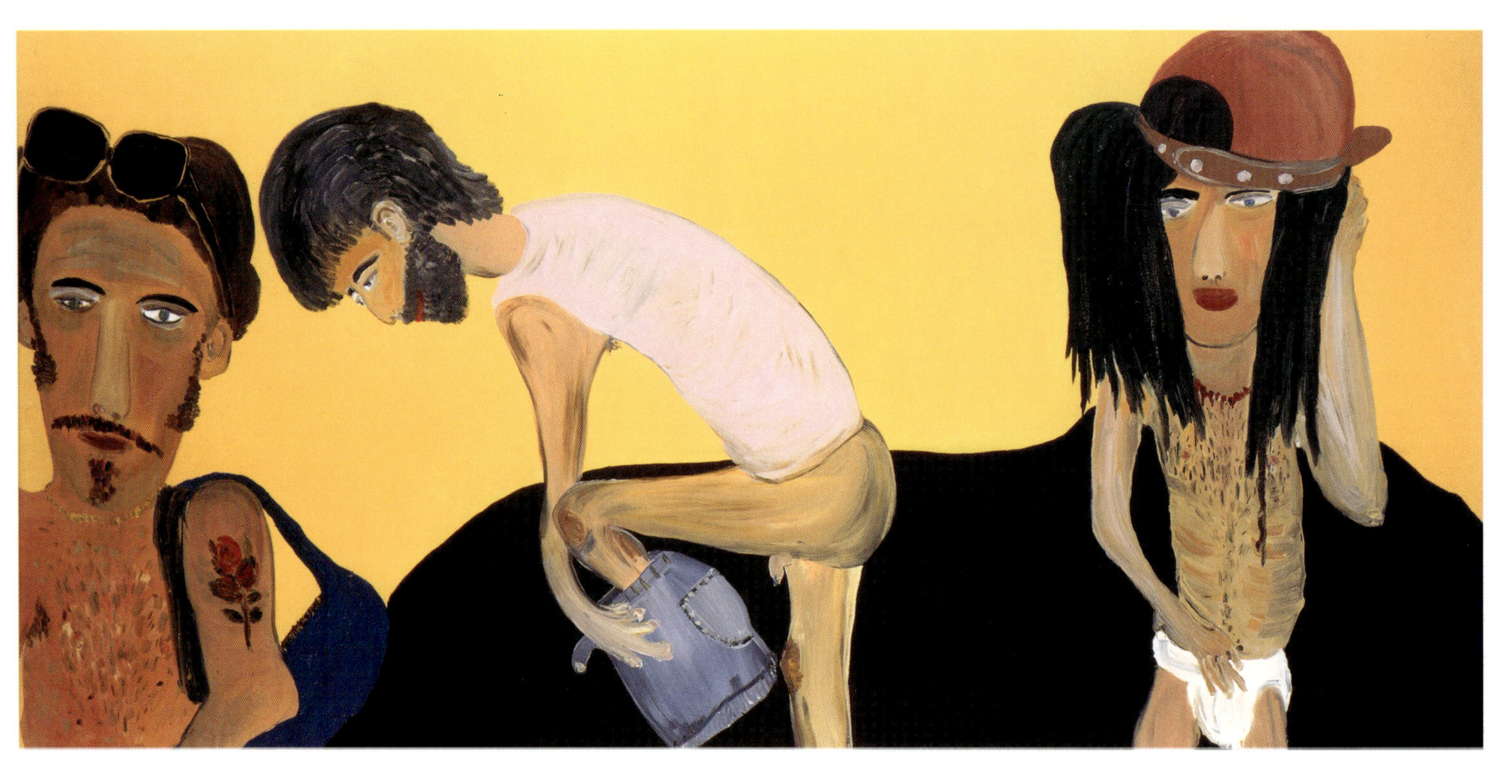

MARTIN MALONEY

A Conversation Piece #3: Getting Dressed 1998
oil on canvas
172 x 348cm/67³/₄ x 137in

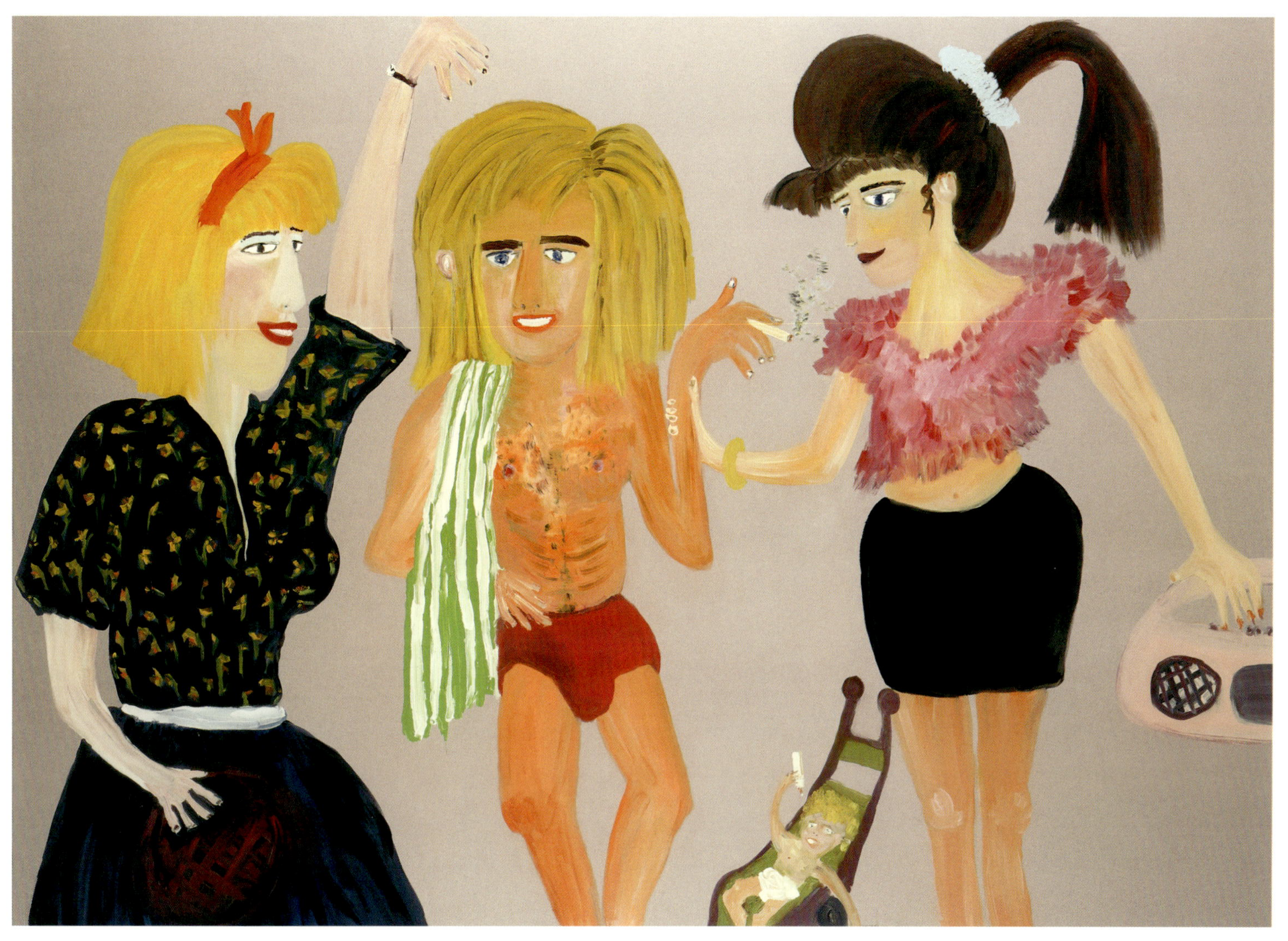

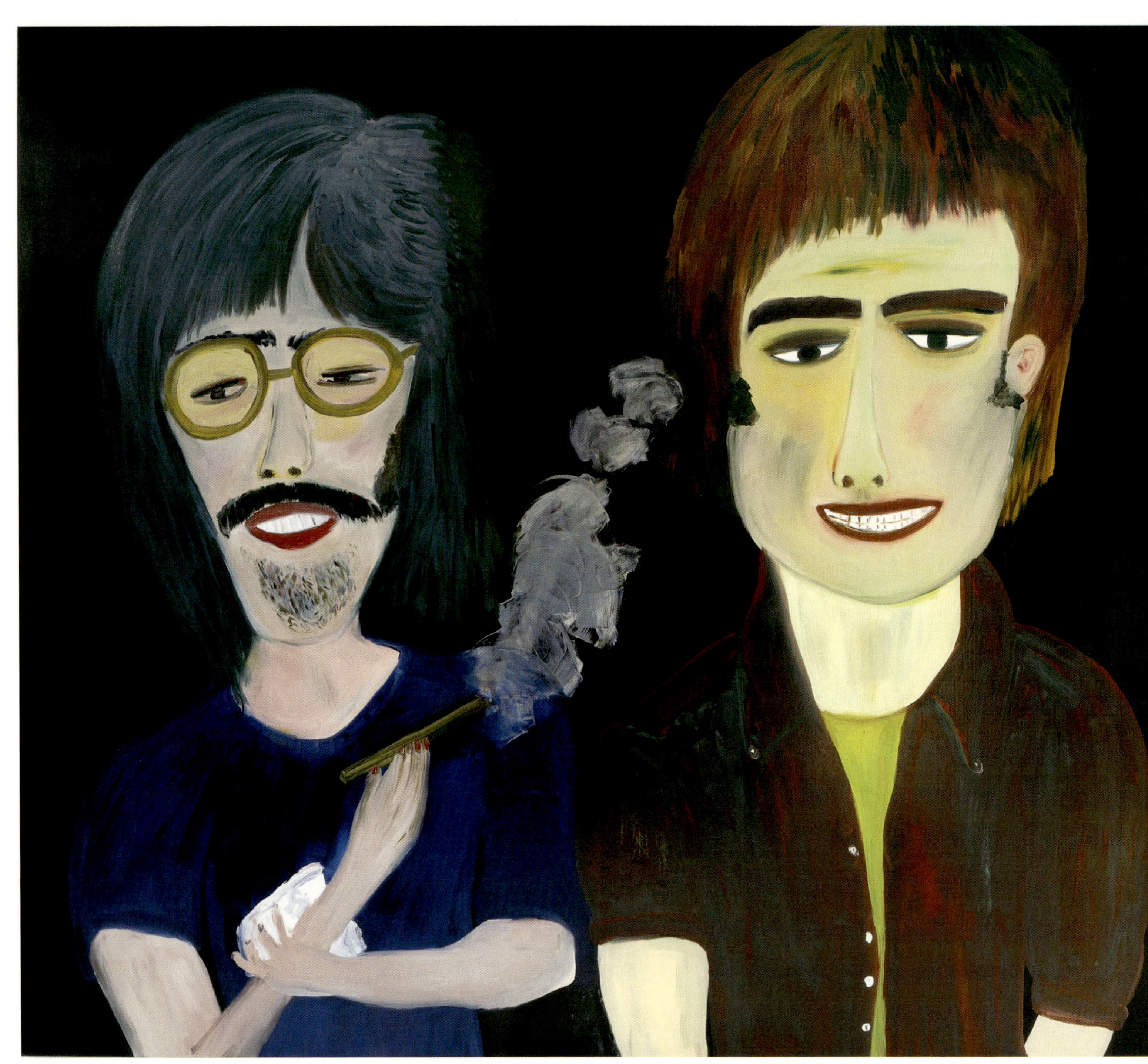

MARTIN MALONEY

Sex Club (M&S-S&M) 1998
from a series of 12 paintings
oil on canvas
274.3 x 609.6cm/108 x 240in

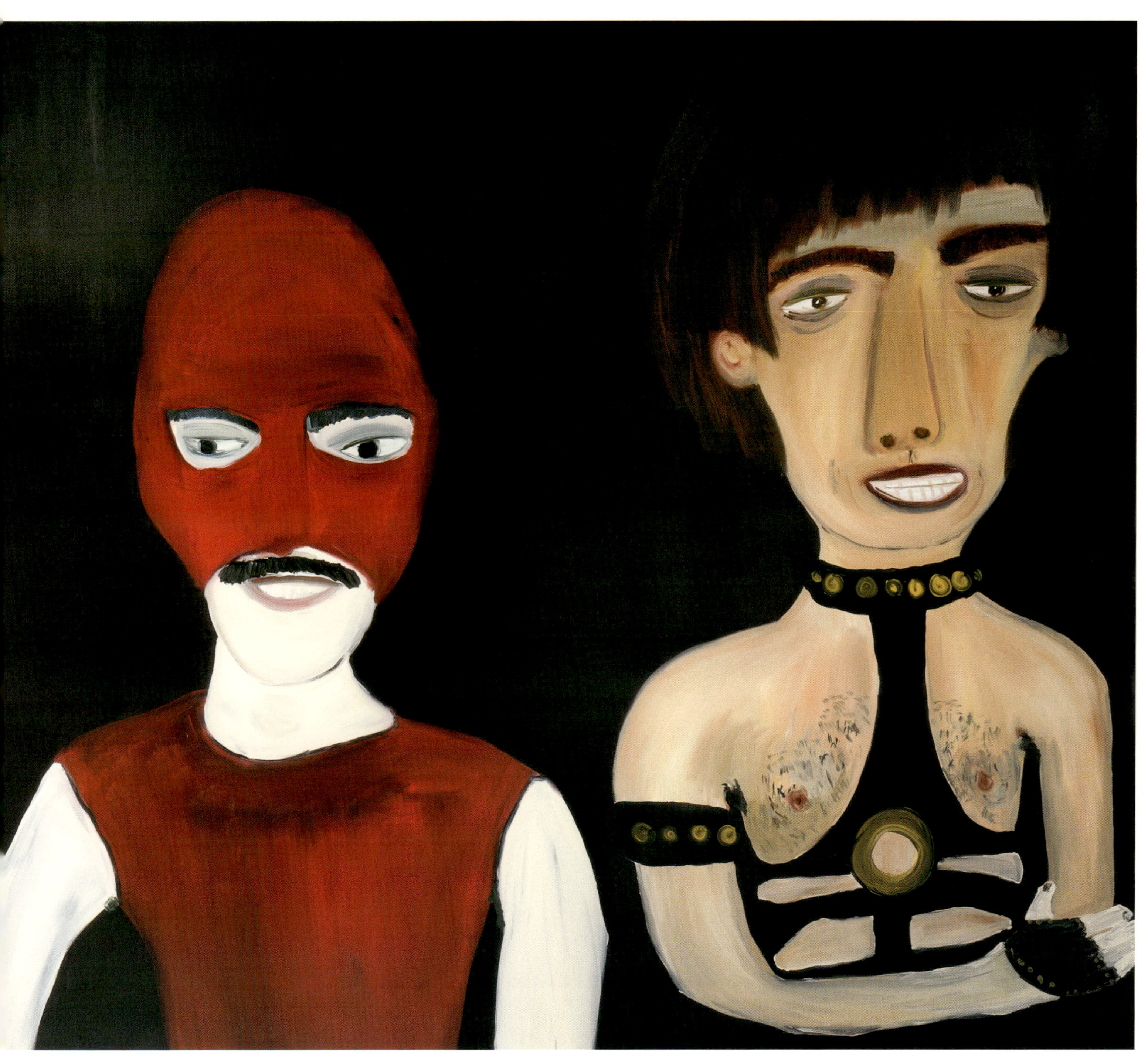

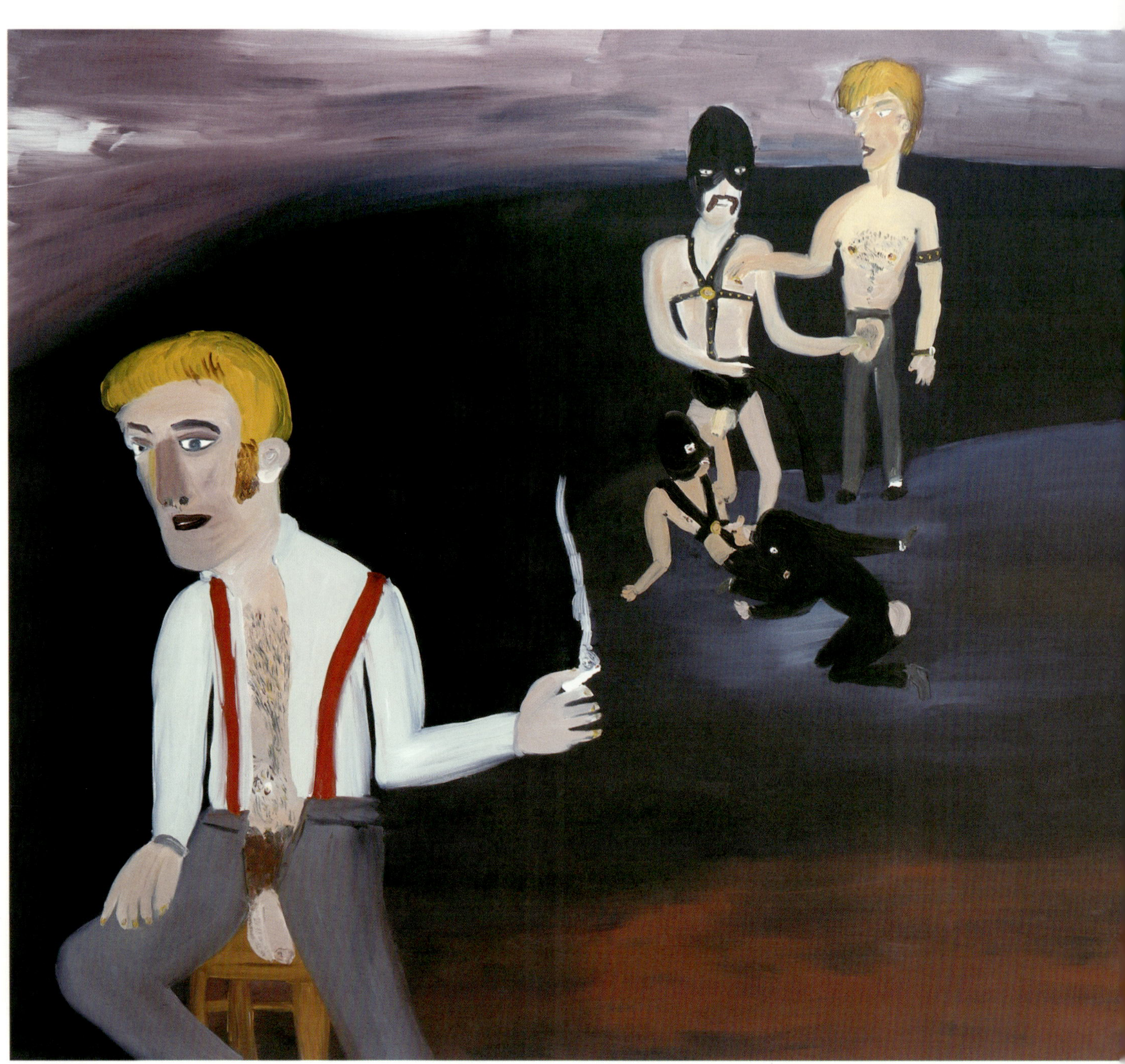

MARTIN MALONEY

Sex Club (Cowboys) 1998
from a series of 12 paintings
oil on canvas
274.3 x 609.6cm/108 x 240in

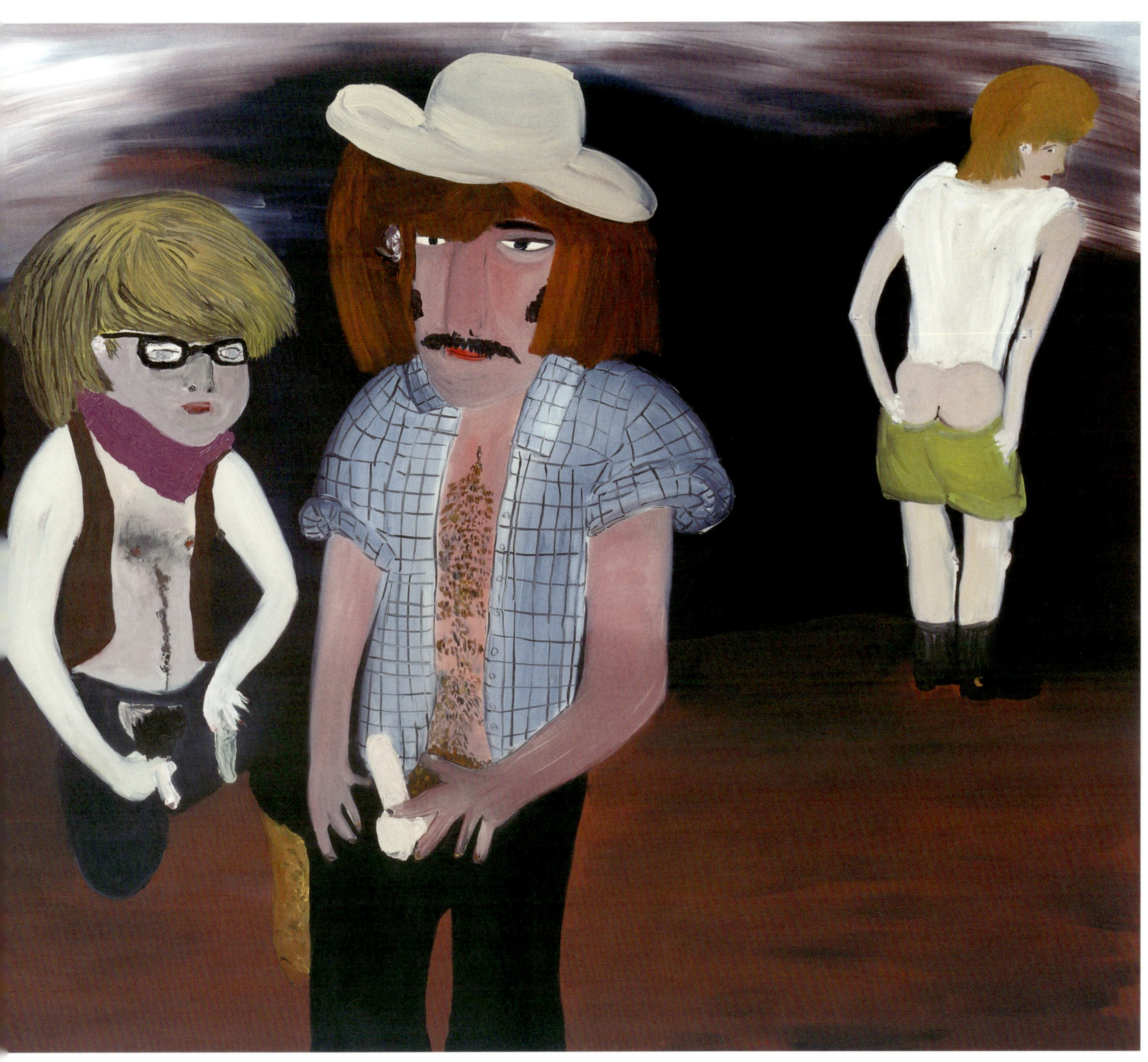

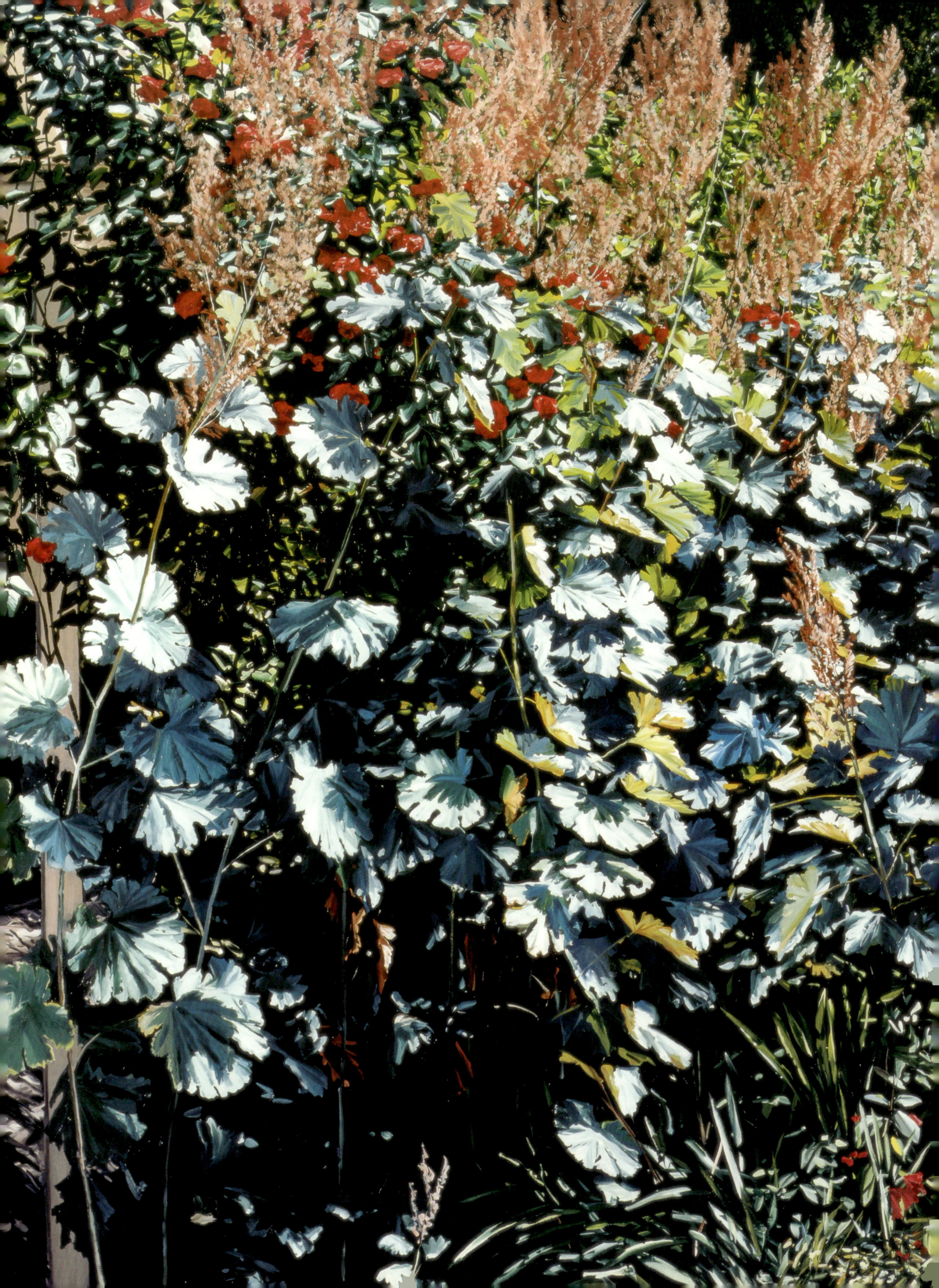

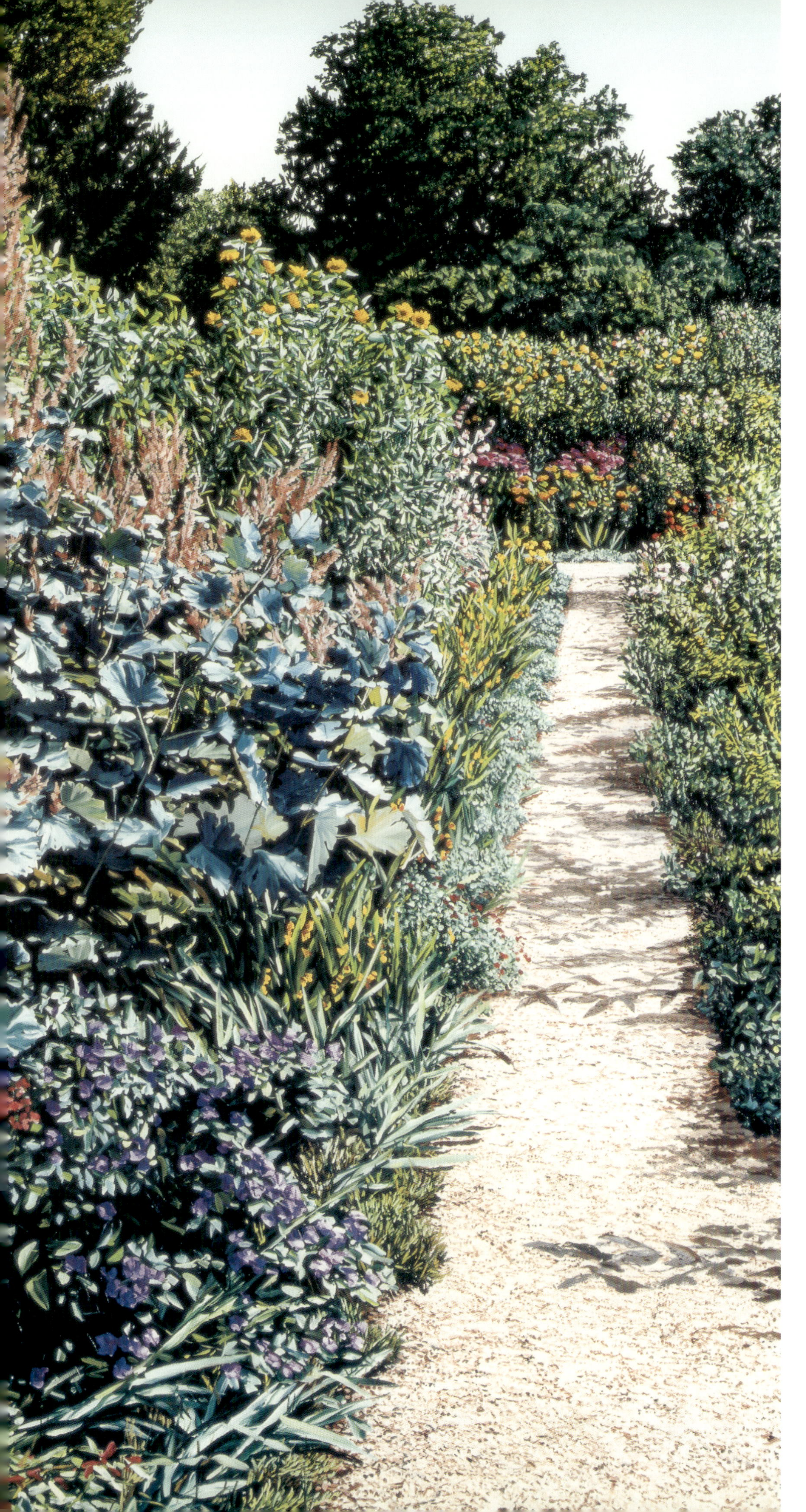

KARL MAUGHAN

Plume 1997
oil on canvas
200 x 250cm/78³/₄ x 98¹/₂in

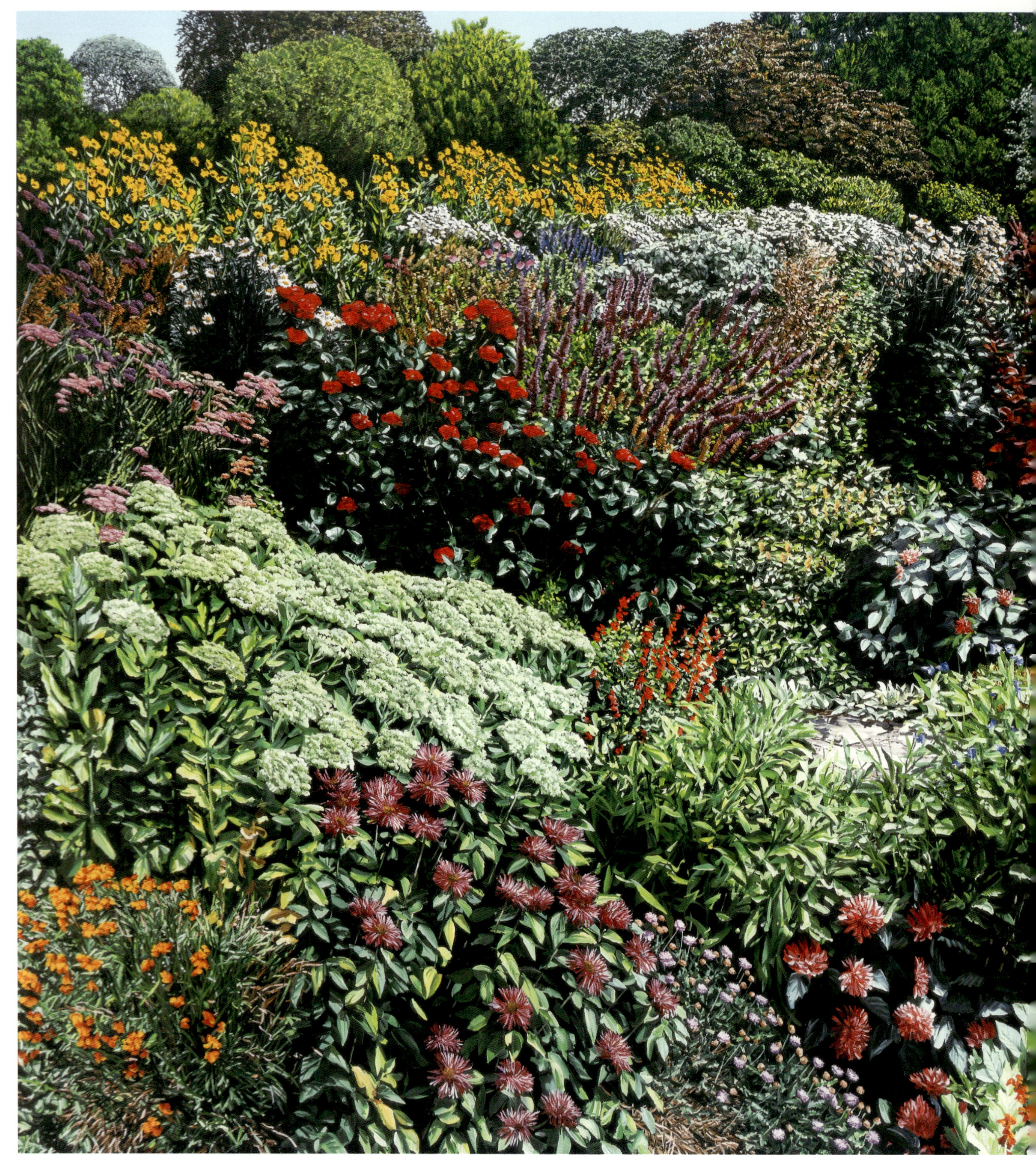

KARL MAUGHAN

Ashhurst 1998
oil on linen
182.9 x 304.8cm/72 x 120in

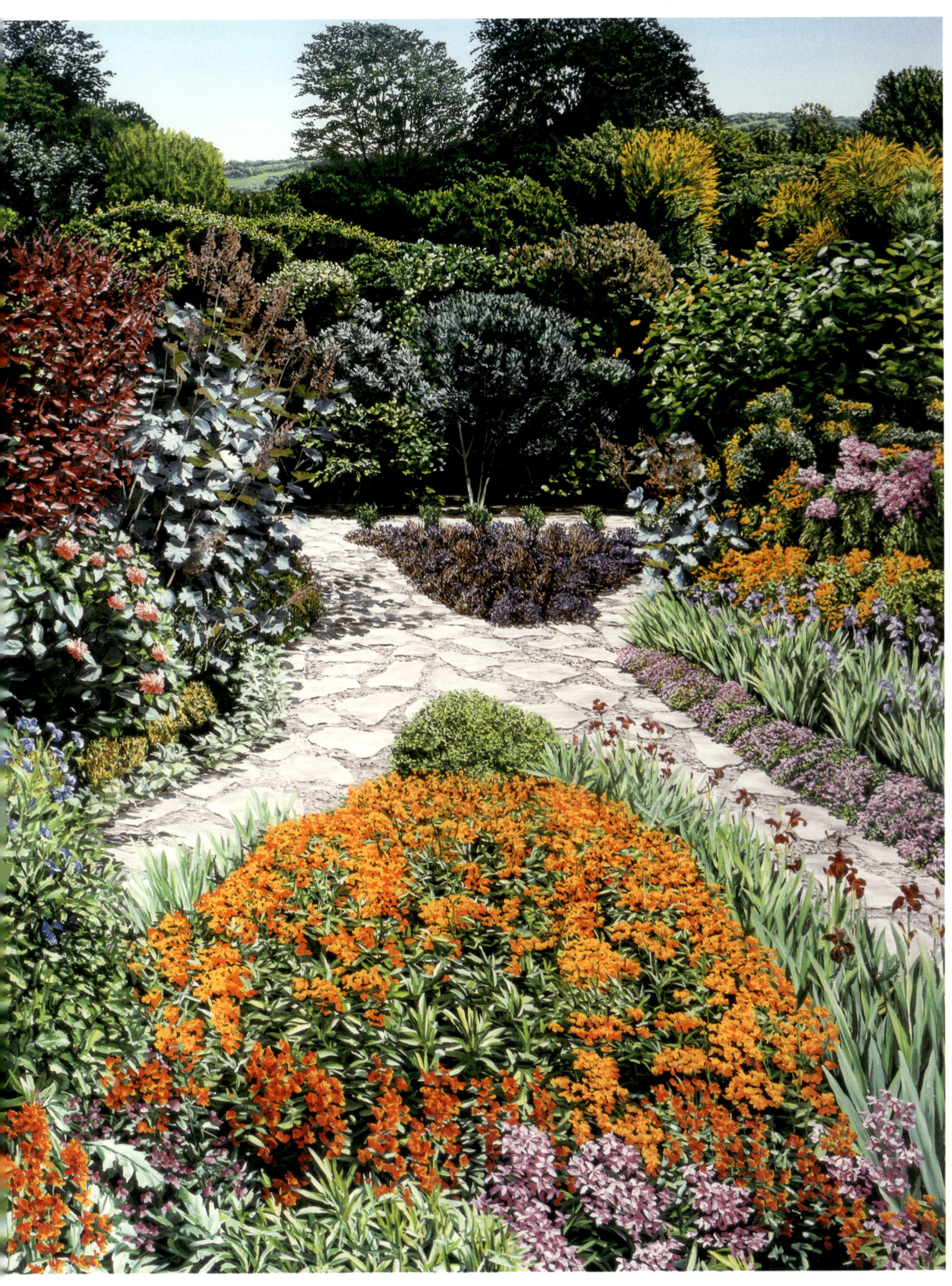

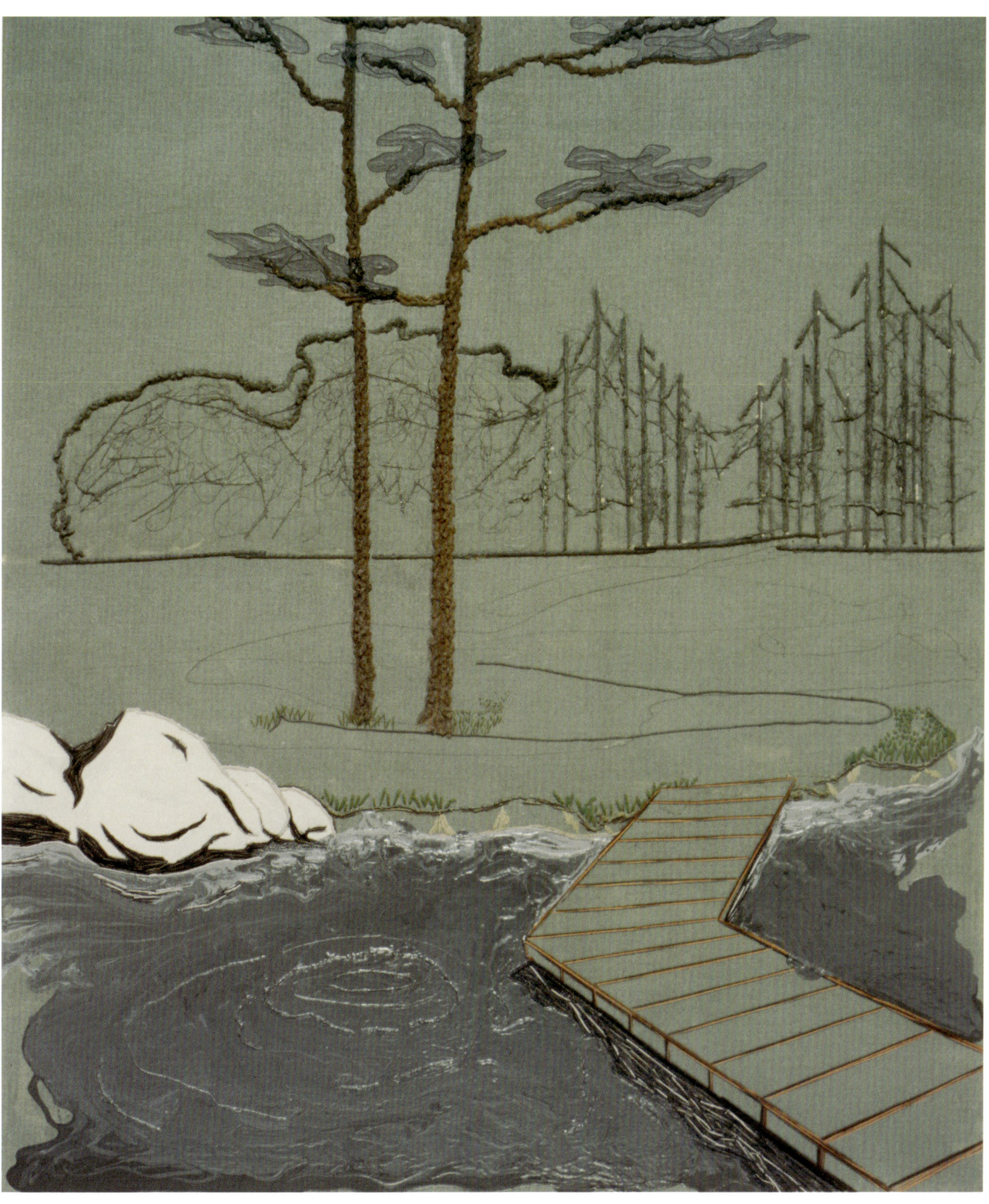

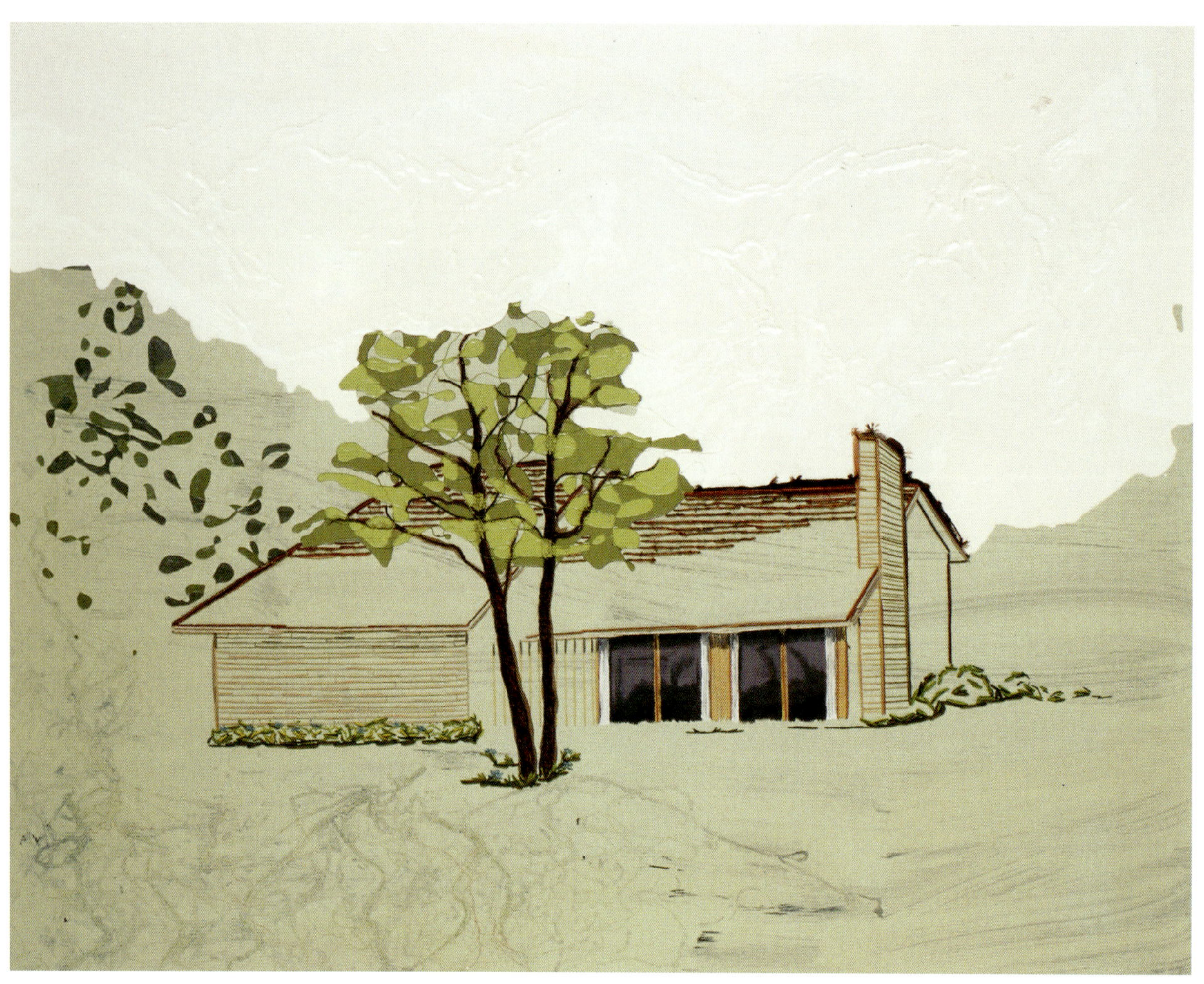

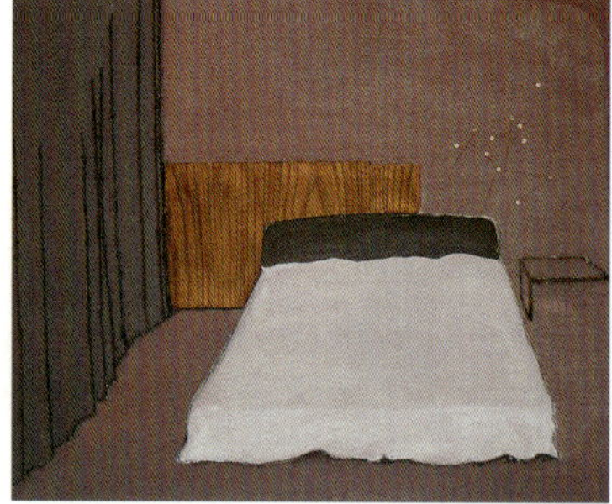

Room 2 1997
oil, acrylic, veneer and thread on linen
55 x 65cm/21$\frac{1}{2}$ x 25$\frac{1}{2}$in

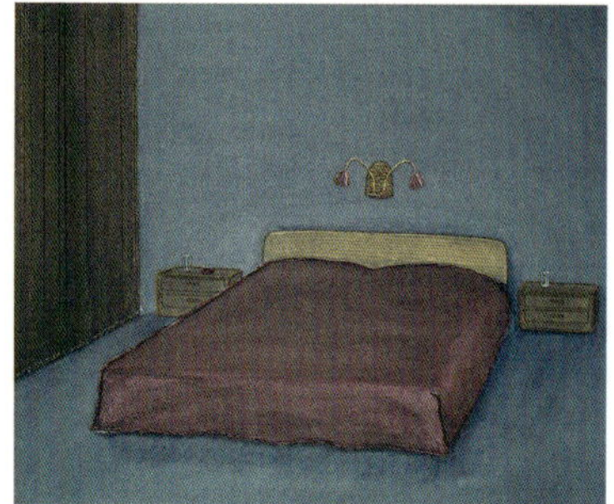

Room 5 1997
oil, acrylic, veneer and thread on linen
60 x 70cm/23$\frac{1}{2}$ x 27$\frac{1}{2}$in

MICHAEL RAEDECKER

Occluded 1997
acrylic and thread on linen
120 x 160cm/47$\frac{1}{4}$ x 63in

right:
Perspective 1997
acrylic, thread, veneer on linen
137.5 x 169cm/54 x 66in

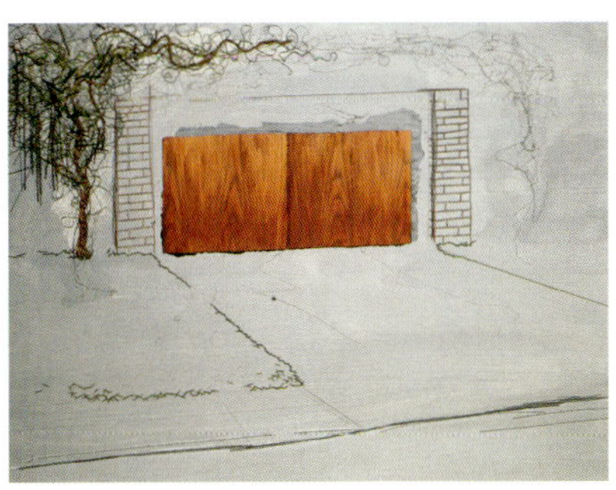

Still 1997
oil, acrylic, veneer and thread on linen
120 x 160cm/47$\frac{1}{4}$ x 63in

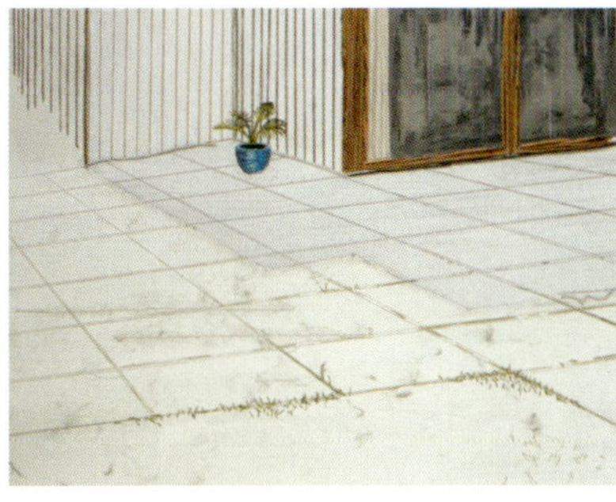

Shot 1997
oil, acrylic, veneer and thread on linen
50 x 70cm/19$\frac{3}{4}$ x 27$\frac{1}{2}$in

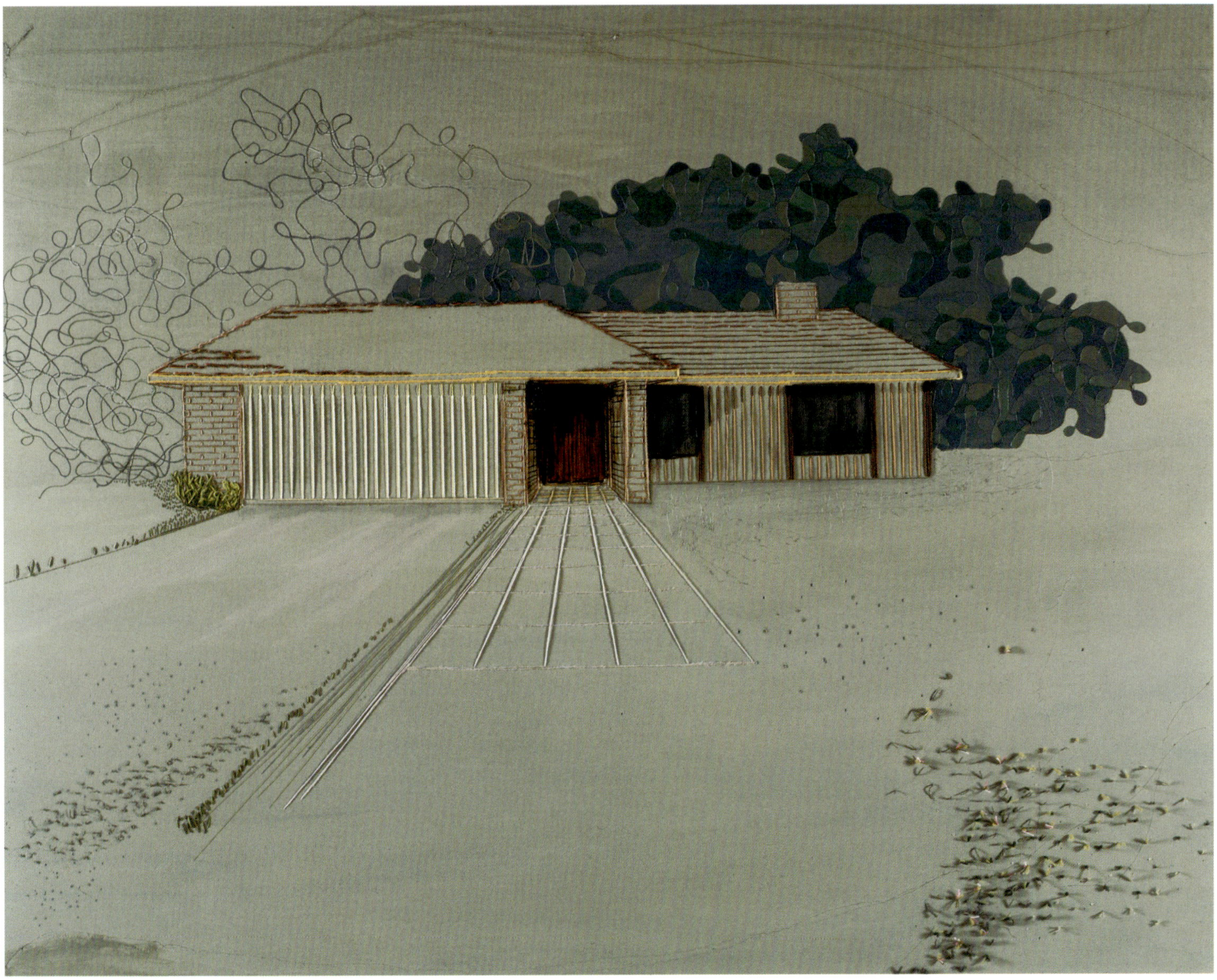

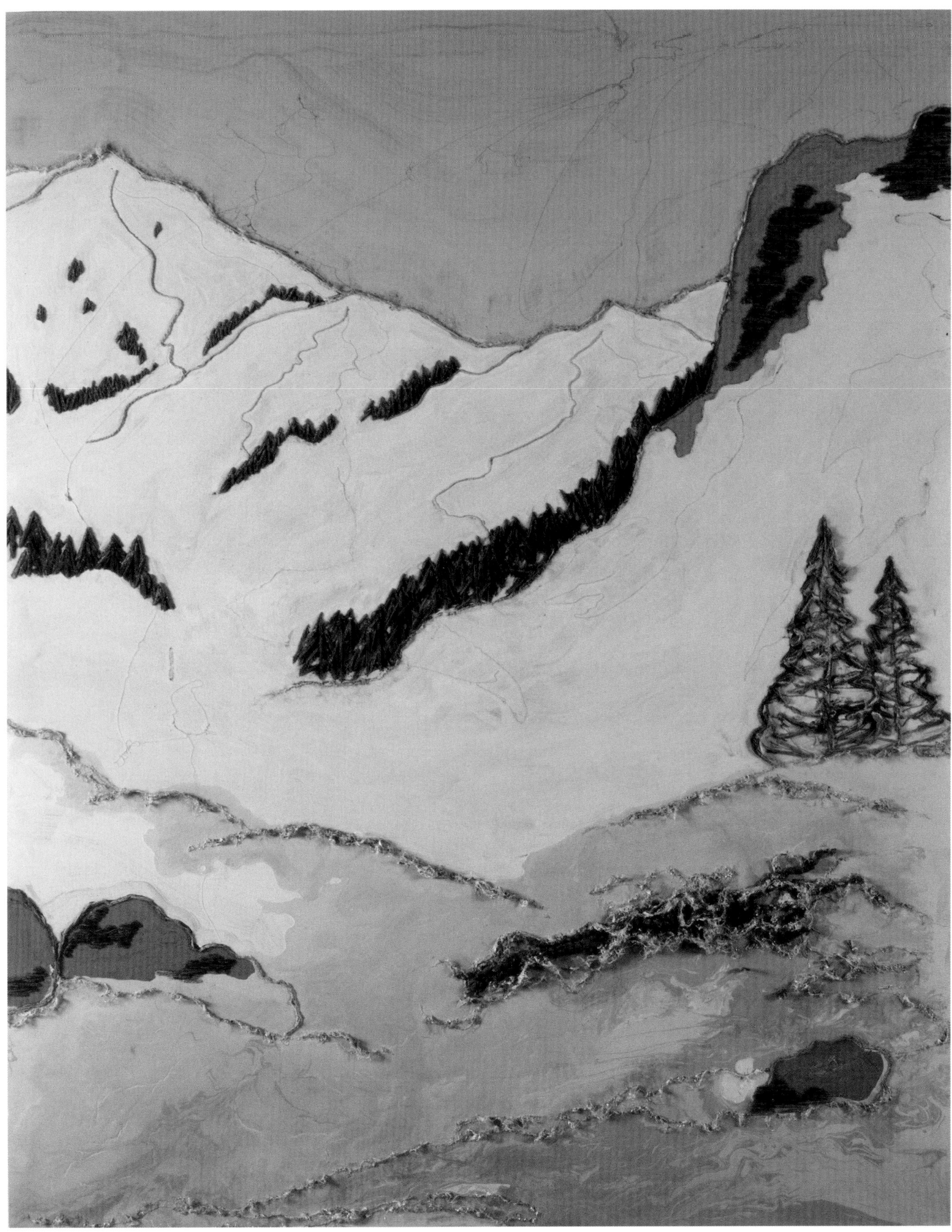

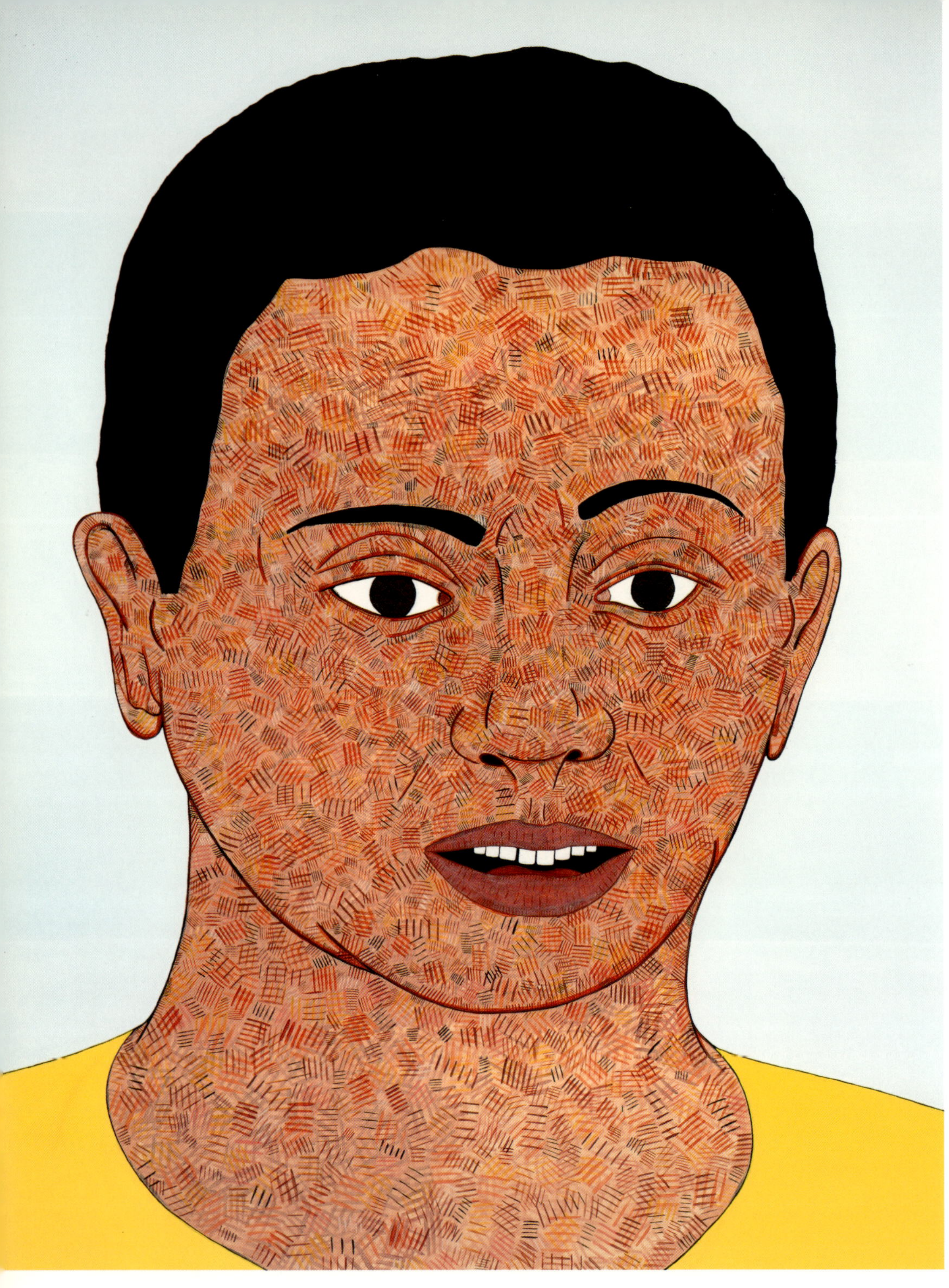

RICHARD REYNOLDS

Large Head (2) 1996
acrylic on canvas
270 x 200cm/106$\frac{1}{4}$ x 78$\frac{3}{4}$in

right:
Mine's Bigger Than Yours 1998
acrylic on canvas
270 x 200cm/106$\frac{1}{4}$ x 78$\frac{3}{4}$in

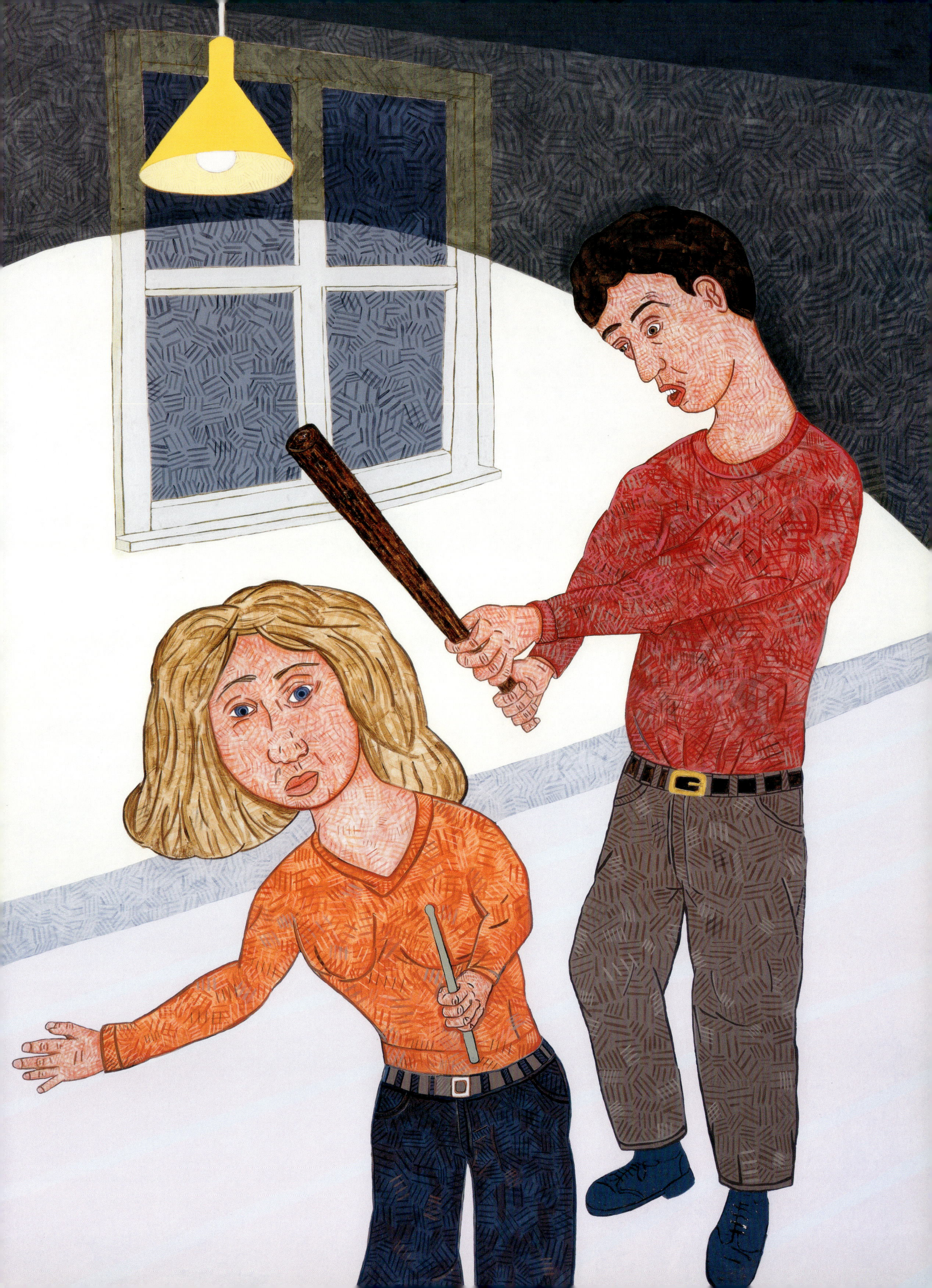

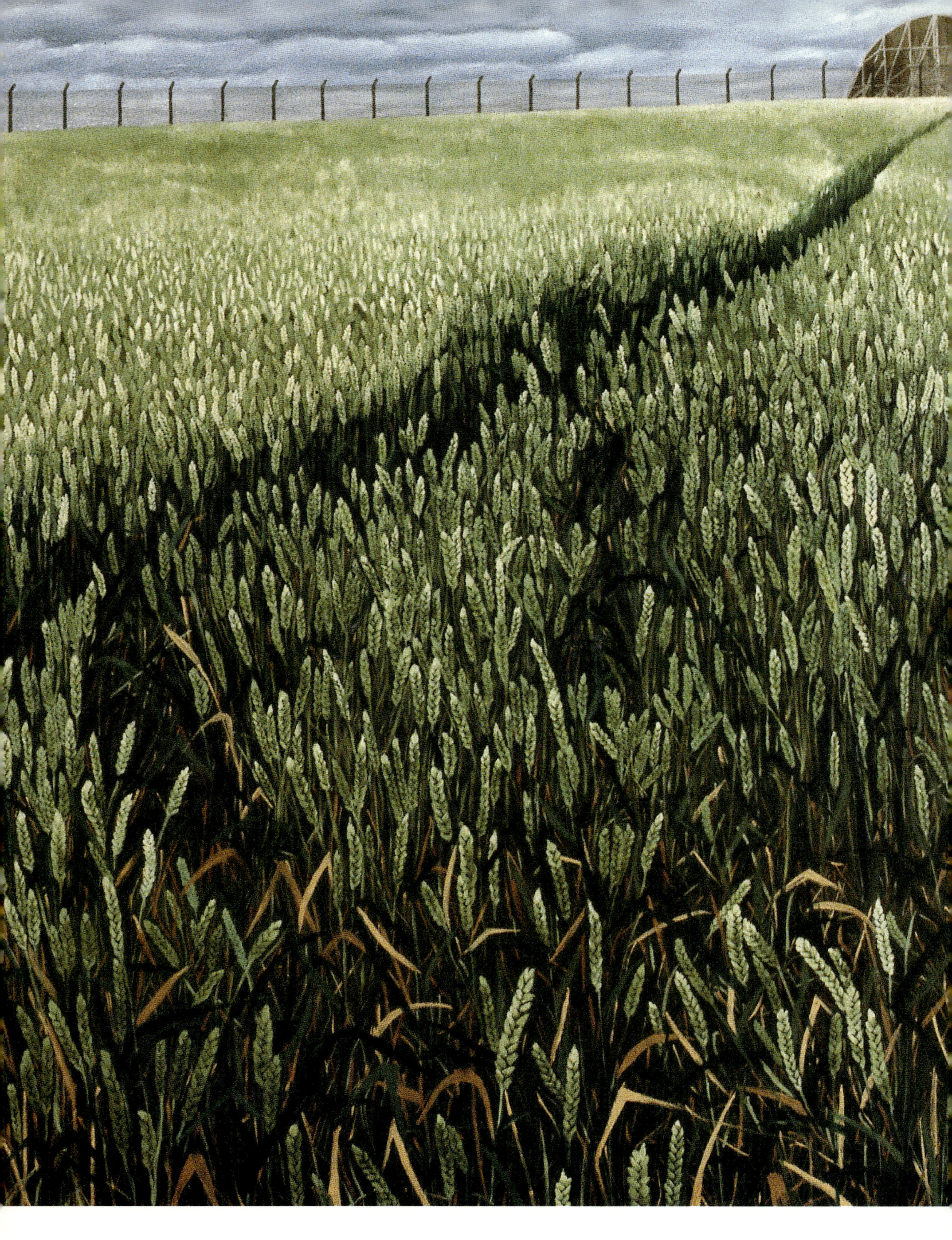

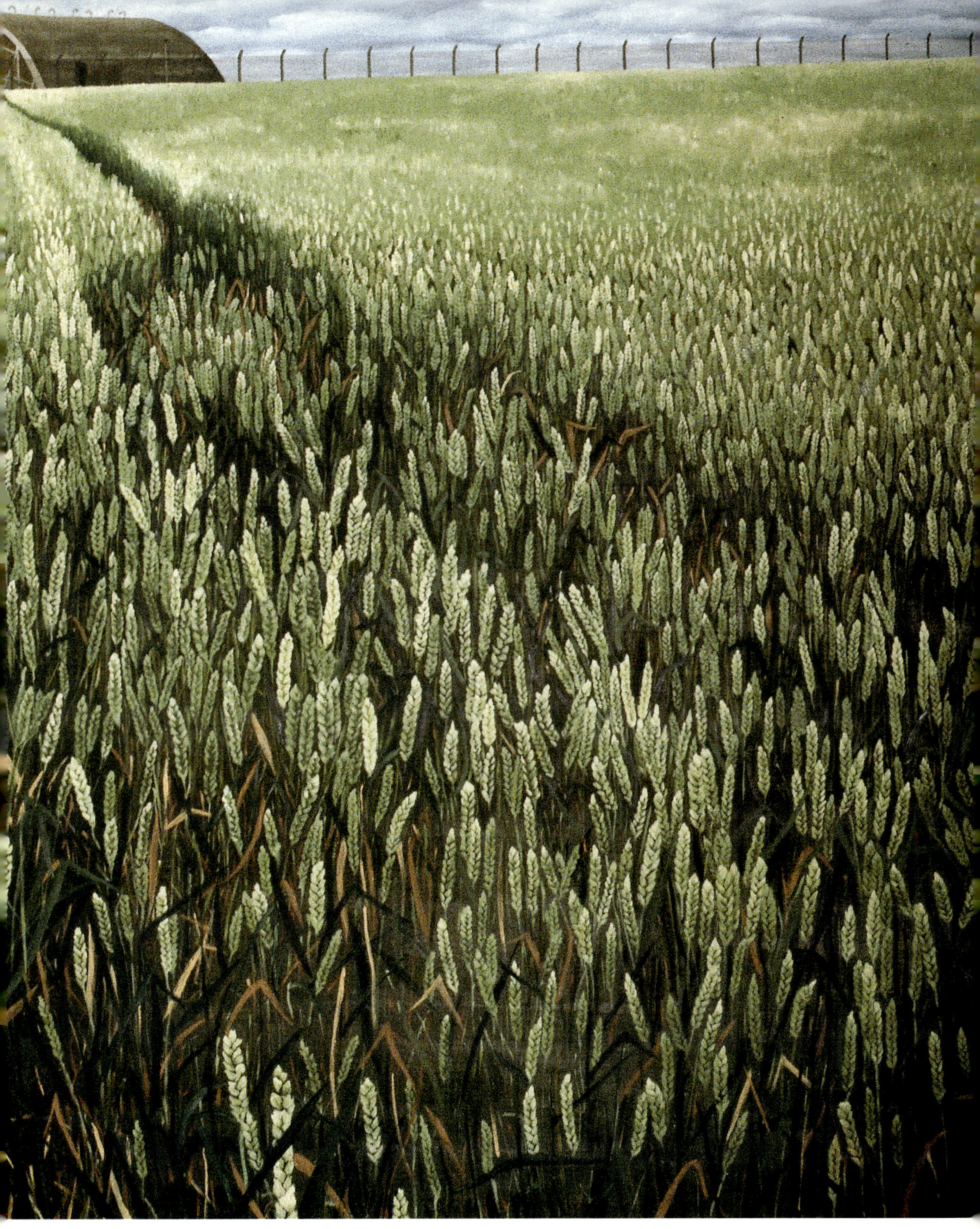

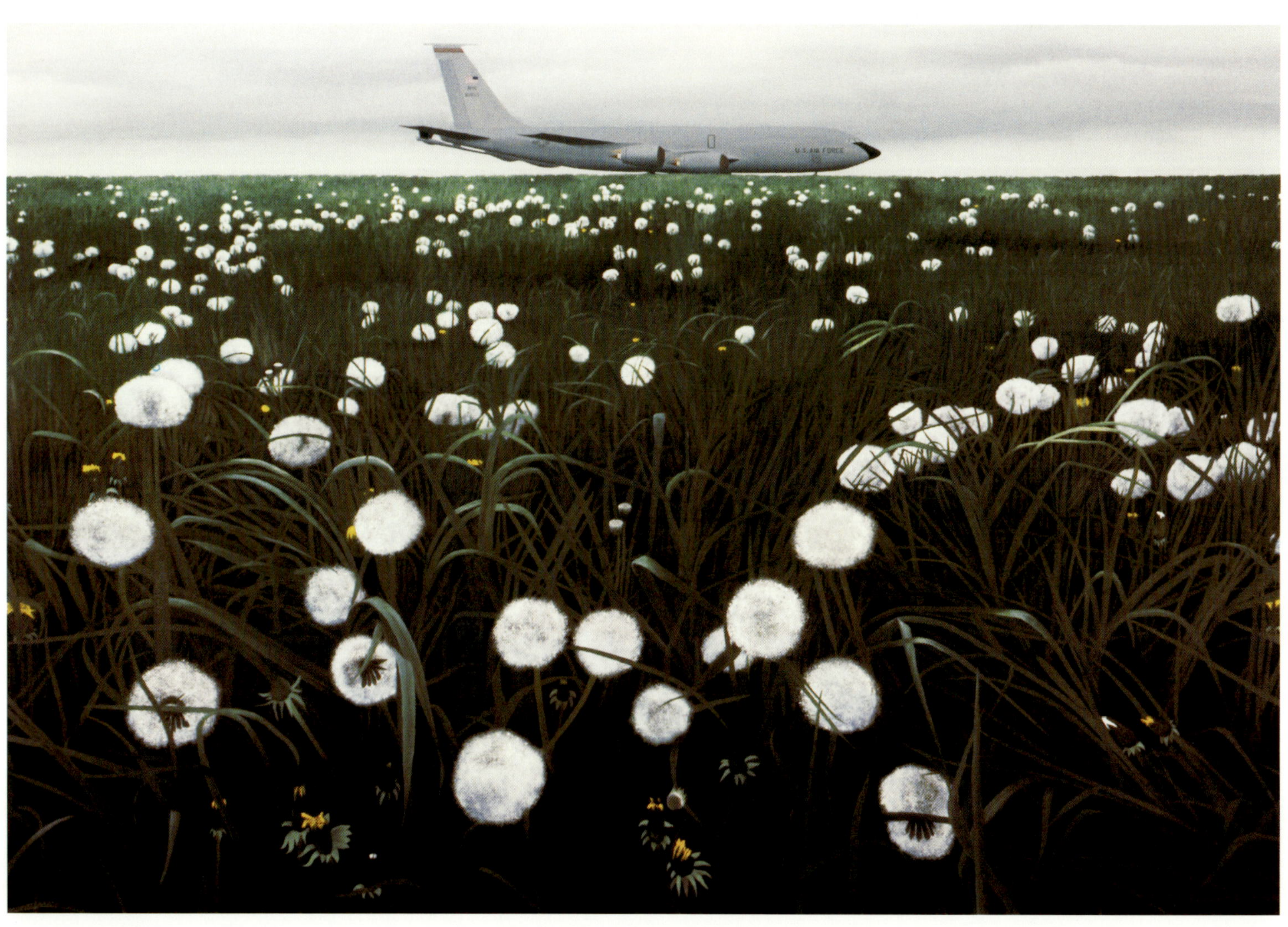

ROSIE SNELL

Marking Time 1997
oil on canvas on panel
120 x 170cm/47¼ x 67in

previous page:
The Hangar 1996
oil on canvas on panel
168 x 275cm/66 x 108¼in

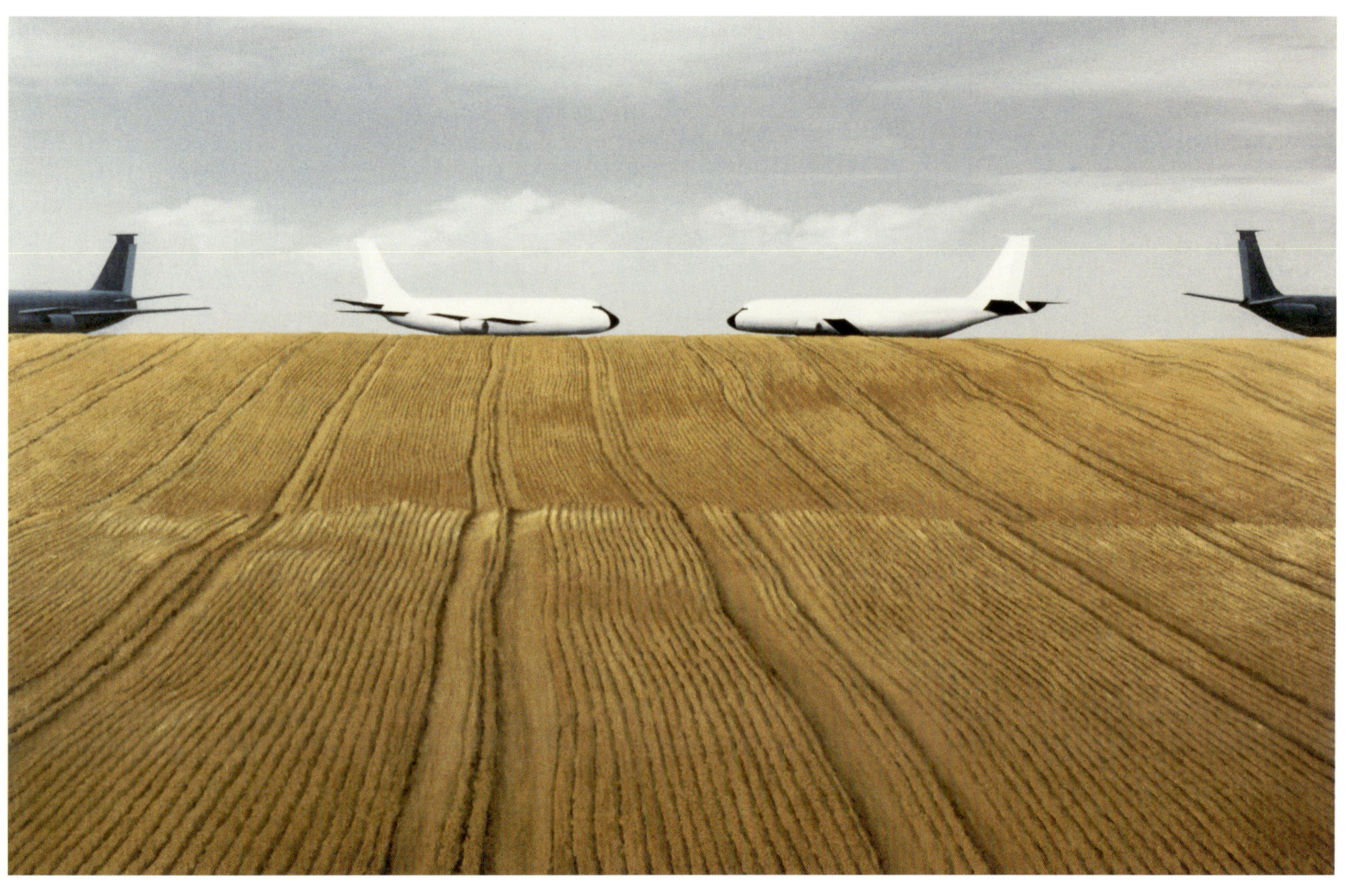

ROSIE SNELL

Ground Clearance 1998
oil, sand on canvas on panel
85 x 130cm/33½ x 51¼in

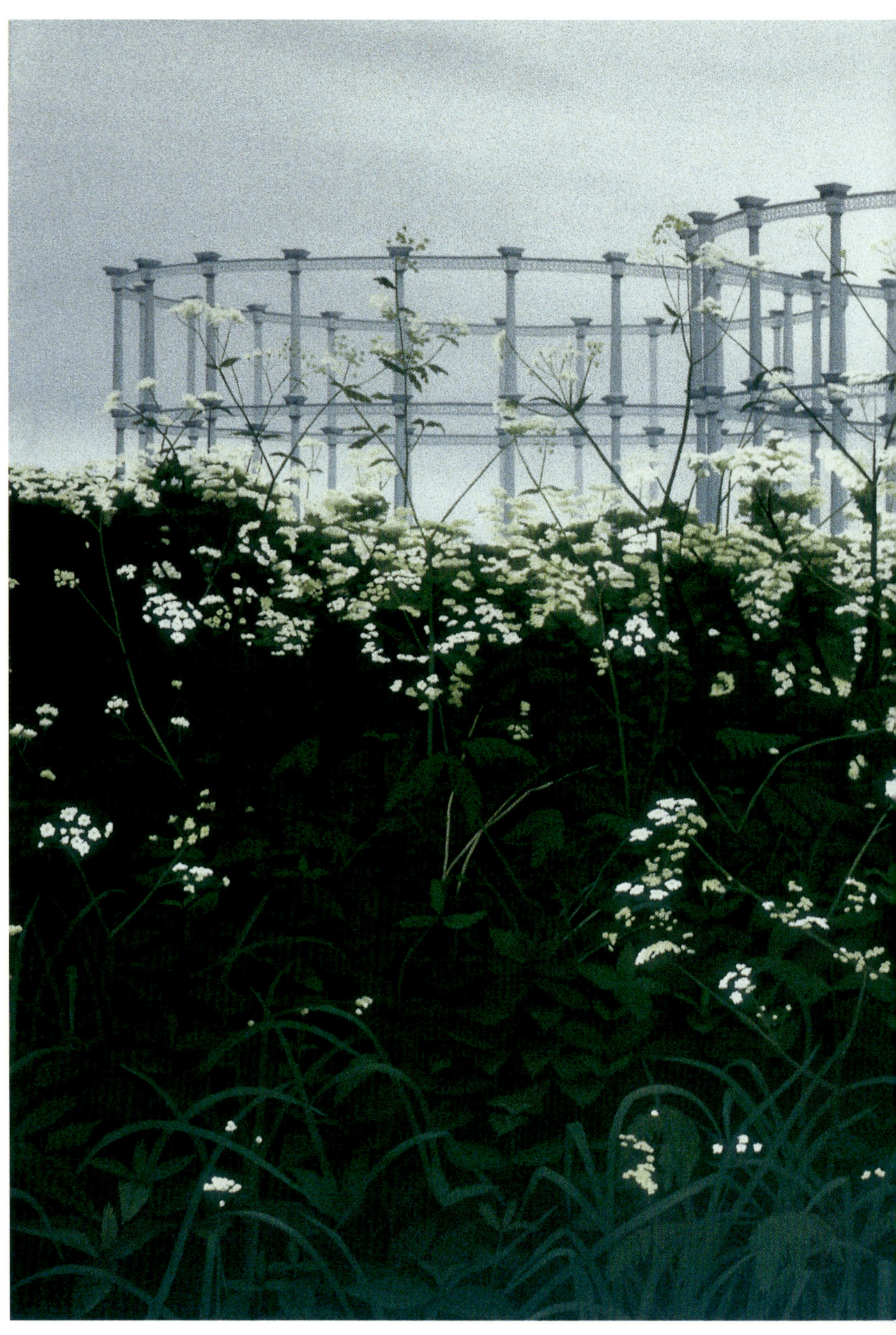

ROSIE SNELL

Exhale 1998
oil on canvas on board
115 x 180cm/45¼ x 71in

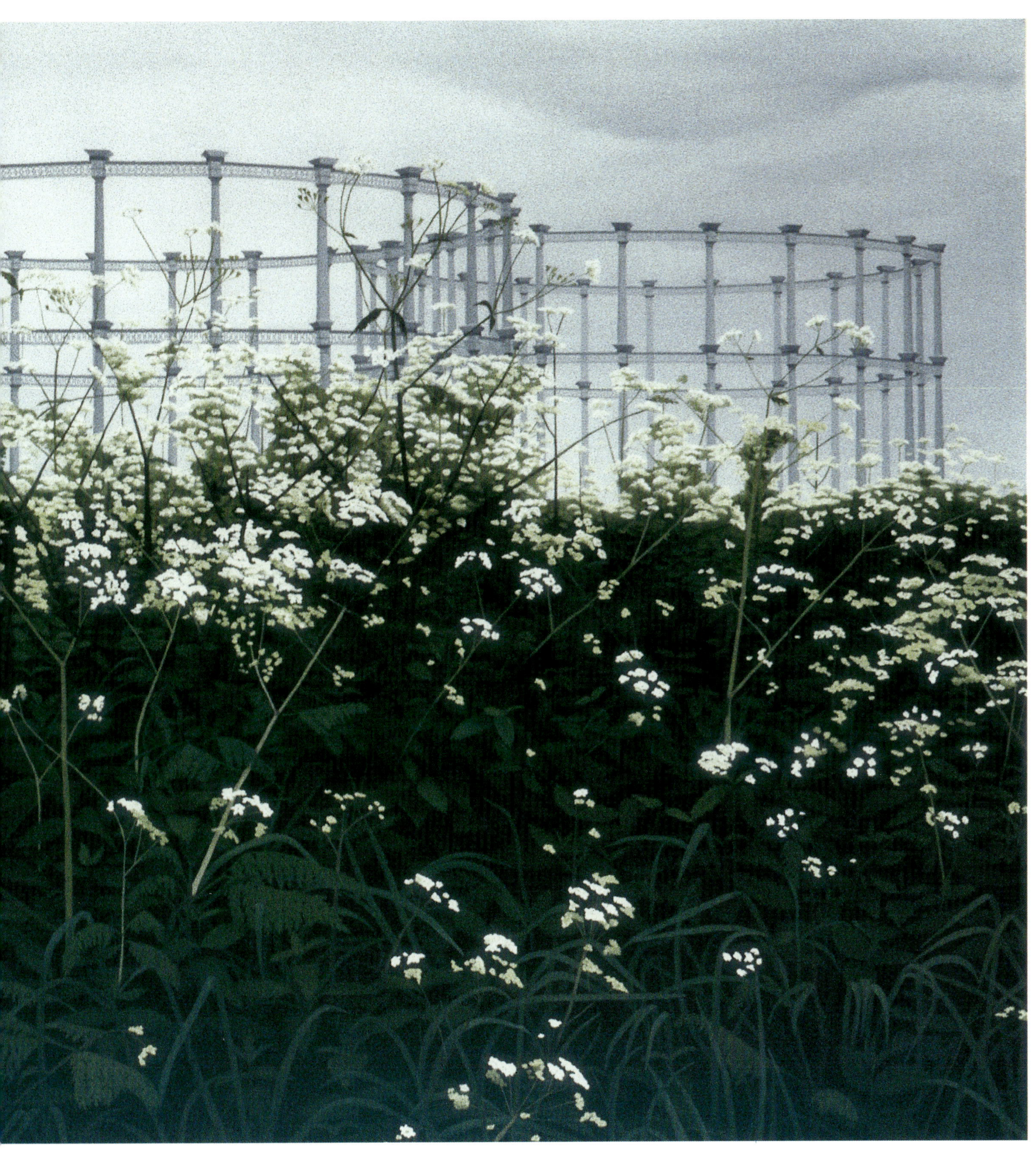

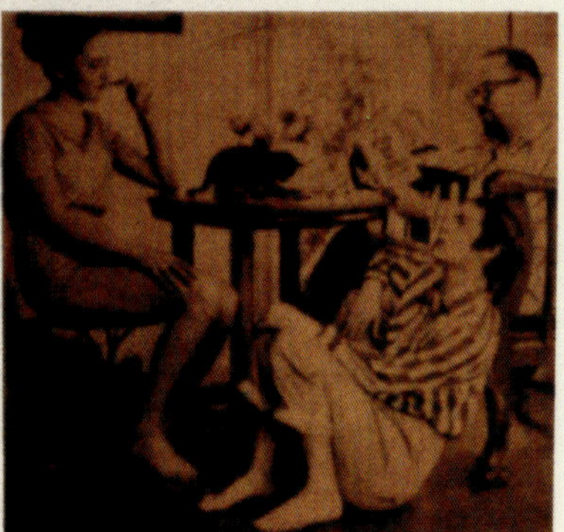

People have long pondered the question of birth.

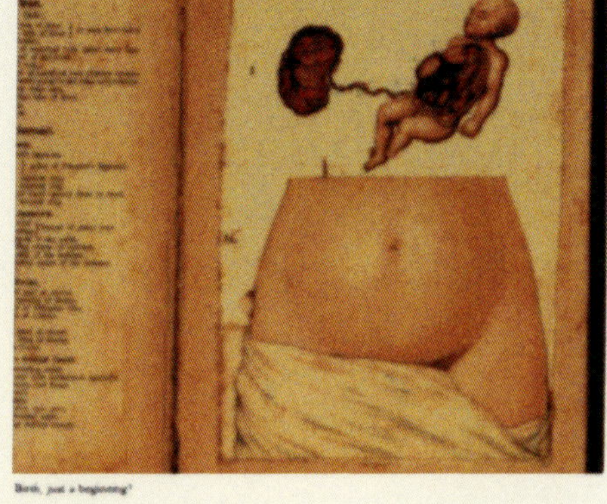

Birth, just a beginning?

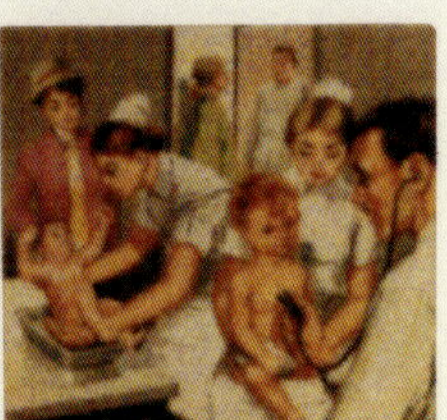

The psyche, related to the soul

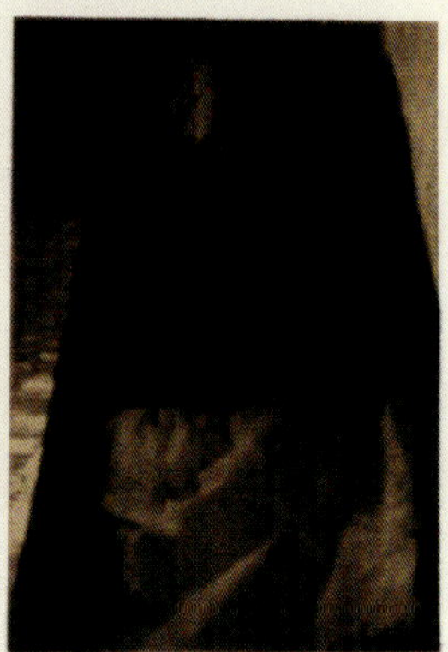

Scientific authorities today shows us with unerring accuracy that death, birth, consequently all life that is part of the world, the cosmos, has been the same specifically, or more generally speaking

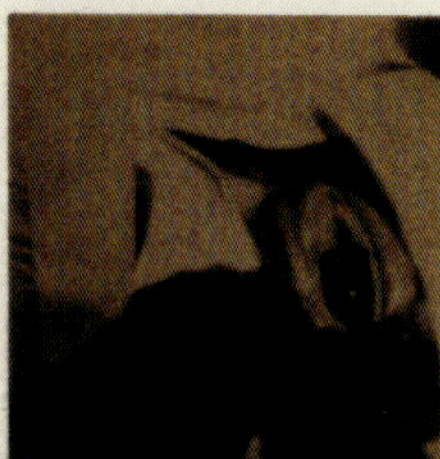

Birth, a complicated, very deep profound subject

BIRTH AND DEATH

Birth and death have been with us as long as world history. None can escape birth. None can escape death. You cannot have one without the other Both events are linked to the psyche, for instance, what does the word psyche mean?

UNANSWERED QUESTIONS

It is a subject that has puzzled humanity for all time. What is birth? What is death? Do we come from anywhere? Do we go to any place? Artist's, writers, philosophers, poets, children, women and men of all sorts have pondered this question. Yet still nobody can say for certain.

AN OBJECTIVE VIEW

The topic is of course a very difficult one to look at without some degree of subjection. This has forced some people to make various analogies. For example we could say; birth and death are like book ends, (the books in the middle being life) this enables us to get a more objective over-view of the whole subject.

DREAMS, LIFE OR DEATH?

Dreams could be thought of as central to our understanding of being alive and being dead, as they are a bit like both. These two important events in everybody's life are very deep, very profound, and we find that if we take each of them on there own we can focus in with more clarity. Looking at them in the generally accepted order of birth first, to be followed by death.

THE BEGINING OF LIFE?

Birth is in fact a beginning, but does it also represent the start of life itself? When do we begin life? Is it when we are born? Before, when still in the womb? Maybe even before that, when we are spermatozoa or ovum. The very subject is one fraught with great danger in the world today. With far reaching implications for the human race even in feild of political science.

A DARK MYSTERY

Death is a more sombre subject, seen as an end, it is final. Because the exact time of death is vague and uncertain, relative to the predictability of birth, it becomes more important for some the longer they live. Although there are many more ways to die than to be born, being dead is the same.

DEATH IN ART

Artists in the West, since the Renaissance, have focused on death more than birth. And we find, the Memento mori, the crucifixion, *Madame Recamier de David*, consequently all great art going on into time itself. The Mishnah anybody who is familiar with the Mishnah (one of the seven books of Moses) finds as in art, many things, very deep very profound. Death itself is also depicted as allegory. In fact the whole cycle from birth to death is allegorised throughout the Western world in film, great art, poetry, in fact all human endeavour.

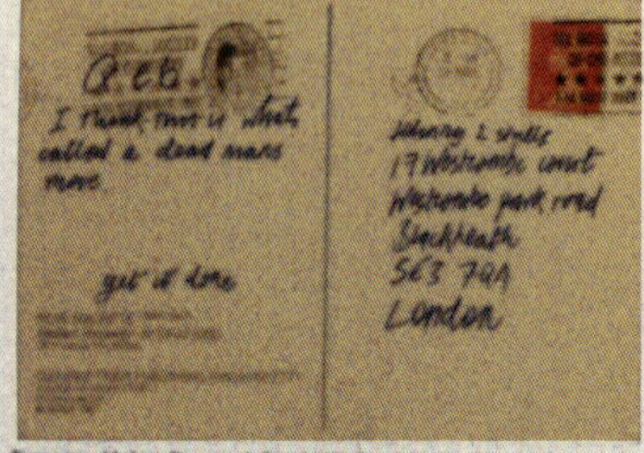

Perspective: *Madame Recamier de David* 1951 René Magritte 1898—1967

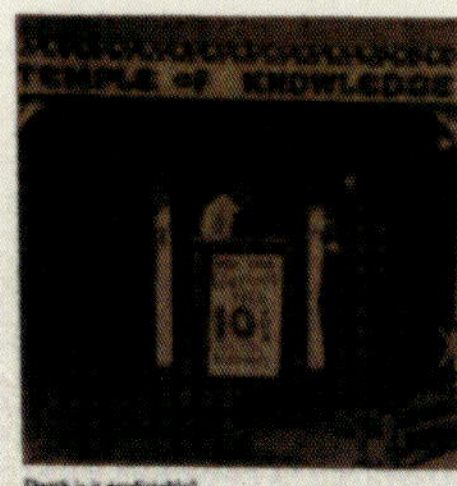

Death is it predictable?

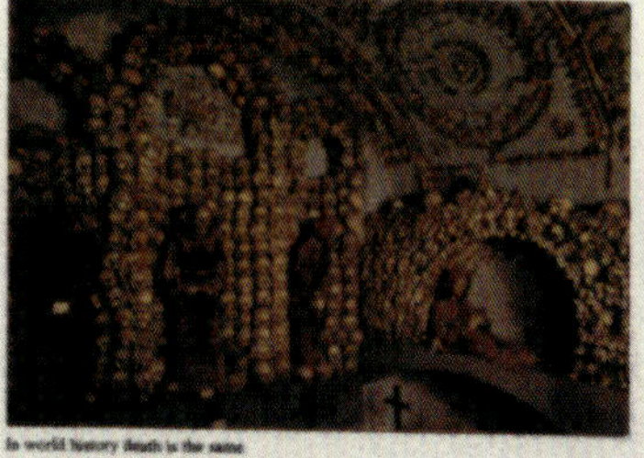

In world history death is the same

JOHNNY SPENCER

Birth and Death 1995-6
laminate, paper on panel
81 x 57cm/32 x 22½in

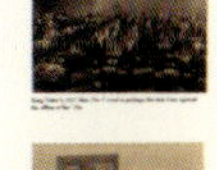 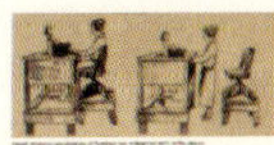 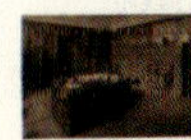
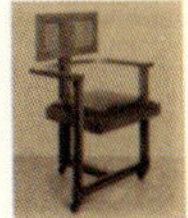

A HISTORY OF OFFICE FURNITURE

Office furniture has a history that barely extends back to the 19th century. The development of distinct designs for the office evolved rapidly. As organisations and the technology they used became increasingly sophisticated, so did the furniture.

Furniture in the office is usually a visible sign of hierarchy and status. Interestingly, the most advanced furniture was frequently associated with the bottom rungs of an organisation work force. Executive furniture, for the most part, had changed little since the 19th century.

The attempt to make the work of the growing army of office clerks more efficient, were all pressures that led to the development of furniture designed specifically for the office. The roll-top desk that evolved was a visible demonstration of organisational efficiency.

The increasing complexity of the organisations eventually had a simplifying affect on their furniture. When clerks were responsible for a range of tasks, including filing, their desks needed to cope with demanding storage and organisational requirements. The trend, however, became the reduction of work to simple highly repetitive tasks, and the furniture began to reflect this.

Two distinct strands of thought could be seen in the 20th century. One, the most visible, was technology led, in response to new materials like tubular steel and laminated wood or the technology such as the typewriter, telephone and desktop computer. An alternative strand had started from an analysis of organisations themselves, and the people who work within them.

The most significant advance was the 1904 Larkin building, Buffalo, New York. Designed by Frank Lloyd Wright, the building contained, amongst such innovations as, air-conditioning and the central skylit court, the first metal furniture.

By the middle of the 20th century some European office designers were taking issue with the American approach. The large ordered office space that dominated American corporations did not prove so satisfactory in Europe. Bürolandschaft, a design geared to counteract the anonymity of open plan was devised in Germany. Bürolandschaft, or office landscaping, came to represent the democratisation of the workplace. The simple, mobile furniture designed for the landscaped office was an attempt to be solely functional, without regard for visible marks of status.

One of the most decisive events in the development of office furniture came through Robert Propst in 1958. Propst foresaw the effects of the information revolution in the office and in 1964 produced for Herman Miller the 'Action Office'. The office was based on the concept, in Propst's words, that *"it is natural for people to seek responsibility and….they enjoy it. Performers at any level need challenge and encouragement to gain top performance."*

The altruistic genesis of Bürolandschaft, and, later, of 'Action Office' and its many clones, was overtaken by the need for believable commercial benefit. The original aims of providing what in turn were a more humane workplace was replaced with analyses of efficient use of office space. At the end of the 20th century the pendulum had begun to swing back, with the office planning and architecture as in Centraal Beheer. Crucially were moves (before the demise of the whole system) by furniture manufacturers to satisfy the failing market. Herman Miller's 'Ethospace', with its intention of forming individually controllable spaces within the office, and Castelli's 'Nine to Five', with its stress on privacy and personal possession of the workplace.

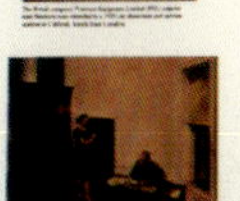 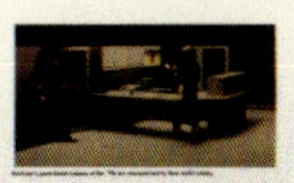 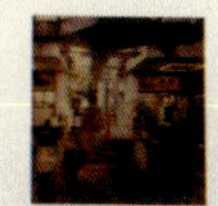

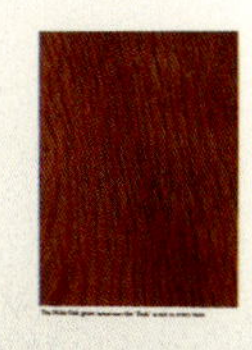

THE HOLM OAK

Family FAGACEAE   *Quercus Ilex*

The holm oak or ilex is a large, ever-green tree which, in favourable environment, will attain a height of 70 to 90 ft., and carry a large, rounded crown that may measure as much in diameter as the height.

TREE AND LEAF

It is a native of the countries around the Mediterranean Sea, but was first brought into cultivation in Great Britain in the early 19th Century. Its forest conditions the stem is tall and slender, but, as grown in open conditions, is much shorter and of greater diameter. The leaves, which are so closely set on the twigs as to produce a very dense mass of foliage, are somewhat variable in shape, but generally elliptical with a long exit three times the breadth.

FRUIT

The young twigs and young leaves are downy but the down soon disappears from the upper surfaces which become a dark, glossy green, the lower remaining felted with matted grey or tawny hairs. The acorns are from ½ to ¾ in. long in Britain, and are borne on short, downy stalks either singly or two or three on one peduncle.

BARK AND FLOWERS

The tree thrives best on a warm, light soil and is liable to frost damage in the colder parts of the country. The bark is deeply fissured and often cross-fissured into rectangular plates. It is not corky, as that of *Quercus suber* which is also native to the Mediterranean region, but it is rich in tannin. The male flowers are in numerous, slender catkins, 2 to 3 in. in length.

WOOD

The wood is hard and heavy, of a reddish-brown colour, and differs from that of the common oak in having no pore rings. In other respects the structure of the Holm, is similar to that of ordinary oak, and, when cut on the quarter, it shows the bold silver grain that is characteristic of oaks generally. It is not as resistant to decay as the heartwood of English oak, needs some care in seasoning to prevent splitting and warping, and in working because of its density. In England trees are grown mainly for shade or ornament in gardens, and has been used for furniture and similar purposes in the form of quarter-sawn stock, with satisfactory results, although the 'very bold "chink" or "flash" is regarded as rather too florid to suit some tastes.

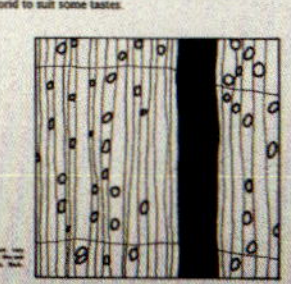

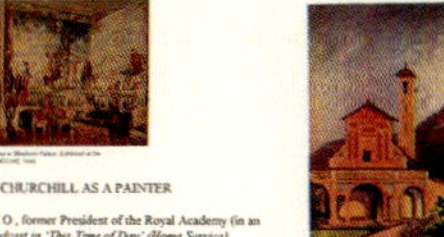

WINSTON CHURCHILL AS A PAINTER

By SIR GERALD KELLY, K.C.V.O., former President of the Royal Academy (in an interview with Hugh Moran). *Broadcast in 'This Time of Day' (Home Service).*

MORAN : Sir Gerald – what sort of painter was Sir Winston?
SIR GERALD KELLY : He was jolly good. Hang it all! He painted exactly like I paint. We both did our best. We both enjoyed it. And he wasn't an artist, he was a painter. I'm not an artist, I'm a painter.

MORAN : And what's the difference?
SIR GERALD KELLY : I don't know. I don't understand art. And when they talk to me about art, it's terrifying. But painting is putting a few things in the right place, on the great Degas said.

MORAN : Do you think Sir Winston would have been recognised as a painter if he hadn't been called Sir Winston Churchill?
SIR GERALD KELLY : If he had become a painter – a professional – as he became a politician – I should have thought he would certainly have been. He painted a lot of jolly good pictures. And he painted well. Now, when I became President I had a friend who was a great friend of Sir Winston's called Edward Marsh, who filed pictures and collected them, and I said to Eddie, 'Look here, the pictures Winston sent to the Academy last year were not much good.' And he said, 'Come with me, I'll take you down to Chartwell and you shall have it out with him.' So down we went. Had a jolly lunch, and he laughed- so gay! Of course, I was frightened and … but you couldn't go on being frightened of Winston especially as we both talked about painting.

MORAN : Did you criticise any of his paintings then?
SIR GERALD KELLY : No more than I would criticise anybody else's paintings. No. I looked and then when I liked one I said how very nice it was. And I saw what I think is his best picture. I think it is one of the best pictures painted in England in my lifetime.

MORAN : What's that one Sir Gerald?
SIR GERALD KELLY : Snow at Chartwell. That was painted in 1924. It is an absolute smasher. It's one of the coldest pictures. I dont know that I would have wanted to have painted it, because I would have been so cold. But it's quite marvellous. Marvellous.

MORAN : How long had Sir Winston been painting at that time - 1924?
SIR GERALD KELLY : I think he'd been painting for a very long time. Eddie Marsh told me he'd been painting for forty-five or fifty years.

MORAN : What did he think of himself as a painter?
SIR GERALD KELLY : He liked it, you know. He liked doing it. I want you to understand that Winston was naturally a painter and he painted, and the word 'art' was never mentioned.

MORAN : When he came to the Royal Academy to look at paintings how did he behave? What sort of paintings did he look at?
SIR GERALD KELLY : Oh sweet - he was absolutely sweet. I used to take him round and we used to stroll round after the dinner, you know, but I never noticed him looking very much at other people's pictures.

MORAN : He looked at his own most of the time?
SIR GERALD KELLY : No more than I would criticise anybody else's paintings. I have never seen a man with great care and he complained if they were not hung exactly as he liked them. And then he strolled on round the rest and I don't think he was very interested. I have seen more famous painters than Sir Winston Churchill behave in exactly the same way.

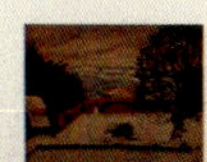 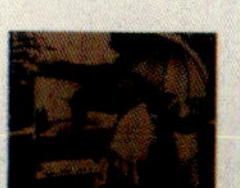

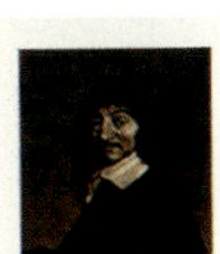 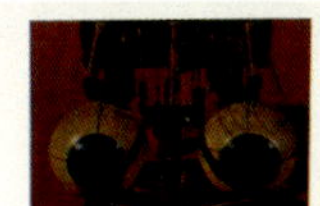

RECOVERY FROM BLINDNESS

Perception of the blind was described by Descartes, in the *dioptrics* (1637). He imagines a blind man discovering the world with a stick.

> …without long practice this kind of sensation is rather confused and dim, but if you take men born blind, who have made use of such sensations all their life, you will find they feel things with such perfect exactness that one might almost say they see with their hands.

John Locke (1632-1704) received a celebrated letter from his friend Molyneux which posed the question: 'suppose a man born blind, and now adult, and taught by his touch to distinguish between a cube and a sphere of the same metal…'

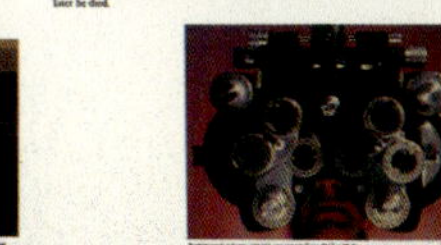

THE AMAZING CASE OF S.B.

ALL THAT REMAINS IS NOW GONE

 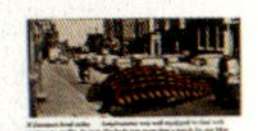 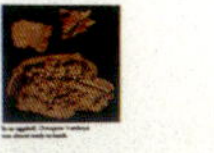 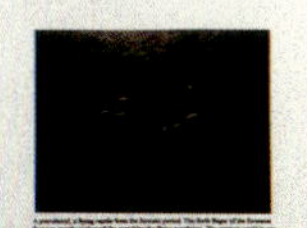

TERRIBLE LIZARD

DINOSAURS came into existence around 220 or 230 million years ago, flourished for about 160 million years then suddenly disappeared. The word dinosaur, from Greek words meaning 'terrible lizard', does not have any scientific meaning. It was not until 1841 that the name 'dinosaur' was first invented. This was done by the brilliant anatomist and palaeontologist Richard Owen.

THEOLOGY OR PALAEONTOLOGY

IN 1711, the well-preserved skeleton of a fossil giant salamander was identified as that of a sinner drowned in the Deluge. Elephant bones found near Paris, France, were generally accepted to have been those of giants.

BETTER ANALYSIS

THE first fossil of a giant reptile to have been identified as such was a set of jawbones full of jagged teeth discovered in a quarry in the Netherlands in 1770. They were identified by an anatomist as those of a giant lizard. Then, in 1795, the anatomist George Cuvier proclaimed that it was some kind of huge sea lizard.

AT LAST THE DINOSAUR

THE study of dinosaurs really started in Great Britain in the early 1850s. The dinosaur bones found in the first half of the 19th century were only odd fragments. With nothing to compare them with, it was impossible to make an accurate reconstruction of the full skeleton.

BONE MADNESS

IN the second half of the 19th century the most remarkable dinosaur discoveries were made in North America by two men, Othniel Charles Marsh and Edward Drinker Cope. There was no co-operation between these two men. In fact, they loathed one another. Each was determined to out do the other, following up reports of fossil bones being found in the foothills of the Rockies. Each one made offers of money to anyone finding significant fossils, to try to ensure that the museums were kept out of the rival's hands, and secured times the opposing expeditions had a knuckle.

EGG PUZZLE SOLVED

KNOWLEDGE is constantly being renewed. In 1923, an expedition from New York found the first *Oviraptor* skeleton in a nest of eggs in the Mongolian desert. The scientists thought the elongated lizard belonged to *Protoceratops*, whose fossils were common in the area. They chose the name "egg stealer" *Oviraptor* because they assumed the animal was trying to eat the eggs when it was caught in a sand storm and died. But the discovery in the back decade of the 20th century of a very similar egg containing a tiny *Oviraptor* skeleton, almost ready to hatch, cleared the name of "egg stealer".

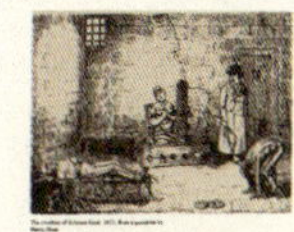

INCARCERATION

INCARCERATION, whether regarded as a reformatory or merely as a punitive process, is not a very ancient method of dealing with crime. In ancient Athens and Rome it was resorted to either as a means of securing the persons of those who awaited trial or were doomed to execution than as an end in itself. At Athens persons who owed money to the State, or were unable to pay fines, could be placed in prison until the obligation was discharged. These continued to be the main uses of prisons until the 19th century.

In England, as in other countries, the condition of prisons became a grave social evil, which went on increasing till it ended the reforming energy of John Howard. When Howard made his first journey through England, in 1773, he found that most of the gaols were loathsome underground dens, in which the prisoners were kept in half-starved and almost naked condition, with nothing to lie upon but filthy and rotten straw. No distinction of sex was observed, and the inmates were completely at the mercy of the gaolers.

AT this time the commonest form of punishment was death, which might be incurred by petty larceny no less than murder. The only other penalty for grave offences was transportation, which originated in the Vagrancy Act of 1597. After the establishment of American independence it became necessary to devise some new method of punishing criminals, unless the death penalty was to be still further extended. An Act (1776) was therefore passed substituting hard labour at home, and two years later the Penitentiaries Act, which was partly the work of Howard.

IN this Act all the principles now recognised in prison legislation – including solitary confinement, care for the health of the prisoner, and the attempt to effect his reformation – are very clearly enunciated. It was nearly 40 years, however, before any penitentiary of the kind suggested was actually completed. In the meantime the hulks established in 1778 (and not entirely discontinued till 1857) formed a very inadequate substitute. The discoveries of Captain Cook revived the idea of transportation, and in 1788 the first batch of Australian convicts was landed at Port Jackson.

MILLBANK the first of a new class of prison, was at first opened in 1816. William Crawford had returned from a mission to the United States, in which he had been much impressed by the salutary effects of the "Pennsylvanian System," which provided for the complete seclusion of each prisoner. The government determined to adopt it, but this could only be done gradually, owing to the expense involved in erecting buildings containing so many separate cells. Pentonville Prison, opened in accordance with the new plan, was opened (sic)in 1842.

BY the end of the 20th century the prison system had developed to the two extremes of the open prison, usually for the rich and privileged, and the maximum security prison. The United States Penitentiary Marion, Illinois, an example of the latter, USP Marion, commonly referred to as "The New Alcatraz" has been "locked down"(meaning that all inmates are confined to their cells) since October 1983.

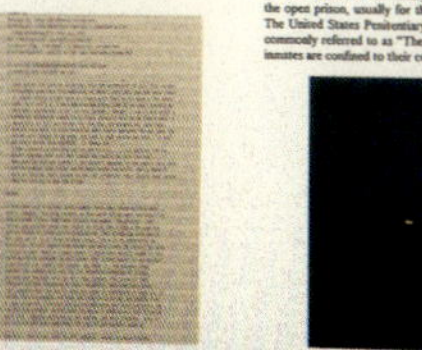 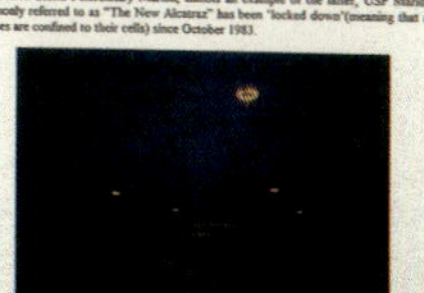

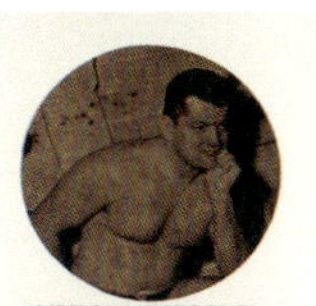 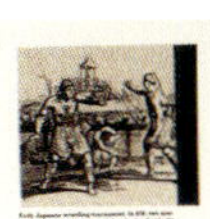 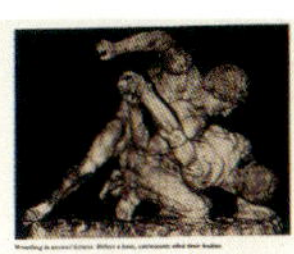

OLD WORLD WRESTLING

WRESTLING is one of the oldest and most elemental of sports, with a history going back to the beginning of recorded time. It was a pastime that ancient man thought fit for the gods, and medieval man regarded as the prerogative of princes.

THE BIG FIGHT

THROUGHOUT the ages wrestling has been practised all over the world. In Japan an empire was wrestled for, in ancient Greece and Israel the wrestling champion was the most important of men. Beowulf, the hero of the Anglo-Saxon epic poem, wrestled with a fiendish monster for the blessings of men. Another story is told in the 32nd chapter of Genesis in the Old Testament: 'And Jacob was left alone, and there wrestled a man with him until the breaking of the day'. In this instance Jacob's opponent turned out to be an angel, not a man. Today this is read as metaphor, not unlike the idea of someone wrestling with the awesome subject matter of contemporary art. The morality of wrestling is simple, there are heroes and villains, and usually it is the hero who carries the day.

WRESTLING TAKES A FALL

THE period between 1900 and 1914 could be called the golden age of wrestling. During these years professional wrestling became the major sport with the greatest audience pull in the English-speaking world. The 20th century was also witness to a decline of the sport, as predicted by professional grappler Jack 'Death Wish' Allen. Believing that all physical contact sports are doomed, Allen from Milwaukee USA, proclaimed in 1967, "We're heading into a sophisticated age in which all sports will be mental."

BRITISH FIGHTERS

THE first mention of wrestling in the British Isles occurs in the *Book of Leinster* 1825 BC that refers to the sport being excluded in the Tailtin Games in County Meath. The sport became unfashionable during the days of William the Conqueror, who thought wrestling was strictly for peasants. The upper levels of society preferred jousting tournaments, so wrestling went underground and became the sport of common people. The sport re-emerged, however, and gained supremacy in the 13th century. At the famous meeting between Henry VIII and Francis 1 of France, at the Field of the Cloth of Gold, Henry, flush with the success of the English wrestlers, prompted a challenge from Francis to a personal wrestling match. The two monarchs actually clinched for a few moments before their courtiers separated them.

GOOD CLEAN FUN FOR GRANDAD

BY the 1950's professional wrestling bouts had shrunk to one hour from nine and showmanship and gimmickry were rampant. Villains were the most popular with audiences. There were hundreds of cavemen, murderers and executioners strutting around the ring. One such villain, Crusher Lisowski, who swaggered into the ring smoking a cigar and waving a beer bottle, suffered more injuries from incensed spectators than at the hands of opponents. Next to the villains the most popular form of gimmickry was the masked wrestler, with the promise of unmasking if defeated. A list of all the gimmicks used by these artists would fill a book. They ranged from the gruesome, as with The Mummy, who wrestled swathed from head to foot in bandages, to 'Pretty Boy' Pat Patterson who would come into the ring dressed as a woman. There have been clean-limbed heroes, too good to be true, Red Indians, storm-troopers, cavemen and African princes, midgets fighting each other as well as tag-team matches and even bouts between women wrestling in mud.

MONEY AND GIRLS

WOMEN'S wrestling was a controversial element in the late 20th century forbidden in some states of America. One claimant to the world title was The Fabulous Moolah, thus named because of her often repeated claim that she was only in it for the moolah, or money. Born Lillian Ellison in Johannesburg, South Africa, she started out in wrestling as an adjunct to a male wrestler known as 'Elephant Boy'. The Elephant Boy would enter the ring dressed as an Indian Prince, and the young Moolah would follow as his second, scantily clad as a member of a harem and known as the Slave Girl. The big gimmick of this combination lay in a cloak worn by Elephant Boy and cured for between rounds by Slave Girl. The cloak, it was claimed, had belonged to Catherine the Great, Empress of Russia, and was said to be insured for a million dollars.

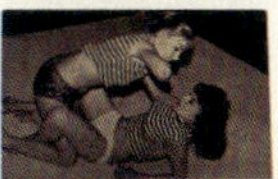 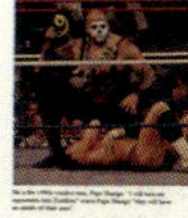 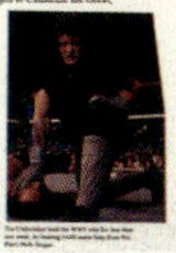

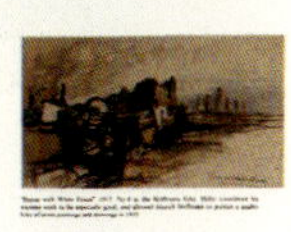 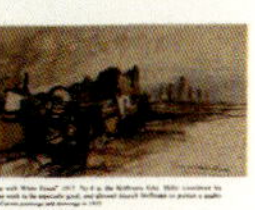 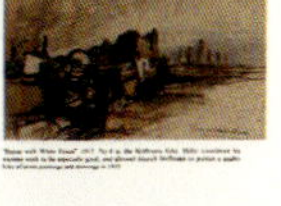 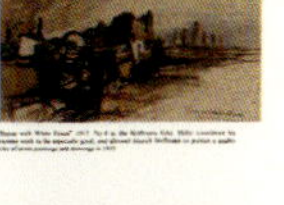 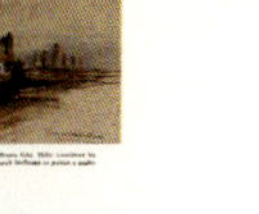 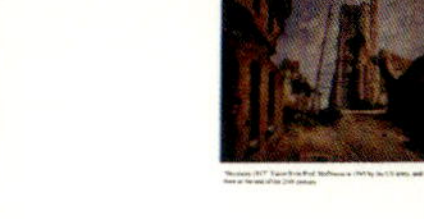

THE ARTIST

Up to the age of thirty Adolf Hitler called himself an artist. He confidently listed his profession as artist on official documents. As a young man, he told his friends he would be a "great artist" someday. Hitler was fascinated and preoccupied with the fine arts — painting, sculpture, music and architecture. His aspirations and years of artistic endeavour produced a considerable amount of work. The estimated total of between 2,000 and 3,000 drawings, sketches, water-colours and oil paintings attests to the seriousness of his intentions.

ART SCHOOLS

In October 1907, at the age of eighteen, Hitler applied for admission to the Vienna Academy of Fine Arts. Two days of examinations were required. Officials who failed him wrote: "Few heads (drawn?). Test drawing unsatisfactory." Of the 113 applicants, only 28 were accepted for first year studies. Failure was neither uncommon nor proof of inability. Acceptance by the Academy, however, virtually guaranteed recognition by the closed circle of artists in Austria and made critical and commercial success easier. Hitler took art lessons from a Viennese sculptor and made a second attempt to enter the Academy the following year. He was rejected again.

TRYING TIMES

HITLER was determined to succeed as an artist on his own. During these years in Vienna, often in poverty, he read voraciously and attended lectures, concerts, the opera and the theatre. To earn a living, he painted and sold his works in various frame makers' shops and on the street. One of his loves, classical music and opera, appeared as a frequent theme in his art, and he often designed stage scenery and costumes for opera productions for his own pleasure.

THE FINE ARTS

THROUGHOUT his life Hitler frequently commented that art and architecture dominated his personality. He was profoundly influenced by the Italian Renaissance and 19c Neo-classicism. He believed that the essence of art was derived from the technical ability to show "clear" and "realistic" representations of life as well as of symbolic subjects. When Hitler was shown drawings by the painter Franz Marc that were precisely and "traditionally" executed he commented, "He could even draw properly, so why didn't he do it". Hitler also felt that the subject matter must be understandable for the masses. "Healthy" art has a "healthy soul," he claimed. It should be "uplifting,""noble," and "idealistic."

THE PAINTINGS

Hitler's works having being bought for high prices in 1920/30s, a fact that outraged the Fuhrer, means many have survived. Rudolf Hess, Hitler's deputy, organised an official systematic search for his art from 1935 to 39. Pictures were bought or borrowed for documentation and copies made (these were given a secret identification mark). Many works were confiscated by the Americans in 1945, and have since found there way into the large personal collections of the Marquis of Bath and Billy F. Price.

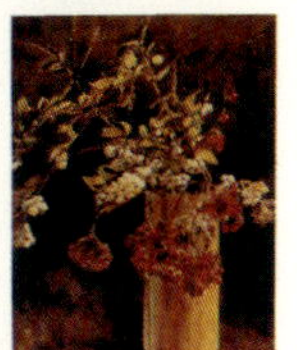 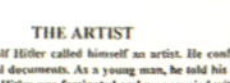 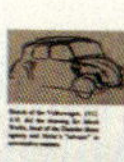 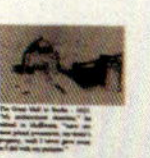

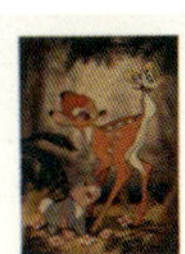 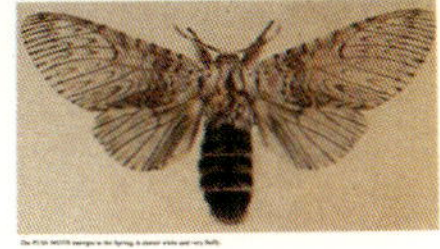 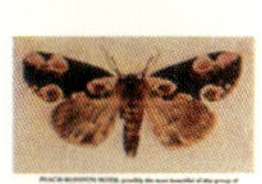

A PUSS MOTH EMANATES

Some time in 1943 Mr. A. Colin hatched a puss-moth egg in his London flat. The caterpillar was fed on poplar, and in due course spun a cocoon from which, in the summer of 1944, a female puss-moth emerged. It was allowed to fly about the room during the night.

A MALE ARRIVES

The next morning Mr. Colin was astonished to find a male puss-moth clinging to the window-ledge outside. Astonished, because this was on the sixth floor of a block of flats in Westminster. It may be, of course, that there were wild puss-moths breeding on the willows by the lake in St. James's Park or on the poplars planted in some of London's residential squares, but, even so, the quick location of the fresh emerged young female behind a closed window is sufficiently remarkable.

MOTHS AROUND A FLAME

Fluttering around burning candles or blundering onto glowing light bulbs, moths seem bent on self-destruction. In fact, they are driven by their mating instinct. It is not the illumination that we see that attracts them, but the ultraviolet light of radiant heat. Ultraviolet vision helps moths get together in the dark. Their body temperatures soar when they are in flight, and they home in on one another like heat-seeking missiles. Warmth from the flame of a candle must seem to them like an overwhelmingly powerful summons. Within range of a female moth of the right species, the male's sense of smell takes over. His antennae detect the sex-attractant odour given off by a suitable mate.

DYING FOR IT

In France during the 1914-18 War, to relieve the tedium of a period of comparative inactivity, *The Times* Correspondent at GHQ (Mr; later Sir, H. Perry Robinson) sent home for some cocoons of the emperor moth, from one of which a female emerged. Without much hope of attracting males—it was quite unsuitable country—he placed the young thing in an empty jam jar and put this out in a potato field. Towards the end of the next day the first male emperor arrived, so exhausted that it died soon after, clinging to the muslin at the top of the jar. Others followed.

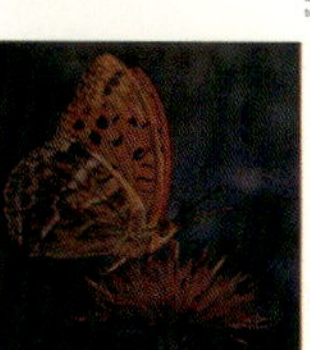 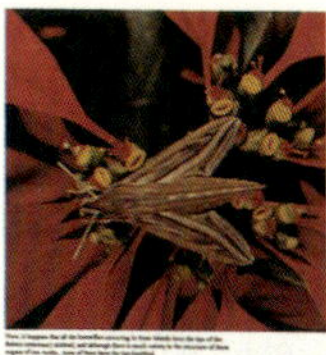 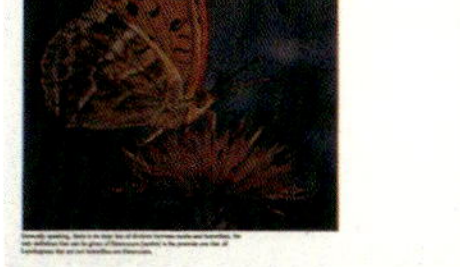

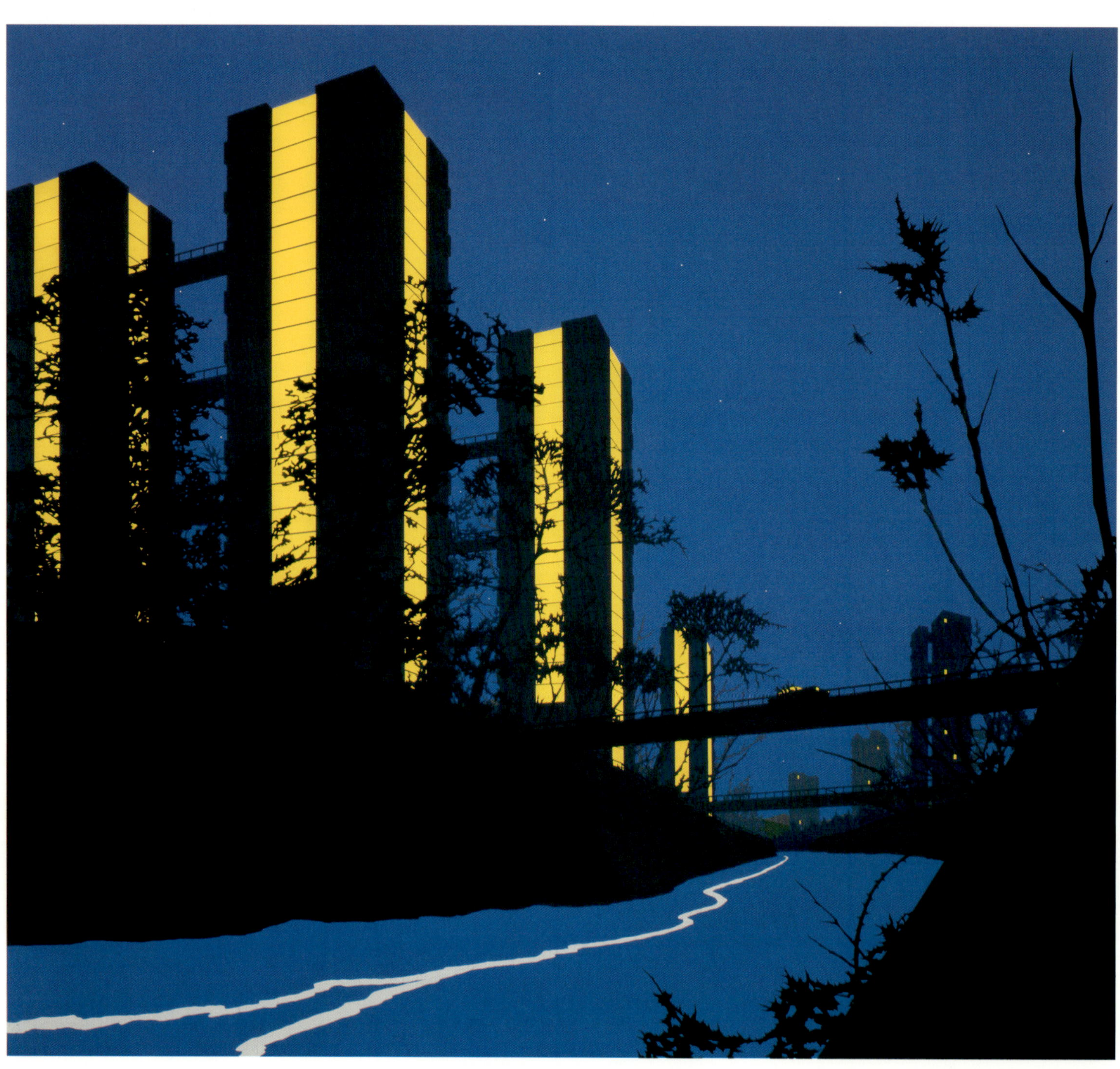

DAVID THORPE

Forever 1998
paper cut-out
136 x 144.5cm/53½ x 57in

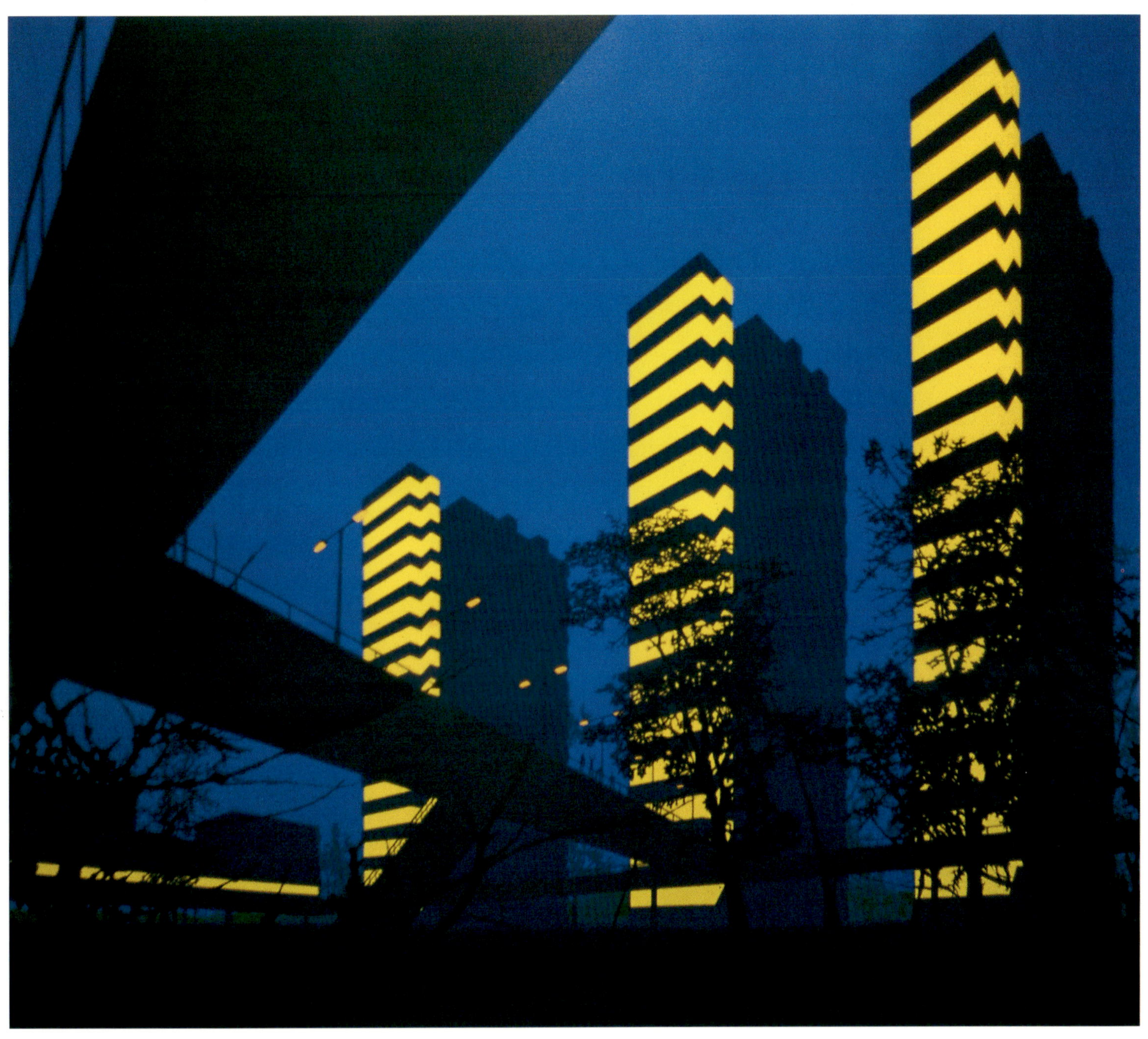

DAVID THORPE

Kings of the Night 1998
paper cut-out
149 x 168cm/58½ x 66¼in

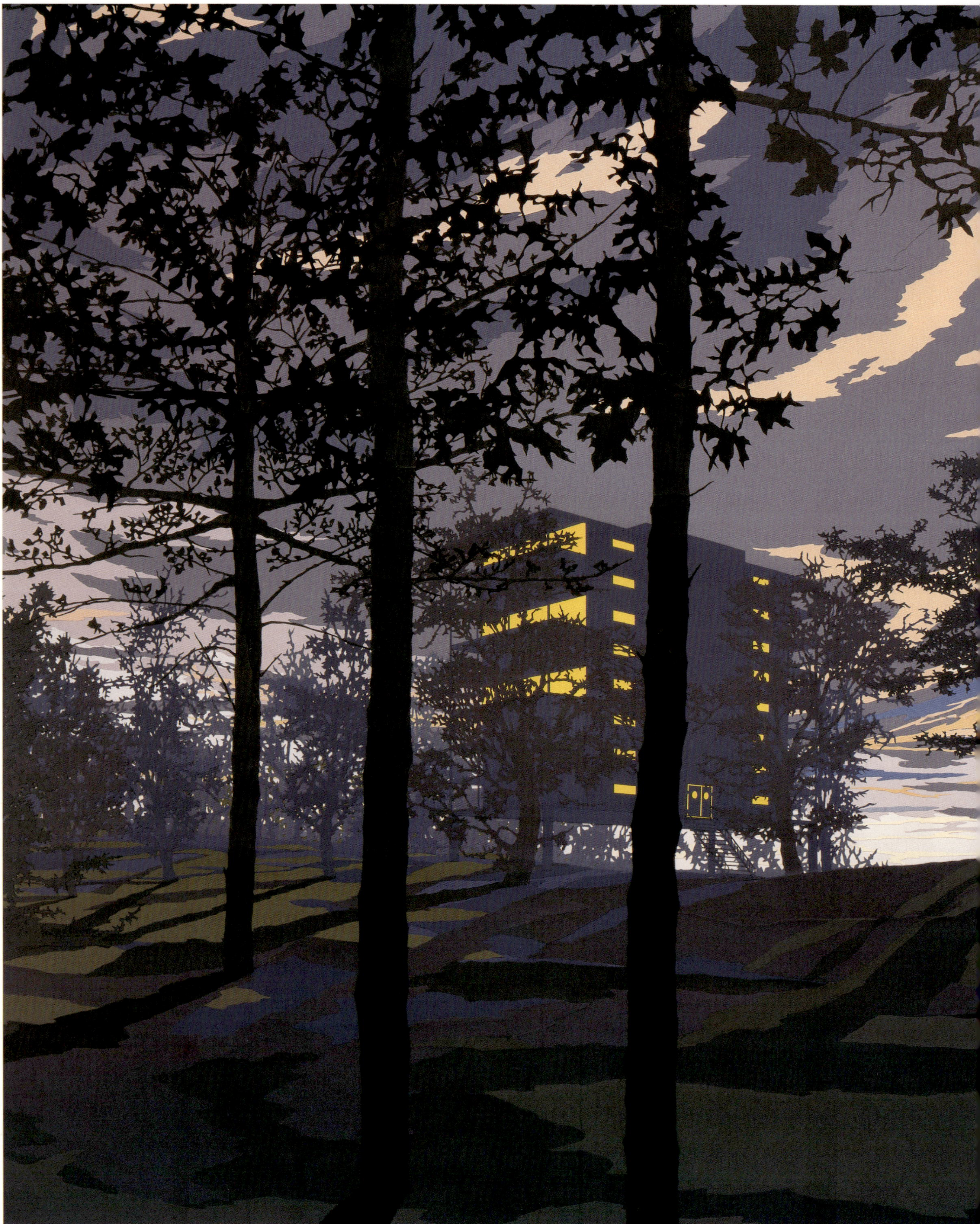

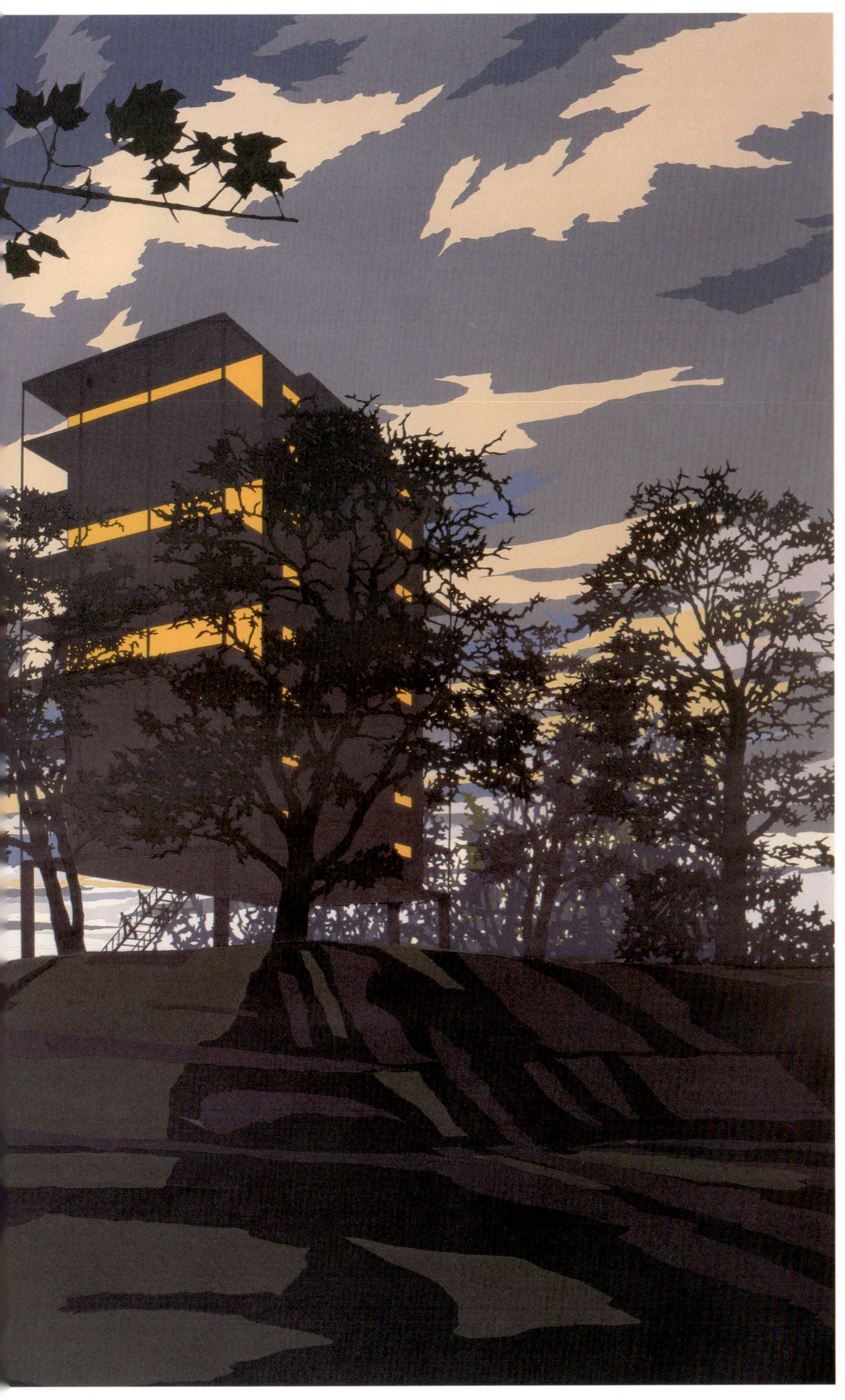

David Falconer

1967	Born Newcastle
1994	MA Art Theory, Goldsmiths College, London
	Lives and works in London

Solo Exhibitions

1998	*Stacked*, Chapman Fine Arts, London

Steven Gontarski

1972	Born Philadelphia, Pennsylvania
	Lives and works in London and New York

Education

1994	BA, Brown University, Providence, Rhode Island
1997	MA, Goldsmiths College, London

Brian Cyril Griffiths

1968	Born Stratford-upon-Avon
	Lives and works in London

Education

1989-92	BA Fine Art, University of Humberside
1995-96	MA Fine Art, Goldsmiths College, London

Roger Hiorns

1975	Born Birmingham
	Lives and works in London

Education

1991-93	Fine Art Foundation, Bournville College, Birmingham
1996	MA Fine Art, Goldsmiths College, London

Mark Hosking

1971	Born Plymouth
	Lives and works in London

Education

1990-93	BA Fine Art, Chelsea College of Art and Design
1993-95	Slade School of Art, London
1997	Rijksakademie van Beeldende kunsten, Amsterdam

Ron Mueck

1958	Born Melbourne, Australia
	Lives and works in London
	Formal education ended at High School

Solo Exhibitions

1998	Anthony d'Offay Gallery, London

Tim Noble

1966	Born Gloucester Lives and works in London

Education

1985-86	Foundation Course, Cheltenham Art College
1986-89	BA Fine Art, Nottingham Polytechnic
1989-92	Residency at Dean Clough, Halifax, West Yorkshire
1992-94	MA Sculpture, Royal College of Art, London

Sue Webster

1967	Born Leicester

Education

1985-86	Foundation Course, Leicester Polytechnic
1986-89	BA Fine Art, Nottingham Polytechnic
1989-92	Residency at Dean Clough, Halifax, West Yorkshire

Two-Person shows

1996	*British Rubbish*, Independent Art Space, London
1997	*Home Chance*, 20 Rivington Street, London

Andreas Schlaegel

1966	Born Kinshasa, Zaire Lives and works in London

Education

1988-94	Studies of Painting and Sculpture with Per Kirkeby and Georg Herold at the Staatliche Hochschule für Bildende Künste, Städelschule, Frankfurt am Main, Germany
1996-97	MA Fine Art, Goldsmiths College, London

Solo Exhibitions

1995	*Barbar*, Galerie Fruchtig, Frankfurt am Main, Germany
1996	Galerie am Schlachthaus, Karlsruhe, Germany
1998	Galerie Dogenhaus Projekte, Berlin, Germany Museum Pfalzgalerie, Kaiserslautern, Germany

Tomoko Takahashi

1966	Born Tokyo

Education

1985-89	BA Fine Art, Oil Painting, Tama Art University, Tokyo
1990-91	Intermediate Certificate Course, as Foundation
1991-94	BA Fine Art, Goldsmiths College, London
1994-96	Higher Diploma, Postgraduate Study in Sculpture, Fine Art, Slade School of Art, London

Solo Exhibitions

1997	Beaconsfield, Vauxhall, London Claydon Heeley International, Battersea, London. Curated by David Lillington and Gillian Dunn ('*Company Deal*')
1998	*Clockwork*, Hales Gallery, London

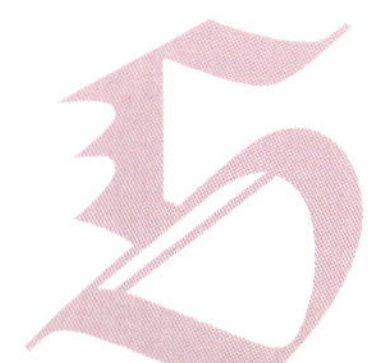

Keith Wilson

1965 Born Birmingham
    Lives and works in London

Education

1984-85 Foundation, Bournville College of Art, Birmingham
1985-88 BA, Ruskin School of Art, Oxford
1988-90 Higher Diploma, Slade School of Art, London

Luke Gottelier

1968 Born London
    Lives and works in London

Education

1988-89 Maidstone College of Art
1989-90 Exeter College of Art
1990-92 Hull College of Art

Tom Hunter

1965 Born Bournemouth
    Lives and works in London

Education

1994 BA Photography, The London College of Printing, London
1996-97 MA Photography, The Royal College of Art, London

Solo Exhibitions

1994 *The Ghetto*, Sutton House, Hackney, London
1996 *Portrait of Hackney*, Alba Gallery Cafe, Hackney, London
1997 *Persons Unknown*, Holly Street Public Arts Trust Gallery, Hackney, London
    Persons Unknown, and *Travellers*, Alba Gallery Cafe, Hackney, London
    Tom Hunter *Retrospective*, Photofusion Gallery, Brixton, London

Sarah Jones

1959 Born London
    Lives and works in London

Education

1978-81 BA, Goldsmiths College, London
1994-96 MA Goldsmiths College, London

Solo Exhibitions

1987 F. Stop Gallery, Bath
1988 Watershed Arts Centre, Bristol
1993 Hales Gallery, London
1995 *Consulting Room, (Couch)*, Camerawork Gallery, London
    Consulting Room, Galerie du Dourven, France (Office Departemental de
    Developement Culturel, Mission Arts Plastiques)
1997 Maureen Paley Interim Art, London
    Le Consortium, Dijon, France

Katia Liebmann

1965   Born Halle, Germany
               Lives and works in London

Education

1995   BA, Kunsthochschule Berlin-Weissensee
1996-97   State University of New York
1997   MA, Royal College of Art, London

Paul Smith

1969   Born Bradford-on-Avon
               Lives and works in London

Education

1991-95   BA Fine Art, Coventry
1995-97   MA Photography, Royal College of Art, London

Solo Exhibitions

1994   The Miners Institute, Blackwood, Gwent
               The Photographers' Gallery, London
               Royal Concert Hall, Glasgow

Hannah Starkey

1971   Born Belfast
               Lives and works in London

Education

1992-95   BA Photography and Film, Napier University, Edinburgh
1996-97   MA Photography, Royal College of Art, London

Solo Exhibitions

1995   *Hannah Starkey, Scottish Homes*, Stills Gallery, Edinburgh
1998   Maureen Paley Interim Art, London

Jason Brooks

1968   Born Rotherham
               Lives and works in London

Education

1988-91   BA Fine Art, Cheltenham & Gloucester College of Art & Design
1991-92   MA Fine Art, Chelsea College of Art & Design, London

Solo Exhibitions

1997-98   Entwistle, London

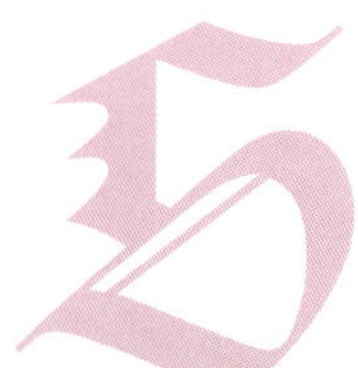

Cecily Brown

| 1969 | Born London |
| | Lives and works in London |

Education

| 1985-87 | B-TEC Diploma in Art and Design, Epsom School of Art |
| 1989-93 | BA Fine Art, Slade School of Art, London |

Solo Exhibitions

1995	Eagle Gallery, London
1997	Deitch Projects, Storefront Gallery, New York
1998	Deitch Projects, New York

Daniel Coombs

| 1971 | Born London |
| | Lives and works in London |

Education

1989-92	BA Ruskin School of Fine Art and Drawing
1992-94	MA Painting, Royal College of Art, London
1994-95	Rome Scholar in Painting, British School in Rome

Solo Exhibitions

| 1997 | *Daniel Coombs, Three New Paintings*, The Approach, London |

Victoria Chalmers

| 1970 | Born London |
| | Lives and works in London |

Education

| 1990-93 | BA Fine Art, Falmouth School of Art and Design |
| 1994-96 | Postgraduate Higher Diploma in Fine Art, Slade School of Art, London |

Dexter Dalwood

| 1960 | Born Bristol |
| | Lives and works in London |

Education

| 1981-85 | BA St. Martin's School of Art, London |
| 1988-90 | MA Fine Art, Royal College of Art, London |

Solo Exhibitions

1992	LTG Gallery, New Delhi, India
	Pundole Gallery, Bombay, India
	Clove Building, London
1995	Galerie Unwahr, Berlin

Peter Davies

1970	Born Edinburgh Lives and works in London

Education

1988-89	Foundation, Central School of Art & Design
1989-92	BA Fine Art, University of Brighton
1994-96	MA Fine Art, Goldsmiths College, London

Solo Exhibitions

1998	*New Paintings,* The Approach, London

Dan Hays

1966	Born London Lives and works in London

Solo Exhibitions

1991	*Silent Partner,* The Coffee Shak, London
	Abandon, The Arched Space, London
1992	*Flock,* Alternative Art Gallery, London
	S.A.S. Office, London
	Visage, Bulstrode Place, London
1996	Laure Genillard Gallery, London
1998	30 Underwood Street, London

Nicky Hoberman

1967	Born South Africa Lives and works in London

Education

1986-89	BA Modern History, Worcester College, Oxford University
1989-93	BA Fine Art, Parsons School of Design, Paris
1992	Yale Summer School of Art, USA, Battel Stoeckel Fellowship
1994-95	MA Painting, Chelsea College of Art and Design

Solo Exhibitions

1996	*Sweet Nothings,* Entwistle Gallery, London
1997	*Chrysalis,* Studio d'Arte Cannaviello, Milan
1998	*Truly Scrumptious,* Mario Diacono, Boston

Chantal Joffe

1969	Born St. Albans Lives and works in London

Education

1987-88	Foundation, Camberwell School of Arts and Crafts
1988-91	BA Fine Art, Glasgow School of Art
1992-94	MA Fine Art, Royal College of Art, London

Felicia Larsson

1967	Born Sweden Lives and works in London

Education

1992-95	BA Fine Art, Chelsea School of Art
1995-97	Postgraduate Diploma, Slade School of Art

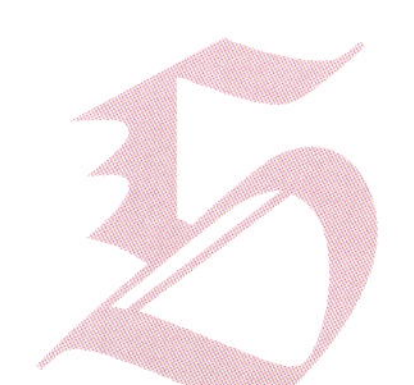

Martin Maloney

| 1961 | Born London |
| | Lives and works in London |

Education

1980-83	University of Sussex
1984-85	London College of Printing
1988-91	Central St. Martin's School of Art and Design
1990	School of Visual Arts, New York
1991	Nova Scotia College of Art and Design, Halifax, Canada
1991-93	Goldsmiths College, London

Solo Exhibitions

1991	*Sex Shop*, OO Gallery, Halifax, Canada
1996	*Portraits*, Habitat, Kings Road, London
1997	*Genre Paintings*, Robert Prime, London
1998	*Conversation Pieces*, Claudia Gian Ferrari Arte Contemporanea, Milan
	Domestic Arrangements, Johnen & Schöttle, Cologne

Karl Maughan

| 1964 | Born Wellington, New Zealand |
| | Lives and works in London |

Education

| 1983-87 | The Elam School of Fine Arts, Auckland, New Zealand |

Solo Exhibitions

1988	Gow Langsford, Auckland, New Zealand
1989	Brooker Gallery, Wellington, New Zealand
1991	Gow Langsford, Auckland, New Zealand
1992	CSA Gallery in conjunction with Gow Langsford, Christchurch, New Zealand
1994	*Romance and Irony*, Gow Langsford, Auckland, New Zealand
1995	*Green Triumph*, Brooker Gallery, Wellington, New Zealand
1996	*Day Night*, Gow Langsford, Auckland, New Zealand
	Love Lies Bleeding, Milford Gallery, Dunedin, New Zealand
1997	*The Great Outdoors*, Tinakori Gallery, Wellington, New Zealand

Michael Raedecker

| 1963 | Born Amsterdam |
| | Lives and works in London |

Education

1985-90	BA Fashion, Gerrit Rietveld Academie, Amsterdam
1993-94	AIR, Rijksakademie, Amsterdam
1996-97	MA Fine Art, Goldsmiths College, London

Solo Exhibitions

1995	Galerie Nouvelles Images, The Hague
1996	Galerie Nouvelles Images, The Hague
	Cover, Stedelijk Museum Bureau, Amsterdam
1998	*Michael Raedecker, New Paintings*, The Approach, London

Richard Reynolds

1967	Born Shropshire, England Lives and works in London

Education

1985-86	Foundation, Shrewsbury College of Arts and Technology, Shropshire
1986-89	BA Fine Art, University of Northumbria, Newcastle upon Tyne
1994-96	MFA, Slade School of Art, London

Solo Exhibitions

1997	*Narrative Paintings*, Habitat Gallery, London

Rosie Snell

1971	Born Littlehampton, West Sussex Lives and works in London

Education

1988-90	Northbrook College of Art and Design, Horsham
1991-94	Loughborough College of Art and Design
1994-95	Norwich School of Art and Design

Solo Exhibitions

1996	Merchants' Court, Norwich Jarrolds Department Store, Norwich *The Undertow*, Islington Arts Factory, London
1997	Royal Bath and West of England Show, Shepton Mallet, Somerset *The Lie of the Land*, Paton Gallery, London *The Promised Land*, Bond Gallery, London

Johnny Spencer

1954	Born Tonbridge Lives and works in London

Education

1978	Foundation, Goldsmiths College, London
1980-83	BA Fine Art, Camberwell School of Arts

Solo Exhibitions

1986	Leo Studios
1991	Richmond's, Soho, London
1993	The Agency, London
1995	Poster Studio, London
1996	Anthony Wilkinson Fine Art, London
1998	The Top Room, London

David Thorpe

1972	Born Greenwich, London Lives and works in London

Education

1990-91	Foundation, Chelsea School of Art, London
1991-94	BA Fine Art, Humberside University
1996-98	MA Fine Art, Goldsmiths College, London

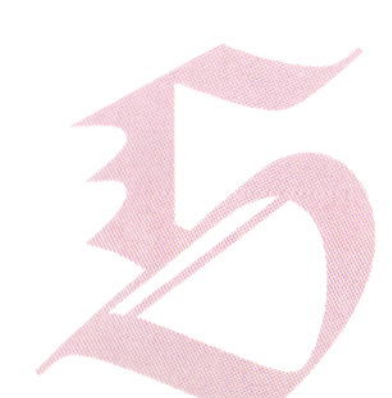

Acknowledgements

We gratefully acknowledge the kind assistance ot the artists for all their assistance in putting together this book. Also the following individuals and galleries for their help:

Anthony Reynolds Gallery; Anthony Wilkinson Gallery; Chelsea School of Art; Sadie Coles; Jeffrey Deitch; Entwistle Gallery; Laure Genillard; Goldsmiths College of Art; Habitat; Hales Gallery; Simon Hedges; Interim Art; Michael Janssen, Cologne; Lisson Gallery; New Contemporaries; One in the Other Gallery; Paton Gallery; The Photographers' Gallery; Robert Prime; The Royal College of Art; Karsten Schubert; David Sylvester; 30 Underwood Street Gallery; The Trade Apartment; Tram Depot Gallery; Walker Art Gallery, Liverpool; Whitechapel Art Gallery.

We extend sincere thanks to Dick Price for his essay.

We are also grateful to the following artists, photographers and galleries for the use of their photographic material:

The Approach; Mike Bruce; Victoria Chalmers; Daniel Coombs; Prudence Cuming Associates Limited; Dexter Dalwood; Peter Davies; Anthony d'Offay Gallery; David Flower, National Galleries and Museums on Merseyside; Laure Genillard Gallery; Steven Gontarski; Luke Gottelier; Marcus Hardy; Lynn Hewett; Mark Hosking; Tom Hunter; ICA; Yasu Ichige; Chantal Joffe; Sarah Jones; Andy Keate; Chris Leinhardt; Katia Liebmann; Anthony Oliver; Richard Paul; Robert Prime; Michael Raedecker; Andreas Schlaegel; Lothar Schneps; Miki Slingsby; Oren Slor; Paul Smith; Rosie Snell; Hannah Starkey; Simon Starling; Eric Steemsa; Tomoko Takahashi; David Thorpe; Peter Thuring; Peter White; Stephen White; Anthony Wilkinson; Gareth Winters; Edward Woodman.

Publications Director and Curator	Jenny Blyth
Assistant Curator/Registrar	Nigel Hurst
Archivist	Linda Copperwheat
Picture Researcher	Janice Kerbel
Installations Consultant	Martin McGinn

right: Robert Wilson
Festival 1996 oil and gloss on canvas 183 x 244cm/72 x 96in
Ointment 1996 oil and gloss on canvas 183 x 244cm/72 x 96in
Sunflower 1996 oil and gloss on canvas 244 x 244cm/96 x 96in
Yaffle 1996 oil and gloss on canvas 213 x 244cm/84 x 96in

overleaf (1): Ian Dawson *171 Elements* 1998 20 Bread Crates, 8 Garden Chairs, 1 Salt Bin, 4 Large Bowls, 16 Medium Crates, 9 Buckets, 3 Bins, 38 Small Chairs, 2 Tricycles, 1 Tray, 4 Small Buckets, 2 Stools, 3 Pushalongs, 1 Tool Trolley, 1 Activity Gym, 1 Garden Table, 1 Tractor, 2 Traffic Bollards, 1 Scooter, 1 Garden Rocker, 16 Washing-up Bowls, 1 Dog Bowl, 7 Coathangers, 1 Pushchair, 3 Baby Baths, 3 Baby Seats, 10 Blocks, 1 Helicopter, 1 Small Stool, 9 Fruit Bowls 160 x 160 x 230cm/63 x 63 x 90in

overleaf (2): Martin Maloney *Choosing A Tie* 1996 acrylic on canvas
64 x 61cm/26 x 24in

overleaf (3): Ron Mueck *Big Baby 2* 1996-97 polyester resin and mixed media
85 x 71 x 70cm/33 x 28 x 27in

Big Baby 3 1996-97 polyester resin and mixed media 86 x 81 x 70cm/34 x 32 x 27in

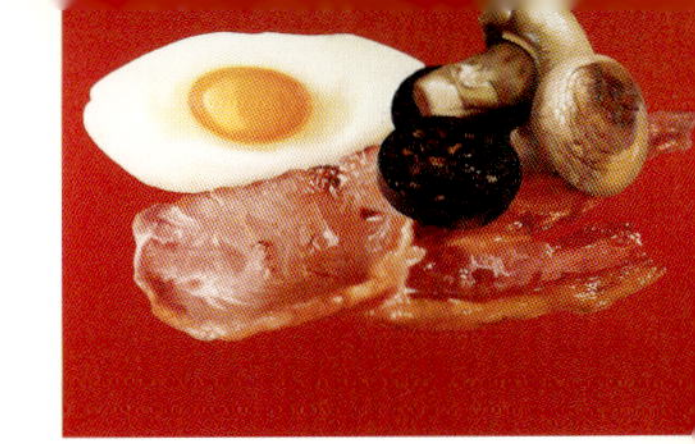
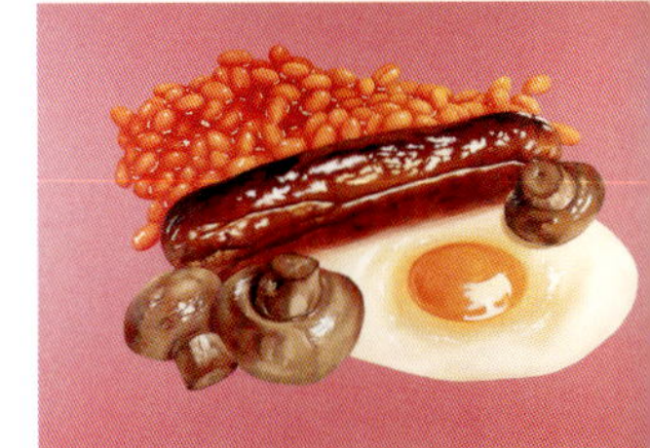
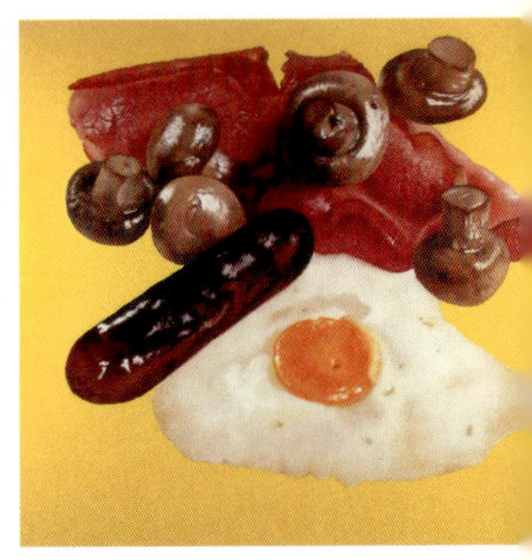
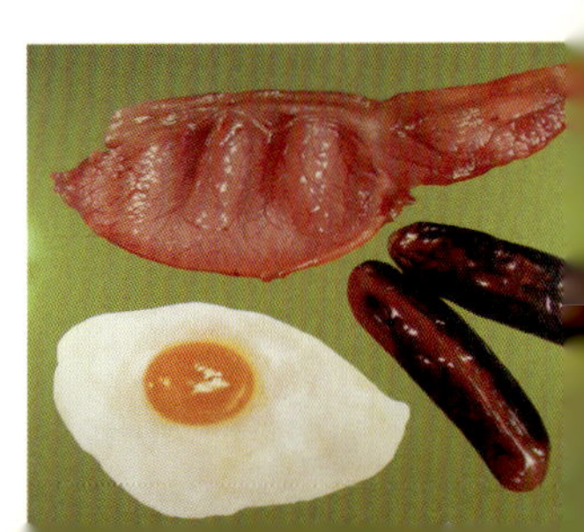

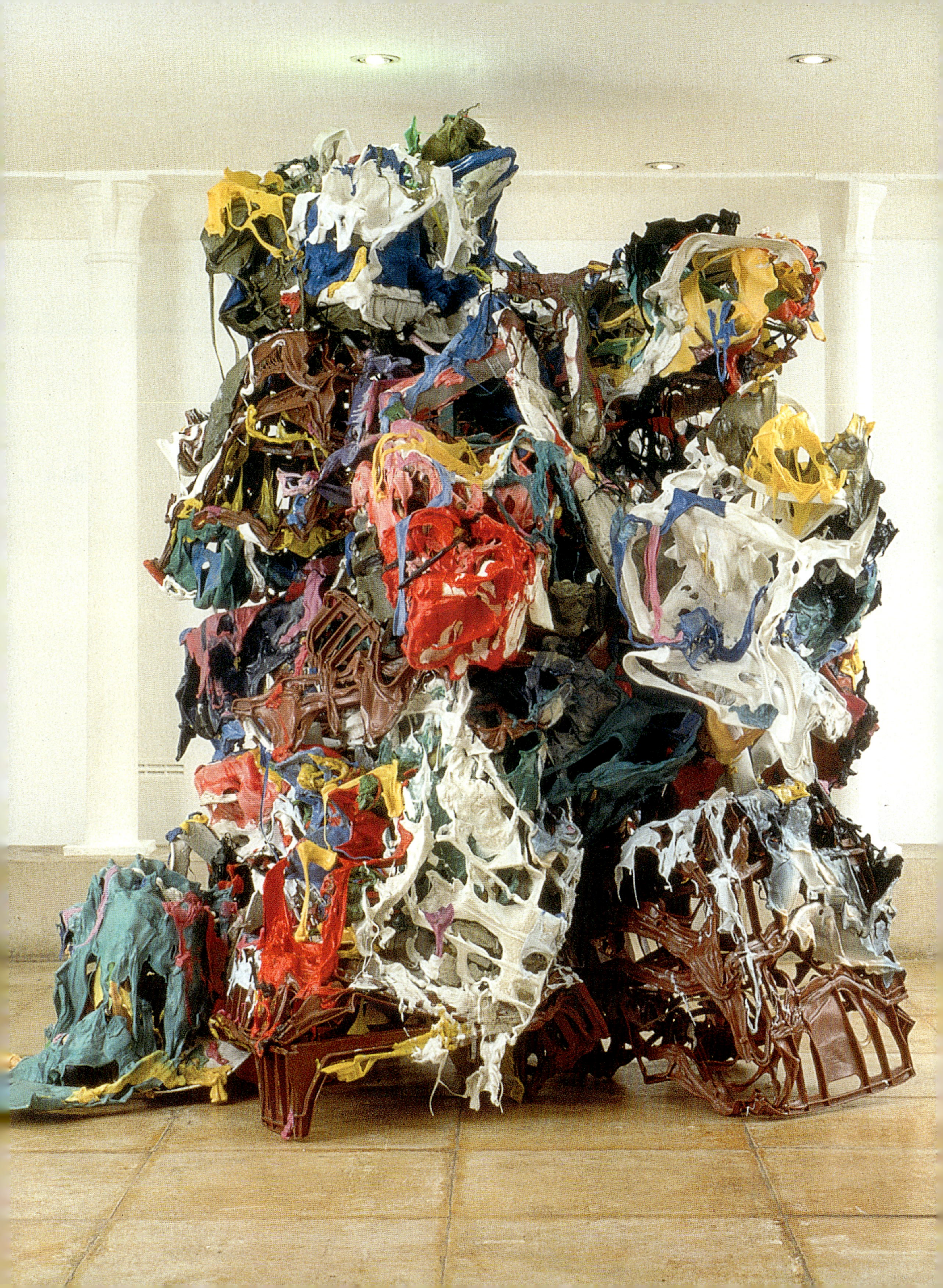

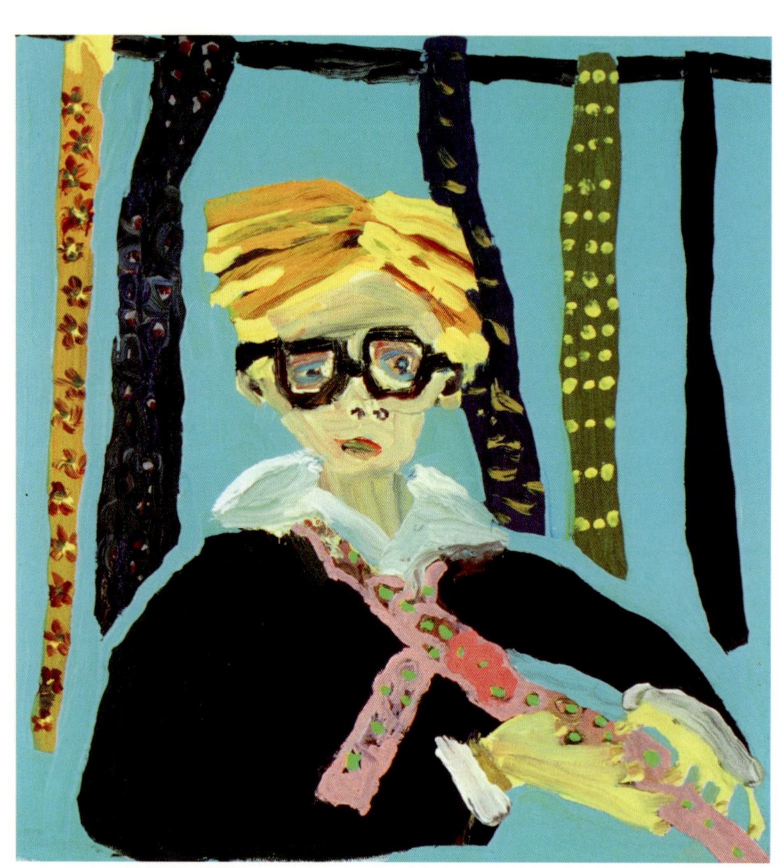

Previous Exhibitions at The Saatchi Gallery

March – October 1985	Donald Judd, Brice Marden, Cy Twombly, Andy Warhol
December 1985 – July 1986	Carl Andre, John Chamberlain, Dan Flavin, Sol Lewitt, Robert Ryman, Frank Stella
September 1986 – July 1987	Anselm Kiefer, Richard Serra
September 1987 – January 1988	'New York Art Now' (Part 1): Ashley Bickerton, Ross Bleckner, Robert Gober, Peter Halley, Jeff Koons, Tim Rollins & K.O.S., Haim Steinbach, Philip Taaffe, Meyer Vaisman
February – April 1988	'New York Art Now' (Part 2): Ashley Bickerton, Carroll Dunham, Robert Gober, Peter Halley, Tishan Hsu, Jon Kessler, Jeff Koons, Allan McCollum, Peter Schuyff, Doug & Mike Starn
April – October 1988	Leon Golub, Philip Guston, Sigmar Polke, Joel Shapiro
November 1988 – April 1989	Jennifer Bartlett, Eric Fischl, Elizabeth Murray, Susan Rothenberg
April – October 1989	Robert Mangold, Bruce Nauman
November 1989 – February 1990	Leon Kossoff, Bill Woodrow
March – November 1990	Frank Auerbach, Lucian Freud, Richard Deacon
January – July 1991	Richard Artschwager, Cindy Sherman, Richard Wilson
September 1991 – February 1992	Mike Bidlo, Manuel Ocampo, Andres Serrano
March – October 1992	'Young British Artists I': John Greenwood, Damien Hirst, Alex Landrum, Langlands & Bell, Rachel Whiteread
October – December 1992	'Out of Africa': Contemporary African artists from the Pigozzi Collection
February – July 1993	'Young British Artists II': Rose Finn-Kelcey, Sarah Lucas, Marc Quinn, Mark Wallinger
September – December 1993	'American Art in the 20th Century' presented by The Royal Academy of Arts, London
February – July 1994	'Young British Artists III': Simon Callery, Simon English, Jenny Saville
September 1994	'A Positive View' 20th Century International Photography presented by Vogue
November 1994 – February 1995	Paula Rego, John Murphy, Avis Newman
April 1995 – June 1995	'Young British Artists IV':John Frankland, Marcus Harvey, Brad Lochore, Marcus Taylor, Gavin Turk
September – December 1995	'Young British Artists V': Glenn Brown, Keith Coventry, Hadrian Pigott, Kerry Stewart
January – May 1996	'Young Americans': Janine Antoni, Gregory Green, Jacqueline Humphries, Sean Landers, Charles Long, Tony Oursler, Richard Prince, Charles Ray, Kiki Smith
June – July 1996	'Stephan Balkenhol' Sculptures 1988 –1996
September – December 1996	'Young British Artists VI': Jordan Baseman, Daniel Coombs, Claude Heath, John Isaacs, Nina Saunders
January – April 1997	Fiona Rae and Gary Hume
April – August 1997	Duane Hanson
September – December 1997	'Young German Artists 2': Thomas Grünfeld, Andreas Gursky, Stefan Hablützel, Martin Honert, Thomas Ruff, Thomas Schütte
January – April 1998	Alex Katz 'Twenty Five Years of Painting'
April – July 1998	'Young Americans 2' Part One: Ashley Bickerton, Carroll Dunham, David Salle, Jessica Stockholder, Terry Winters
September – November 1998	'Young Americans 2' Part Two: Michael Ashkin, John Currin, Tom Friedman, Martin Kersels, Clay Ketter, Robin Lowe, Josiah McElheny, Sarah Morris, Laura Owens, Elizabeth Peyton, Monique Prieto, Brian Tolle, Sue Williams, Lisa Yuskavage
January – April 1999	'Neurotic Realism' Part One: Steven Gontarski, Brian C. Griffiths, Martin Maloney, Paul Smith, Tomoko Takahashi

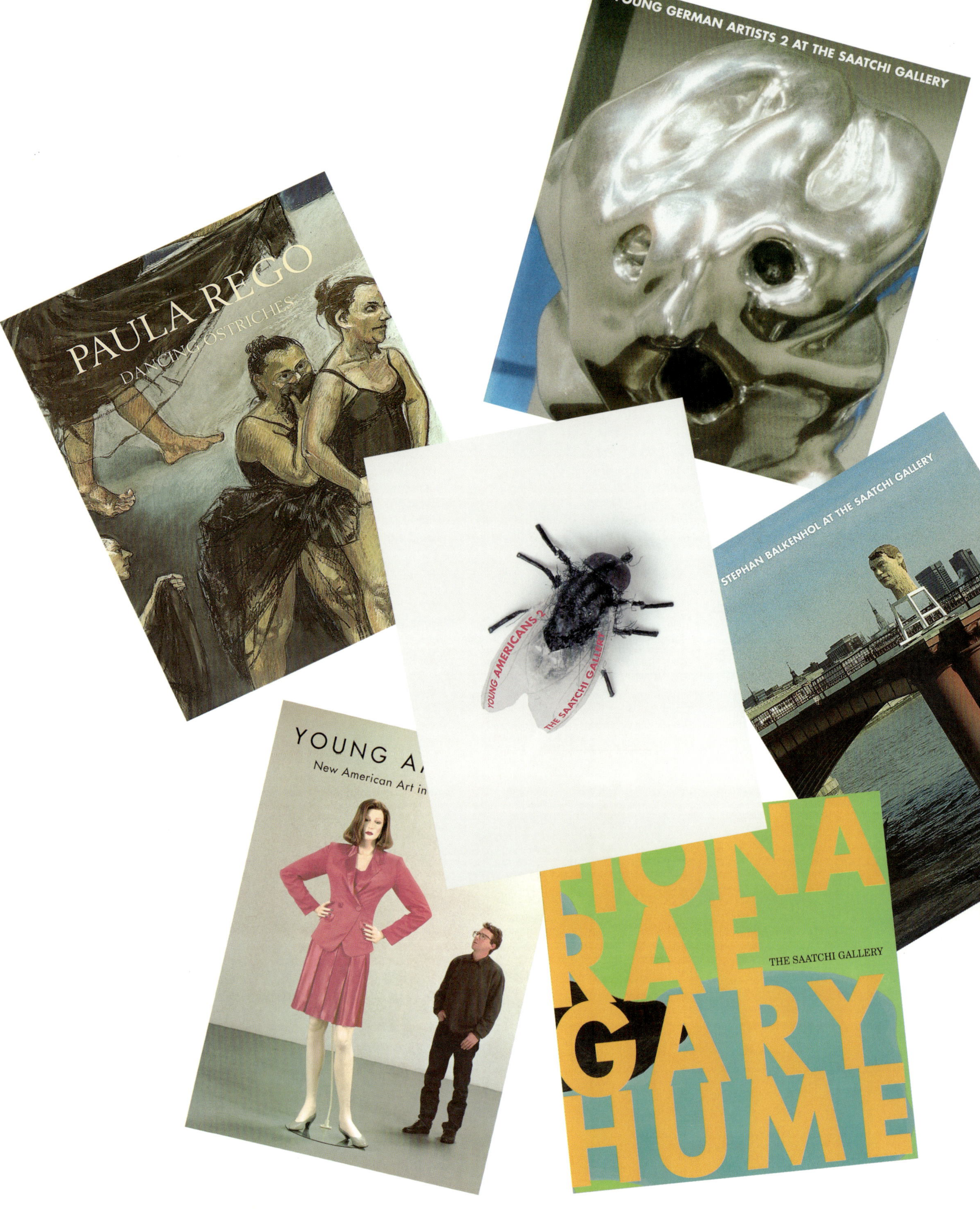

YOUNG GERMAN ARTISTS 2 AT THE SAATCHI GALLERY
PAULA REGO
DANCING OSTRICHES
STEPHAN BALKENHOL AT THE SAATCHI GALLERY
YOUNG AMERICANS 2
THE SAATCHI GALLERY
YOUNG A
New American Art in
FIONA RAE
THE SAATCHI GALLERY
GARY HUME

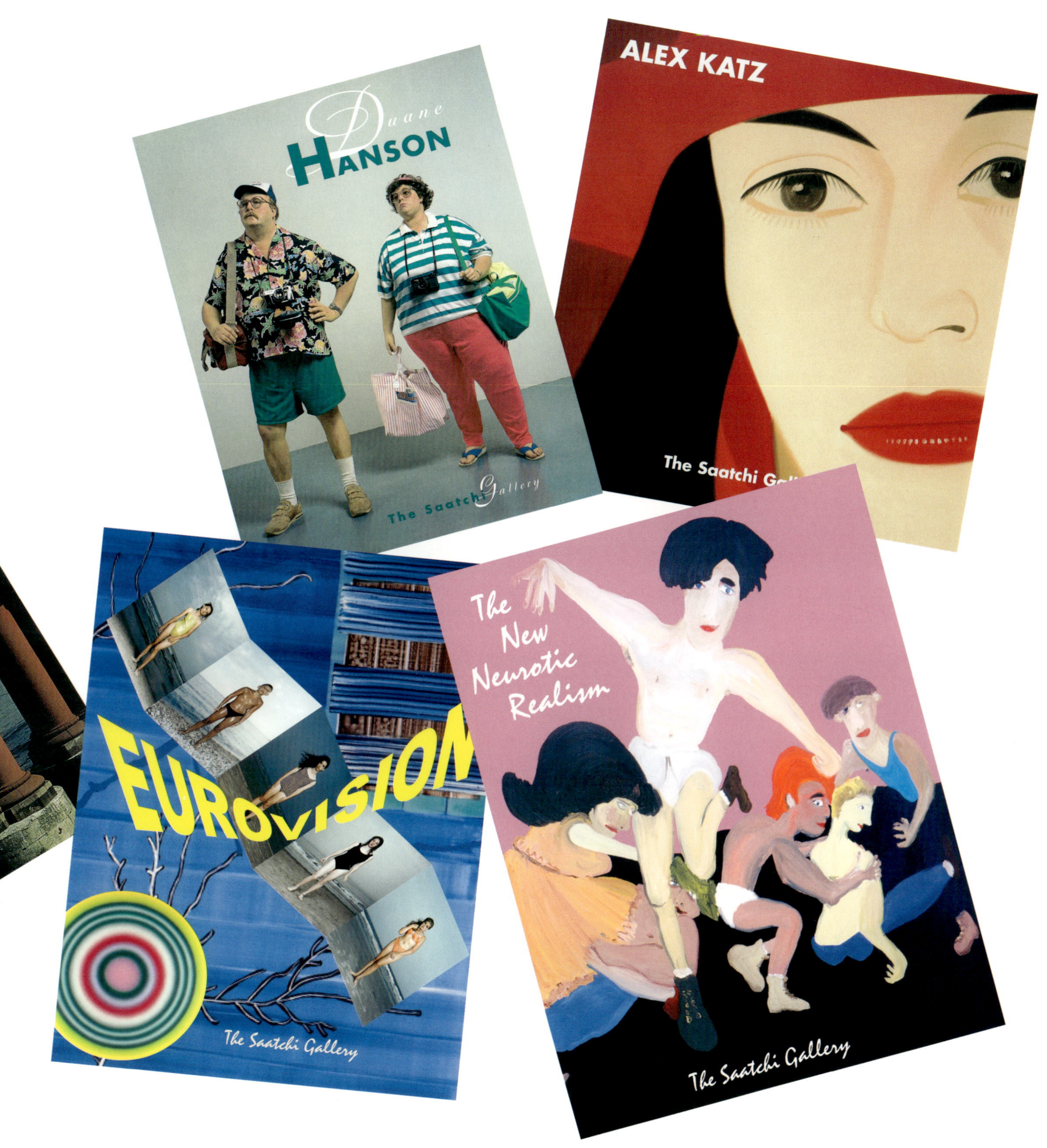

Saatchi Gallery Publications

Duane
HANSON
The Saatchi Gallery
ALEX KATZ
EUROVISION
The Saatchi Gallery
The New Neurotic Realism
The Saatchi Gallery

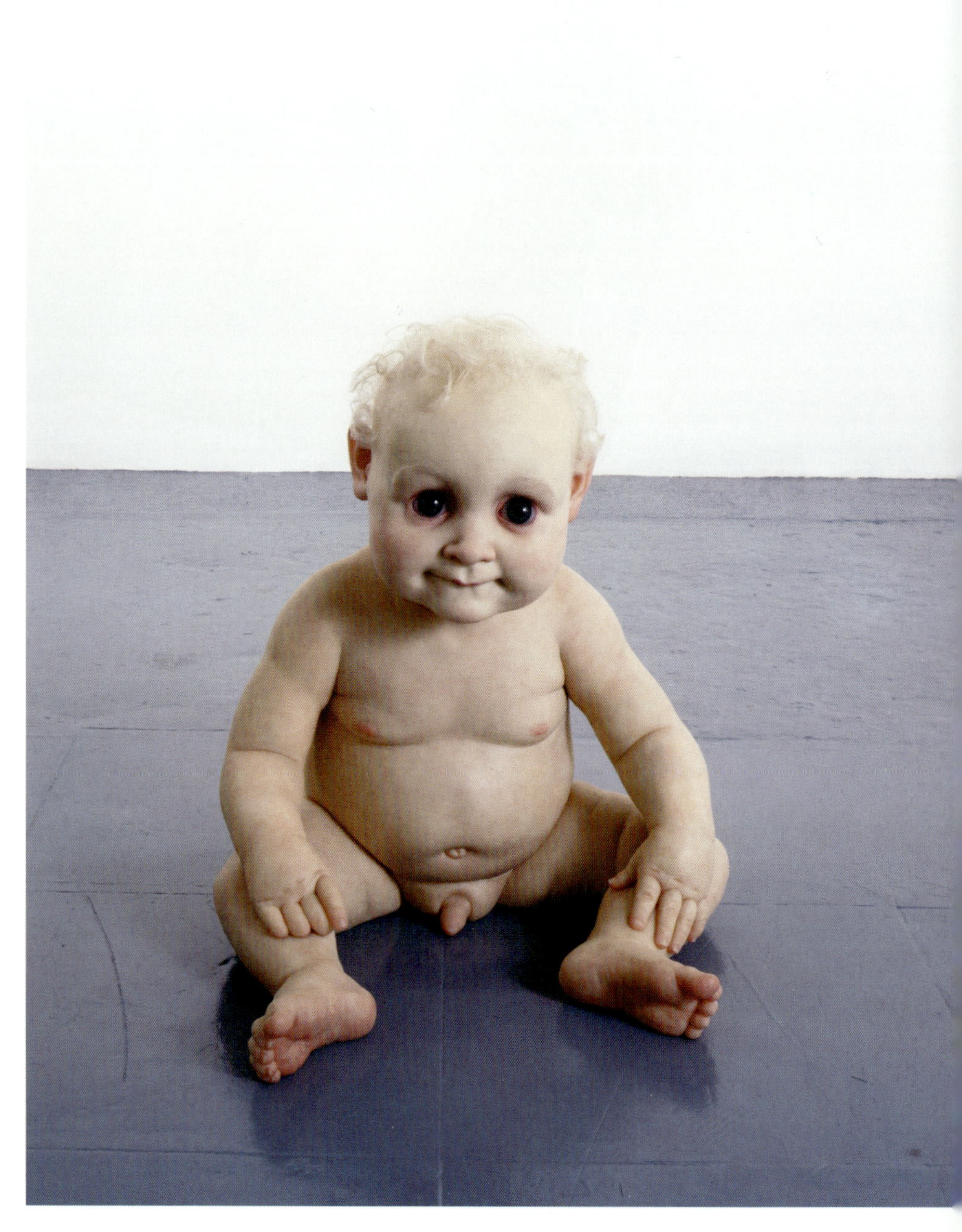

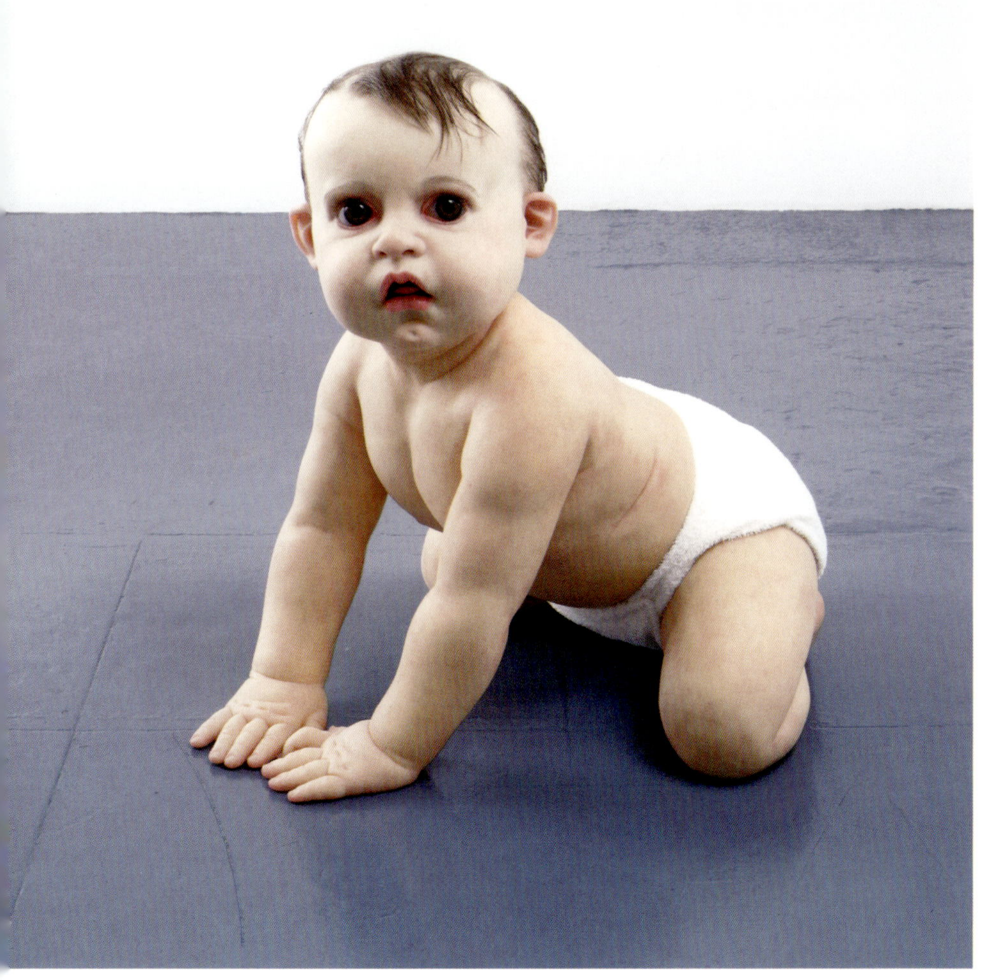